Transatlantic Liverpool

CRITICAL AFRICANA STUDIES:

African, African American, and Caribbean Interdisciplinary and Intersectional Studies

Series Editor

Christel N. Temple, University of Pittsburgh

Series Editorial Board

Martell Teasley, Kimberly Nichele Brown, Jerome Schiele, Marquita M. Gammage, and Bayyinah S. Jeffries

The Critical Africana Studies book series features scholarship within the emerging field of Africana studies, which encompasses such disciplines as African studies, African diasporan studies, African American studies, Afro-American studies, Afro-Asian studies, Afro-European studies, Afro-Islamic studies, Afro-Jewish studies, Afro-Latino studies, Afro-Native American studies, Caribbean studies, Pan-African studies, Black British studies and, of course, Black studies. The Critical Africana Studies book series directly responds to the heightened demand for monographs and edited volumes that innovatively explore Africa and its diaspora employing cutting-edge critical, interdisciplinary, and intersectional theory and methods.

Recent Titles in the Series

Transatlantic Liverpool: Shades of the Black Atlantic, By Mark Christian
AfroLatinas and LatiNegras: Culture, Identity, and Struggle from an Intersectional Perspective, Edited by Rosita Scerbo and Concetta Bondi
African Sovereigns: The Workings of Diaspora in Jamaican Maroon Communities, By Mario Nisbett
Race, Identity, and Privilege from the US to the Congo, By Brenda F. Berrian
Ama Mazama: The Ogunic Presence in Africology, By Molefi Kete Asante
The Afrocentric Pan Africanist Vision: Afrocentric Essays, By Molefi Kete Asante
Branches of Asanteism, By Abdul Karim Bangura
Transcendence and the Africana Literary Enterprise, Edited by Christel N. Temple and foreword by Molefi Kete Asante

Transatlantic Liverpool

Shades of the Black Atlantic

Mark Christian

LEXINGTON BOOKS
Lanham • Boulder • New York • London

Published by Lexington Books
An imprint of The Rowman & Littlefield Publishing Group, Inc.
4501 Forbes Boulevard, Suite 200, Lanham, Maryland 20706
www.rowman.com

86-90 Paul Street, London EC2A 4NE

Copyright © 2022 by The Rowman & Littlefield Publishing Group, Inc.

All rights reserved. No part of this book may be reproduced in any form or by any electronic or mechanical means, including information storage and retrieval systems, without written permission from the publisher, except by a reviewer who may quote passages in a review.

British Library Cataloguing in Publication Information Available

Library of Congress Cataloging-in-Publication Data

Library of Congress Cataloging-in-Publication DataNames: Christian, Mark, author.
  Title: Transatlantic Liverpool : shades of the Black Atlantic / Mark
    Christian.
  Other titles: Critical Africana studies.
  Description: Lanham : Lexington Books, [2022] | Series: Critical Africana
    studies: African, African American, and Caribbean interdisciplinary and
    intersectional studies | Includes bibliographical references and index.
  Identifiers: LCCN 2022029757 (print) | LCCN 2022029758 (ebook) | ISBN
    9781793652638 (cloth) | ISBN 9781793652652 (paperback) | ISBN
    9781793652645 (ebook)
  Subjects: LCSH: Gilroy, Paul, 1956- | Christian, Mark--Family. | Christian
    family. | Black people--England--Liverpool--History. | Black
    people--England--Liverpool--Social conditions. |
    Racism--England--Liverpool--History. | African diaspora. | Africa--Study
    and teaching (Higher) | Critical theory. | Liverpool (England)--Race
    relations.
  Classification: LCC DA690.L8 C493 2022 (print) | LCC DA690.L8 (ebook) |
    DDC 305.896427/53--dc23/eng/20220630
  LC record available at https://lccn.loc.gov/2022029757
  LC ebook record available at https://lccn.loc.gov/2022029758

Dedication
For my wonderful sister:
Rita Christian (1957–2021)

Contents

Acknowledgments	ix
Introduction	1
Chapter 1: Theorizing Transatlantic Liverpool and the Black Atlantic Paradigm	23
Chapter 2: Life and Times in a Liverpool Black Atlantic Family—the Christians	71
Chapter 3: Schooling, L8 Community Football, Grassroots Education, and Mainstream Miseducation	119
Chapter 4: Anti-Black Riots, Resistance, and Black Organization Demise 1919–2000s	165
Chapter 5: A Tale of Two Freedoms: Contemporary Self-Reflexivity and the Memory of Frederick Douglass	221
Appendix A	251
Appendix B	255
Appendix C	269
Appendix D	271
Appendix E	273
Appendix F	275
Appendix G	277
Appendix H	279
Appendix I	281

Appendix J	283
Appendix K	285
Appendix L	287
Bibliography	289
Index	323
About the Author	337

Acknowledgments

This study in essence represents forty-plus years of research, and involves a lifetime of gratitude to many persons. Those who can be deemed family and friends, mentors, colleagues, and associates. Because there are literally hundreds of persons I have learned from, I shall keep this brief but only to share that often one learns more from those whom I disagree with in life, rather than those with whom I have a healthy rapport. Let it be stated at the outset that this study has involved a great degree of retrospection regarding having grown up in and left the City of Liverpool for pastures new due to a distinct lack of opportunity. It was serendipitous my departure from the city; too many things fell into place for me to end up first in Ohio and later in New York. I have to therefore thank my mentor, Dr. William E. Nelson Jr., whom I met first in 1990, and we developed a friendship that lasted till his transition in May of 2013—without his guidance in all things African Diaspora this work may not have ever been completed.

The Black British ancestors to whom I owe a great debt for guiding me as a young man are: Ron "Babatunde" Phillips, Eric Lynch, Dorothy Kuya, Len Garrison, and Bernie Grant. Having spent time with these giants of Black Britain could only benefit my desire to make a small contribution to the struggle of Black Britons—whether in Liverpool or within the context of the transatlantic sphere. Indeed, we literally stand on the shoulders of those who have struggled before us. Too often we disregard past generational resistance to the social forces of discrimination and this is certainly an unforgiveable act. I am eternally grateful to those who gave so much and received so little in their lifetime resisting racialized oppression, particularly in Liverpool, England.

In relation to the present, there are two persons I need to acknowledge for their brilliant research skills, and the information they shared with open collegiality. Hyder Jawad graciously passed on obscure cricket articles that situated my father, Gladstone Forbes Christian, with the great Trinidadian cricketer Learie Constantine in the 1940s war years. Without his input I may never have known this crucial knowledge about my father and his cricket prowess during the second world war after he arrived from Jamaica in August of 1941. Then there is Alvin Christie, a digital chronicler of Liverpool's forgotten history of Black musicians and social clubs. His research should be also turned into a book for future generations of Liverpudlians to learn from. After we exchanged information, it turns out that his father too was one of the African Caribbean munitions workers brought to Britain, like my father, during the second world war. What a small world it is in regard to "six degrees of separation." So to both Hyder and Alvin: thank you!

Moreover, librarians and archivists specifically based at the Central Library in Liverpool were helpful in my pursuit of rare information relating to the Liverpool Black experience—particularly Vicki Caren and Helena Smart. However, it should also be stated that gaining information from the Liverpool City Council itself and directly related to the "Slave Trade Apology" proved rather cumbersome. There needs to be a definite improvement in general transparency regarding this aspect of the city's history, particularly for the public to gain easy access to such important historical materials.

There are too many Black Liverpudlians for me to name here, yet I do mention many of the community activists of relevance to this study throughout. Along with my former football teammates from Liverpool 8, far too many to name individually but who emanated from two main teams: Caribbean F.C. and Saana/Yemen F.C. between 1978 and 1987. Reflections on our triumphs within the "beautiful game" continue to bring a smile to my face when no one around me even understands why I am smiling. Great days indeed, some of which are captured herein.

I want to thank Dr. Christel N. Temple, the series editor for Critical Africana Studies for Lexington Books, who offered me sanguine encouragement to complete this research on a complex Black British topic that involved a semi-autoethnographic approach. It was a difficult task, but her editorial insight made it much easier for me to delve into aspects of my past that would be employed to illuminate the essence of this Africana transatlantic study. One criticism that may be leveled at me is in my evocative prose. I suppose this style emanates from the very fact that my people have endured such social discrimination, but it also derives from my reading of Frantz Fanon, Richard Wright, James Baldwin, Malcolm X, Ida B. Wells, Martin Luther King Jr., Fannie Lou Hamer, and many other Africana activists who shared their experiences in comprehending racism and oppression. In point of fact, there is no "elegant way" to write about the impact of racism on the lives of human beings who do not deserve such stigma. Anyone who suggests one can write "elegantly" on such visceral subject matter could not derive from an oppressed and racialized social group. Therefore, my prose is authentic and evidential to the history/biographical that has molded my personality—resistance to racism and its ugliness. In view of this, I make no apology for writing with a degree of resistance that can be found also in most writers who have covered similar terrain and fought for the humanity of Africana peoples. Lastly, all names from my "schooldays" and university affiliation in Liverpool have been changed for anonymity, and quotes from Levi Tafari, *Liverpool Experience* (Lautertal, West Germany: Michael Schwinn, 1989), are reprinted with author permission. Any errors contained are the sole responsibility of the author.

Introduction

This is an Africana transatlantic case study, written within the context of semi-autoethnography; which is no different than many other writers on Black experiences. For example, James Baldwin who wrote as a "witness" to how his people forged their lives within the context of his hometown in Harlem, New York and elsewhere in the United States. Baldwin also noted his travels to France to "escape" American racism and find breathing space to reflect and conduct his writing from a safe distance. Yet he was always involved in comprehending the emancipation of his people back in the United States. Indeed, Baldwin's non-fiction essays in his celebrated *Notes of a Native Son* reveal what are in essence a compilation of autobiographical notes revealing his deep-seated, visceral, autoethnographic insight into life as an African American in twentieth century North America and France.

On the art of writing, and in his inimitable manner, Baldwin stated, "One writes out of one thing only—one's own experience. Everything depends on how relentlessly one forces from this experience the last drop, sweet or bitter, it can possibly give." It is difficult to argue with this point of view on how one should speak to the world through prose. Moreover, within this context Baldwin claimed forthrightly, "I want to be an honest man and a good writer" (Baldwin 2012, pp. 7–9). Yet, to be candid within an Africana critical studies framework is inevitably to be counter-hegemonic to the cultural hegemony that has sustained white supremacy within the world of ideas. To put it another way, Africana critical studies is to engender Black liberation from oppression wherever one encounters it (Bassey 2007, p. 914). Therefore, herein like Baldwin, my aim is merely to be "an honest man, and a good writer" in offering this research that intertwines personal history, life experience, primary and secondary source material, to both substantiate and validate what at times may prove to be a "uniquely horrific" journey for the average reader. In this sense, the narrative within this account of an Africana critical studies investigation will be mostly expressed in the third person unless the prose is related directly to my life history—no different than a

James Baldwin, Richard Wright, Malcolm X, or any other man of color author endeavoring to articulate racialized oppression.

That stated, the transatlantic experience from the era of European enslavement through to colonialism and beyond in the so-called "New World" was invented between the fifteenth and nineteenth centuries. This era would bring forth tremendous socioeconomic transformation, cultural exchange, and human misery for millions born of and who could claim African heritage. Ana Lucia Araujo in her insightful study, *Paths of the Atlantic Slave Trade: Interactions, Identities, and Images*, put the immense upheaval involved in the transatlantic pathways this way:

> The [Trans-] Atlantic exchanges and their effects were critical to the economies of regions surrounding the Atlantic slave ports, and such exchanges also decisively influenced the centers located in the interior of the European, African, and American continents. In both the North and South Atlantic, as well as the Caribbean basin, the various forms of the internal slave trade were an additional factor to be considered. The process of enslavement did not end with arrival on the American shores; in this context, the different paths taken by the individuals and groups who were victims of the Atlantic slave trade were influenced by a myriad of factors—including the disembarking region, the kind of work performed, gender, age, religion, and language. These elements very often oriented the paths toward freedom available to these men and women (Araujo 2011, p. 4).

After centuries of unbridled Eurocentric oppression on the African continent, Caribbean, and "New World" regions, there would follow the Indigenous freedom struggles for Independence between the satellites and metropoles in the twentieth century. This history left a myriad of dissimilar yet similar communities of Africana heritage across the globe. That stated, the focus of this study involves a transatlantic Black British experience, connected to a once major slaving port located in Liverpool, England in the northwest region of Britain. Considered within an Africana critical studies frame of reference, it is without denial a complex social and cultural history reaching back centuries. Certainly, Liverpool is regarded as one of, if not the, oldest Black settlement in Britain/Europe (Costello 2001). Yet, the major Black British scholars that emerged in the 1970s to 2000s were arguably Stuart Hall and his former student Paul Gilroy. They were each prominent in disseminating transatlantic knowledge relating to Black British heritage that can be deemed "London-centric" in terms of overall analysis. Neither Hall nor Gilroy ever focused on the City of Liverpool in their influential body of works. For example, Gilroy's *The Black Atlantic* never mentions Liverpool at all, but his academic admirers within transatlantic discourse often engaged his ideas to substantiate *their* specific studies on Black experience in the city (Belchem

2006a, 2006b, 2014; Brown 2005). Likewise, Hall has had major influence on what it is to be "Black and British"—yet he failed to consider one of its longest standing Black communities: Liverpool. Instead, viewing Black presence in Britain as starting from the arrival of the 1948 *Empire Windrush* (Hesse 2000) via the docking of this ship that brought over eight hundred persons mainly from Jamaica, Trinidad, and Bermuda in the Caribbean region. This fact alone should be enough to warrant a study that relates specifically to both an understanding of the longevity in regard to Black heritage in Liverpool, England, and how it has connected with the broader experience involving Africana peoples in terms of involuntary and voluntary migration throughout the transatlantic domain. This introductory chapter will map out the logic and methodology in studying Liverpool, England, as a major transatlantic case study—while revealing some of the key aspects that have shaped Black settlement in the city.

COLLIDING COUNTER-NARRATIVES IN BLACK BRITISH HISTORIOGRAPHY

In 2005 a number of events serve to underline the relevance of this contribution to Africana critical studies. First, in the *Chronicle Review*—a supplement to the *Chronicle of Higher Education* (January 7, 2005), Paul Gilroy penned an article titled "From a Colonial Past to a New Multiculturalism" which focused on Black presence in Britain in the post-9/11 era and the "war on terror" relating essentially to the "clash of cultures" thesis between the "West and the Rest"—so to speak. Throughout this piece he pushes the idea of an "emergent convivial culture" that offsets the notion that there is no hope in the seemingly "unbridgeable gulf" between civilizations. Again, Gilroy is largely London-centric and ahistorical in the sense that he fails to acknowledge older Black British communities that are expressed as supposedly "cosmopolitan" and yet still mired in racialized discrimination—Liverpool, England, being one notable case in point (Belchem 2006a, 2014). Moreover, there is nothing "convivial" when one considers the historical trajectory of Black presence in Liverpool. On the contrary, it has been a harsh existence for Black and brown people and often incredibly racist, with a tremendous amount of institutional racism that cannot be deemed in any form as an "emergent conviviality" because of its longevity (Gifford, Brown, and Bundey 1989; Christian 1998b, 2002d). As for its cosmopolitan look, there have been Africans, African Caribbean, African American, Arab Muslim, and an array of other cultural groups, that have settled, mingled, and lived out their lives in Liverpool under a siege of resentment from the majority white population—historically.

This is not to suggest Gilroy is completely mistaken, just partly, because he raises some very important points in his article—it is the ahistorical aspect in regard to Black British presence that is problematic. Melancholia is another word that Gilroy is fond of in relation to the British Empire and its past glories being encapsulated in racialized hierarchies that stifle his notion of an "emergent convivial" multicultural Britain. To put it another way, the British establishment had become mournfully nostalgic about its loss of Empire and found itself grappling to hold on to a colonial past, a racialized hegemony. To make matters worse, the "colonized descendants" had emerged unfortunately on its doorstep in the metropole causing considerable angst to the "British Way of Life"—that was viewed as "white" of course. Concomitantly, there developed an insidious white British resistance to a "Multicultural Britain"—as Gilroy contended:

> Britain's postcolonial, or postimperial, melancholia is different from an older, simpler melancholy for glories past. . . .
> The disruptive and unwelcome presence of Britain's many aliens has always been explained in racial terms as an invasion. The current manifestations of that unsavory rhetoric derived from the populist interventions of Enoch Powell, a Conservative member of parliament, during the 1960s [Powell's 1968 "Rivers of Blood" speech warning of Black and Asian presence on British soil gave rise to the far-right movements still alive in 2020s Britain]. But it is still at work, presenting the white working class as a wounded victim of government policy, expected to protect the nation against the intrusion of what Powell liked to the call "the alien wedge" (Gilroy 2005, p. B8).

One cannot disagree with Gilroy's perspective in regard to the British nostalgia for its disintegrated British Empire, and how it scapegoats the former descendants of various colonized communities that are in the metropole, that have been born and raised in Britain. This is correct, and the racism of Enoch Powell is a manifestation of the broader white racism that is ubiquitous in all areas of British society. Gilroy had elaborated on the topic of Britain's loss of empire in his 2004 book, *After Empire: Melancholia or Convivial Culture?* His argument overall makes sense, but the problem is in Gilroy's analysis being deemed "new" when in fact it was ahistorical in relation to cities such as Liverpool, Manchester, and Cardiff. To be sure, Black Liverpudlians have been Black and British for centuries, and within this context is a multicultural and multifaceted experience that predates the *Empire Windrush* era of 1948 by decades (Christian 1998b; Hesse 2000). Moreover, Black Liverpudlians have suffered consistent racialized onslaughts indirectly due to the British "losses"—not only of its Empire but due to an economy that floundered—Liverpool was once "The Gateway to the British Empire" (Belchem 2006a). Essentially, it is this overall historical oversight by Gilroy, Hall, and others that will be somewhat rectified within the chapters of this book. Again, this is not to dismiss the ideas and viewpoint of Gilroy and Hall, who have offered insightful thoughts on British racism and how to combat it. The main point here is merely to supplement and extend the historical terrain of Black British presence that has great significance. Because, quite frankly, Gilroy and Hall could be deemed making the Liverpool Black experience "invisible" and that is unacceptable due to the historical relevance it holds to an understanding of multiracial Britain.

Second, in 2005 I was commissioned by the *Times Higher Education Supplement* to write an article on the exodus of Black scholars from Britain titled "Why Do We Go Abroad? There Are No Opportunities for Us in Britain"—it was self-explanatory. During the early 2000s there was what could be deemed a "group" of young Black British scholars leaving Britain for jobs abroad, mainly in the United States. Even a Gilroyesque scholar like Barnor Hesse, once based in London, would leave Britain for greener pastures at Northwestern University. Perhaps he left racist Britain for a more optimal economic package, and for the greater freedom involved in pursuing his academic ideas under less stressful circumstances than are found in Britain. No doubt it was similar for other Black British scholars, as the dire lack of a multicultural curriculum, and the job insecurity, made it an easy option to seek a professional academic life overseas. Ironically, Gilroy at this time was heading back to Britain in order to take up a prestigious position in sociology at the London School of Economics, after a short sojourn at Yale University. His Yale opportunity had been orchestrated by his postmodernist peer from the UK Birmingham University, Stuart Hall school of thought, Hazel Carby—another "Black British" scholar who was by then established at Yale University. Gilroy and Carby were certainly elite "tokens" of Black British success who basically did not challenge the racialized academic hegemony in their works. They generally espoused a growing avoidance of racialized oppression for a diluted "intersectionality" that down-played, and often eliminated, Black empowerment perspectives articulated by other Black British scholars (Christian 1998a; Graham 2007).

Yet the exodus of Black British scholars from Britain was something that resonated in 2005 in the British higher education sphere. To be sure, there were few very successful Black British academics—after the late Stuart Hall, Gilroy is arguably the most well-known today; yet paradoxically also the most criticized among Africana critical studies scholars. He is most often critiqued because his ideas do little to empower Black grassroots communities. Gilroy offers more of an abstract utopian vision of a non-racialized world. This perhaps is commendable but it is an unrealistic outlook to comprehend the ubiquitous reality of racism encountered in every sphere of Western societies. The fact of white nationalism raising its ugly head across

Britain/Europe and the United States in the 2020s endorses the point. Even after the uncouth racist presidency of Trump (2017–2021) had left the White House in political turmoil, the effluvia of his racist rants continue to reek across the nation. Certainly, while Trump lost his attempt to be re-elected for a second term, after being impeached an unprecedented two times, he *still* amassed almost seventy-five million votes in the Presidential election of 2020. This social fact should provide more than a caveat as to what may lay ahead in the coming years in terms of white nationalist fever and its concomitant racism—in Europe and North America. The forecast remains bleak for racialized relations and this has both historical and contemporary roots that can be understood within the context of Africana critical studies and the transatlantic paradigm.

The circumstance of Black British academics leaving for the United States back in the early 2000s may indicate to the reader just how bad it was in Britain from a Black scholar's racialized standpoint—overwhelmingly was the distinct lack of opportunity to write from a Black perspective. Undoubtedly, to have preferred the racism of the United States over the British variety should be quite illuminating in an intellectual sense. Moreover, those British scholars who wrote on racialized issues from the 1970s to 1990s, specifically Hall and Gilroy, were often too abstract in their prose and produced largely inaccessible studies for those embedded in the everyday living or day to day realities of British racism. Such dense studies are exemplified by Stuart Hall et al. in *Policing the Crisis: Mugging, the State, and Law and Order* published in 1978. Even Paul Gilroy's first book from 1987, *There Ain't No Black in the Union Jack: The Cultural Politics of Race and Nation* that attempts a "race" and class analysis in regard to Black Britain yet fails to write one iota on Liverpool is telling. Given the fact that Gilroy took the name for his book from a racist chant sung by England football fans against a prominent Black Liverpool Football Club player, John Barnes—who repeated whenever he played for England, "There Ain't No Black in the Union Jack, Johnny Barnes! Johnny Barnes!"—adds curiosity if not gall to the invisibility of Black Liverpool promoted by Gilroy. The racist English fans were stating categorically that they did not want a Black player representing the England football team.

In regard to this situation whereby Black British academics like Hall and Gilroy were essentially divorced from the Liverpool Black and grassroots actualities, certainly in terms of analysis and communication due to the highbrow abstraction of their collective analyses, I contended in the March 4, 2005, issue of the *Times Higher Education Supplement* that the situation was at best problematic:

Arguably, the most respected Black scholar to emerge in the 1970s, and one who would come to dominate any "race-related" analysis in the British academy, was Stuart Hall, who can be considered the "godfather" of Gramscian cultural theory. He led the way, with his students, Paul Gilroy, [Hazel Carby,] and others, following and building on his mantra: "Down with essentialism and the naïve craving for black solidarity." From this group came volume after volume of largely inaccessible writings that attacked any idea of commonality among Black peoples struggling to overcome the reality of everyday white supremacy. Instead, we were to think of ourselves as individuals divorced from any sense of collective Black experience (Christian 2005a, p. 21).

Therefore, the need to both reflect on the Black British experience in the 2020s as being far more deeply rooted than the standard *Empire Windrush* of 1948 is important. Moreover, from an Africana critical studies perspective the reader should note that Black British writers differ in style and content just as any other cultural group. Yet Stuart Hall and Paul Gilroy, along with their acolytes, have had far too much airplay over the last thirty years. A study such as this will hopefully expand discussion and provide readers with greater scope in comprehending another point of view regarding Black British academic thought. Indeed, when I decided to leave my family and friends in Liverpool to take up a full-time academic position at Miami University of Ohio in 2000, I had little choice in regard to creating a successful career as a Black studies scholar. Even having published my first solo book, *Multiracial Identity: An International Perspective* in 2000, there were few, if any, opportunities for a full-time academic career open to Black scholars in Britain relating to Africana critical studies. This point was borne out by the exodus of other Black British scholars who would depart or were already in the United States in the early 2000s.

In addition, it is not as if there was not a foundation for Africana critical studies in Liverpool: the Maritime Museum based on the Albert Dock would be opened by none other than Maya Angelou in October 1994; later to be renamed the International Slavery Museum in 2007 and reopened formally by the Reverend Jessie Jackson—two African American souls from the 1960s and beyond opening a museum in Liverpool dedicated to remembering the historical nightmare of enslavement is quite an irony, given it was the transatlantic slaving era that actually provided the economic foundation for the city to grow its wealth and to become a powerhouse in the eighteenth and nineteenth centuries. The International Slavery Museum is now dedicated to preserving this legacy; along with teaching existing and yet unborn generations of its historical significance to the City of Liverpool and beyond.

Lastly, a significant moment related to this study that occurred in 2005 and of importance to the reader relates to the murder of a Black Liverpudlian,

Anthony Walker (1987–2005). He was an eighteen-year-old of Jamaican parentage but himself born in Liverpool, who lived in a predominantly white area as a lone Black family in Huyton, Liverpool. His aunt, Juanita Walker, had worked in the Charles Wootton College in an administrative position before the Liverpool City Council withdrew the funding for this Black grassroots educational establishment in 2000. Anthony Walker, on July 29, 2005, was walking his white girlfriend to a bus stop with his cousin, another Black youth, when two racist thugs threatened them with violence. The two Black boys and the white girl walked on to another bus stop to keep clear of them, but the racists followed in a car, the girl and cousin were able to run to get help, but Anthony was struck in the head with an ice pick. It was embedded so deeply in his head it caused him to be brain dead. He was formally pronounced deceased the following morning in hospital. This murder was openly motivated by racism, in line with other violent attacks on Black Liverpudlians in previous times, some which are covered in later chapters, but this was different because he was in a middle-class part of Huyton, and he was a very good student with immense potential. It can be assumed that Anthony had to cope with microaggressions being the only Black pupil in his school. Nevertheless, by all accounts, he was doing very well in his schoolwork. This racist murder was clearly unprovoked and completely vicious by all measurements of violence. Thankfully, the killers were arrested by the police fairly rapidly and would be eventually sentenced to life in prison—given the history of assaults on people of color in the city that went unpunished this was a minor victory.

There were no complaints about the police and how they conducted the investigation, unlike with a similar gratuitous racist murder of a young Black man, Stephen Lawrence. Also, eighteen years of age and a talented student, his murder occurred in London, April 1993. Stephen was set upon by at least five racist thugs while waiting at a bus stop with a friend. The police in this case were found highly negligent and corrupt in their pursuit of justice for the Lawrence family. Back in 1993 this caused Stephen's parents to fight for justice in the case of their son. Briefly, in what would become known as the Stephen Lawrence Report or the McPherson Report (1999), it was found that institutional racism was rife throughout the police force in British society—along with most other British institutions. The findings were a major victory for Black British communities throughout the country, but again it was a case of the recommendations for change not being implemented that has since frustrated Black Britons. To make matters worse it took many years before the killers of Stephen Lawrence were brought to justice. Stephen's mother, Doreen Lawrence, shared her story in seeking justice for her son in a book titled *Doreen Lawrence: And Still I Rise, Seeking Justice for Stephen* (2006). Without her courage, and that of the father Neville Lawrence, Stephen would not have received justice. His body was returned for burial to Clarendon in Jamaica where the Lawrence family still have roots.

In the 2005 Anthony Walker case in Liverpool there was swift reaction from the police to apprehend his killers, unlike with Stephen Lawrence. Yet, the murder of Anthony again demonstrated in graphic horror that racism was still festering in British society. There was never a surprise to this viciousness of racism in Liverpool among Black Liverpudlians, even though there manifested a degree of outrage for such a senseless murder from the majority of Liverpudlians. There remained still the evidence of the Liverpool City Council taking funding away from organizations that assisted Black Liverpudlians in their fight against racism—so the "outrage" for Anthony was not fully sincere from those who occupied positions of power in the city that could genuinely help fight institutional and individual acts of racism.

Crucially, one requires a degree of perspicacity to comprehend the Liverpool Black experience in terms of its historical and contemporary trajectory. Hence, this study aims to provide the reader with a tour de force in relation to the City of Liverpool and its historical Black presence. There is an effort to place the analysis firmly within the paradigm of an Africana critical studies perspective with a determination to explain the history and culture from the point of view of Black Liverpudlians, who have been at the center of so much racialized discrimination without ever fully gaining recompense or acknowledgment for such historical abuses. Ultimately, this contribution to Africana critical studies is designed to provide readers with an insider's account of a Black British experience. Indeed, there are few accounts of Liverpool Black history that are written within the context of Africana critical studies. Arguably, William E. Nelson Jr.'s 2000 publication, *Black Atlantic Politics: Dilemmas of Political Empowerment in Boston and Liverpool*, has given the most insightful twentieth century account on Black politics in Liverpool, while comparing it with another transatlantic case study, Boston. William Ackah and Mark Christian's 1997 volume on *Black Organisation and Identity in Liverpool* stands currently as the most useful interpretation of Black community organizations in the city at that time period. In addition, grassroots resistance to institutionalized racism went hand-in-hand with the formation of Black Identity in a regional sense known colloquially as Liverpool Born Blacks or LBBs—in response to the historical and scurrilous term "half-caste" (Blacks of mixed heritage)—which deemed and stigmatized their various African heritages, whether African continental, Caribbean, or African American (Christian 2008a; Ackah and Christian 1997; Small 1991).

THEORETICAL GROUNDING IN AFRICANA CRITICAL STUDIES

One cannot begin to write a book that speaks to complexity of a Black British experience without having a theoretical foundation that allows for the reader to comprehend the writer and what he or she has absorbed in an epistemological sense. In following an Africana critical studies paradigm there are philosophers one should read in order to have a competent comprehension in the experiences of those who had fought for both physical and mental liberation of African peoples—wherever they endured the might of the European oppressor (Bassey 2007). For example, if one is to grasp the notion of the "Colonizer and the Colonized" or the "Oppressor and the Oppressed" then one has to have consulted the works of such writers as: Frantz Fanon, Amilcar Cabral, Albert Memmi, and Aimé Césaire. Why? Simply because their studies collectively have reached the core, both physically and psychologically, to what Africana peoples suffered under a Eurocentric colonial regime. Moreover, each of those selected writers had experienced life and education under such colonial structures. They were able to write viscerally about the delusions of grandeur emanating from those who had the power to control those who did not have the power under colonialism. The same can be stated in relation to these writers comprehending the intricacies of self-hatred among the colonized—something that continues to be grappled with today in postcolonial times. Frantz Fanon's *Black Skin, White Masks* personifies the psychological problems of internalized racism—it cannot be underestimated.

Of course, the writers mentioned above are not an exhaustive list but they are certainly a "representative example" of a counter-hegemonic contribution that profoundly offered an understanding of racialized hierarchy and oppression. In turn, this "racialism" was an integral aspect of European colonialism in Africa and the Caribbean regions, whereby most Black Britons emerged. Because the Black settlers into Britain had firsthand knowledge and experience of a colonial setting. This ingrained colonial mentality was then transferred from the satellite to the metropole; each Black settler brought with them a view of British colonialism. Though Fanon, Cabral, Memmi, and Césaire had come out of French and Portuguese colonial heritages, the basic dimensions of "oppressor/oppressed" remain similar, if not the same. Therefore, as an Africana critical studies scholar there should be a theoretical grounding in thinkers who have shared ideas and concepts that fit within an epistemological paradigm that can be employed by the researcher—which this study has provided.

To be grounded in the British colonial legacy there is herein an engagement with writers and thinkers, beyond Stuart Hall and Paul Gilroy, such as: C. L. R. James, Learie Constantine, Samuel Selvon, George Lamming, Linton Kwesi Johnson, Beryl Gilroy, Benjamin Zephaniah, Levi Tafari, A. Sivanandan, Buchi Emecheta, Zadie Smith, Caryl Phillips, and others. A caveat, merely a few of those writers have ever focused on the Liverpool Black experience, apart from the poets Zephaniah and Tafari—the latter having been born in Liverpool of Jamaican parents. It would be apt to describe Levi Tafari as the Black Poet Laureate of Liverpool. Part of his poem "Liverpool Experience" reads:

> Yes living inna Liverpool
> is living in hell
> especially if you are
> black as well
> yuh should hear
> some a the stories that
> we can tell
> nuh wonder the youths
> them did have to rebel (Tafari 1989, p. 73)

Indeed, maybe that is why so many of the Black British writers have focused on London-centric themes. Despite the fact that those authors are geographically distanced from Liverpool, they too link into the transatlantic experience because the legacy of colonialism knows no boundaries for Black and brown people in Britain. There are the same themes related to "otherness" and alienation. When considered from an Africana critical studies perspective it is necessary to view each Black experience as unique but similar, which may sound incongruous but on the human level it is not. The tentacles of racialized hierarchies are widespread and even the simplest thing such as access to travel is bound up in it. What is unique to Liverpool is in the longevity of Black settlement and the development of an Indigenous Liverpool Born Black community that has been socially excluded and stigmatized over decades by institutional forces stemming from the Liverpool City Council, law enforcement, and even university studies with dubious social science disseminated racism (Christian 2008a; Zuberi and Bonilla-Silva 2008).

To be able to uncouple oneself from the avalanche of misconceptions derived from a Eurocentric worldview is itself a task every Africana critical studies thinker has to grapple with. Reading contemporary Africana philosophers such as Charles Mills is a fundamental necessity if one is to develop a liberated mind that can cope with Eurocentric ideas. His book *The Racial Contract* reveals how the European expansionism over the last five hundred years created the debilitating nomenclature most scholars have to deal with today: "whites" and "non-whites" via racialized hegemony.

Basically, Mills skillfully articulates the manner in which Eurocentric notions of Enlightenment were ingrained, juxtaposed, by a system of racial hierarchy that swept through all aspects of epistemology in Western universities. Today, we still largely have this same situation. Mills published *The Racial Contract* in 1997, and he opens it up with the prophetic words:

> White supremacy is the unnamed political system that has made the modern world what it is today. You will not find this term in introductory, or even advanced, texts in political theory. A standard graduate philosophy course will start off with Plato and Aristotle, perhaps say something about Augustine, Aquinas and Machiavelli, move on to Hobbes, Lock, Mill, and Marx, and wind up with Rawls and Nozick. It will introduce you to notions of aristocracy, democracy, absolutism, liberalism, representative government, socialism, welfare capitalism, and libertarianism. But though it covers more than two thousand years of Western political thought . . . there will be no mention of the basic political system that has shaped the world for the past several hundred years (Mills 1997, p.1).

Twenty years later in his *Black Rights/White Wrongs: The Critique of Racial Liberalism,* Mills continued to contend that Western liberalism has been essentially an exclusive club for whites; though it seeks to articulate a "creed of fairness" there has always been the oppression of Africana peoples wherever they have existed under European imperialism. Mills is certainly an important philosopher in the field of Africana critical studies that indirectly informs this study. There are other Africana philosophers, such as Molefi K. Asante, who is arguably the most prolific writer in the contemporary Africana world. He has also traveled to most parts of the globe speaking to literally thousands of people relating to Africana philosophy, what he deems now as Africological and/or Afrocentric thought. Indeed, Asante in August of 2007 gave the Slavery Remembrance lecture at the Liverpool Town Hall, and he opened up his talk with these words:

> Whenever I am in the City of Liverpool I feel quite connected to it like I am in an American city, a city with familiar images, histories, and dynamics. In many ways it is like Charleston, Savannah, Baltimore, and my own city, Philadelphia. Of course the link is truly historical but Liverpool has a visceral impact on me, a descendant of enslaved Africans whose ancestry goes to Sudan and Nigeria. I will never know if the ships that took my ancestors to the Americas were built and outfitted here at the Mersey (Asante 2007c).

Theoretically, the importance of Asante's words relates to the profound linkages between Africana peoples the world over. The boundaries are rather superficial, despite differences in how we may speak, how we have been forged as humans under rather similar degrees of racialized hierarchies (Asante and Dove 2021; Walvin 2022). Therefore, Molefi Asante as an African American can comfortably link his life to that of Liverpool, England because there is something in the historical past that has resonance with the contemporary—this is something we should keep in mind. The transatlantic experience was a way to exchange, intermix, and forge different Africana experiences, but still there is something much deeper that allows visceral connections to foster and that is why Maya Angelou and Jessie Jackson too can come to Liverpool, England from the United States and speak on issues that connect us all as humans. That is why a Frederick Douglass and many other fugitives from bondage seeking freedom could plead their case in Britain, though ironic as this is given its profound slaving past. Therein lies the incongruity of a Black traveler who can find his or her freedom in a place where "freedom" is withheld to Indigenous Blacks.

Consequently, there is arguably no Africana researcher that has not dealt with unraveling in his or her mind notions of racialized hierarchy. Whether it be those Black or brown persons who were raised in Africa or the Caribbean, or have been born in Britain or the Americas, the specter of racialized experience is in perpetual flux and this can be validated from reading the works of the writers and thinkers already touched upon. Yes, this study delves into the world of Black Liverpudlians—but it cannot divorce itself from the broader manifestations that have impacted Africana peoples, and other people of color, historically under colonialism and its profound legacy under what is most often deemed: postcolonialism.

However, to go back to enslavement and its debilitating impact on the Black mind and body. In this sense, the use of Frederick Douglass and his peers in this research is extremely illuminating for getting grounded in the horrific nature of what the enslaved endured under that inhumane barbarity. Reading the works of many Douglass scholars, too numerous to name here but provided in the extensive bibliography, who have engaged with the life and times of Frederick Douglass has been a boon in terms of walking in the shoes of this great historical transatlantic figure. Moreover, the fact that he arrived in 1845 and left out of Liverpool in 1847 allowed for Douglass to be juxtaposed with the Liverpool Black mixed heritage experience in the city. Writers like Charles Dickens and Herman Melville provided even broader relevance to Liverpool of the nineteenth century. When one reads these authors in conjunction with Frederick Douglass it is intensely moving because as peers, they were living markedly different social statuses—Douglass being a fugitive in Britain on the run from enslavement in America, while Dickens and Melville were writing in relative comfort in comparison. One can take that metaphor of Douglass in the nineteenth century and compare it with a Black Liverpudlian scholar writing in the twenty-first century—compared to his white peers, who have "scholarly privileges of access" to historical data that are far easier to obtain, he has far greater difficulty in accessing basic historical data in archives based in the Liverpool City Council. This study will elaborate on the "dilution" by the established order to the truth in terms of Liverpool and its deeply racist historical past. Making it difficult for a researcher to do his or her work in the twentieth and twenty-first centuries by withholding documentation is akin to Douglass not having his freedom to live his best life while Dickens and Melville could write and think within a framework of access to all areas of life and liberty.

Again, relating to Douglass' era as a Black man in nineteenth century Britain, it is also important to consider Karl Marx and Frederick Engels' *The Communist Manifesto* because it was first published in 1848 and these two men were peers of Douglass—that is in age but certainly not circumstance. Yet when one delves into the reading from an Africana critical studies perspective one finds no connection between Marx and Douglass, even though the latter was making a powerful impact among all who listened to him during his tour of Britain between 1845 and 1847. This juxtaposition of Marx and Douglass deserves further scrutiny, as within the context of this study it was a very important exercise to consider the "working class emancipator" in relation to the African American fugitive from enslavement who spoke in Liverpool, October 19, 1846, to an audience of 2,500 on a Monday evening at the Concert Hall in Lord Nelson Street—quite outstanding given Douglass was on that evening openly criticizing the Christian Church for its hypocrisy in being inextricably woven into the bondage of Africans in America, at that very hour. Moreover, given the fact that among Liverpool merchants there would later be major support for the Confederates during the forthcoming American Civil War, along with the Anthropological Society of London (Fryer 1984, p.179). Yet here we have speaking boldly in 1846 a fugitive and by law still enslaved, speaking in a city engulfed in the history of enslavement and its profits—quite astounding as this was fifteen years prior to the outset of the Civil War. Indeed, the presence of Frederick Douglass in Liverpool in 1846 suggests he was there at a time when many Liverpool merchants and institutions such as the Christian Church were inextricably woven into the fabric of American slavery. Douglass was a brave soul to speak out in Liverpool, England, while so vulnerable in his capacity as a fugitive from bondage. However, even after his freedom was secured, he continued to fight for the rights of his people and women generally up to the last day of his life—literally. In all of this, he was intertwined with autoethnographic research—linking his life experience to that of the broader issues encountered by those who struggled for liberty and justice.

Introduction 15

WHAT IS AUTOETHNOGRAPHY?

Within the context of qualitative methodology in Africana critical studies (Conyers 2016, section IV), this study employs what can be deemed a "semi-autoethnographic" framework by integrating aspects of a Black family from Liverpool: The Christians. A Black Liverpudlian family that can put some "meat on the bones" of what it was like to grow up in the City of Liverpool in the mid-to-late twentieth century. Given the profound discrimination associated with the city, and with the author being part of the Christian family, there requires some methodological validation. This self-reflexivity can emerge from the qualitative method known as "autoethnography"—which is defined by Christopher Poulos, an expert of autoethnography, in this manner:

> *Autoethnography* is an autobiographical genre of academic writing that draws on and analyzes or interprets the lived experience of the author and connects researcher insights to self-identity, cultural rules and resources, communication practices, traditions, premise, symbols, rules, shared meanings, emotions, values, and larger social, cultural, and political issues (Poulos 2021, p. 4).

The reason I employ "semi" before "autoethnography" is because this is primarily an academic piece of work that simply sheds light on an area that has been neglected—especially from an Africana critical studies perspective. Nor has any writer ever employed a transatlantic analysis by linking what Gilroy has deemed *The Black Atlantic* with a greater emphasis on a Black British grassroots point of view. The use of autoethnography is very helpful and it does not diminish the social analysis. On the contrary, it enhances what has been stated and states what has never been stated, yet needs to be, in regard to the Liverpool Black experience. Having interacted with many of the key Black grassroots organizations and actors in Liverpool, for example, merely enriches the semi-autoethnographic aspect. Moreover, having traveled, lived, loved, lost, and found, across the transatlantic divide between Britain and North America for over three decades, in the capacity of being an Africana critical studies scholar, there is much to share in my semi-autoethnographic leanings that only add to the authenticity of the narrative. Of course, the interpretation of events is no different than that of a James Baldwin explaining his thoughts or experiences during the Civil Rights Movement era; or a Frederick Douglass sharing his life and times while under the yoke of enslavement. Being Black in Liverpool is also another example of the Black Atlantic paradigm in motion and it should be considered authentic from the vantage point of those who have lived and endured such a life.

In an interesting take on the transatlantic experience of Africa and the slaving port of Liverpool, the celebrated Black British writer Caryl Phillips, who was raised on a working-class estate in Leeds, Yorkshire, in his book *The Atlantic Sound* dedicates a chapter to the city titled "Leaving Home" which is fictitious in part but based on historical knowledge. In addition, Phillips adds to the chapter his own practice of visiting Liverpool, and learning about its slaving past in relation to offering a contemporary view of the city. For his visit he has a Liverpool Born Black guide, Stephen, and in reading the account of their interaction one gets the impression that Phillips is condescending and ill-informed, taking liberty with his prose to give the impression of his "enlightened mind" compared to that of the Black Liverpudlian. Indeed, he explains to the reader that Stephen is merely twenty-three years old, and left school at sixteen years of age—but he has a passion for Black history. Part of the characterization Phillips portrays of Stephen could well fit Mark Christian—the only difference is that the latter attended three universities, one abroad, gaining the bachelor's, master's, and doctorate degrees, unlike his fellow Black Liverpudlian.

What is very curious about Caryl Phillips' prose is in him being a Black British writer who was raised within a working-class context in Leeds, Yorkshire—which he explains in another one of his books, *Color Me English: Migration and Belonging Before and After 9/11*, published in 2011. Phillips was brought up in relative poverty on a council estate, which is about seventy miles from Liverpool. In other words, he is not that far removed from Stephen's life and times other than a seventy-mile divide. Yet in *The Atlantic Sound* he writes on Liverpool as if he is a traveler from overseas who does not comprehend Black British experience—this is implicitly disingenuous. In the latter part of his chapter where he is on a guided tour of Liverpool 8, the main area where Black Liverpudlians reside, he writes:

> Liverpool 8, or Toxteth, appears to me to be no different from scores of other British inner-city areas that have entered a stage of terminal decline [like the estate in Leeds where he was raised]. Stephen and I drive down streets and along avenues that were clearly once grand, and we pass by the elegant single-family residences that have, over the years, been divided up into units which now provide immigrants with shared accommodation. The white population has withdrawn to other parts of the city, and it is clear that the social services now pay scant attention to cleaning and upkeep. The present-day "immigrants" are from both Africa and the Caribbean, and they have slowly, but not without some considerable difficulty, attempted to blend in with the proud LBB [Liverpool Born Black] population which was originally made up of West African seamen, former slaves from the Americas and others connected to trading in both goods and humans (Phillips 2000, p. 110).

The ignorance in the above extract from *The Atlantic Sound* from the pen of Caryl Phillips in regard to Black settlement in Liverpool is glaring. What makes it worse is in the fact that he literally emerged from "down the road" in Leeds—a one hour and fifteen minute journey with decent traffic. First, and it is so ingrained it needs to be finally put to rest, African seaman were not the *only* sailors to be connected to Liverpool and its port; there were Caribbean sailors and African American sailors explained by Herman Melville in his book *Redburn* published in 1849. Moreover, there were rarely any large settlements of "former slaves" in the city, which is humbug history. There were African American soldiers, especially from WW2, who interacted with the local population producing "brown babies" (Sherwood 1995; Christian 1995/96b). Also, to suggest the Liverpool Born Blacks were "against African and Caribbean migrants" is to state they were in a sense against their fathers—which is ridiculous. Now, of course, there are incidences of "outsiders" being unwanted in any community. But overall, the Liverpool Black experience has opened its doors to peoples of African heritage from all over the transatlantic world. Just as there are some light frictions between the Caribbean Island peoples—mostly in humor—this should not be taken out of context as Caryl Phillips has taken liberty with his stereotypical prose on Liverpool Born Blacks. It is for this reason that authentic Liverpool Black writers should tell their stories. The problem then is in Liverpool white historians and researchers like John Belchem (2014, p. 271) employing the ideas of Phillips without any critical response to his unsubstantiated comments. For example, how does Phillips validate such a claim that "Blacks from other parts of Britain have often been made to feel unwelcome in Liverpool"? This is akin to Black Liverpudlians going to London and feeling "unwelcome" when in fact it depends on many factors, such as whom one interacts with and where one goes to socialize. Crucially, it is a rather subjective comment that is not backed up with empirical data. In reading Benjamin Zephaniah's *Inna Liverpool* from 1992, a Black British writer of Jamaican heritage raised largely in East London, there is nothing but respect for Black Liverpudlians. There are many other "outsiders" from around the globe who could be deemed friends of Blacks in Liverpool. What is important to note here is the old adage: do not judge a people, community, or situation before finding out first for yourself.

The problem is in a researcher comprehending the deeply rooted ostracism encountered by Black Liverpudlians that Belchem acknowledges in one sense, then denies in another. For example, he clearly notes the demise of Black grassroots organizations in Liverpool 8 that helped give Black Liverpudlians life chances and a degree of social recreational activities, yet he fails to critically question the establishment, those in the Liverpool City Council who made these decisions to defund, the role of Gideon Ben-Tovim as an influential actor in the Liverpool 8 scene with his undeniably paternalistic hold on Black grassroots politics. None of this is assessed by Belchem

2014. Other researchers, like Diane Frost (2000, 2021) and Jacqueline Nassy Brown (2005), fail miserably to get to the core of why Black Identity constructs created by Liverpool Born Blacks were so important in the resistance to stigma of their humanity via white racism. Thankfully, Dave Clay (2020) offers a condensed historical visual with commentary of what should be focused upon in regard to authentic Black experience in Liverpool. His research also has an autoethnographic element and it shows because there is a genuine depiction of what Black Liverpudlians had endured in the city from 1919 to 2019. The problem is in Clay's work not being referenced by such researchers, particularly those based at the University of Liverpool who most often dilute the essence of Black Liverpudlian resistance to the forces of oppression in the city. This is not hyperbole as this study will show in the following chapters; there has been a systemic denial of the deeply rooted racism that has stifled Black empowerment in the city, especially from those who have had significant institutional power to effect change and/or disseminate social research with veracity.

As for being an outsider in terms of one's research output, I would never, for example, be arrogant enough to write about the nuances of being Black, say, in Leeds, Yorkshire, or being Black and female in London—there are certain aspects of identity that researchers should leave the interpretation to those who have encountered stigma and racism firsthand. In this sense, Caryl Phillips, Jacqueline Nassy Brown, as Black writers, and John Belchem, Diane Frost, and other white researchers should always be aware of the shades of difference in Black settlement, and *how* Liverpool Born Blacks have consistently fought back any attempt to stigmatize their collective lives. In assessing Phillips' *The Atlantic Sound*, for example, it is a "sound" distinctly lacking harmony with the nuances of Liverpool Black experience. Holding the entire Liverpool Born Black community accountable based on a young Black Liverpudlian male guide's personality and knowledge is a dishonorable approach to research. Overall, his assessment of the Black experience in the city merely offers an extension and proliferation of unnecessary and arcane stereotypes. In, for example, the closing of his "Leaving Home" chapter, Phillips lets the reader know exactly what he thinks about Liverpool, as he states:

> At Lime Street Station I sit and wait for my train. . . . A train pulls in and I can hear the uncivilized braying of football fans readying themselves for a Saturday afternoon of revelry. I am glad I am leaving. It is disquieting to be in a place where history is so physically present, yet so glaringly absent from people's consciousness (ibid., p.117).

Clearly, Phillips is glad to be leaving Liverpool, after staying in a plush hotel and being escorted around the city by a local guide, a young Black Liverpudlian, which must have been very difficult for him (Phillips 2000, p. 98). Facetiousness aside, Phillips was right about one thing; it "is disquieting to be in a place where history is so physically present, yet so glaringly absent from people's consciousness." It is therefore the aim of this study, via a semi-autoethnographic framework, to shed greater light on a largely hidden or misunderstood transatlantic history. To be sure, it is the researcher's experience and insights that will provide an added nuance that is often missing from those who have written on Black Liverpudlians—as mentioned earlier. It may be unsettling to the reader who has no understanding of Liverpool and its Black heritage.

In addition to autoethnography, the sociological perspectives of Erving Goffman, exemplified in two of his studies, *The Presentation of Self in Everyday Life* (1959), and *Stigma: Notes on the Management of Spoiled Identity*, are useful in comprehending the unique aspect of Black Liverpudlian identity being stigmatized (Christian 2008a). Goffman explains a stigmatized person/group in this manner:

> By definition, of course, we believe the person with a stigma is not quite human. On this assumption we exercise varieties of discrimination, through which we effectively, if often unthinkingly, reduce his [/her] life chances. We construct a stigma-theory, an ideology to explain his [/her] inferiority and account for the danger he [/she] represents, sometimes rationalizing an animosity based on other differences, such as those of social class (Goffman 1986, p. 5).

In the Goffman sense of "stigma" it is contended historically that Liverpool Born Blacks have been stigmatized, making their life chances more difficult to attain. The writers that have indirectly or directly agreed with this researcher emanate from the Liverpool Black experience and their works are contained within the chapters of this book. In addition, C. Wright Mills' *The Sociological Imagination* provides a compelling paradigm for understanding the history/biography of anyone born in a particular time and place. It is the juncture between one's birth (year) and the history of the day (era) that often determines how life unfolds for the person connected to a specific cultural group. C. Wright Mills argued: "Neither the life of an individual nor the history of a society can be understood without understanding both" (1959, p. 3). Therefore, in combining Goffman's ideas with that of Wright's is an important methodological strategy that has been employed to facilitate a smoother narrative that is found sometimes implicitly or explicitly in this study.

Moreover, extensive research has been conducted over the span of thirty-five years—and many interviews have been conducted with prominent

Liverpool Born Blacks or persons who have spent time in Liverpool from the continent of Africa, the Caribbean, and the United States. Indeed, to name a few I have either interviewed on numerous occasions or have spent quality time with discussing the Liverpool Black experience, some of which have sadly transitioned: Eric Lynch, Dorothy Kuya, Wally Brown, Dave Clay, Steve Smith, Ben Agwuna, Ron Babatunde Phillips, Ijou Thompson, Maria O'Reilly, Solly Bassey, Richard Benjamin, Ibrahim Thompson, Adam Hussein, Gloria Hyatt, Stephen Small, Ruby Dixon, Joe Joel, Tony Ford, Peter Bassey, Eddie Amoo, Dave Smith, Ray Quintal, Alvin Christie, William Ackah, Ray Costello, Isaac Mensah, Barnor Hesse, Ray Quarless, Yinka Yusef, Paul Smeda, Eugene Lamb, Michael "Spongy" Prendergast, Michaela Amoo, Manneh Brown, Michelle Spooner, Louis Julienne, Michael Greenidge, Wally Brown, Eugene Weaver, Ann Carney, Liz Drysdale, Ivan Freeman, Tony Bessman, Howard Gayle, Abdul Gayle, Ken Drysdale, Brian Khader, Lorraine Riley, John O'Connor, Joe Farrag, Laurence Westgaph, Karl Smith, Vickie Nurse, William E. Nelson Jr., and Patricia Reid-Merritt. There are certainly others, many souls, who have helped me directly or indirectly understand Liverpool and Black settlement in the city that goes back centuries—this book is therefore an amalgamation of all the above scholarly knowledge, the Christian family, life experience, and social interaction with friends and colleagues who comprehend the nuances of Black heritage in *Transatlantic Liverpool: Shades of the Black Atlantic*.

REMAINING OUTLINE OF BOOK

Chapter one considers the theoretical scope of the "Black Atlantic" as articulated by Paul Gilroy due to its continued influence on transatlantic Africana experiences. The main aim is to extend the paradigm and allow for other areas to be examined and to expose some weaknesses in Gilroy's perspective. In other words, there should be room for other areas to be explored, such as Liverpool, England, as it has a rich legacy in both transatlantic history and Black British settlement. Chapter two covers the Christian family to give an insight into what other Black Liverpudlian families ordinarily encountered living and surviving in the city during the mid-to-late twentieth century. What transpires in this chapter can be buttressed by the broader Liverpool Born Black experience, so there is an effort to cover the migration and settlement aspect, along with sharing how a family grew to be famed for both musical and educational achievement. Chapter three examines areas such as schooling and social recreation for Black Liverpudlians, drawing from historical primary documentation from grassroots organizations that provides authentic evidence that has too often been ignored or dismissed. Education reports and academic studies elucidate the chapter's themes and topics. Those who led grassroots organizations or wrote reports are highlighted because of their relevance in knowing how they functioned under often adverse funding conditions. In terms of community recreation, and despite the constant pressure for survival, Black Liverpudlians also found ways to take the pressure off with a focus on amateur football in Liverpool 8. Chapter four focuses on the history of anti-Black riots in the city, along with the uprising of 1981 that is viewed as being the worst urban disturbance on record for the British homeland. There is also an analysis relating to the demise of Black organizations that flourished in the 1980s to 1990s before an outright assault on the funding by the city council. In addition, there is an analysis of the official City of Liverpool Slave Trade Apology that was sanctioned by the Liverpool City Council in December 1999. This "apology" offered an unreserved act of contrition regarding the historical legacy of the slave port and all that followed; it promised to work with Black communities and to fight institutional racism. However, in reality during the 2000s, Black grassroots organizations fell like a pack of cards largely due to the Liverpool City Council reneging on its promises to Black communities etched into the Slave Trade Apology. What is more egregious is the fact that the cuts in funding began in the following year after the apology was authorized.

Finally, chapter five considers the lives of two men of Black mixed heritage, from opposite sides of the transatlantic who encompass the essence, incongruously, of seeking liberation generations apart and in different eras. Frederick Douglass traveled by steamship from Boston to Liverpool as a fugitive on the run from enslavement in 1845, disembarking in Liverpool. Not only does he find his liberty in Britain, he is never the same again due to his sojourn across the British Isles speaking out loudly against bondage and slaveholding. His time in Liverpool is of particular importance to this study as it provides an insight into nineteenth century Liverpool. On the other hand, when I left Liverpool in 1992 to pursue a master's degree at Ohio State in the United States it was to pursue academic freedom. That experience led me to intellectual growth and development that would never have been possible as a Liverpool Born Black individual—opportunities for Black scholars were limited and largely unsustainable.

The irony is in the fact that I, like Douglass, was pursuing the prospect of a better life. Certainly, I was not a fugitive like him, but neither was I able to fulfill my potential and have a decent professional life in Britain as an academic who focused on Africana critical studies. Perhaps, after the reader contemplates this entire study, it will be easier to comprehend why I simply had to leave Liverpool in order to develop positively as a Black British scholar. Liverpool *still* does not offer a viable option for teaching full-time in the university system if focused on Africana critical studies. Frederick

Douglass fought all his career after being manumitted to improve the lives of his people; I too have spent the lion's share of my vocation defending the humanity of Africana peoples. One may ask, at bottom, what then is the real difference in these two lives beyond time and place, as C. Wright Mills explained in *The Sociological Imagination*? Crucially, this transatlantic study will be of interest to anyone interested in expanding their notion of the Black Atlantic, and who is keen to discover the historical struggle of Liverpool Born Blacks. Time and place do offer different ways to view the life experiences of individuals, but often there is relative similarity that creates a rather telltale curiosity that gives sociological food for thought.

Chapter 1

Theorizing Transatlantic Liverpool and the Black Atlantic Paradigm

This chapter will explain through a myriad of historical and cultural theorists the complexity of transatlantic contours that has led to both the hybridity and bastardization of Africana cultures over the course of centuries. As an opening caveat, endeavoring to encapsulate the experience of millions of Africans dispersing to the Americas and the Caribbean regions in the fifteenth to nineteenth centuries, via transatlantic routes, and later in the twentieth century throughout Europe due to the relations of "colonizer and colonized" is an unfathomable task. To take a francophone literature scholar, for example, the Caribbean writer Édouard Glissant in his *Poetics of Relation* (1997) speaks, among other things, to the complexity of Blackness and its relationship to otherness. Yet, compared to his compatriot Frantz Fanon (1925–1961), a fellow native of Martinique, Glissant is largely apolitical in his search for alterity meaning. Both Fanon and Glissant were arguably skeptical about the Negritude movement and its writers, such as Aimé Césaire (1913–2008), whom they implicitly considered "essentialist" for wanting African history re-centered in cultural *and* political discourse. This perspective would be carried forward by the likes of Gilroy and others who gained implicit encouragement via the status quo.

However, one could argue that both Fanon and Glissant were a tad hasty to dismiss Negritude as essentialist without taking account of its *essence*: to shine a light on the hypocrisy of the European colonizer and to restore ultimately the humanity of the African and her descendants strewn, hybridized, and culturally bastardized across continents over centuries of European violence and domination. Césaire (1972) can best put his critics in place with his own words by speaking to those who suggested he advocated a "return" to the past. Far from it being a return, it is simply acknowledging that there is a past to be proud of in postcolonial eras. This is necessary because the colonizer created such an inferiority complex that Fanon profoundly noted, as Césaire contended:

> It seems that in certain circles they pretend to have discovered in me an "enemy of Europe" and a prophet of the return to the ante-European past ["ante" whereby Africa had once democratic and fraternal societies until destroyed by imperialism].

He continues,

> For my part, I search in vain for the place where I could have expressed such views; where I have ever underestimated the importance of Europe in the history of human thought; where I have ever preached a *return* of any kind; where I ever claimed that there could be a *return* (p. 23).

The point in his work, it seems, was merely to emphasize the barbarity of European colonialism and to show with reference and detail the tremendous hypocrisy entailed. He was not denying Europe its civilization or contributions, but he was underlining the manner in which it denied Africa its offerings to the world in terms of invention, arts, and culture. Césaire was writing his truth, his insight, into how European colonization of lands inhabited by Indigenous peoples had brought great devastation to their cultures and ancient traditions. He also explains in *Discourse on Colonialism* the tragedy of Africa has been its place in history that coincided with European conquest, "It was our misfortune to encounter that particular Europe on our path, and that Europe is responsible before the human community for the highest heap of corpses in history" (p. 24). In other words, Africa was unfortunate to meet and engage with European traders in African humanity and later colonizers and exploiters of their lands, as it was the onset of a domination that proved devastating beyond scope for peoples of African heritage (Davidson 1961, 1992; Rodney 1970, 1972).

EUROPEAN HEGEMONY CREATED COUNTER-HEGEMONY

Keep in mind that Césaire was an African Caribbean man who endured under French colonialism. The point here is in the fact that one does not necessarily need to have direct association with Africa to comprehend the unsavory impact of enslavement and colonialism. Nor does one have to speak French, English, Spanish, Dutch, Portuguese, Danish, or German to comprehend European colonialism and its hegemony. That stated, the salient features of all writers are the continued conundrum in how to explain the experiences of populations who can be deemed descendants of Africans and their historical interaction with Europeans. After all, this is the essence of Africana critical studies in wanting to extrapolate how peoples of African heritage, in all their cultural and physical complexity, have survived the onslaught of European domination. One can read Glissant or Fanon in different ways; this again stems from both the manner in which a writer chooses her topic and perspective on European domination. If one is to be critical, to be honest as a writer, then there is a need to be conscious of one's understanding of history. Indeed, as noted in the introduction, James Baldwin writes in *Notes of a Native Son*, "I want to be an honest man and a good writer" (2012, p. 9), and this can be attested in his writings related most evidently to the African American experience. The same can be stated in relation to Césaire and those who experienced the colonized practices in the Caribbean or Africa during the early twentieth century. One can disagree with a writer's truth and accept another's but *any* author is accountable to veracity. In real terms, European colonialism was at best evil; this can be determined merely in regard to how it was broadly administered. It was a cruel system in terms of profound oppression of Indigenous peoples, turning their lives literally upside down—while attempting to destroy their cultures. Césaire, does not shirk his responsibility to accuracy and authenticity as an anticolonial writer in his influential essay first published in 1955, *Discourse on Colonialism*:

> That if I am attacked on the grounds of intent, I maintain that colonialist Europe is dishonest in trying to justify its colonizing activity *a posteriori* by the obvious material progress that has been achieved in certain fields under the colonial regime—since *sudden* change is always possible, in history as elsewhere (p. 24).

Clearly, Césaire like other Negritude contemporaries of the 1950s sought to put a mirror to the face of European colonialism. Francophone Africans and Caribbeans were living through a time of growing anticolonialism on the continent and shared their ideas, along with praxis, as African centered intellectual activists. The field of colonial and postcolonial studies reveals a continuum of writing that delves into the vicissitudes of transatlantic experiences. Ideas and interpretations continue to yield dialogue; just as the above took into account a sliver of the francophone insight, this book is focused largely on British colonialism and its former territory, the United States. The point is to note how "European Colonialism" had diverse nations involved with a degree of variance in how each colonizer operated, but on the whole the outcome was the same. Again, we turn to Césaire who viewed colonialism as universal in its outcome:

I look around and wherever there are colonizers and colonized face to face, I see force, brutality, cruelty, sadism, conflict, and, in a parody of education, the hasty manufacture of a few thousand subordinate functionaries, "boys," artisans, office clerks, and interpreters necessary for the smooth operation of business (p. 21).

The reality of racialized European domination from the fifteenth century, with its concomitant discrimination, is that it has trailed through successive generations to find its way comfortably into the twenty-first century. The trauma involves enslavement, rape, cultural genocide, Indigenous religions crushed, cultural artifacts stolen, miseducation of African history and contributions to world civilization, to name some of the key forms of subjugation and terror. Though today European cultural hegemony is more diluted in its form, yet as deadly as ever in its outcomes, it has created widespread social inequality among peoples of color in the majority of Western*ized* societies. Wherever it may be in the transatlantic sphere there is the specter of racialized relations that haunts the lives of peoples of Africana heritage. Comprehending the impact of such is the role of those in Africana critical studies; sometimes this may be characterized as "critical race theory" if one focuses on the aspect of law and constitutional rights. Regardless of the type of lens one employs to dissect the longevity of racialized hierarchies, they continue to manifest and cause great social dysfunction. One cannot deny in all good conscience that there is a problem haunting humankind in relation to the legacy of enslavement and colonialism.

TRANSATLANTIC HYBRIDITY ROOTS AND ROUTES

Although this study will focus mostly on a Black British perspective in transatlantic experience, it is difficult not to encounter in part theorists such as Césaire or Fanon, and other writers foreign to British culture because colonialism and postcolonial realities have encompassed similar aspects whether it be French, British, Portuguese, or other European colonizers. For example, the work of Walter Rodney (1942–1980) in his groundbreaking book, *How Europe Underdeveloped Africa*, published in 1972, almost two decades after Césaire, is a definite complementary text to *Discourse on Colonialism*. Yet Rodney was raised under British colonial rule in Guyana and educated partly in London, England, not Paris, France like Fanon or Césaire. Although from a working-class Guyanese background he was a brilliant scholar, gaining a doctorate in African history from the University of London at the tender age of twenty-four years. His doctoral thesis was on the slave system in relation to a West African region under Portuguese colonialism, Guinea-Bissau, and later turned into a book first published by Oxford University Press in 1970 titled *A History of the Upper Guinea Coast: 1545–1800*. Rodney can also be deemed a scholar-activist in the similarity of a Frantz Fanon, who took on European colonialism and explained not only the exploitative nature of enslavement and colonialism, but unsavory elements such as Africans of mixed Portuguese heritage in Upper Guinea who would go on to participate during the slave system as "middlemen" for the Portuguese and other European enslavers. Chapter eight, "The Rise of the Mulatto Traders," is of interest to this study as it involves the reality of mixed heritage Africans, something that is largely overlooked by historians who have studied enslavement and colonialism. Rodney (1970) writes covering the Portuguese interaction with Upper Guinea from 1545 to1800 and its African mixed heritage population:

> Even if there was a high degree of in-breeding among the mulatto population, they would eventually have been swallowed up by the preponderance of Africans. This explains why most of the mulattoes were very dark and sometimes indistinguishable from Africans. It is also the case that many blacks who were considered"Portuguese" had no Portuguese ancestry whatsoever, for racial origin was by no means the only criterion which set successors to the *lacados* [a small group of white Portuguese convict migrants to Upper Guinea in the sixteenth and seventeenth centuries] apart from the mass of Africans (p. 202).

Rodney reveals a number of salient points ordinarily unheeded by transatlantic scholars; for one, the Portuguese interacted with the local Africans intimately enough for there to develop a distinct African mixed heritage population *on the continent* and this kind of analysis is usually confined to the Caribbean and the Americas. What is also significant is the development of a "middleman class" of Africans, *compradors*, who could either claim Portuguese heritage, or actually not. The ambiguity of racialization raises itself via Rodney's scholarship and it is worth considering the absurdity of the racism that would emerge emanating from Europe—often perpetuated for reasons only to justify their barbarity and exploitation of African peoples. Another irony is in the fact that many "dark Portuguese" today are in fact members of that lineage of African hybridity that emerged on the continent. It is an odd irony to consider the Portuguese claiming superiority over the Africans in Upper Guinea yet amalgamating with them physically *and* later in trade. Transatlantic history between Africans and Europeans has been violent, messy, contradictory, and conniving (Césaire 1970; Fanon 1986; Gilroy 1993; Rodney 1972).

A major activist of the continent, not the African Diaspora, was Amilcar Cabral (1924–1973) who was born in Guinea-Bissau. He would be educated in Cape Verde, and Lisbon in Portugal. He was an agronomist by training, but would go on to be an anticolonialism theorist and revolutionary. His writings and speeches were to inspire many African Diaspora thinkers such as Maulana Karenga, who frequently cites him in his own writings (Asante 2009, p.9). This again shows the deep-rooted connection between African intellectuals from the continent and the African Diaspora within the context of African liberation and resistance. Amilcar Cabral's writings and speeches are captured in his posthumous publications: *Return to the Source* (1973), alongside his *Unity and Struggle* (1979). Interestingly, Rodney's historical analysis of the devastating slave system in Upper Guinea, and his later work covering *How Europe Underdeveloped Africa* are an excellent foundation for comprehending the ideas and practice of Cabral's anticolonial theories and activism. Liberation for both these scholars stems from the empowerment of the masses. Cabral in particular inculcates an analysis of colonialism that breaks down its structure of domination and explains, ultimately, that real freedom can only be achieved when the masses are involved with the struggle.

Cabral argued intensely that one of the key errors colonizers made was to "ignore or underestimate the cultural strength of African peoples" (1973, p. 49). His phrase of "return to the source" came from an address he gave at Lincoln University in October of 1972 after receiving an honorary doctorate. It is a powerful speech still worth reading, titled "Identity and Dignity in the Context of the National Liberation Struggle." Cabral pulled no punches in his demolition of European imperialism as a greedy conglomerate monopolizing and preying on other people's land and resources. No doubt this kind of rhetoric put his life in jeopardy, but that is the nature of speaking truth to power. Much like the authentic scholar in academia, Cabral struggled initially in his role as a native "petite bourgeoisie" clerk within the colonial structure. He states in *Return to the Source*:

> For this reason arises the problem of "return to the source" which seems to be even more pressing the greater is the isolation of the petite bourgeoisie (or native elite) and their acute feelings of frustration as in the case of African diasporas living in the colonial or racist metropolis (p. 62).

Cabral linked the African continental struggles with that of the African Diaspora. He understood the need that many peoples of African heritage seek to link with their ancestral roots given the experience of enslavement and colonialism. African Americans may not have suffered the colonial experience as in Africa or the Caribbean, but they endured the long night of oppression in the United States under enslavement and segregation. When writers like Cabral and Fanon connect with African heritage peoples in the West, it is a visceral reaction to the racialized worlds they also inhabit, whether it be in Lisbon or Liverpool, Paris or Philadelphia. The global reality of the colonizer and the colonized has touched home with most African heritage persons. Of course, as Gilroy and others would argue, there has been great hybridity and difference in how one colonizer may have met its colonized population, but the outcome of racialized hierarchy and social oppression has not been too dissimilar.

Indeed, a person born in Liverpool, England of Black mixed heritage can share profound similarities with someone born in another part of the world that has racialized hierarchy within its societal borders. This is not rocket science, it is simply a unity of experience without uniformity in how white racism has impacted his or her life chances. Therein lies the conundrum within transatlantic knowledge: how do we consider difference while endeavoring to overcome such racialized negative forces that have most Black communities suffering from this extensive legacy of enslavement and colonialism. To think of unity is not naïve or illusory. Africana critical studies has different schools of thought within the discipline. Yet there should also be a defining core of knowledge that sets it apart from any other discipline—otherwise what is the point in having this field of knowledge if it is not unique? If it does not find ways in providing a consensus in eliminating racialized discrimination that has plagued the world for centuries then it is not being authentic. Cabral, Fanon, Rodney, and many other scholar-activists have provided a way to overcome the legacy of Eurocentric domination of Black and brown lives.

Of course, Black communities located in the West may not today be struggling for an independent nation as in the 1950s to 1970s Africa and Caribbean, but the descendants from that generation of activists still contend with the legacy of racialized discrimination. This is evident in *any* community or profession one puts a social analysis to, and it is why the fight for social justice continues in varied societies across the transatlantic world. To be sure, when Frantz Fanon introduced the reader to his first book published in 1952, *Black Skin, White Masks*, he cited Césaire's *Discourse on Colonialism*, "I write of millions of men who have been skillfully injected with fear, inferiority complexes, trepidation, servility, despair, abasement" (Fanon 1986, p.9). Well, successive generations of scholars have sought refuge in the words of Fanon and Cabral and Rodney, and of course many other counter-hegemonic intellectuals of similar ilk.

Drawing from the legacy of Frantz Fanon, a contemporary scholar, Nathalie Etoke exemplifies the postcolonial necessity in Africana community reflection in forging a positive global Black identity. Her recent book, *Melancholia Africana*, expands on Fanon's ideas as she considers the twenty-first century realities of racialized hierarchy. She writes:

> Africans and people of African descent have made their entry into a global world through an experience rooted in loss and mourning. Still, this double

negative does not prevent us from affirming the absolute superiority of life. . . . Delving into suffering reveals that this experience can create a common humanity. Those who are subjected to suffering and those who inflict are inseparable (2019, p. 71).

Etoke offers a profound human spirit above all else, writing as an African woman who belongs to the Sawa people of the Cameroon, reflecting on the trauma of enslavement and colonization. Yet, the essence of Fanon envelops her writing because his insight into the African condition in regard to enslavement and colonialism was literally unequaled for its time and place—and continues to be so. Etoke, however, builds on Fanon via spirituals, jazz, and modern African literature. To be sure, she offers insights that capture the essence of Fanon with poetic zeal. Her comprehension of historical trauma encountered by Africans and their descendants is something present and future generations of Africans and its African Diaspora must grapple with, especially Black communities throughout Europe who offer close-up realities of the former colonizer and decolonized in France, Britain, Germany, Holland, Spain, Portugal, and other European nations. Moreover, African and Caribbean nations have only pseudo-Independence from European rule in the twenty-first century, because these regions rely heavily on the global economy, which is still controlled with a vice-like grip by Europe and North American financial institutional power. Also, China has a growing presence on the African continent and this does not bode well for African nations wanting to establish a future free of foreign economic exploitation and interference. It is important to comprehend the past and to consider the future as the struggle for African mental and physical liberation continues to be as relevant now as it was in the 1950s under anticolonial confrontation.

Given that the transatlantic experience from the fifteenth to twentieth centuries has involved enslavement and colonialism involving numerous European nations, and too often Europe is seen as a "block" rather than individual geo-political entities, it is important to know of these writers who have endeavored to empower through Africana resistance. In this sense, they have collectively in the course of decades developed a counter-hegemonic epistemological framework that brings Africana humanity to the forefront of the analysis, as for too long there has been a preponderance of white scholarship to undermine such work. Cabral was aware of this reality when he spoke to a group of African Americans in New York on October 20, 1972; in a speech titled "Connecting the Struggles" he stated:

> We try to understand your situation in this country. You can be sure that we realize the difficulties you face, the problems you have and your feelings, your revolts, and also your hopes. We think that our fighting for Africa against

colonialism and imperialism is a proof of understanding of your problems in this continent. Naturally the inverse is also true. All the achievements toward the solution of your problems here are real contributions to our own struggle. And we are very encouraged in our struggle by the fact that each day more of the African people born in America become conscious of their responsibilities to the struggle in Africa (1973, p. 76).

For Cabral, there is a connection that is undeniable between the African continent and its African Diaspora. The struggle for African liberation from European colonialism was always inextricably interwoven with peoples of African heritage outside the continent and from within. The Pan African movement started in the African Diaspora by intellectuals and activists based in the United States, the United Kingdom, and the Caribbean. Africans educated in the West, like Cabral, Fanon, Nkrumah, and many others, would come to be key anticolonial African leaders. This fact gets lost too often in much of the scholarship that emanates regarding the transatlantic experience. Incredulously, Gilroy does not cite either Walter Rodney or Amilcar Cabral in his study on the Black Atlantic—even though they both contributed immensely to the anticolonial struggle with both scholarship and activism within a transatlantic context. In point of fact, Cabral and Rodney were each assassinated for their political beliefs and involvement in the politics of liberation. Crucially, the ideas of these men continue to resonate today as their writings are widely used in Africana critical studies circles.

AFRICANA BRITAIN AND ITS COMPLEXITY

In terms of Black Britain, Stuart Hall offered a rather poignant viewpoint in regard to the many stories that have yet to be told; this in turn gives credence to the need for greater comprehension of Black experiences forged within the confines of enslavement and colonial-transatlantic pathways to find settlement and residence in many geographical regions. In relation to this complexity, Hall stated:

> Black experiences and black identities are more complex than they were. There is no one story that encapsulates the black experience, there is no "the black experience," any longer. There are black experiences, there are a rich variety of ways in which blacks are now deeply part of the fabric of British life (cited in Phillips and Phillips 1998, p. 380).

To attest to Hall's point of view, a key part of this chapter is to consider the "Black" or African heritage aspect within the context of transatlantic Liverpool; yet given the micro-element of this study it would be further truncated without noting the macro-element of the previously cited scholar-activists who laid the foundation in comprehending African and European relations in colonial and postcolonial times. Indeed, employing an Africana critical theory entails examining the complexity of Blackness in relation to the African Diaspora and its dissemination of peoples of African heritage outside of the African continent from the fifteenth to twentieth centuries (Asante 2007a). Perhaps the most widely known mainstream academic scholar, mentioned briefly earlier, renowned for his "Black Atlantic" thesis is Paul Gilroy. His study has been lauded by conventional academia, titled *The Black Atlantic: Modernity and Double Consciousness* (1993a). He is a Black British scholar of Guyanese and Jewish heritage who was born and raised in London. This is important to note for international readers as the City of Liverpool is geographically and culturally different from London in terms of accent and how the two cities are perceived across British society. For example, Liverpudlians have what is deemed a "scouse" diction, whereas Londoners have a "cockney" drawl. This is in reference to the broader working classes who reflect the majority of persons raised in either British city—with no reference to the "posh" upper crust British accent most readily known in the United States. Put another way, Liverpudlians speak ordinarily like the Beatles, and Londoners speak mostly like the Rolling Stones. Within that scenario there are also Black Liverpudlians and Black Londoners—who each have distinct accents.

The reason to highlight this basic cultural difference is to give the reader some sense of diversity *within* the British context of Blackness too. Therefore, it is important to adopt Gilroy's Black Atlantic as a way of opening up varied Africana experiences rather than accepting it as a "hold all" analysis. There will be a more reflective and specific account of Gilroy later, but for now it is important to decouple *his* Black Atlantic paradigm from that of critical Africana studies because it is not directly associated with the genre—beyond its premise that African experiences are in fact *hybrid* in form since the arrival of modernity. That is, from approximately the 1700s European Enlightenment era through to the industrialization and the origins of mercantile capitalism, when enslavement was well established, on up to roughly the postmodern era from post–World War Two onward. In other words, it is fundamental to accept that there has been a fluid and cultural Africana human experience in the concomitant racialization of the world. Due to those initial European voyages of "discovery" led by Columbus and others, with their attendant feature being the conquest of other peoples' culture, land, and resources, through acts of genocide and/or enslavement. Alterity would become a reality *within* the context of the "colonizer and the colonized" whereby "otherness" was espoused by a pervasive rise in European pseudoscientific racism—specifically within the British and North American context (Fryer 1984, p.133; Painter 2010).

In the period when European colonizers, the first being the Spanish and Portuguese in the late 1400s–1600s, called the lands of the Caribbean and Americas *their* "New World," we know in hindsight that it was actually an "Old World" inhabited by Indigenous peoples who had occupied the lands and/or islands for millennia. Europeans would go on to create the tangled human mess we are in today when it comes to the long legacy of racialized exploitation, ethnocentrism, and pseudoscientific racism (Asante and Dove 2021). Indeed, the argument that Africans, and their descendants in the Caribbean, the Americas, and in fact Europe have not been met with human and cultural hybridity would be folly. This is an acceptable theory within Gilroy's Black Atlantic paradigm—we shall consider the problematic aspect of his thesis further on—which is perhaps a tad more political in scope than it is cultural. Indeed, writing on Black historical experiences is profoundly political due to the nature of racism and prejudice.

LIVERPOOL AND SLAVERY

In terms of Liverpool, a famous port city built primarily on African exploitation, it is not unlike a New Orleans in the United States or a Cape Town in South Africa whereby the creolization of its people is also a part of its legacy in racialized discrimination (Christian 2000; Biko 1996). Specifically, the Black experience in Liverpool is often characterized as having one of, if not the oldest continued presence of peoples who can claim African heritage as part of their human identity in Europe (Fryer 1984; Christian 1995/96b, 1997a, 1998b, 2000; Costello 2001). With the focus of this study being essentially on the City of Liverpool there is a need to make clear the uniqueness of the Black experience therein. This is largely due to how the Black population developed from the 1700s in regard to the transatlantic experience in the enslavement of Africans, the apogee of British involvement was arguably the mid-1700s to the latter (Walvin 1999, p.105). This is a period also whereby Liverpool took over from the other two major slave ports in Britain, London and Bristol, as the major purveyors of slave ships that took Africans to the Caribbean and the Americas from the African continent. In point of fact, in a book titled *Liverpool*: *Capital of the Slave Trade*, the authors, Gail Cameron and Stan Crooke, emphasize how the city capitalized on the transatlantic enslavement system by calculating the number of slave ships that left British ports. Cameron and Crooke (1992) write:

> By the 1780s there were nearly twice as many slaving vessels clearing from Liverpool each year as there were from London and Bristol combined. Three out of every four slaves shipped to Jamaica in this decade were carried on Liverpool ships, and all but three of the 19 most important British firms engaged in slave trading were based in Liverpool. By 1795 . . . a quarter of the ships belonging to Liverpool were engaged in slave trade. Liverpool had control of over 60% of the British slave trade, and over 40% of the entire European slave trade (p.1).

The statistics offered by Cameron and Crooke are not readily found in British history books related to the City of Liverpool as it sheds great historical shame on its past. Generations of white historians airbrushed the fact that the city had a deeply rooted connection to the enslavement of millions of African souls. Even the contemporary doyen of Liverpool history based at the University of Liverpool, John Belchem, merely notes the extent of the city's involvement in the slave system. Of his edited volume, *Liverpool 800* published in 2006 to mark the eight hundredth year of its existence, one can only describe the book as euphemistically downplaying the role the city had in regard to its slaving legacy. Indeed, the closest chapter in the book that deals remotely with its slaving history is written by Jane Longmore titled "Civic Liverpool: 1680–1800." This chapter camouflages the essence of Liverpool's notorious role and growth as a fundamental and crucial slave port. What is incredulous about the analysis is in the fact it covers the century whereby Liverpool rose to become the key slave port of Europe. It is unutterably sad that historians, who wield a lot of power at presses by policing what gets published in regard to Black Liverpool experience, continue to camouflage, dilute, and obfuscate the authentic historical record of the city. One could choose many parts of Longmore's vague and sanitized chapter on Liverpool slave merchants to show how problematic this kind of historical writing can be in mystifying a contemptible and heinous past, but let us consider this following extract:

> Amid this fluidity [the growth of a migrant Liverpool population between 1660 and 1760] the key social group was the mariner-merchants. They bound together Liverpool society, linking politics, trade and finance to build a commercial community. They were major catalysts in economic development, moving easily between different forms of money-making, investing in voyages, purchasing shares in industrial concerns and engaging in property speculation. . . . The domination of local government by a cohesive mercantile group was therefore inevitable and was to run in tandem with the interests of the port (p.119).

Well, there you have a typical mainstream Liverpool historian's account of the growth in the city's slave merchant class. What is disturbing is in the fact that this is writing and historical interpretation from the twenty-first century.

Yet one has be rather adept at obscuring the historical fact when it comes to Liverpool's dishonorable past with so much more knowledge available. Let us unpack the above citation from the chapter now with a degree of clarity and greater veracity. One, the major social group to emerge in Liverpool in the 1700s was a slave-merchant class. Two, they consolidated their power in the city by monopolizing local politics, banking, insurance, slave ship building, and related outfitting businesses. Three, the slave-merchants would construct lavish real estate in the city, invest in the burgeoning industrial revolution, and oversee the city's mercantile expansion based primarily on slave voyages, slave products grown on plantations in the Caribbean and North America, while producing sugar refining, tobacco, and cotton factories in Liverpool, Manchester, and further afield. Therefore, Longmore's camouflaged, euphemistic, prose from her "Civic Liverpool: 1680–1800" chapter is typical of how Liverpool historians have in the past and continue to downplay the notoriety of a city whose wealth and growth came fundamentally from its heritage as an undeniable and formidable slave port (Fryer 1984, pp. 36–37; Christian 2002d; Walvin 1999, p. 87). We will return to John Belchem's *Liverpool 800* volume on Liverpool later in this book as it deserves further critical scrutiny.

Briefly, from the mid-1700s up to the outset of the 1800s, the lion's share in the British participation in the enslaving system was held by Liverpool, easily outpacing both Bristol and London. Overall, there is no doubt that the city was built fundamentally because of its profound involvement in enslavement. What is often overlooked is the immense related businesses that it spawned: banking, shipping outfitters, a cotton exchange, manufacturing, a sugar refinery, cotton factories, local stores, law firms, and insurance companies—to name a few. For historians to develop historical amnesia in regard to Liverpool's past is unacceptable but it is commonplace. It would be more appropriate to deal honestly and forthrightly with what is the true legacy in order to forge a better future that is free of mendacity and airbrushing of notoriety. There is no doubt that this is a painful, emotional, and rather inhumane journey to consider. But without an assessment that is free of historical sanguine mythology one cannot move beyond such an ugly slave port past. Truth will only linger and fester in the basements of archives, museums, and libraries waiting to be liberated from falsehoods and historical misrepresentations. The past does not have to determine the future, but it should shed light on how societies have developed, and why some things have not changed—such as racialized discrimination in all areas, professions, and institutions in Western society. Perhaps Liverpool offers a way of untangling the transatlantic experience in ways one would not ordinarily encounter. The author having traveled far from his roots over many years knows only too well that the City of Liverpool is famous globally for two major cultural offerings: The

Beatles and Football. Very rarely has anyone opened up a conversation about Liverpool the Slave Port in my three decades being abroad.

This is why it is important to bring such historical knowledge to the forefront as we map out a bygone context of the transatlantic impact on the city. Without hyperbole, Liverpool would never have existed to the extent it has unless it had developed strong links with the transatlantic slave system. Successive mayors, local and national politicians had strong links to the enslavement and exploitation of African humanity. As Peter Fryer stated: "At least 26 of Liverpool mayors, holding office for 35 of the years from 1700–1820, were slave-merchants or close relatives" (1984, p. 41). When one considers the past, it should be noted that those with the power to interpret it often are those who benefit from it most. Black British history has been largely marginalized in the British education system. If the Liverpool slave port history had been taught in British schools, facts shared by Fryer (1984) would be less shocking to the core of one's being because they would at least be widely known. Instead, there has been widespread denial and a muddying of Black British history to either dilute it or completely whitewash it out of existence.

TWO LIVERPOOL SLAVE SHIPS

Let us consider two slave ships that left the port of Liverpool engaged in the trafficking of enslaved Africans; both are notorious examples in the history of the city but rarely are they considered as relating *specifically* to the history of Liverpool. First, the *Brookes* slave ship was built in 1781 and named after a Liverpool slave-merchant, Joseph Brooks Jr. The ship would become a symbol for the abolitionist movement due to its draconian, hellish, packing of enslaved Africans like sardines in its hold. Marcus Rediker's profound account of this ship can be found in chapter ten of his acclaimed *The Slave Ship: A Human History*. Poignantly he writes:

> The *Brookes* had a long life as a slaver, making ten successful voyages over almost a quarter of a century. Its captains purchased an estimated total of 5,163 Africans, 4,559 of whom they delivered alive, giving the ship a mortality rate of 11.7 percent, close to the average for ships over four centuries of the slave trade (2008, p. 311).

To consider the human misery behind the bland statistics offered by Rediker is inestimable. But a deeper reading of his study reveals a vile and unimaginable horror that enslaved Africans encountered. Those who found it easy to defend this cruelty were pushed on merely by economic profit rather than any moral compulsion to contemplate the treacherous barbarity involved. Such were the lucrative gains from the transatlantic slave system as it would remain for centuries—enhanced by larger and more superior profits for those involved. Slave merchants were avaricious for greater profits and did not consider the traffic in African humanity across the Atlantic as anything other than carrying wood or any other inanimate object. The callousness involved within the context of transatlantic slave ship accommodation was tantamount to murder on the high seas (Rediker 2008; Walvin 1992, pp. 11–22). In fact, there is no other way to describe the slave-merchants other than a minority bursting with zeal for capital gain, regardless of the human misery involved. Rediker's prose captures the depth of despair involved in a slave system that only truly benefited a small minority of wealthy white men. The poorer white working-class sailors were often brutal, yes, but poor and underpaid for their dastardly work on board the slave ships. As Rediker (2008) explains:

> A voyage into this peculiar hell begins with the human seascape, stories of the people whose lives were shaped by the slave trade. Some grew prosperous and powerful, others poor and weak. An overwhelming majority suffered extreme terror, and many died in horrific circumstances. People of all kinds—men, women, and children, black, white, and all shades in between, from Africa, Europe and the Americas—were swept into the trade's surreal, swirling vortex (p. 14).

The "prosperous and powerful" were the slave-merchants who gained vast sums of wealth, passing it on to generation after generation of white privileged families, while the poor and the weak, from Europe, were those who did the dirty work, following the sea captains' orders while also taking advantage of the enslaved in barbaric ways from rape to murder. Those who suffered the "terror" in absolute form were the enslaved Africans. Those who survived were stronger than strong mentally and physically—one can only describe it as super-human strength given the details of slave ships related by historians such as Marcus Rediker and James Walvin, both of whom are respected white historians with no axe to grind other than veracity in historical interpretation. Combining these two books, *The Slave Ship* and *Black Ivory*, will give any reader with an ounce of compassion chills because the depiction and prose is so graphic in regard to the inherent cruelty involved in the transatlantic slave system.

Life on board such vessels was atrocious—filled with disease and dis-*ease* for the enslaved. One should never forget this was a human enterprise; we should not simply allow this to be deemed a "slave trade"—a term that again euphemistically undermines the extent of the atrocities that took place. To present more clarity, it is apt to give an insight into two slave ships, from hundreds, which emerged from the notorious history of Liverpool's transatlantic involvement in slavery. Indeed, it is imperative to allow the human misery to be fully understood as often it can be lost in the fog of historical narrative.

Joseph Brooks Jr. (1746–1823) was one of many Liverpool slave-merchants to enrich his coffers by indulging in what amounted to an African holocaust. It is without hyperbole a disturbing account of what Africans endured on those slave ships for centuries. The English abolitionist of the British slave system, Thomas Clarkson (1760–1846), traveled to the British slave ports and further afield collecting data and objects related to enslavement to display during his presentations to abolish the barbarity. He came to Liverpool in 1787 to speak to sailors and gather more experiential evidence. Many of them willingly gave horrid stories about life and death on board the slave ships. Clarkson received severe pushback from the Liverpool slave-merchants and captains, who refused to speak to him, as they were those who earned the most from slavery and favored its expansion rather than abolition. Nevertheless, Clarkson gained a model of the *Brookes* slave ship that displayed the enslaved Africans on board as being so tightly placed together it was akin to them lying in coffins. The description and chart broke down inch by inch the enslaved quarters on slave ships; and this visual aid would be employed as a powerful propaganda tool by the abolitionists to evoke moral outrage in the public sphere. As Walvin contends in his book *Black Ivory*:

> Even contemporaries began to feel queasy at the sight of crowded Africans on British ships. Of all the imaginative publicity coups organized by the abolitionists, few were as successful—or better remembered to this day—as the pictures of the *Brookes,* the Liverpool slave ship. It was a vessel of about 320 tons, a very large slaver indeed for the period: in 1787 only twenty-five of Liverpool's seventy-two slave ships were 200 tons (p. 46).

Indeed, the visual depiction of this slave ship looked like a sailing morgue rather than a vessel that transported live human beings. Every inch of the *Brookes* graphically showed space being used to harbor enslaved Africans. There is an immediate sensation of claustrophobia when one looks at the dimensions and padding of human cargo. Walvin adds more anguish by stating: "Although the visual allowed for 454 slaves, in 1783 the ship had transported 600" (p. 47). By this time, 1780s, slave ships had made the journey thousands of times ferrying African souls across the Atlantic, literally delivering them to the so-called "New World" and the plantation economies thrived through the blood, sweat, and tears of forced and involuntary labor—grueling and soul-destroying toil would continue for enslaved Africans well into the nineteenth century.

However, in England in the late 1780s the *Brookes* would come to symbolize a slave system that had no place in so-called civilized societies. Abolitionists alongside Clarkson fought tenaciously to end the British slave system against a backdrop of staunch resistance from slave-merchants. The formerly enslaved African Olaudah Equiano (1745–1797) played a massive role in the abolitionist movement, alongside Granville Sharp (1735–1813), and later William Wilberforce (1759–1833), who would arguably become the most famous of the British abolitionists. In regard to the passion for an ending of the British role in the transatlantic slave system, Rediker correctly states:

> The opponents of the slave trade thus began an intensive campaign to make the slave ship real to the reading public, to bring the vessel that had long operated beyond the bounds of civil society in the glare of public scrutiny and, they hoped, under new political control (p. 308).

Unfortunately, one cannot imagine beyond the confines of slave ships what depth of inhumanity took place. Yet beyond the squalor and sordid mistreatment, claustrophobia, and malnutrition of most slave ships there could be even worse incidents of inhumane treatment. Again, emanating from the slave port of Liverpool, if the *Brookes* slaver was bad enough publicity for Liverpool slave-merchants, it only got worse with the public becoming aware of another slave ship named the *Zong* of 1781. This slaver was owned by a syndicate of Liverpool slave-merchants, led by a Liverpudlian, William Gregson (1721–1800), and his two sons John and James Gregson. William Gregson was the mayor of Liverpool between 1762 and 1763, and later his son following his father as mayor in 1784–1785. Briefly, the *Zong* owners were inextricably tied to Liverpool's civic, banking, insurance, and other business life for over three decades. Significantly, William Gregson and the Gregson Syndicate would become responsible for the murder of Africans who were enslaved and on board the *Zong* for one of its middle passage voyages. The members of the Liverpool slave-merchants syndicate were: William Gregson, John Gregson, James Gregson, Edward Wilson, and James Aspinall. Moreover, the Gregson Syndicate, whether individually or as a group, frequently operated out of Liverpool and had owned numerous slave ships over the course of their careers, though it is the ownership of the *Zong* from 1781 that brought a more focused spotlight on their notorious involvement in slaving.

The story of the *Zong* is similar to most other slave ship journeys, but this one turned more macabre when its captain Luke Collingwood, who had previously been a surgeon before captaining a slave vessel, led from the front a murderous assault on his captured African cargo. The slave ship had set out from Liverpool in March of 1781 for the Gold Coast region of

West Africa and picked up at least 440 enslaved Africans at two locations, before embarking for Jamaica in September of 1781. It was during this three-month-plus route between West Africa and Jamaica that things began to go wrong. With seven crew members dying and over sixty enslaved Africans perishing, Collingwood explained to his officers that if their "cargo" died of natural causes then the insurers would be duty bound to reimburse the cost to Gregson and his syndicate. Though one of the officers, James Kelsal, disagreed with Collingwood, it was in vain as he personally chose nearly one hundred and forty captured Africans to be thrown overboard to drown or be eaten by sharks—they were duly cast overboard. The *Zong* massacre would in the end favor the Liverpool slave merchants who eventually received recompense for the loss of their human cargo. Solicitor-General John Lee, representing the owners, claimed at the time:

> What is all this vast declamation of human people being thrown overboard? The question after all is, Was it voluntary, or an act of necessity? *This is a case of chattels or goods.* It is really so; it is the case of throwing over goods; for to this purpose, and the purpose of insurance, *they are goods and property: whether right or wrong, we have nothing to with* (Fryer 1984, p. 128).

What should be noted here are two major realities: One, the Liverpool slave-merchants have yet to be truly made accountable for the iniquities; and two, neither has there been made reparations to those Africans and their descendants for what was in a sense trafficking humanity in ways that should only be deemed inhumane. What can be gleaned from the contemporary court case and commentary is the idea that Africans were indeed no more important than tossing over decayed meat into the ocean. Juxtapose this with modernity rationalism and *Eurocentric Enlightenment* and it is a cruel jest to consider this a period of such. What is evident, however, is the callousness and inconsideration the British court system had for African humanity in the case of the *Zong*. In hindsight, it is a barbaric act that should not be airbrushed out of Liverpool history as has been done for centuries. Indeed, one has to dig deep to find that the *Zong* owners were Liverpool slave-merchants. This fact alone should warrant reparations to those descendants of such a tragic episode in which the city has largely denied ever took place.

Nevertheless, both Liverpool slave ships, the *Brookes* and the *Zong*, gave the British public and beyond clear knowledge of the barbarity involved in the entire slave system. Yet it would take the abolitionists and their political advocates over a quarter of a century to end the long nightmare of formal transportation of enslaved Africans in international waters—which occurred in 1807. This did not, however, end British slavery in its colonies, only in international waters. Enslavement continued to 1833/4 and never ceased for up to fifty more years in other parts of the Americas. There would be enslavement connected to every cotton garment worn, every cigarette or cigar smoked, and every English cuppa with sugar in it up to the 1890s. When all things are calculated, Liverpool was from the mid-1700s to the early part of the 1900s the "Gateway to the British Empire" and its dominions replete with sheer exploitation and unabashed cruelty (Lane 1987; Belchem 2006a).

GROWTH OF LIVERPOOL BLACK EXPERIENCE

With increasing pressure from abolitionists Liverpool's slave-merchant class had to find new ways in accruing profits. A move from indirect enslaving through trafficking to the direct colonization of African, Caribbean, and American territories were consolidated, especially in the 1800s to early 1900s. With the transatlantic flow of goods, capital, and culture, the British Empire continued to pour through the Liverpool slave port. In a sense, it could be deemed the Liverpool Black Atlantic because of the importance it had in the overall flow of mercantilism.

After the 1807 British abolition in the international trading of African humanity, through the 1800s and 1900s indirectly it created a distinct Black Liverpool experience, with a concomitant affluent city (Brown 2005; Christian 1995b; Fryer 1984, p. 33). The settlement of various Blacks stem from Africans brought in the city to be educated, though few, and often they were sons of African chiefs who would be inculcated with British viewpoints, some even to act as interpreters for the colonizers (Fryer 1984, pp. 5–6; Costello 2001, p.10). Some Africans were also brought over as servants for the aristocracy in the seventeenth and eighteenth centuries; and later arguably the most sustained group to arrive in Liverpool were African seamen. After 1807 the sea routes still operated and Africans were employed as cheaper labor for ships that sailed frequently to the colonial outposts of the British Empire. As Frost (1995) contends, "West Africans generally, and Kru seaman in particular, had found their way to Liverpool as individuals from at least the early nineteenth century" (p. 50). Essentially it was the seaport employment culture that brought Africans to Liverpool, and it is the transatlantic routes that took commerce back and forth creating a greater transcultural reality too. This scenario relates to Gilroy's thesis: "The history of the black Atlantic yields a course of lessons as to the instability and mutability of identities which are always unfinished, always being remade" (1993a, p. xi).

Gilroy's perspective is correct in many ways, but still there is also something that always *combines* people of color in relation to a racialized society that has fostered hierarchy and social exclusion. Liverpool is a city based primarily on a "race and class" social system. Africans who came to live permanently were subject to the racism that was manifest in Africa and the Caribbean regions. We must also remember that British popular culture fed into the racism as Christine Bolt argued in her book, *Victorian Attitudes to Race*, that British racism and pseudoscientific theories would proliferate mainstream popular culture. Comprehending the diversity and growth of Liverpool from the 1700s to the 1900s is to accept a hybridity or mixed heritage Blackness—what could be deemed no different than what occurred throughout other parts of the African Diaspora.

Therefore, a pivotal aspect in comprehending the City of Liverpool is not to merely note it as an insignificant port *until* its involvement in the transatlantic system in enslaved African humanity. There should also be acknowledgment that after the formal abolition of international trading in African humanity in 1807 there continued to be the sea routes and commerce between colonies. Thus, bringing vast amounts of wealth into the city particularly during the Victorian era as it was the "Gateway to Empire" from Liverpool. To give some context, in 1700 the population in Liverpool was merely five to six thousand and by 1800 it had risen to around eighty thousand, and by the beginning of the 1900s it was just under seven hundred thousand. In all measures, this is a rather staggering demographic growth to the city over two centuries. Fryer (1984) points out in *Staying Power: The History of Black People in Britain* that the city's "pride" during the earlier years was in its lucrative involvement in enslavement as it "flooded" the city with wealth (p. 33). This in turn provided it with an economic and business foundation that would become the envy of other British cities by the mid-1700s to the early 1900s.

Indeed, though rarely expressed due to the hidden aspect of historical data, and frankly the "airbrushing" of its slave past largely by the city's twentieth and twenty-first century mainstream historians, until arguably the 1980s, without slavery and its concomitant businesses the City of Liverpool would probably have continued to be an insignificant port. On the rise of Britain's overall involvement in the transatlantic slave system the renowned British historian James Walvin (2000) in his book *Making the Black Atlantic: Britain and the African Diaspora*, who is one of the best chroniclers of British enslavement history:

> A host of British ports rushed to join the lucrative trade in humanity, from Workington to Poole, from Lancaster to Lyme Regis. But the bulk of the trade continued to be dominated by London, Bristol and Liverpool. Until the early eighteenth century, finance from London funded the majority of British slave voyages. But between 1750 and 1780 almost three-quarters of the British slave trade was financed by Liverpool merchants. The City of London, however, remained critical to the Atlantic slave system throughout, its merchants and financiers guaranteeing and remitting bills of exchange used by West Indians,

Americans and Liverpudlians. Moreover, they often financed the cargoes of ships from other British ports bound for the slave markets of West Africa (p. 27).

British involvement in the exploitation and subjugation of Africans and their descendants is now well documented, but its ownership of such atrocity is less so. Common to this is there being a deadly silence and stifling of Black communities by local white power structures. If one seeks to learn the history of Black Liverpool, for example, a researcher has to dig deep to find an Africana critical studies point of view. Black Liverpool perspectives have been limited to the power and local hegemony of white scholars largely based at the University of Liverpool. Most often it has been a diluted version masquerading as authentic Black Liverpool that is severely lacking in grassroots veracity and comprehension (see Belchem 2014; Frost 2000, 2020).

However, Black Liverpool from a grassroots point of view offers a unique insight into the vast complexity involved in transatlantic hybridity in culture and human contact. As Costello writes, "The Liverpool Black Community is an example of a distinct people having the appearance of almost complete invisibility for more than two hundred years" (2001, p. 8). That is a rather harsh assessment of mainstream Liverpool's assault on the Black experience from Costello, and with him being a Black Liverpudlian historian his words should be acknowledged as authentic. Indeed, I can also attest to what Costello contends, in that the Liverpool Black experience stands as an example of a Black mixed heritage community being made socially invisible due to racialized exclusion. Moreover, its Liverpool Born Black population over centuries has largely been ostracized and dealt with severe social omission, stigma, and second-class citizenship throughout the twentieth century leading to the twenty-first (Christian 2008a, 2002b, 1997a; Clay 2020; Nelson 2000; Small 1991).

Moreover, there is something tangible in regard to there being a need to focus on why there has been a history of social exclusion for those deemed "Liverpool Born Black" (Christian 1997b) and this will unfold as the reader continues the journey through this book. Regardless of the racialized discrimination that has been a permanent feature of Black presence in Liverpool, it has produced many persons of talent in music, arts, education, and sports—particularly from the mid-to-late twentieth and early twenty-first centuries. In point of fact, Costello in 2007 published a book titled *Liverpool Black Pioneers*; though rather superficial with credible omissions, it does reveal some interesting Black persons from the city who had broken barriers, a number of them being known to the author. One interesting entry is on a "James Brown" who was a Black man who settled in Liverpool and was born around 1750. Costello (2007, pp. 32–33) reveals more information on one of his sons, James Brown Jr. (1815–1881), and after training as a printer he joined the *Liverpool Mercury*—now the *Liverpool Echo*. He later would get involved in the Chartist movement that fought for better voting rights, working conditions, and for social justice between 1838 to the late 1850s. James Brown Jr. supported Chartism with his writings, speaking truth to power for working-class Liverpudlians. The story of the Browns reveals the longevity of Black presence in Liverpool and its impact on the life of the city. Additionally, without historical and biographical context regarding the lives of individuals like the Browns one can get lost in the fog of white history—putting Black lived experiences in comprehending the social background of Liverpool also helps enliven its human aspect. To use a more modern phrase, *Black Lives Matter* when grasping the depth and scope of history—especially within the context of transatlantic Black experience.

One cannot explain the Liverpool Black experience without the context of transatlantic enslavement as it is fundamentally due to that experience that the city created a community made up of diverse African Diaspora peoples who would intermingle with local white women who had in turn brown babies. Why? The main reason is quite straightforward, the African migration into the city was based primarily on Black men mainly from Africa, but not solely, as seamen (Brown 2005; Christian 1998b; Frost 1995/6). Later in the twentieth century there would be African Caribbean men and African American men who were part of both world war efforts (Wilson 1992). Out of this amalgamation of African and African Diaspora humanity came what is known as the Liverpool Born Black community (Brown 2005; Christian 1997a, 1997b, 2000, 2002d, 2008a; Costello 2001). There will be an effort to unpack the social reality of the Liverpool Black experience through the strong connection the author has to the city in the following chapters, while integrating that knowledge with historical data and scholarship that is local, national, and international in scope. Indeed, the heritage and depth of Liverpool Born Blacks is rather unique and it has been described by another scholar born in the city as "a harbinger for other British Black experiences" (Small 1991). There are other Black British cities that have longstanding presence, Cardiff, Bristol, and London are salient in this regard, but there are also communities such as Moss Side in Manchester that have had longevity in terms of diverse Black mixed heritage communities having been borne out of British Empire connections and slave port history.

GILROY'S BLACK ATLANTIC AND THE POLITICS OF ALTERITY

As indicated earlier, the Black British scholar Paul Gilroy is associated with coining the term, via his book *The Black Atlantic,* which was first published in 1993. In essence, he posits the idea that "race" is a fluid concept in relation to comprehending what connects "Black communities" within the Atlantic sphere and via the history and development of the "New World." There is what he deems "hybridity" in the cultural flow of not only ideas but bodies too. African humanity and culture, in a sense, has been bastardized via the flow of enslaved Africans within the context of the Black Atlantic experience. There is no single or homogeneous cultural experience, for Gilroy all is a mix, a hybrid amalgamation of human interaction brought about by the enslavement era in the Americas and Caribbean regions. Enslavement and the plantation economy, with a concomitant growing mercantile industrialization, was at the heart of this multilayered cultural exchange.

The prose is often dense, often vague, and if taken holistically it appears to be a postmodernist approach to understanding the Black Atlantic experience. In the parlance of the 1990s academic spiel, it is an anti-essentialist thesis. Yet, when all is considered, it is hard to find a writer who would not disagree that the enslavement era did not usher in human and cultural hybridity. Babies were snatched from the breasts of their African heritage mothers, sold at whim, and deprived of human worth. The white enslavers physically abused and raped women on ships and on plantations; the enslavers mentally suffocated the lives of the Africans they enslaved (Douglass 1994). It is rather curious to consider this historical trauma to be anything other than the creation of a "new people" born out of both resistance and resentment. One can be fanciful about it or logical in relation to this subject matter. It seems that Gilroy is endeavoring to delineate a historically specific cultural hybridity on something that obviously had such elements. So what else is he suggesting in his Black Atlantic paradigm? That cultural nationalism in terms of resistance is flawed? That the idea of a global Black experience that aims for solidarity is myth-making?

To consider these questions it is important to briefly explore Gilroy's lauded paradigm for analyzing the Black Atlantic—largely by white liberal postcolonial theorists in academia. Particularly, Gilroy puts forth the notion that Afrocentric epistemology, the centering of African peoples' cultures in relation to Eurocentric intellectual dogma and pseudoscientific racism, is essentialist and mythical. It is worth noting that *The Black Atlantic* was published almost three decades ago; at the time of its publication there was a rise in Black consciousness with the re-emerging focus on Malcolm X's ideas on

Black liberation. This was personified by the euphoria created with the biopic movie starring Denzel Washington, *Malcolm X* (1992), directed by the noted filmmaker Spike Lee. Moreover, in the academic sphere there was during this period a growth and development in Afrocentric perspectives that further challenged the cultural hegemony of Eurocentric canons of knowledge (Asante 2002). In short, the early 1990s was an era of intellectual cultural resistance on behalf of Black communities across the globe, but particularly in nations such as Britain and the United States.

In a sense, it could be contended that Gilroy was addressing what he deemed as rigid cultural Black Nationalism; what he claimed as an unchanging static cultural heritage. Another term he is fond of is "ethnic absolutism," the notion of static cultural affiliations particularly among Black communities. This perspective of Gilroy's has been the mainstay in academia for over a quarter of a century from what can be loosely considered the "liberal cultural theorists" in academia, mainly white scholar elites praising the fragmentation of the Africana world. One can read Gilroy as a sophisticated anti-Black unity pessimist when it comes to a committed resistance to white cultural hegemony. Indeed, for Gilroy, anything remotely coming close to Black solidarity is akin to promoting ethnic absolutism and should be rejected as intellectual naïveté. Yet, ironically, given Gilroy's deeply entangled prose, one could return his critique in kind. Indeed, by his own admission, his thesis relies on the help of some stellar and lesser-known European intellects, to name a few: "Michel Foucault, Marshall Berman, Richard Sennett, Fredric Jameson, Jurgen Habermas, Stuart Hall [his teacher]"—the list is a cadre of rather Eurocentric-based intellectual epistemology—with Cornel West and bell hooks adding some African American leftist/feminist flavor to his cohort of thinkers. After his list of largely European thinkers he includes, as if wanting to rubber stamp his intellectual foundation, "as well as a good dose of the classics [Europeans of the Enlightenment]" (1993a, ix). This is merely a point to emphasize his rather slanted view toward European intellectual heritage—rather than employing thinkers like Frantz Fanon, Amilcar Cabral, Walter Rodney, A. Sivanandan, C. L. R. James—who could have countered anything critically compared to the modernity double conscious aspect of Gilroy's study. The fact that the latter are men of color does not negate women; he could have employed Claudia Jones, Anna Julia Cooper, Ida B. Wells-Barnett, or even Angela Y. Davis, who is steeped in Eurocentric classics yet has a discerning knowledge regarding anti-Black sentiment. It is telling how Gilroy's elevation to academic stardom replicates his use of the "master's tools" to downplay Black intellectual resistance. Certainly, authentic Africana Studies scholars would not ordinarily be found in such highly held esteem by the liberal status quo in academia—as Paul Gilroy undoubtedly is. One must ask why this is so? It is certainly not because he empowers

Black unity across the transatlantic experience; on the contrary, his perspective is one of fragmentation (Gilroy 1993a, p. 2).

If indeed Gilroy considers the Black Atlantic to be viewed as a mixed bag of cultural amalgamation, emanating from the transatlantic enslavement experience onward, why should this weaken an argument for Black cultural unity without uniformity and resistance? Social theorists with a Pan Africanist approach from the past to present, though different in their perspectives, like W. E. B. Du Bois, Marcus Garvey, Ida B. Wells-Barnett, Walter Rodney, Kwame Ture, Amiri Baraka, Molefi Asante, Assata Shakur, and Clenora Hudson-Weems, to name a few, have each recognized the reality of the Eurocentric impact on the physical make-up of the Black body. Yet there is an African proverb that states, paraphrased: "A log can lay on the bed of a river, change color, shape, even its look, but it is still deemed a log." This maxim can be used to also explain that Blackness is not merely a color, it is not associated with ethnic absolutism, and it is akin to a sharing of a cultural experience, a consciousness, a way of life that has been undermined constantly in the Western world. Whether it be in London or Liverpool, Philadelphia or Pittsburgh, Cape Town or Johannesburg, city to city, or nation to nation, the impact of a racialized world shares both similarity and dissimilarity. Actually, it is rather inane to not acknowledge the differences within Black experiences, there are many nuances that clearly are relevant. However, to dismiss the similarities is just as ridiculous because there are so many situations whereby Blackness is shared across cities, nations, and even continents—that is a given. Whether it be culturally in music, or dress, or generalities in the social experience of being in a predominately white setting, there are comparable ways in which Blackness manifests itself. It is folly to suggest that because one African person speaks Wolof and another Ibo they do not share a common Africanness; or an African American cannot share similarities of experience with that of a Black British person. We have come too far in history to get bogged down in the diversity of Blackness. It was Malcolm X who suggested emphatically, to paraphrase: "They don't kill you because you're a Muslim, or because you're a Christian—they kill you because you're Black!"

BLACK DIVERSITY WITH UNITY

Let us consider a more micro-contemporary scenario of what can be an example of unity in a diverse Black experience. Five Black persons are standing at a bus stop in New York City, two women, three men. One woman has braids in her hair, brown skin, and is wearing a leather jacket, a t-shirt with Aretha Franklin on it, and a pair of jeans with heels. The other woman is light skinned, like a creamy vanilla; she is sporting an Afro hairstyle, a dashiki, with a black skirt to her knees, and flat black shoes. The three men, one is very dark skinned, melanin rich, with a shaved head, one is brown skinned with reddish hair and short Afro, and the other is a light skinned brother with corn-rowed hair. Each of the men is dressed casually but very smart and clean-cut—smooth.

A car drives by the bus top with a number of white youths shouting obscenities from the side windows: "Niggers! Wogs! Coons! Get back to Africa!" and "Make America Great Again!" The startled group of Black persons in the bus stop stare at each other in dismay and disgust; one of the men tries to run after the car but it speeds off out of sight weaving in and out of traffic lanes. This of course is a fictitious scenario, but one that has happened to the author in Liverpool, England a few times in varying degrees. The point here is that there can be differential phenotypes, styles, shades, and human shapes of Black humanity. Just as those standing in the bus stop offered such diversity, but they were seen as a collective group of Black persons in the opinion of the car load of white racist youths shouting obscenities. According to racist ideology and to those racist youths who yelled the deleterious epithets, the five diverse Black persons standing in the bus stop were all "niggers" and relevant to their ignorance to be targeted for hate speech and name-calling. This may be a crude way in explaining something that is very obvious to grassroots Blacks, but it seems to go over the head of an intellectual like Gilroy.

In addition to the diversity of Blackness mentioned above, the differences between Black persons can delve even deeper. For instance, one of the two women was born in Kingston, Jamaica, the other was born and raised in Brooklyn, New York; while the men were born in England, Nigeria, and Guyana. Only one from the five was actually born in the United States. This in a sense is a typical example of the diversity within African Diaspora experience: a variety and sameness exist in relation to the *white world*—especially when living in any Western nation. No one can tell where anyone is from most often until a person reveals his or her cultural heritage and geographical origin. Those fictitious five Black persons were all standing in the bus stop waiting to be taken to various spots in New York City. They did not happen to know each other personally, yet they occupied the same cultural space when the racist bigots passed by them. They were viewed as a *collective* group of Blacks, united in their Blackness according to ignorant racism. In turn, the collective experience of racism was felt by the group of Blacks in that bus stop scenario.

This can be gleaned for comprehending and critiquing Gilroy's argument that a Black commonality is in fact a flawed concept. It may well be that there is *difference* among Black folks, but this pales into insignificance when Blacks actually share their individual and collective experiences of life in white controlled societies. It is too simplistic to make the contention that when one considers Black unity one is promoting ethnic absolutism or essentialism. There is variance between a Black British person born in Liverpool, compared to one born in London, yet could they not also both be deemed variants of what it is to be Black British? Can we not find modification between an African American born in Atlanta, Georgia compared to one born and raised in Philadelphia, Pennsylvania? Yet could they also be considered of African American origin? One could go on and on with these examples of difference yet *still* sameness, both within nations and between nations where Blacks of African heritage (and those blended with another cultural lineage) reside in the Western sphere.

GILROY'S ESSENTIALIST BLACK ATLANTIC PARADIGM

Interestingly, Gilroy's Black Atlantic thesis has held sway fundamentally on the basis that it has espoused an assault on Black cultural solidarity, on cultural nationalism and the idea that representing Blackness in this manner is akin to ethnic absolutism. This is an erroneous and false premise because cultural nationalism or Black Nationalism has merely represented self-determination in the face of often brutal systems of oppression. Moreover, what is also inaccurate is in the notion of Black Nationalism being synonymous with white nationalism. This could not be further from the truth, because the former has only ever sought solidarity among varied Black cultural groups, it has not espoused violence, certainly not in the sense that humanity has witnessed from white nationalism. For sure, one could argue that Black Nationalists have often stood for self-defense in the face of physical assault, but not the pursuit of violence for violence's sake. White nationalism on the other hand has sought to instill fear, intimidate, and emasculate Black humanity. This took place during the onset of Gilroy's Black Atlantic model, and has continued in various forms for over five hundred years.

To be sure, the Black Atlantic is a site of tremendous intellectual intrigue and interest. Of course, there are cultural differences among Black peoples of African heritage, and mixtures of genes with those that oppressed them. This is not particularly earth-shattering knowledge-wise and it begs the question why such an idea held has been a central and lauded part of Gilroy's thesis. He also relates that the eras of modernity, capitalism, and industrialism being determining factors in the identity of millions of exploited Black peoples across the contours of the Black Atlantic forming a "counterculture" but clearly not one that is unified and unchanging. Yet clearly the essence of the culture itself is *change*; it is not particularly novel to consider Black culture ever-changing because racism too is also ever-changing, both brutally and subtlely.

Curiously, he opens his famed book with a problematic sentence, if one reads it from the perspective of Africana critical studies: "Striving to be both European and black requires some specific forms of double consciousness" (Gilroy 1993a, 1). This needs unpacking on a number of levels. First, and throughout his Black Atlantic paradigm, there is no Africa. There is European first, and a *striving to be,* with a lowercase *black.* Lowercase black is an apolitical Black for those unaware of the nuance. It is instructive to note that Gilroy is both right and wrong. Right about the obvious cultural mix within the African Diaspora, but fatally incorrect when it comes to that still not being a site for potential cohesion and understanding when it comes to responding to the myriad assaults on Black humanity. Unity without uniformity is what an Africana critical studies perspective can strive for within Black experience.

As with all art, and Gilroy is fundamentally an academic writer, one can read into his work from the lofty heights of Ivory Tower privilege, because he clearly does not write from the standpoint of wanting to reach the Black grassroots communities like an A. Sivanandan or a Walter Rodney. Therefore, Gilroy's *The Black Atlantic* has been lauded primarily within mainly elite academic circles, and largely rejected instinctively and logically by those on the ground in grassroots communities, so to speak. This is a major relevancy that has not been considered enough by critics. Indeed, indirectly Gilroy has had a precarious impact on Black communities seeking a unity without uniformity in their response to combating racialized hierarchical structures. Moreover, due to his fragmentation and stereotyped views on many Black scholars who support, for example, Afrocentricity. However, authentic Africana critical studies advocates, without apology, endeavor to empower by liberating Black communities from the myriad realities of white supremacy dogma.

To be sure, Africana/Black studies emerged as a discipline first in the United States as part of the 1960s Civil Rights Movement and student activism. It did not exist in a vacuum but in the social reality of Black struggle for human and civil rights. Always within this context is the need for mental liberation. This was not ethnic absolutism but an acknowledgment, among other things, that European centered epistemology was largely ethnocentric and biased against the humanity of African heritage peoples—most definitely from the fifteenth to twentieth centuries—and *still* it impacts communities of color which should be noted.

Moreover, without serious comprehension in how white cultural hegemony operates, one could read his take on the Black Atlantic as a hidden resistance for Black peoples' struggle for and resistance against the forces of white privilege. In terms of mutation and Blackness in the African Diaspora, as stated earlier, "a log is still a log" if it is left in a river for a hundred years. The modern African Diaspora has certainly morphed just as the work songs, spirituals, and gospel mutated into the blues, jazz, rhythm & blues, soul, funk, and rap music—while *still* having remnants from the origins of its essence—African rhythms. Certainly, we can also trace the past in Sankofa terms to gauge how these changes in cultural innovation tend to remain fundamentally "Black" and from Black Atlantic experiences. Is not Black music also hybrid and multifaceted? Yet it remains a distinctly Black form of art—with other influences. Alternatively, the Beatles are viewed today as a quintessential rock and roll band, but without the knowledge of Black music at the outset of their careers, aping many songs and cues from Black artists, they would probably not have been who they went on to be. However, their collective *whiteness* is never brought into question. The Beatles appropriated aspects of Black culture but remained "white" in a real sense. Gilroy employs the Frankfurt School's Theodor Adorno (1903–1969), the detester of Jazz (Adorno 1989/90), to bolster his ideas on the politics of Black music—which is clearly a case of cognitive dissonance. Indeed, the influence of Black American music globally is unprecedented in Western cultural history. Though, as an example of variance in Black interpretation, Frederick Douglass (1818–1895) found enslavement work songs too painful and sorrowful to tolerate *because* he lived through the experience of bondage—not because he did not respect his people and their cultural expression in song during the worst of times. Meaning, there can be complexity in how Black people *individually* experience their Black cultural heritage—which is another aspect of hybridity in motion.

Crucially, the Black Atlantic thesis as articulated by Gilroy has been a pillar in academia for way too long without much pushback. It is at best a "third way" of seeing the Black experience of enslavement, colonialism, and resistance in the development of the African Diaspora. This means we are to consider the Black Atlantic as a hybrid cultural phenomenon formed in a crucible of Eurocentric and Afrocentric worlds—but the latter gets overly critiqued by Gilroy if it aims to find a form of self-determination for millions of African heritage peoples. Those that criticize his intellectual foundation are often ignored, dismissed, or castigated as "essentialists" and/or "rigid purists" when in most cases Afrocentric scholars are never read holistically or fairly due to the cultural hegemony within academia favoring always a Eurocentric point of view. To suggest there is not a Eurocentric hierarchy of knowledge and epistemology in academia is erroneous; and if one works authentically within an Africana critical studies paradigm he or she represents a counter-hegemony that inevitably will forfeit the major academic prizes for one's intellectual output. One must therefore consider the success of Gilroy's thesis in mainstream academia in such context—if one reads Gilroy critically from an Africana studies perspective, he is ultimately a defender of European canons and its philosophers. In addition, he is most often dismissive of those Black intellectuals who espouse themes that disavow such Eurocentric ways of thinking about thinking.

Gilroy even aligns W. E. B. Du Bois with Georg Hegel (1770–1831), the anti-African philosopher, with a distinct misinterpretation of the doyen in African American intellectual history (Gilroy 1993a, pp. 134–135). Moreover, Gilroy is too smart not know what he was doing when he also gave the impression that Molefi Asante, who is the leading philosopher of Afrocentric thought, was a scholar who peddled in the notion of racial purity (p.189), when in fact that is articulated by a minority of scholars who speak of melanin having special significance in human biology—even though it actually does in relation to protection from the sun rays, Asante is *not* a racial purist. Reading Gilroy's *The Black Atlantic* is a lesson in how to not understand African centered knowledge, and how to diminish its relevance while standing deep in the waters of Eurocentric canons. He even assails Patricia Hill Collins for using the term Afrocentric, while disregarding any critique of those Eurocentric thinkers who denied her African American ancestors their humanity and worth. Indeed, his defense of Hegel is cringe worthy (pp. 51–53).

It is curious how Gilroy employs essentially African American writers, often with misinterpretation, to articulate the notion of hybridity in his Black Atlantic thesis. Indeed, W. E. B. Du Bois and Richard Wright together command a third of the book as he devotes a chapter to each from his six-chapter study. What is particularly significant is in Gilroy's explicit dismissal and disrespect for African American literature. Take his concluding evaluation of Richard Wright as an example:

> Analysis of Wright's legacy has been impoverished as a result of his being over-identified with the same narrow definitions of racialised cultural expression that he struggled to overturn. *The part of his work which resists assimilation to the great ethnocentric canon of African-American literature* have been left unread, and much of it now out of print [*Italics* my emphasis] (p.186).

It is not clear what Gilroy means by "ethnocentric canon" in relation to African American literature; it seems a rather bizarre term to employ in the context. However, there is no doubt that Richard Wright did not enjoy being a racialized human being, nor did Ralph Ellison, James Baldwin, or Zora Neale Hurston, to name a few of the key African American writers. Yet Wright in particular made his reputation writing *Native Son* (1941), a distinctly protest novel in the genre of African American literature. One should not willy-nilly dismiss this as "the great ethnocentric canon of African-American literature" as it shows a distinct lack of understanding of his holistic work. Of course, his later nonfiction work expands and delves into areas of Pan African politics, specifically employing an anticolonial perspective. His *Black Power* from 1954 looks at Ghana's rise out of a colonial stranglehold, with the hope of freedom and empowerment for Black Africa. Moreover, Wright's friendship with the then Prime Minister Kwame Nkrumah, who would in a few years become the first president of an African nation free from colonial rule, surely deserves Gilroy's attention as it emphasizes his deep connection to African struggles. Indeed, Richard Wright had close acquaintances among the newly emerging leaders of African anticolonial rule. The following letter dated May 4, 1953, to Wright from Nkrumah is testimony to their deep friendship, whereby it is a reference for visa status to visit Ghana and the African continent during the height of anticolonial protests:

To Whom It May Concern:

This is to certify that I have known Mr. Richard Wright for many years, having met him in the United States.

Mr. Wright would like to come to the Gold Coast to do some research into the social and historical aspects of the country, and would be my guest during the time he is engaged in this work.

To the best of my knowledge and belief, I consider Mr. Wright a fit and proper person to be allowed to visit the Gold Coast for reasons stated above.

Kwame Nkrumah
Prime Minister
(See Wright 1995b, p. v)

Though clearly any worthwhile understanding of Richard Wright would move him clear of any notion of "racial purity" or Black racial superiority, he was a man who fought openly against the tentacles of white supremacy as a force in the lives of peoples of African and Asian heritage. The late and noted Marxist scholar Cedric Robinson, whom Gilroy fails to cite in *The Black Atlantic*, wrote the 1995 Introduction to Wright's *White Man Listen!* which incidentally is dedicated to another Pan African thinker, Eric Williams, who as a Caribbean historian and political leader of the People's National Party in Trinidad and Tobago led his nation to independence from British colonial rule in 1962. Williams also published his acclaimed *Capitalism and Slavery* in 1944 which explained, among other things, the economic foundation of enslavement in the transatlantic world and how white historians had played down this fact. Richard Wright, like Eric Williams, was an anticolonialist in the mold of his younger contemporaries, Fanon and Cabral. Cedric Robinson goes further to explain the intellectual depth of Wright's connections to anticolonial struggles:

Wright's subject matter [in *White Man Listen!*] was not of his own choosing. Indeed, he appears to have sutured the concerns found in the writings of many of his contemporary Black radical intellectuals—Frantz Fanon, Aimé Césaire, George Padmore, C.L.R. James, and Amilcar Cabral, to name the most illustrious [how Robinson did not add Kwame Nkrumah and Eric Williams defies logic in relation to Wright as the three were, as indicated, very close friends]. They, too, determined to trace the sociopsychological genesis of the historic appearance of a new social force: the revolutionary Black nationalist (1995, p. xiv).

Now we have a much deeper comprehension of Richard Wright, rather than the selective insight of Gilroy. Robinson situates Wright in the vanguard of anticolonial struggle with the best thinkers and activists of the time. Gilroy overlooks this aspect of Wright to advance his avoidance of Black Nationalist struggle being at the heart of all during his lifetime. Yes, in hindsight there was undoubtedly problems with African leadership after the colonizers departed physically as outward colonial administrators. But the relevance of Black Nationalist thought and support of it by Richard Wright was obvious if only by his profound connections to Nkrumah and Williams.

It is rather disappointing reading Gilroy and his selective interaction with thinkers such as Du Bois and Wright, there is always lurking in his prose the ghost of Eurocentric thought hovering over the analysis. Twisting and contorting any semblance of Africana resistance to the forces of European racism—Gilroy is a consummate apologist for Black Nationalism, hence his lofty standing among in elite circles of academia. Ultimately, he is the guardian of all things Eurocentric in terms of epistemology. His work omits scholars of credibility (Fanon, Rodney, Cabral, Sivanandan, Césaire, among others) and substance who fought openly against white supremacy, alternatively, while lauding the likes of Hegel, a profoundly racist thinker. To be sure, Gilroy is quick to pounce on anything remotely radical in Black thought—Marcus Garvey being one of his favorite Black Nationalist targets for overt criticism, even using an exaggerated misrepresentation of Garvey from C. L. R. James to prop up his attempt to stigmatize the entire Garvey movement as fascist (Gilroy 2000, p. 231). On the contrary, Hegel's overt racism is conveniently ignored by Gilroy who fawns over the dialectical insights of Hegel merely to aid his hybridity thesis. The point here is Hegel gets a pass on his deeply held views on African inferiority but Garvey is lambasted, overtly taken out of historical context, and is literally defamed as anti-Semitic. Interestingly, Gilroy avoids any discussion of Malcolm X (1925–1965) in *The Black Atlantic*, which is another glaring omission in terms of an insight into Black political thought and the Black Atlantic. Malcolm X was a traveler and a Pan African thinker and not to mention his contribution to the Black Atlantic struggle is a major oversight—but again, any Pan African theorist that counters Gilroy's thesis is carefully omitted from *The Black Atlantic*.

Another flaw is in the manner Gilroy sets up Europe implicitly as a monolithic block of nations, while conveniently omitting its extreme diversity, centuries of internal conflict, and its variety of languages and culture (Painter 2010). Moreover, Europe can be a totality for Gilroy without questioning its diversity. Yet the African Diaspora is forthrightly deemed a mutated semblance of fragmented peoples unable to ever view themselves in terms of a group dynamic experiencing similar historical and contemporary socio-economic and cultural forces. Gilroy's Black Atlantic is at best myopic, and at worst profoundly hypocritical. One must consider the transatlantic enslavement experience and the development of the plantation economy as a conglomerate of white Europeans, contending African, Caribbean, with North and South American interests. Racism and exploitation shifted in shape and style from one region to another. Nothing was ever truly stable, especially the African humanity that was ripped from the continent into a physical and cultural melting pot of African Diaspora Blackness. Out of this emerged some of the most ardent peoples the world has witnessed. Armed with cultural resistance and an unshakeable resilience that lives on to this today in the hearts and minds of the liberated Africans on the continent and in the Diaspora. There is more to be achieved in terms of freeing the minds of the miseducated, misdirected, and misinformed. Significantly, if we consider the Black Atlantic with an authentic Africana critical lens, and not via hackneyed trivia, all roads will lead us ultimately back to Africa. No matter how hard some try to destabilize its importance to modernity, the African in the Black experience should never surrender to the whim of those who endeavor to mistreat its profound relevance in terms of its socialized solidarity in various form.

One of the strongest critics of Gilroy is Laura Chrisman (2003), and her essay "Journeying to Death: Paul Gilroy's Black Atlantic" provides another critical insight into the numerous omissions that have already been discussed. The clarity of the essay is very useful in breaking down Gilroy's illusive thesis that fundamentally looks at the Enlightenment lightly to connect the terror of African enslavement. In other words, modernity for Gilroy was inextricably interwoven with the era of African slavery but this has often been overlooked in notions of modernity. Also, for Chrisman, Gilroy tends to let the Enlightenment philosophers off the hook—once his African slavery terror is connected. Not only this, he comfortably employs Eurocentric philosophers via a "good dose of the classics" (p. ix). In addition, there is a rather superficial but incessant critique on anything "too Black" and nationalist in scope, whether in political or popular form. Chrisman (2003) makes an insightful observation at the outset by explaining the subtle, if not insidious, popularity of Gilroy's book:

It licenses an easy armchair condemnation of black politics; it enables academics to feel justified in not taking seriously the challenges posed to their institutional privilege to hegemonic forms of knowledge production by black and Third World nationalisms (p. 74).

Chrisman makes a valid argument in the sense that the elite academic community are able to manipulate their way out of many aspects of Black political resistance. Gilroy, by employing this mish-mash "we are the world" philosophy whereby a racialized world no longer exists. This Black Atlantic perspective is distinctly abstract in its efficacy, because on the ground in Black communities dealing with individual and institutional acts of racism it has little significance. However, as Chrisman alludes, the popularity of Gilroy's thesis theoretically stifles the attempt to foster Black solidarity in the face of racialized oppression, and gives power to those who can sit back and write in academic comfort and discuss largely incomprehensible things that have no bearing on day-to-day Black life. Whereas in his notion of Black cultural nationalism being trapped in its camp, he overlooks that Eurocentric forms of institutional power have most often limited opportunities for Black communities to escape such "camps" or urban boundaries. There is too little thought placed on the continued social exclusion, mass incarceration, excessive unemployment, poor educational outcomes, and draconian policing of Blacks in Britain and in the United States. Disapprovingly, he fails to critique the structures of racism that foster such isolation and discrimination among Black communities.

Chrisman also picks up on Gilroy reaching out to Jewish concerns of anti-Semitism in *The Black Atlantic*, "a connection he makes explicit in the book" (p. 74), while diminishing Black community attempts to forge consensus and unity. She regards this aspect of Gilroy coming out of the early 1990s "Holocaust Studies" whereby there was an upsurge, an academic popularity, in focusing on the Nazi atrocities. This is plausible, but again it is rather telling too that Gilroy would "sell-out" his Black heritage for thirty pieces of silver—so to speak. To put it another way, he offers himself openly to the cause of Jewish interests while doing all he can to project his disavowal of Africana/Black studies as it is "too Black" and nationalist in scope. Of course, this is ridiculous but so is much of what Gilroy offers for genuine contemporary grievances and social isolation experienced by Black communities across the Black Atlantic region is problematic. Wherever one travels in the contemporary Black Atlantic one encounters poverty and discrimination limiting progress in communities of color. This is clearly a legacy that goes back to the eighteenth and nineteenth centuries where Gilroy starts his study. Chrisman's essay reveals the "academic elite" aspect that often gets buried in Gilroy's overall model. *The Black Atlantic* is truly an exercise in academic abstraction, elitism, and could well be deemed a *counter-counter-hegemonic* standard when all things are considered. Yet he produced an intellectual tour de force in camouflaging this aspect of his Black Atlantic, for example, by using selective insights from the W. E. B. Du Bois and Richard Wright archives of ideas. Indeed, unless one is invested in seeking out the broader writings of Du Bois and Wright then it is easy to overlook Gilroy's adept manipulation of their complicated and profoundly anticolonial philosophies.

Another useful critique of Gilroy comes from Babacar M'Baye (2003) whereby he argues Gilroy overemphasizes "essentialism" and "ethnic absolutism" in Black cultural nationalism as his perspective gains favor with white power structures without considering the broader implication in how white domination can be enforced on peoples of color without any pushback. Moreover, there is no doubting the Black Atlantic he speaks of is clearly heterogeneous in form and culture but actually uniform in terms of the experience Blacks and other peoples of color encounter due to racialized hierarchies. M'Baye is singing from the same hymn sheet as other scholars located in Africana critical studies who find Gilroy's Black Atlantic attempting to stifle a broad Black coalition whereby there can be varied forms of unity among disparate Black communities. M'Baye considers this "strategic essentialism" and a necessary antidote to the virulent and insidious racism that manifests in most regions of the Black Atlantic. As M'Baye states:

> [Gilroy and others of his ilk] over-emphasize anti-essentialism, hybridity, and ambivalence in African-American culture. I would suggest that they need to go beyond the reducible concepts of anti-essentialism and examine the importance of strategic essentialism in African-American resistance against racism (p. 151).

The point of view that M'Baye posits regarding "strategic essentialism" relates to having a sense of community among Black communities in the struggle against racism and its related discrimination. There can be no reason to suggest "strategic essentialism" to be out of the ordinary—most communities that encounter racialized enmity have a sense of solidarity in that situation. After all, following an ongoing historical struggle, during the 1960s there were groups of African Americans and groups of Black Britons fighting the good fight against racialized oppression. Progressive whites would sometimes join forces, even with radical groups like the Black Panthers. This was a solidarity based on fighting institutionalized oppression brought on by centuries of enslavement, disenfranchisement, and second-class citizenship. In the 1960s, some Black organizations in the United States were overtly radical (e.g., Black Panther Party, BPP) and others more liberal (National Association for the Advancement of Colored People, NAACP), while others (e.g., Southern Christian Leadership Conference, SCLC) were perhaps a mix in philosophy and activism.

Whereas, in the United Kingdom, the Campaign Against Racial Discrimination (CARD) was a mix of left wing and progressive liberal activists. Some may be surprised to know that there was a British Black Panther Party (BBP) formed in 1968 to about 1973 in London made up of Black British Caribbeans and South Asians. Again, one can gauge the transatlantic *unity* from this fact alone not mentioned in Gilroy's study. But ultimately what pulled these diverse groups together in one direction back then was the spirit and determination to end the long night of racialized discrimination globally. Black cultural nationalism may have found its way, in part, in all the organizations—especially after the mid-1960s. Yet this again was part of the broader anticolonial struggles raging on the African continent and in the Caribbean region at the same time. Gilroy does not adequately connect these elements in his Black Atlantic paradigm as he is focused primarily on drawing them apart.

Gilroy's reading of Afrocentricity is particularly rather shallow; he engages superficially with this field of knowledge, writers of profound intellect who could be deemed in part Afrocentric—those scholars who focus on the experience of Africa and its Diaspora historically and *centrally*, not locating it in the margins of world history as Eurocentric epistemology has largely placed it, scholars such as: John Henrik Clarke, Ivan Van Sertima, Clarence Munford, Ronald Walters, William E. Nelson Jr., Jacob Carruthers, Marimba Ani, Patricia Reid-Merritt, Nah Dove, Clenora Hudson-Weems, Maulana Karenga, Asa Hilliard III, *along with* Molefi K. Asante, to name just a few who are not considered in *The Black Atlantic*. Therefore, his take on Asante is far too selective and narrow (p. 20). For example, Asante created the first doctorate in philosophy in African American Studies while at Temple University in 1987, and all the Ivy League schools soon followed suit, including Yale University where Gilroy spent time as a visiting scholar. Asante has gained the *top* scholarly prizes in both his fields of communication and Africana studies. Moreover, his scholarship in terms of publications is closing in on a staggering one hundred books—not to mention hundreds of journal articles and book chapters. Indeed, a more recent book by Asante, written with Nah Dove, and published in 2021 titled *Being Human Being: Transforming the Race Discourse* is an exemplary example of his depth of humanity as a writer in Afrocentric philosophy. Again, without a deeper reading of scholars in Africana critical studies one cannot expect to comprehend the essence of this profound body of epistemology.

This is merely mentioned because Gilroy is rather flippant in his dismissal of Afrocentricity and it is contended that it was done purposely. To suggest, for example, that Asante is a "racial purist" via melanin is erroneous (p.189).

Those who tend to laud Gilroy in elite academia *never* cite a broader range of scholars in Afrocentric studies, apart from Howe (1998) who is rather myopically Eurocentric in his analysis. To put it simply, Gilroy has not read deeply in Afrocentric philosophy, but what he has been able to do is produce a superficial account that allows Eurocentric philosophy to flourish within his body of work.

In essence, Gilroy claims to be neither Eurocentric or Afrocentric but a "hybrid intellectual" who draws from Eurocentric modernity to add his "counterculture narrative" of enslavement, akin to a "third way" of assessing Black cultural expression. Yet, to emphasize, it does not show in his scholarship and bibliographies that he has deeply read anything other than a caricatured comprehension of Afrocentric thought and Asante, who is Gilroy's main target of critique. At the very least if one does not share the ideas of a specific scholar the minimum one should do is be fair in the reading of him or her. Crucially, Gilroy is largely dismissive of Black intellectuals who are "at home" being Black. Any sign of comfort in a Black scholar being a cultural nationalist and Gilroy turns to his Eurocentric cabal of thinkers for reassurance, which is evident fundamentally in his critique of Asante (1993a, p. 189). This is a salient feature in all of his published works, he is indeed a consummate Eurocentric thinker who happens to have an interest in Black cultural expression in relation to modernity. From the perspective of Africana critical studies, and to use an antinomy in relation to Gilroy's first major publication from 1987, *There Ain't No Black in the Union Jack*: there ain't no Black empowerment in *The Black Atlantic*.

WRITING BLACK BRITAIN IN THE TRANSATLANTIC CONTEXT

Ordinarily, if one endeavors to study Black British writers from the twentieth century there is a list of the usual suspects that align with an erroneous date of "arrival" of Black Britons with the famous *Empire Windrush* ship from Jamaica that disembarked in 1948 at Tilbury Dock on the River Thames in London. This book is testimony to such a date being incorrect and extremely misleading in regard to Black British history. Nevertheless, expatriates from the British colonies who made their way from a satellite to the metropole, being London, have largely been regarded as the foundation in Black British writing. Writers such as George Lamming, Samuel Selvon, Beryl Gilroy (the mother of Paul Gilroy), E. R. Braithwaite, and Linton Kwesi Johnson, to name some of the key migrant Black British writers—who incidentally happen to have also been *born* in the British Caribbean colonies. Between

1948 and 1960 there was an influx of African and Caribbean migrants who fled their respective colonies to seek success in the British "mother country" as they had largely been fed such lofty ideals about "Great Britain" through a colonial education. Part of which was to inculcate the British Empire and its metropole as being paved with silver and gold. Sadly, most African and Caribbean migrants merely encountered the harsh realities of British racism and its gloomy cold weather.

George Lamming arrived in London, England from his native Barbados in 1950 and personifies those Caribbean writers who came during this period from the British colonies to the metropole in search of fame and fortune. However, it is important to point out that talented men (initially it was mainly male migrants, who would later send for their families) such as C. L. R. James arrived in England in the early 1930s seeking his fame as a writer, residing with his friend due to pennilessness, the Jamaican cricketer Learie Constantine (chapter two will cover more of this connection); the importance here is to note that transatlantic travel for African and Caribbean human ability has had longevity—do not think of 1948 and the *Empire Windrush* as the starting point of Black Britain or Black British writing. That stated, Lamming was just twenty-three years old when he published his first novel in 1953, part autobiographical, titled *In the Castle of My Skin*. Essentially, it covers his childhood growing up under British colonial rule in a small village in Barbados. Among other themes, he narrates the story through the eyes of a young boy from age nine up to his late teens. His experiences depicted a colonial education and racialized class tensions under British rule in Barbados. Lamming wrote the novel while residing in England as a hungry writer suffering the cold chill of British racism and relative poverty.

Looking back, in an article from the *Guardian* (October 23, 2002), he considered his former years, mentioning his close friend and fellow novelist, Samuel Selvon; who wrote another acclaimed novel about Caribbean migrants struggling for life again in a bitterly cold and racist London, aptly titled *The Lonely Londoners*, published in 1956. Lamming reflected on *his* generation and the younger, what he deemed as the "third generation" of Black Britons; he juxtaposes the poetry of his peer Derek Walcott with that of a younger poet, Linton Kwesi Johnson, who arrived in England aged ten years in 1963 from Jamaica. Yet herein lies something significant to note, which George Lamming overlooked in his sociocultural analysis of the two British Caribbean poets, in that Johnson though young *still* had ten years of life, his first ten years, in Jamaica before arriving in England. That can be important as he would have missed five years of primary schooling in Britain whereby the school system tended to destroy the creative energy of young Black boys (Christian 2005b; Coard 1991). To emphasize this point, Linton Kwesi Johnson would graduate from Goldsmiths, University of London, with a degree in sociology in 1973, at the average age of a middle-class white person, twenty-one years old. Now, this may indicate a young Black boy who was able to withstand the slings and arrows of misfortune in England at a very young age due to his ten-year grounding in Jamaica. Even though young Linton Kwesi Johnson would also join the British Black Panther Party as a teenager and write rather radical poetry expressing his disdain with British racism, he was *still* well beyond the average Black Briton *born* in England in terms of educational achievement for 1973.

This social analysis is something missed by George Lamming and other Caribbean writers in regard to Indigenous Black Britons compared to the migrant Caribbean writers. Nevertheless, Lamming expresses a pertinent reality about his generation compared to the younger who were more evocative in expressing their angst with British racism. Lamming related to the psychological complexity, ambivalence, whereby he alluded to his generation offering greater scope for conciliation between white British society and its colonial migrants of Caribbean heritage, as he explained in the *Guardian* (10/23/2002):

> This colonial entanglement makes for a complex relation between colony and metropole—a psychic entanglement that is often beyond the understanding of a third-generation British citizen of West Indian ancestry. Their relation to England is experienced as a racial assault that allows little space for a dialogue that would humanise the conflicts that arise from a perception of the other's difference.

Lamming cited the dub poetry of Linton Kwesi Johnson to show how the newer generation of Caribbean writers were unwavering in representing a counter-hegemonic Black British culture that was resistant to British racism. Johnson's "Inglan is a Bitch" (1980) comes from his dub poetry album *Bass Culture*—which was distributed by Island Records, who were also responsible for bringing Bob Marley's music to the broader world. Johnson's dub poetry in *Bass Culture* is quintessentially British Caribbean resistance to Margaret Thatcher's harsh and draconian policies of the 1970s and 1980s that engulfed the Black British experience. Lamming picked out the core of "Inglan is a Bitch" (Inglan is Jamaican patois for England):

> Inglan is a bitch
> dere's no escapin' it
> Inglan is a bitch

Clearly, as Lamming expressed, there was little room for dialogue between the British colonizing hegemony and its younger generation of Black British cultural artists experiencing racialized life on mainland Britain by the 1970s.

What is underplayed by Lamming is the fact that his generation were raised to see everything British as culturally superior, grand, and something to aspire to. After all, this was the home of Shakespeare, Chaucer, Woolf, Hardy, Dickens, Austen, Shelley, to name just a few of the celebrated white British writers. Lamming and his peers were "fed" in the Caribbean schools a deeply-rooted colonial education that most often obscured overt British racism. It was not until he arrived in Britain in 1950 that he unraveled the pretentiousness and folly of his brainwashed colonial education. A love of Queen/King and the British Empire was instilled into the minds of young Caribbean men and women during the British colonial rule. Lamming portrays this type of education insightfully in his novel *In the Castle of My Skin* whereby he uses a speech of a school inspector given to Caribbean schoolboys in order to convey the hidden ideology of British colonial brainwashing:

> My dear boys and teachers, we are met once again to pay our respects to the memory of a great Queen [Victoria, 1819–1901]. She was your queen and my queen and yours no less than mine. We're all subjects and partakers in the great design, the British Empire, and your loyalty to the Empire can be seen in the splendid performance which your school decorations and the discipline of these squads represent. We are living, my dear boys, in difficult times. We wait with greatest anxiety the news of what is happening on the other side of the world [lead- up to World War Two]. Those of you who read the papers may have read of the war in Abyssinia [Italian-Ethiopian war of 1935–1937]. You may have seen pictures of the King of Ethiopia and the bigger boys may have wondered what it's all about. The British Empire, you must remember, has always worked for the peace of the world. This is the job assigned it by God, and if the Empire at any time has failed to bring about that peace it was due to events and causes beyond its control . . .
>
> The boys and teachers applauded and his voice was lost in the noise. The inspector waited till the shouting died down and concluded: "Barbados is truly Little England!" (Lamming 1991, 38–39).

Lamming reveals the reality of a British colonial education that camouflaged its real intent—to rule parts of the world it had no fundamental right to rule. That its primary purpose was to exploit the land and its peoples of the Caribbean and regions of Africa. It would have been difficult for young minds not to be impressed with the pomp and ceremony of the British Empire ingrained in almost every school activity. Lamming represents the generation of Caribbean writers who were in "both camps" and who experienced a colonial upbringing and a postcolonial psychological awakening in the metropole. The Black British generations that followed his generation did not have to endure such overt brainwashing in the British education system. Instead, most often the offspring of the once colonized, many of whom were also of

Black mixed heritage origin having white mothers, entailed being labeled educationally subnormal, being excluded for misbehavior, or being labeled as problem children (Coard 1991; Christian 2005b).

This is not to dismiss colonial migrants as empty vacuums as themes relating to African rebellions struck a chord, such as the Mau Mau uprising in Kenya in the 1950s and the British atrocities that took place to quell it that were present in the poetry of Dereck Walcott, a peer of Lamming from St. Lucia. George Lamming employed Walcott's poem "A Cry from Africa" juxtaposed by Linton Kwesi Johnson's "Inglan is a Bitch" to show how poetry from each generation of African Caribbean poets resonated with similar protest—even if Johnson may have had a more radical tone. Part of Walcott's "A Cry from Africa" reads:

> I who am poisoned with the blood of both
> Where shall I turn, divided to the vein?
> . . .
> Between this Africa and the English tongue I love?
>
> (Derek Walcott cited in Lamming, 2002).

Walcott in his poem alludes to what he considers a psychological dilemma being a descendant of African heritage mixed with the British Caribbean origin of his birth. Again, this shows both hybridity and connection that deserves attention; "How can I turn from Africa and live?" is a question asked by Walcott, who cannot turn his back from the evil of British colonialism and the violence it is inflicting on the Kenyan nationalists who fight for their right to control the future free of the colonizer. Jomo Kenyatta (1894–1978) was the leader of the Mau Mau uprising and a Pan African thinker who attended the Pan African conference in Manchester, England in October of 1945 to strategize the decolonization of Africa from European colonial rule. Derek Walcott, George Lamming, C. L. R. James, and other African Caribbean intellectuals were influenced by these times and it emerged in their writings in the 1950s.

Another younger Caribbean author, who migrated to England as a child with his parents from St. Kitts is the celebrated writer Caryl Phillips, who was just four months old on his arrival in 1958. He clearly, unlike Linton Kwesi Johnson, can be deemed Black British as he grew up entirely in England, mainly in a working-class environment in the Leeds/Yorkshire area. Among his celebrated books are: *Crossing the River*, *The Atlantic Sound*, and *The European Tribe*. Phillips deals with the transatlantic themes of enslavement, the middle passage, belonging, loss—basically all things related to the Black Atlantic paradigm. He defies the norm of the post-1970s writer because his life trajectory is pretty much a "rags to riches" story. Raised on a working-class estate in Leeds, his mother and father divorced and he was sent out to foster homes, before his mother was able to reunite him and his siblings. A pretty grim typical Black British working-class start in life. However, at primary and secondary school in Leeds, he was a talented scholar in the disciplines of English and History and by sheer will power, and no doubt luck, he managed to get into Queens College, Oxford in 1976 at the age of eighteen years. A remarkable achievement given his start in life. What is more interesting is his talent for exploring Black Atlantic themes.

In *The Atlantic Sound*, published in 2000, he shares his experiences of traveling to Liverpool, England; Accra, Ghana; and Charleston, South Carolina: three points on the transatlantic voyages that exemplify the essence of the "triangular slave system" and its related horrors that have been covered throughout this chapter. Phillips, as with many of his predecessors, has traveled to various cities and nations for both psychological and physical freedom from racialized oppression. Never quite finding "home" is also something felt by the author of this book. Indeed, Phillips could certainly be deemed a peer of mine. Leeds is merely seventy miles from Liverpool; he was born in 1958, I was born in 1961; he supports Leeds United Football Club passionately, as I do Liverpool Football Club. Both of us have found a sense of intellectual freedom in the United States; yet we neither feel "at home" there or in England.

However, the fact that he left Leeds for Oxford University at eighteen years of age, then living later in London and New York, seems to have impacted his writing making it a tad pretentious at times, certainly in regard to his analysis of Liverpool. In a chapter titled "Leaving Home" from *The Atlantic Sound* he narrates a vision of Liverpool that yields both truths and perceptible stereotypes. Noticeably he asks questions about the city's wealth through its involvement with enslavement via its monumental architecture. He is also curious about the invisibility of Black presence in the city. There is a superficial characterization of a guide to show him around the city named "Stephen"—a Black Liverpudlian. Here we have a Black writer from Yorkshire, Phillips, and his Black character from Liverpool, Stephen. Phillips has risen to the heights of minor author celebrity from humble British inner-city origins in becoming a noted writer, but clearly, he does not comprehend the experience of Blacks in contemporary Liverpool being excluded from opportunities in education (Swann Report 1985) when he describes the young Black Liverpudlian. What is rather galling is his implicit put-down of Stephen for not having gone to university, yet having a deep interest in literature and the Black history of Liverpool. It could be the very fact that he did *not* go to a British university that encouraged his interest in Black history. Nor should one ever underestimate the profound knowledge that can be found in grassroots communities rather than university settings. Phillips depicts the Black Liverpudlian in this manner:

> Stephen is a strikingly tall young man of twenty-three. He left school at sixteen and began to work, but although he is erudite and clearly interested in literature, he never went on to university. His passion is Liverpool's hidden history; its black history, and in particular the city's relationship to the slave trade (p. 98).

This characterization could have been myself at the age of twenty-three in Liverpool. What is disappointing is in the way Phillips implicitly undermines and patronizes the character of "Stephen" as the interaction between the two unfolds. For example, a guide should at least be given the benefit of the doubt in terms of his local knowledge, yet Phillips is dismissive of the claims Stephen makes about being part of an exploited Black community in the city. This is important because it shows the degree of difference *within* Black British experiences—something I have alluded to earlier and will continue to highlight throughout later chapters. Regardless of Phillips' cardboard cut-out of his Black Liverpudlian character, "Leaving Home" is a worthwhile read and it gives further insight into the Black Atlantic, Caribbean heritage in Britain and its relationship to the transatlantic geographical framework. However, his comprehension of Black experience in Liverpool could be improved greatly as it lacks historical context.

Another writer related to having been born and raised in Britain, and who has gone on to be famous for her output, is Zadie Smith. She was born in London in 1975, of Jamaican and English parentage. Her first novel speaks to multicultural and multiracial Britain in postcolonial-postmodern times. *White Teeth* was published in 2000 to worldwide acclaim that catapulted her to fame and fortune—as with Phillips at Yale University, Smith has taught at Harvard. Both of these Black British writers came from humble origins, working-class communities, yet managed to get into the elite universities in Britain to study for the BA degrees. Phillips gained his degree from Oxford in 1979; Smith graduated in 1998 with a BA in English Literature from King's College, Cambridge. Her work focuses on the intricacies of interracial life in Black Britain; what is unique is she creates characters, white, South Asian, and Black. There is a fluidity in her prose ingrained with humor, irony, and pathos.

Zadie Smith, however, like most of the writers before her on Black British experiences, focused *White Teeth* within a London multiracial context. That's what is refreshing about Caryl Phillips' works as opposed to the London-centric Black British authors—he often delves into an interactive historical experience of the Black Atlantic. In a telling section of *The Atlantic Sound* Phillips speaks inadvertently about the Liverpool Black experience, as he reflects on the city while sitting in a pub:

The barman has a solid boulder for a stomach, and as he pulls my pint I realize that I have now spent a whole morning walking, sitting and talking in Liverpool, and aside from a few solitary faces in the street, I have not encountered a single black person. Where on earth is the Liverpool Black population? (p. 107).

The deeper response to Phillips' question will be answered in other chapters, but what he reveals is an age-old vision of Liverpool: "Where are the Black folks in the city centre region?" The fact is we are there in the city and have been for centuries. It is noticeable from reading the *The Atlantic Sound* that "Stephen" appeared not to walk around the Black areas of Liverpool with Phillips where the history of Black settlement was largely located— Liverpool 8 or Toxteth is one of the main areas. It seems from reading the chapter that they merely drove through sections of Liverpool 8 where Black Liverpudlians tend to reside. It should be pointed out that the Black experience in Liverpool has "spread" outward to areas such as Smithdown Road, Kensington, and Aigburth where Black Liverpudlian families live. They have been dotted around the entire area of Liverpool too; it is fallacious to think of there being only one area of concentration. Liverpool Black families, in short, are more integrated than they used to be, but still the history of Black settlement from the 1900s would take us from Liverpool 1 to Brownlow Hill, to Liverpool 8, and then further outward to places like Cantril Farm, Kirby, Speke, Halewood, Netherley, Norris Green, or more centrally in the case of Tuebrook and West Derby.

THE TRANSATLANTIC IN CONTEXT TO THE BLACK ATLANTIC PARADIGM

This chapter has covered the importance in comprehending the development of the transatlantic enslavement and colonial experience, considering anticolonial writers and activists, and later engaging with Paul Gilroy as a major theoretician of this topic. In addition, there has been an effort to explain the City of Liverpool in terms of its development within the context of the slave system leading to Black presence, which will be affirmed continuously throughout the book—hopefully the reader can gauge that it is a city not sealed off from the broader context of Africana experiences. Different, yes, but connected; hybridized, yes, but within a Black settlement paradigm; regionally and historically specific, yes, but not isolated from global racialized realities.

As Barnor Hesse, a Black British scholar, has contended, " If our objective is to illuminate the [Black] political, its institutions and modalities, inevitably we encounter experiences and events from 'other' narratives, from elsewhere or another time" (2000, p. 78). Clearly one cannot study the Black British experience without linking the broader African continent and its Diaspora. Therein lies the conundrum, because Gilroy would argue that there is nothing that connects Black experiences in fundamental terms of a unified, multifaceted oppression. Or to put it another way, as a continuum and at times integrated by Black Nationalism or Pan Africanism on international terms. Such political resistance that was created as an antidote to white international racism and oppression is something Gilroy appears to reject because it maintains "sealed camps" and causes further conflict. In another book that is a collection of his essays, *Small Acts: Thoughts on the Politics of Black Cultures,* Gilroy incorrectly employs sensationalist homogeneous-race purity labels, among other things, to some Black scholars in order to peddle his fragmentation of a Black unity thesis, as he writes:

> The fundamental, time-worn assumption of homogenous and unchanging black communities whose political and economic interests were readily knowable and easily transferred from everyday life into their expressive cultures, for example, proved to be a fantasy. To make matters worse, the ideal of racial purity, the appeal to phenotypical symmetry and the comfort of cultural sameness have never been more highly prized as attributes of black social life than they are today (1993b, p. 1)

Gilroy was writing in the early 1990s, a time when Afrocentricity was very popular in grassroots communities, and when there was a revival of Malcolm X's ideas. One must add that this was also the period when a young, middle-class Black man, Stephen Lawrence (1974–1993), was murdered by a group of white racists in London after a knife attack. This was a murder that outraged Black communities across Britain and galvanized them to fight against racism. When one considers Gilroy's idea in this context, on a grassroots level of Black experience, it appears that he is lost in some abstract thought and not thinking from a day-to-day level of British Blackness in all its complexity. One can also gauge why Gilroy finds himself so appreciated by the white cultural hegemony in liberal academia because he assails any attempt to forge a Black unified front which he regards as "fantasy" and ethnic absolutism. Gilroy continues to emphasize his fragmentation thesis:

> The idea of a common, invariant racial identity capable of linking divergent black experiences across different spaces and times has been fatally undermined. The increasingly desperate assertions of homogeneity that flow out of black vernacular culture can neither conceal nor answer this transformation. Homogeneity can signify unity but unity need not require homogeneity (p. 2).

Gilroy never offers concrete examples of his "desperate assertions of homogeneity" and if he believes all Black thinkers think alike in a given discipline then he is profoundly mistaken. There are tremendous differences of opinion *within* Africana studies. Indeed, there are schools of thought that this author has recognized (Christian 2006a). Too often the critical insights from Africana studies scholars have been subdued by an avalanche of white liberal intellectual praise for Gilroy, while ignoring the problematic aspects of his limited view that emphasizes mere *difference* over *significance* in the disparate Black lives galvanized within the cauldron of the Black Atlantic experience. Yet, again, to counter Gilroy is to contend that there can be *unity* without *uniformity* among the millions of peoples of African heritage who make up the African Diaspora. Also, one should note that Gilroy largely omits Africa and African continental thinkers from the Black Atlantic experience.

This is akin to a European writer, say Hegel or Adorno, omitting Europe when writing about the migration of their peoples to the so-called "New World" that was only new to them, and not to the Indigenous peoples that were inhabiting the Caribbean islands, the Americas, and other geographical regions outside of Europe for thousands of years. In short, without looking at Gilroy from an authentic Africana studies perspective to comprehend his ideas on the Black Atlantic one can easily get lost in his European-derived analysis of Black history and culture. To be fair to Gilroy, he states humbly that at the outset of his study "there is nothing definitive here. . . . I have done scarcely more than put down some preliminary markers" (p. xi). Given Gilroy's veracity here, why does his Black Atlantic thesis continue to have such traction? This question was partly answered earlier through Laura Chrisman (2003); to paraphrase, *The Black Atlantic* allows the white controlled academy to "escape" the critical insights of Africana studies scholars because Gilroy gives them an excuse to call anything "Black" essentialist and dogmatic. It is as simple as that—all neophyte scholars of Black experience are introduced to his problematic and naïve thesis.

BLACK ATLANTIC TRAVEL—
INVOLUNTARY TO VOLUNTARY

A major aspect of transatlantic history has been the reality of travel itself. It is a salient fact in the long history of human and cultural exchange over centuries. It is something central to the ebb and flow of Africans from the continent and into what would be termed its African Diaspora. Perhaps a book that captures the essence of this theme is the 1998 edited volume by Alasdair Pettinger titled *Always Elsewhere: Travels of the Black Atlantic*. There are *many* names missing who could be in this book, yet it is still a volume that seizes an important aspect of the transatlantic experience. Certainly, another book on the same theme adds more famous names to the list of Black Atlantic travelers: *A Stranger in the Village* also from 1998, edited by Farah Griffin and Cheryl Fish, has Angela Davis, James Baldwin, Countee Cullen, and June Jordan who are missing from Pettinger's volume. Again, no one volume could amass those famous individuals who have traversed the transatlantic to share their insights. It is simply impossible to catalogue all the famous souls who have traveled within the Black Atlantic sphere. Two glaring omissions from both of these important volumes are Paul Robeson and Malcolm X—each share tremendous participation in the freedom of African heritage peoples through their respective travels across the transatlantic historical vortex.

When one considers the enslavement era up to the mid-twentieth century and the collapse of direct rule in the British colonies, there was the mass involuntary aspect of bondage, followed by individuals who shine a light on the notion of *traveling for freedom*. Indeed, a precarious pursuit of freedom that could lead to despair or joy—it was always a gamble to pick up and leave a place of origin—whether it be from enslaved quarters (Frederick Douglass to New York from Maryland in 1838) or leaving a colonial satellite for the metropole (C. L. R. James to London from Trinidad in 1932), there was always a risk involved. Yet these individual acts of courage, forged with singular talent, are examples of the human spirit ever wanting freedom and the right to exercise it to the fullest. Freedom as a concept is tricky—what exactly is freedom? Maybe it is better to think of it as *free-from* whatever plagues one's soul at the time of departure from one place to another. For Frederick Douglass in 1838 it was a desire to escape bondage; for C. L. R. James in 1932 it was to depart the confines of a Caribbean Island to seek the world of Shakespeare and Chaucer. A British colonial education had filled him with delusions of grandeur for England's pleasant land.

Neither Frederick Douglass nor C. L. R. James, for example, knew for sure what they would eventually encounter after reaching a destination of their choice—it was merely a courageous urge to travel from a place they were at that stifled life aspirations and personal growth. To be sure, we are merely considering two major historical figures for the sake of clarifying Black Atlantic travel. There are indeed many reasons why individuals seek to travel from their place of origin. However, one should keep in mind too that the majority of people live out their lives within a two-mile radius of where they were born. Those who travel to seek a broader experience do so often out of desperation, and what could be more desperate than wanting to escape from bondage? Or wanting to find a better life economically, supposedly, beyond the confines of a British colony? It does not take much imagination to share empathy with those many thousands of African and Caribbean migrants who sought their specific sense of freedom from whatever suffocates the human spirit.

In conclusion, the Black Atlantic articulated by Gilroy is in need of refinement, addition, not subtraction. In considering a number of anticolonial writers and activists not mentioned in *The Black Atlantic,* this book is one such addition. Undeniably, the Euro-intellectual foundation of his thesis makes it rather incongruous to suggest a "third way" beyond it and African centered analysis because he is firmly encamped intellectually in a Eurocentric epistemology—a "third way" could never emerge when he mainly employs one set of canons. Hence, the need for an Africana critical studies perspective is imperative if only to explain the theoretical flaws embedded in Gilroy's offering. Moreover, most cultural studies scholars would agree that there has been an interactive flow of humanity and with it cultural exchange that speaks profoundly to this reality. Yet, to diminish Blackness to the point of endless fragmentation given the constant *changing same* of racialized discrimination is absurdity. There still has been, no matter how one describes it, a unity between the disparate African and Caribbean nations that were once colonized. These regions continue to be saturated with English, French, Portuguese, Spanish, Dutch, and other "foreign" languages in having endured under various European colonial regimes. In addition, the men and women of the African Diaspora who have had their blood mixed, voluntarily or involuntarily, with Europeans had their offspring *still* inextricably linked to Black heritage and largely excluded from the white European cultural hegemony. In other words, Blacks of mixed heritage had little choice but to stand with their darker brothers and sisters due to the nature of European racialized oppression. Sometimes they were used as a way to divide and conquer Black experiences, but fundamentally, certainly in the US context, they were part of the "one drop rule" and of African heritage. To develop historical amnesia in regard to this fact may be convenient for an abstract "we are the world" thesis—but it does not meet with the grassroots experience of Blackness across the Black Atlantic. Different shades of the Black Atlantic, from ivory to blue Black, may well be a salient feature—yet this is also a reality that has been a feature on the African continent from time immemorial. The racialized nature of the last five hundred plus years is a fundamentally European invention. Crucially, given the ebb and flow of Black humanity presented in this chapter, and given the tremendous problems facing the twenty-first century in terms of racialized discrimination, a closer look at a microcosm of the Black Atlantic via *Transatlantic Liverpool* is apt due to its many racialized complexities. In the spirit of Frederick Douglass, Ida B. Wells-Barnett, Aimé Césaire, Frantz Fanon, Amilcar Cabral, C. L. R. James, Walter Rodney, and the many thousands of forgotten souls forged in the Black Atlantic, let us now consider the Liverpool Black experience more intimately.

Chapter 2

Life and Times in a Liverpool Black Atlantic Family—the Christians

The essence of this chapter is to integrate a Black British family within the context of the transatlantic experience and its relationship with the City of Liverpool, beginning with the migration of Gladstone Forbes Christian from Jamaica to Britain during World War Two, and his subsequent life with Ada Pitt and their children. A caveat is necessary at the outset: this story of a Black family from Liverpool, England is interconnected with social theory and the reality of racialized relations. The objective is to give a micro-sociological insight into what indeed was experienced by many other Black families in the city. The use of historical primary data to enhance the narrative is a crucial element in order to authenticate the efficacy of what can be deemed "The Christians" and Black Liverpool. There is an effort to weave in and out of family history with sociological analysis that meets with the overall narrative—think of this as *Jazz-writing*. However, to put the Christians as a Black Liverpudlian family in context in regard to the city, two respected writers on Liverpool Black experience, summarize its history in this manner:

> The history of white racism and black settlement in Liverpool has for too long remained hidden beneath the myth of Liverpool's cosmopolitan harmony and the white bias or complacency of local historians. . . . Racist ideas, derogatory images and stereotypes of blackness and black people have been an integral part of local thought and culture since Liverpool itself emerged in the seventeenth century. . . . There is substantial evidence to show that the twin themes of racism and black settlement are integral parts of Liverpool's history and can no longer be ignored. There is still much to be done to record and document this history. (Law and Henfrey (1981, p. v).

GLADSTONE

It was a hot day in mid-July 1941, Kingston, Jamaica. The *Jamaica Producer* was getting set for a transatlantic voyage that would take in Montreal, Canada before disembarking at the port of Belfast, Ireland on the 6th of August. On board were over one hundred young Jamaican men, skilled in various occupations to help the "Mother Country" in her fight against the Nazi axis. Many of these young men had never left their homeland which was in itself nerve-wracking. To add to this anxiety was the thought of the ship being attacked by German enemy U-boats who patrolled the Atlantic seeking out the convoys of merchant shipping that supplied the Allied forces with weaponry and goods. It would not be until later in the year, after the December 7th Pearl Harbor assault, that the United States would enter World War Two (WW2). These were perilous times and the young Jamaican men were decidedly brave souls to leave behind their families to embark on the unfamiliar—the treacherous unknown.

Among these brave Jamaican men was Gladstone Forbes Christian, a thirty-four-year-old technician and fitter. He had been raised in a middle-class family of eight siblings, with a loving mother and father. There was a lawyer, an accountant, nurses, teachers, and a police officer among his siblings—most of whom had made a life between Jamaica and the United States. Their parents had made a life in Columbus, Ohio in the early 1920s; the father George Rupert Christian, was a schoolmaster in Jamaica and later become an organizer within the Marcus Garvey movement, and his wife Ada Jane Christian was his staunch supporter. Of all the siblings, it was only Gladstone who ventured out to Britain during wartime, volunteering as many other African Caribbean souls did to aid the war in Europe, between Europeans.

Gladstone was a stubborn man, he always wanted to create his own path in life. He took the greater chances, and there was no greater challenge than in the summer of 1941 to embark on a transatlantic voyage to Britain during the second world war. Gladstone was a keen cricketer in his homeland, he had made his name in the local league while working on the Kingston railway as an engineer. Confident and courageous, he had been schooled via the British colonial education system that made everything appear as though whatever was British would be the best. With England being the home of cricket, he was enchanted by the thought of being involved in aiding the mother country in its hour of need. Unlike his father, who protested his involvement, Gladstone remained obstinate in his decision to help fight the Nazis and free Britain/Europe from its tyranny.

The *Jamaica Producer* set sail with stomachs churning and hearts beating fast as the transatlantic voyage proceeded across precarious terrain. To

Figure 2.1 Gladstone Forbes Christian and his African Caribbean colleagues circa 1942. Gladstone is in the back row, fourth from the right.
Source: International Slavery Museum and National Museum Liverpool (ISM/NML) using the accession number (ISM.2010.5)

give some context, the final destination was Belfast, and during the months of April and May of 1941 the city had endured what is now regarded as the Belfast Blitz. The Nazi Luftwaffe inflicted tremendous terror on the city in four air riads killing over one thousand souls and injuring far more—the destruction was only beaten by the London Blitz of 1940 (Barton 2015). Considering that these air raids on Belfast took place only three months before the arrival of the *Jamaica Producer*, it gives an indication of the immense bravery it must have taken to have traveled such an arduous journey during these perilous times.

It is no wonder Gladstone's father was pessimistic about his son taking such a risk with his young life to aid in what he considered a "white man's war" that had nothing to do with Jamaicans. Indeed, as noted, George Rupert Christian (1882–1952) was no ordinary Jamaican, being a staunch member of the Universal Negro Improvement Association (UNIA) led by Marcus Garvey. Interestingly, Garvey had died the previous June 1940 in London, so it must have been difficult for Gladstone's father to contemplate his beloved son leaving his homeland for what he considered a cause that was not empowering for Africana peoples. For him, this was just another form of exploitation by the British colonizer to extract what they could from their colonial outposts. Gladstone was not a political thinker like his father, his love of Britain came from his love of cricket—the source of his lifeblood. He was not a student of history like his father and only wanted to do the right thing and help the mother country fight an openly hostile enemy in the Nazis.

It is important to note that not everyone has the gift of historical and political perception to weed from one's mind the miseducation that a British colonial education had wrought.

Those of his fellow compatriots on board the vessel had similar or varied social backgrounds to Gladstone; what they each had in common was their Jamaican heritage and a hope that whatever they encountered in the coming months would lead to ultimate victory. They were collectively optimistic and bursting with the arrogance of youth, they wanted to prove their worth as men of color and to fight for British "freedom" and its democratic principles that had been inculcated into them as schoolboys and young men. This is the type of education that C. L. R. James in Trinidad, or George Lamming in Barbados, or Derek Walcott in St. Lucia had received—in other British Caribbean colonies. Yet Jamaica was a "big island" and a massive sugar and banana producer for the British Empire. Jamaicans prided themselves in being Jamaican, and they tended to have much bolder and stronger personalities than the "smaller island" dwellers—or so the mythology assumes. What was in common among all the British Caribbean colonies related to a colonial education that inculcated a respect and allegiance to the British Empire. To be a good citizen of the British Caribbean colonial structure was to adhere to the key principles of the British Empire—all roads led back to the green and Promised Land of England. Miseducation at its most potent would be imbibed by all gullible African Caribbeans.

During the previous European world war of 1914–1918, young Black men of the Caribbean region were also drafted to fight in France/Europe again for the British cause, and this is something largely hidden from the historical record. Once the war had finished the Black soldiers or seaman, whatever capacity they worked in for the war effort, were no longer wanted on the British homeland. They were treated and regarded as a problem to the British Isles and ports like Liverpool and Cardiff, where Black British populations had earlier developed and where "race riots" occured based primarily on this issue of not wanting the presence of Black labor once the war had ceased (Heneghan and Onuora 2019; Jenkinson 2009). It was a wakeup call for Black Britons on the mainland and in the British colonies. Perhaps this is the insidiousness of the British education system and its ability to erase memory within a generation, but the young men in the British colonies still heeded the call again in WW2 for them to aid in the defense of the motherland. An abusive "motherland" if one is to take on board the historical record without amnesia; yet the previous WWI experience did not stop a multitude of African Caribbean youth wanting to leave their relative safety to participate in the WW2 effort. There is something rather incongruous with this but it has to be related to the power of British seduction to outwit so many while a few see through the two-faced chicanery of the authorities. When in need they plead; when need recedes they renege on the promise of a better life in England for those who put their lives on the line for King and country.

Though testy at times for all on board, Gladstone made the transatlantic crossing without too much angst; there was the inevitable sea sickness brought on by his nervous system being on alert due to the possibility of imminent death via a Nazi U-boat attack. Fortunately, he and his compatriots arrived in Belfast unscathed ready to make a cross ferry trip to Liverpool, England. There the group of African Caribbean technicians were escorted to temporary lodgings while the welfare services found more suitable accommodation. These men were all due to find employment in the armaments factories located in the northwest of England. Gladstone was assigned to the Royal Ordnance Factory based in Fazakerley, located on the northern side of Liverpool near Walton and Aintree. This armament factory was responsible for producing small arms, of which the Sten and Sterling machine guns were among the main production.

Gladstone settled into his accommodation at a large house in Croxteth Road, Liverpool 8, the area where most Blacks in the city resided. He shared an apartment with two fellow Jamaicans. They would reach their top floor home by walking up a long flight of fire escape stairs external to the house that led to the apartment entrance. This home in Liverpool was far from what Gladstone had been accustomed to, it was a far cry from the comfort he had enjoyed in his spacious family home in Jamaica. Nevertheless, he did not complain as it all related to experiencing a new adventure in England. Everything was novel and it made him more flexible to the realities of life during WW2 in Britain. This was a time of sacrifice and the bonding of souls to engage in the fight for eventual victory against a common oppressor—the Nazis and its axis. It is difficult to consider such tremendous courage it must have taken to leave one's homeland to embark on an adventure during a world war. Gladstone Christian was one of many African Caribbean men who took up the burden to save the world from Nazi domination. In doing so he encountered a new life in the cold and blustery winds of Britain.

ADA

As time went by Gladstone would settle into life in Liverpool. He was responsible for making sure the machines worked efficiently for the women in the Royal Ordnance Factory; he took his job very seriously and worked tirelessly to ensure the smooth operation of the machines would not falter for the diligent women workers. After a couple of years there in the summer of 1943, a young attractive woman aged about twenty-one years joined the factory; her name was Ada Pitt. She also came from a family of eight siblings; she had one sister and six brothers. Her father was a Liverpool Merchant Navy captain, Frederick Pitt. Her mother was also called Ada and took care of the Pitt family home. Apparently, Ada's grandmother was Spanish and born in Spain, and this accounts for the deep brown eyes and sallow skin of young Ada Pitt. Interestingly, Ada was also the name of Gladstone's mother. What seemed like an odd couple, Gladstone being a strapping six foot and four inches, Ada being five foot and three inches in height made for a curious connection; juxtaposed by the dark-skinned tone of Gladstone with Ada's lighter complexion they certainly stuck out as a couple in the British chill of winter, spring, summer, and fall.

Ada had six brothers and one sister,; the Pitts were a close-knit family and would sing songs in the parlor room of their home. Like all British children born in the 1920s, Ada left school at age fourteen years. She was expected to marry young and settle down as women were not empowered to be independent as they are today. By the age of ten years her family were also living through the Great Depression, life was not easy for the Pitts during the 1930s but they took care of each other. At the outset of WW2, she was seventeen years old so life had thrown quite a lot of challenges at her for one so young. By the time she was eighteen the call for women to join the war industries sounded in order to help save the nation from Nazi tyranny. Patriotism was in the air and the Pitt family were ready to do their duty. Ada's elder brothers joined the British Army and her father continued to sail the treacherous seas, taking frequent transatlantic voyages for much needed wartime supplies to Britain. Ada was more than pleased to be able to work in the munitions factory as it gave her a sense of involvement in the war effort—she was very proud to be British during this period in her young life.

These two souls, Gladstone and Ada, who were once separated by the Atlantic Ocean: fate and circumstance had now brought them together by the unsavory reality of WW2. Ada was born and raised in the City of Liverpool in a loving family of moderately middle-class status. Her father being a Merchant Navy captain was nothing to be shy about as it involved great courage and leadership skills; but raising eight children on his salary could not have been easy. Nonetheless, she and her siblings had a good life growing up in the Norris Green area of Liverpool, on the North side of the city not too far from the armaments factory. Gladstone and Ada initially made small talk while at the Royal Ordnance Factory, though they began to look for each other during the complexity of the day and its working hours. They were always cordial and professional in terms of social interaction; discreet is the right word, if only due to the respective social realities of time and place and the ever-present specter of British racism hovering over their social world.

WAR ON BOTH FRONTS

An interesting study on Black Liverpool by John Belchem titled *Before the Windrush: Race Relations in 20th- Century Liverpool* and published in 2014 takes into account the period of WW2. Chapter three covers "wartime hospitality and the color bar" which in itself reveals a glaring paradox. That is, in there being hospitality *and* a color bar in unison is either cognitive dissonance on behalf of this historian or a tongue-in-cheek attempt to draw the irony to the reader. The social fact remains that Gladstone Christian was one of 345 technicians and trainees brought over from the British Caribbean colonies to aid in the war effort between February and August 1941. As John Belchem (2014) and earlier Anthony Richmond (1954) have revealed, these men experienced being welcomed by some and scorned by many—particularly in Liverpool. Anthony Richmond was more emphatic in the title of his study concerning Gladstone's social experience in the city, along with that of his Jamaican compatriots: *Colour Prejudice in Britain: A Study of West Indian Workers in Liverpool, 1941–1951*. This sums up the reality of what these young courageous African Caribbean men encountered, prejudice and racism in Britain after taking a treacherous transatlantic journey to aid the nation.

The modern reader maybe confused by the term "West Indians" and this should be explained. Briefly, the term comes from the fact that when Christopher Columbus was looking for a way to the Indies (Asia) in the late 1400s and early 1500s he got lost and his ships ended up in the Caribbean region; hence the name of the area would become known as the "West Indies" in European history. Moreover, this term has been used up to the present time when it relates to the African Caribbean cricket team playing abroad in England or Australia. However, for scholars in Africana critical studies it is more appropriate to call the region African Caribbean when relating to the history of the African Diaspora as in the case of this study. Richmond was a white European scholar, like Belchem, and their epistemological approach was and is most often within the confines of what could be deemed the *colonizer's paradigm*. To put it another way, they analyze Black experiences through the lens of white men and as European thinkers who tend to dilute the depth of racialized discrimination. This is why it is important to have perspectives that also emanate from Black writers, if only for balance. In explaining his study of Gladstone Christian and his fellow Jamaicans from WW2, Richmond explained:

> The West Indians with whom this study is mainly concerned come to this country under a scheme organised jointly by the Ministry of Labour and the Colonial Office, with the object of increasing production, strengthening the bonds between Great Britain and the West Indies, and making a small contribution

towards relieving the unemployment in these Colonies. In Jamaica and other islands of the West Indies men were eager to offer their services to the "Mother Country." At that time [1940s] there were few openings in the armed forces but it was felt that the Colonies could help fill the urgent need for skilled workers in the factories. The view that Merseyside [Liverpool and surrounding area] was relatively familiar with the idea of coloured workers resulted in a policy of employing the majority of the men in this area; later men were employed in Manchester, Bolton, and the surrounding district as well (1954, p. 23).

Richmond appears to be economical with the truth in regard to his point, "there were few openings in the armed forces." What he should have stated is there were few if any openings for African Caribbean men and women initially, much like that in the United States with African Americans, because of institutional racism. But with political insight and necessity the British government gradually changed its stance and opened up opportunities particularly for skilled workers to come over and help and this is the context in which Gladstone Christian and his colleagues found themselves: needed but not really wanted. Moreover, Richmond indirectly alludes to the longevity of Black presence in Liverpool with the phrase Liverpool/Merseyside "was relatively familiar with the idea of coloured workers." In other words, the northwest region of Britain could accommodate the influx of African Caribbean workers in this time of dire need during WW2 as long as there were adequate welfare provisions.

Liverpool being a region that had long been a home of Blacks, a growing community that was actually Indigenous to the area, it was probably the most efficacious reason why the government placed the majority of the African Caribbean technicians there. They would not admit such a strategic move in case it looked as if they were putting them where other "coloreds" resided. For example, the African Churches Missions led by Pastor Daniels Ekarte had been set up in the early 1920s, its premises at 122–124 Hill Street from 1931 was clearly an indication of Black presence in the city (Belchem 2014, p. 67; Sherwood 1995). Ekarte had been present in the city from about 1915 and had arrived as an African from Nigeria to preach. He was a major African character in the city for over thirty years and this had not gone unnoticed by the city fathers. As established, Black Liverpudlians were recognized in the city well before WW2, so it was natural for the British government to consider Liverpool an ideal location for the African Caribbean technicians. The problem was in it not being a welcoming experience for most of them, who suffered on two fronts: from wartime austerity and from institutional and individual acts of racism, not to mention the emotional wrench in leaving their homelands for the cold climate and solemnity that Britain offered.

WELFARE AND FANFARE IN CRICKET

Part of the effort to welcome Gladstone and the other African Caribbean men was to appoint the well-known cricketer Learie Constantine (1901–1971), who was from Trinidad and a close friend of C. L. R. James. Constantine came to England to play cricket in the 1920s and he would develop into a popular celebrity throughout the 1930s with his skills playing for the Lancashire League club Nelson, where he played for over a decade. He was put forward by the Colonial Office as the official welfare officer for the Jamaican technicians in Liverpool; he was specifically responsible for making sure the hostels set up for accommodation were fully compliant with decent housing standards for those technicians that utilized them. There was also a Merseyside Hospitality Council (MHC) to provide a welcoming experience but this was not as hospitable as one would hope due to the overall discrimination apparent in Liverpool even before the arrival of the Jamaican technicians (Belchem 2014, p. 80).

The fact that Gladstone Christian and two of his friends decided to branch out and find independent accommodation in the Liverpool 8 area, away from the hostels, may give an indication that the standard of them was not friendly and accommodating for these overseas transients. Nevertheless, to have a man like Learie Constantine in their corner was formidable and he did his best to ensure there was both respect and recreational facilities for these brave souls. He was a man of great dignity and he carried himself with honor—he was not as politically inclined as his friend C. L. R. James, but he was nobody's fool either. Gerald Howart, a biographer of the great man, sums up Constantine's life and achievements in a manner that was largely denied to peoples of African heritage in British society; he was clearly an exception to the rule, or a man of "rags to riches"—a fabled life:

> Learie Constantine, from the obscurity of slave ancestry and a small cocoa plantation, rose to become one of the great cricketers of his generation, a broadcaster, a cabinet minister, a diplomat, a knight-bachelor and the first Negro to take his seat in the House of Lords.... Constantine's homeland was Trinidad yet it was in the British Isles that he won greater recognition and where he believed he "was accepted and honoured" (1976, p. 11).

Though the writing of Howart is a tad dated one can still gauge the journey that Learie Constantine took from humble origins, having enslaved ancestors not too far back, yet still being able to have risen to the very top of British society. Gladstone Christian and his peers certainly appreciated being in the company of this great cricketer, but not one to be in awe of any human being as he too was a rather talented individual and cricketer himself. In under six weeks after arriving in Liverpool Gladstone was playing cricket *with* Learie Constantine, which gives one an indication of his standing in Jamaican cricket. It appears that some of the best sportsmen were brave enough to travel to Britain to both work and entertain the British public with their varied talents. This can also be assessed due to the interest of the local press. There was a match preview on September 16, 1941 highlighted in the *Liverpool Daily Post* that clearly shows how much these cricketers from the Caribbean were respected. The promotion of this event by the local newspapers gave an enthusiastic welcome to the "West Indies" cricketers who would be playing. Among the team led by Constantine, was Gladstone Christian:

> L. Constantine, E. Achong, E. A. Martindale, C. B. Clarke, F. St. Hill, Musa Beg, C. Roach, **G. Christian**, V. Mason, F. Rhoden, A. W. Whittingham, F. Winter

(*Liverpool Daily Post*, September 16, 1941, p. 3).

What is particularly interesting in this primary source relates to providing contemporary evidence that the Jamaican people were able to listen to the commentary via a transatlantic radio broadcast. When one considers this occurring during WW2, and the Jamaican nation was able to listen to a cricket match being played in the Liverpool, England, just weeks after the *Jamaica Producer* had brought Gladstone Christian over to play his part in the fight against the Nazi axis, it is truly remarkable when one considers the context of cultural life during the war years. Clearly, there appeared to be time for recreation and leisure periods even though it was arguably the most stressful time in the lives of all involved. Nor was this a one-off match; there would be several played on some of the most famous British cricket grounds, including Lords where England played a West Indies XL led again by Constantine and including Gladstone Christian during the summer of 1943. One wonders what was going through his mind as he played cricket with some of the best players in the world holding his own in the mix of talent on display. There were none better than the Trinidadian Learie Constantine who would assist his fellow African Caribbean men to settle into the harsh realities of war-torn Britain.

Certainly, during the war years and with the leadership and direction of Constantine, cricket teams would be assembled under the title the "Learie Constantine XL" and always the name of Gladstone Christian was acknowledged as a firm member of the teams. It is clear that besides the inevitable frustrations of racism and discrimination the Royal Ordnance Factory (ROF) workers from Jamaica and other Caribbean islands did what they could to settle, enjoy, and prosper in Liverpool to aid in the war effort. Another example of the press being interested in the men from the Caribbean is the *Liverpool Echo* who advertised one such cricket match taking place in the same area where the ROF was located in Fazakerley, Liverpool in August 1943. The report offers vibrant publicity to get spectators out to see an exciting match between local cricket rivals. One can gauge from the line-up of players that Gladstone Christian is an established member of a prominent cricket team during WW2.

It also affirms that Gladstone was a top-class cricketer and could comfortably hold his own beside a great like Learie Constantine. The fact that such cricket matches were advertised in the major Liverpool newspapers is an indication of the sport attracting wide public interest. This was a difficult time for the city during wartime, so recreation clearly played a significant part in alleviating tension. Crucially, the public evidence shows a great deal of interest surrounding the African Caribbean men who traveled so far from their native lands to fight for the freedom of British society. A major pastime in Jamaica and the other British Caribbean colonies was the game of cricket, an import from the English to the colonies. It seems that this pastime indirectly created cultural links that would be lasting between the satellites and metropole. Yet there was also the racialized factor that percolated within the colonizer and colonized when cricket was played between England and the West Indies. There was no escaping the tacit competition between the delusional "superior English colonizer" and the rebellious so-imagined "inferior West Indian colonized" teams. However, most often, the West Indies teams demonstrated the colonizer's cricketing frailties—as the colonized contested cricket with verve and passion.

C. L. R. James dedicated his 1963 *Beyond a Boundary,* an analytical insight into the game of cricket, to his friend Learie Constantine, and to one of the English pioneers of the game, W. C. Grace (1848–1915). James straddles both his love of the game and its social significance in terms of the colonizer/colonized heritage. He mentions Constantine a great deal, again giving kudos to the brilliance of the man whom he grew up with in Trinidad. James, of course, was indebted to Constantine for giving him a warm bed and a career start, while in turn Constantine was encouraged by his good friend to write about cricket and his life. The two men were brilliant, one largely in sport, and the other largely in prose and other artistic endeavors. James was far more radical in his political ideas than Constantine, but the two were good friends and respected one another. This is important to note: one can have difference in political opinion but still have friendship. In *Beyond a Boundary* James puts Constantine on a mighty pedestal:

> The rest of the world, England in particular, knows a great and original cricketer, a man of character, shrewd and genial; and, of late years, with a tendency ("rather a pity") to lay emphasis on racial discrimination. Circumstances placed me in a position to observe at its critical stages the development of one the most

remarkable personalities of the day. He belongs to that distinguished company of men who, through cricket, influenced the history of their time (1993, p. 101).

High praise indeed, and in hindsight, it is not misplaced. When Constantine was playing with Gladstone Christian and his peers during WW2 it was effectively for him exhibition matches to keep the West Indian technicians' welfare in the public eye. His name alone could attract a large audience, so to have him as a welfare officer was a boon for those young men settling into wartime Britain. By 1938, C. L. R. James had left England for the United States where he would stay for fifteen years. Therefore, James missed his friend Constantine actually playing during WW2 exhibition cricket with Gladstone and other African Caribbean cricketers against British opposition. Historically, it is unfortunate that James was not in England to witness this era in Constantine's life as it was a political gesture by him to stand with his fellow African Caribbean men during this tempestuous period. He could have easily rejected the offer to watch over the settlement of these technicians but instead put his heart and soul into the task. That was what James meant by him being "a man of character" who was "shrewd and genial" in thought and practice.

James goes on to share something rather salient in regard to the essence of this book: Blackness in complexity. For Constantine, just like Gladstone Christian, was a dark-skinned African Caribbean, yet James writes:

> Constantine is not pure Negro, if that term has any meaning [it actually does not]. Any West Indian who took one glimpse at his father would know that somewhere in his ancestry, and not too far back, there was European blood. The Constantines, however, were black people. Off the cricket field the family prestige would not be worth very much. Constantine was of royal ancestry in cricket, but in ordinary life, though not a pauper, he was no prince (1993, p. 103).

James reveals much about the absurdity of racialized thought and practices by explaining the folly of "racial purity" in any human grouping. Clearly, no matter how dark-skinned a person happens to be, or how much melanin is apparent, if he or she emerged from the transatlantic enslavement heritage then there is likely by ninety or more percent to be some form of mixed blood in the family tree. This is not rocket science but simple historical reality. The fact that Constantine was clearly a Black man in phenotype to the naked eye does not reveal his entire ancestral line. The same with Gladstone, because his mother was very light skinned and evidently had some European heritage in her family background—whether forced or of consensual lineage. To be sure, to think of racial purity is rather facile when it comes to transatlantic racialized history—and this is a sensitive topic for many. But like James articulated, there is racial mixture in the African Diaspora experience, yet it did not make oneself lesser Black in the overall social experience. Whenever the history of Africa and Europe has collided, there has been some form of blending in a human-biological sense. The same, undoubtedly, can be stated in relation to the Liverpool Black experience. Indeed, any region that has an influx of peoples from all over the transatlantic sphere will inevitably encounter cultural diversity and a mingling of various humanity that produces another, often attractive yet maligned, cultural group.

BEYOND RECREATIONAL CRICKET

Whether the African Caribbean technicians during WW2 were truly appreciated is up for continued debate and analysis. It would be wrong to suggest they were outwardly rejected as men of color in a foreign, mainly white, land—but it was far from perfect racialized harmony. Of course, there was the inevitable age-old British racism that Richmond (1954) and Belchem (2014) have both alluded to in their studies of wartime Liverpool and its social interaction with Africans from the Caribbean and the continent, as they experienced life in this famous British city. A freelance historian, Marika Sherwood, wrote a chapter relating to "West Indian Munitions Workers in Britain, 1941–1945" from her book, *Many Struggles: West Indian Workers and Service Personnel in Britain (1939–1945)*. Her research reveals the insidious nature of British colonial racism and its underhand tactics with the African Caribbean munitions workers. Gladstone Christian was fortunate because he arrived fully trained with qualified ability as a tool setter. But there were a number of those brought over who needed extra training to be skilled workers, and it would mean being trained by white men who often resented their presence in the factory. Marika Sherwood cites a Colonial Office official who visited in a hostel named the West Indies House, in October 1942 located at 91 Chatham Street, in Liverpool 8. He found an " atmosphere of discontent and unrest . . . the new warden Mawson unsettled and harassed . . . internal organisation leaves much to be desired . . . discipline not satisfactory . . . some of the residents difficult" (Sherwood 1985, p. 64). The real problem was the men were not adequately taken care of on arrival and not enough effort was taken into consideration regarding their overall welfare. It was not only accommodation set-up, but what did these men have for recreation and entertainment? Not all African Caribbean men were skilled in the game of cricket. There needed to be other forms of outlets that could make their lives a little easier and enjoyable. The British Ministry of Labor was simply draconian and felt that any misbehavior or rebelliousness on behalf of the men would result in repatriation, but the Colonial Office endeavored to calm the waters as there were legitimate grievances from some of the men who had given up so much in the Caribbean to travel so far from home to fight in a war that appeared increasingly not to be *theirs* given the reception and inadequate hostels (Sherwood 1985, p. 65).

As part of an effort to relieve the tension of daily life, beyond cricket, nightlife beckoned that kindled romance between the many lonely hearts longing for some love and affection in a cold clime. Liverpool 8 offered an array of social clubs that were frequented by Indigenous Blacks but it also had visitors from outside the community. The Rialto was one such ballroom-nightclub that offered dances and concerts with big bands—it was a very popular venue. It also contained a cinema, which was a grand architectural feature of Liverpool 8 erected in 1927. During WW2 the Rialto held ballroom dancing with big bands, along with Africans, African Caribbeans, there were now the presence of African American GIs who would travel in from the United States Air Force base in Burtonwood—located a few miles outside of Liverpool. Their presence would sometimes cause conflict between local Liverpool Blacks whose women were literally running off with the charismatic African American servicemen. This could be deemed another side to the broader Black experience: *internal strife*! There was often internal conflict between Africans, African Caribbeans, African Americans, and local Liverpool Blacks—regardless of the broader racism found in society. Unfortunately, it is not surprising to have internal conflict, but it does indicate the complexity of Blackness in any urban context when there is a lack of resources and an array of Black migrant-travelers trying to find a foothold in a profoundly racist society.

Specifically relating to the African Caribbean munition workers in Liverpool, there was an effort to support their settlement by encouraging time-out for dances. Therefore, the factory would organize balls at the Grafton Rooms, a nightclub for dancing and other entertainment activities on West Derby Road in central Liverpool. This was a club where potential love could blossom and spring into life. For example, Ada Pitt loved to dance and Gladstone Christian would recall his Mento days in Jamaica, this was a Jamaican folk music from the 1940s that laid the foundation for Ska and Reggae in the 1950s and onward. A mixture of African rhythms imbued with Jamaican and European influences—early African Diaspora hybridity in music—no different in formula, maybe sound, from what came from the United States out of the bowels of enslavement and segregation. Indeed, Gladstone was exposed to both Jamaican music and that which emanated from the Black artists in North America. Artists such as the Mills Brothers and the Ink Spots with their silky rhythmic harmonies were a favorite of Gladstone's, whereas Ada was a big fan of Bing Crosby—himself being a Jazz aficionado.

Crucially, Ada and Gladstone would dance the night away slowly falling for each other in those difficult days whereby racism raised its ugly head. Gladstone who had come to the aid of the metropole from a colonial satellite found himself fighting on two fronts: the Nazis and the home-grown Nazis of Britain. Sometimes there would be altercations with white men in the Grafton Rooms nightclub because white women would want to dance with the handsome African Caribbean men and African American GIs who often glided across the dance floor. This would bring out the envy of the less rhythmically inclined white men—who fumed and cursed at these cool, slick, young men with melodic foreign accents. Racialized sexual tension has been a feature of relations that has caused great conflict. Indeed, it has to be one of the key factors that has been the cause of resentment among the white community relating to Black presence in Britain. Perhaps sexual envy is something visceral in the human condition, but if one adds cultural ignorance wrapped up in the ideology of racism then we have a very combustible situation that could and did actually lead to riots.

Paul Rich in his *Prospero's Return? Historical Essays on Race, Culture and British Society* draws from racist opinions since the 1920s through British and American writers Frederick Lugard and Lothrop Stoddard, respectively. Each were avid white supremacists, and he states, "Opposition to interracial liaisons and miscegenation was linked to a campaign for racial 'purity' and national homogeneity" (Rich 1994, p. 95). This is the ideological racist backdrop to a deeply rooted British racism that young couples from different racialized cultural groups would encounter. Gladstone and Ada were not naïve, they knew that they would face opposition from family, friends, and outsiders, for example, no different than Frantz Fanon, Amilcar Cabral, or Cheikh Anta Diop who at one time chose white women to be their wives. However, "love" has a way of overriding ignorance. Although far from an easy choice, those that decided to have an interracial relationship in Britain during WW2 were brave souls. The individuals involved in mixed racialized relationships must have had deep affection for each other to withstand the severe social pressure. Though it does not take much to assess either Gladstone or Ada refusing to wilt in the cauldron of racism. They were too strong-minded and independent of thought to allow the pettiness of racism to defeat their affection for each other.

FAMILY—LIVERPOOL BLACKS OF MIXED HERITAGE—AND MUSIC

Therefore, ignoring the ubiquitous racists, there emerged the blending of two "odd souls" who would produce a love affair that endured till Gladstone's transition in June 1978—their union would endure for over thirty-five years. Wally Brown wrote on such unions, being a Black Liverpudlian who is an essential personality in the history of Black settlement in the city, and a community leader who rose to become the first Liverpool Born Black Principal of The City of Liverpool College from 1992 till his retirement in 2008. On mixed relationships between Black men and white women he wrote:

> Racism is a cruel and inhumane entity. The pain and indignity it inflicts on Black people is well documented. What is not so clearly recorded is the pain experienced by White women who marry Black men and who rear Black children (Brown 1997, p. 4).

Whether one considers the experience of Black men or white women in inter-relationships, or less likely back in Liverpool in the 1940s, white men and Black women, the impact on each individual depends on their character and family background. What can be gleaned from mixed racial unions within the British context is that they were largely frowned upon (Collins 1951). The significant aspect of Wally Brown's point of view above is how such a liaison produces "Black children" and that such offspring will live most often as "Black" in a rather racist social world. It does not matter how "light" the offspring may or may not be, one only has to look across to the United States to consider how mixed unions were viewed sociologically to comprehend its "one drop of African blood" predestined considered being Black in America—this shall be discussed more in-depth later. Let us first consider the Christian family as a key thread of Blackness within the Liverpool context.

Out of the conjugal pairing of Gladstone and Ada Christian came thirteen children in the following order: Ian, Pam, Denny, Roger, Tina, Victor, Janet, Garry, Russell, Rita, Kevin, Mark, and Jenny—born between 1945 and 1962—The Christians. Once WW2 came to an end in May of 1945, Gladstone continued to work in Britain as a technician, while Ada adopted the role as full-time housewife and home provider. One of his employers provided a house in the Knowsley area on the outskirts of Liverpool as part of an employment package. It was an area unfettered by urban sprawl, where fields of hay grew and lambs meandered in the spacious land. They kept live chickens and Gladstone would wring the neck off one when it came time to devour it for a festive Sunday dinner. Yes, these were times of relative peace, happiness, and family growth. While Gladstone was at work a mobile library would make its rounds and Ada would take her allotted six books and finish them before it returned two weeks later. Knowsley provided a tranquil milieu for reading and Ada was a voracious reader. After various residential moves, in 1958 the Christian family finally settled on a home at 26 Osborne Road, in the Tuebrook area of central Liverpool. This semi-detached home afforded them ample space for their growing family as it had six bedrooms, and three floors. Plenty of room for a large family who would require sustenance in a rather difficult economic period during the 1960s and early 1970s.

When Gladstone was at the peak of his earning power, he made enough for the family to purchase a summer home near Talacre beach in North Wales. It was a place where the family went for summer vacations and to enjoy the beach in the early to mid-1960s. This was probably the crowning of family memories before Gladstone met with an automobile accident while traveling to work that would deny him the ability to do his engineering tasks; he was an unhappy man to be around due to his nervous condition. He was reduced from being a skilled engineer to working in a factory off Edge Lane in the industrial part of Liverpool. This was also a time when the elder siblings were finding it hard to find jobs in the city due to a very poor economy in the late 1960s to mid-1970s—and of course the inevitable aspect of institutionalized racism.

The lack of household money made life difficult for the Christian family to survive. The eldest daughter, Pam, was lucky to have a job in the city as a clerk, and she was old enough to have seen the Beatles play at the Cavern club while on her lunch breaks with a girlfriend. The eldest sons, Denny and Roger, were seeking fame and fortune as singers in a soul group called the Gems—the name apparently came from Ada's imagination. Roger was a tenor and modeled his singing style mainly off Johnny Moore from the Drifters, while Denny as a baritone/bass took his lessons by listening to Melvin Franklin from the Temptations. There was always music playing at "26" as the family christened the house that sheltered them from the worst elements of life in Liverpool.

The 1960s was a time of protest in the United States and this filtered into British culture within its Black communities fighting for an end to racialized discrimination. Denny and Roger were old enough to have been in the Black Panther Party—but instead they followed their passion for rhythm and blues by covering many of the Temptations' classic songs: "Since I Lost My Baby," "Cloud Nine," "I Can't Get Next to You," or "Ball of Confusion" were favorites of the group, along with "Old Man River"—as the Temptations did a wonderful version of that classic from the American song book. The Gems were a five-piece vocal group, all Black Liverpudlians born in the city: brothers Denny and Roger Christian, Tommy Brown, Lawrence Griffith, and Dave Clay (who would later be replaced by Robbie Ellis). In the summer of 1971, they were advertised in the *Towns' Gazette*, a local paper printed in Great Harwood, Blackburn, as: "The Gems, Fantastic Coloured Show Group, Liverpool's Latest Recording Stars, Radio 1" (June 4, 1971, p. 1). Though a rather dated headline, even for 1971, it does indicate the presence of a Black

British Liverpool soul group during the height of the Black Power era of the United States.

What is also significant is in the fact that two of Gladstone and Ada's boys were now in their early twenties, and being influenced by the sounds of Motown, Atlantic Records, and other labels that produced African American musical talent. This is sometimes overlooked from the North American side of the Atlantic. For most Americans the idea of Black British communities alive and vibrant in the 1960s and 1970s was foreign to the perception of Britain. Perhaps this was because most Black British talent never crossed the Atlantic or were exposed, unlike the Beatles or the Rolling Stones, and other British rock n roll bands. There was no excuse, other than racism, as there were a number of talented Black entertainers in Liverpool who could have found success had they been properly supported and publicized. Before the Gems, for example, in Liverpool there were the Chants, another five-piece soul group that was entirely made up of Black Liverpudlians: Alan Harding, Nat Smeda, Eddie Amoo, along with brothers Joe and Edmund Ankrah. All were raised in the Black experience of Liverpool and were contemporaries of the Beatles, who actually backed the Chants as musicians for a gig at the Cavern (Harry 2000, pp. 251–254). Eddie Amoo recalls the first time the Beatles listened to the Chants during one of the lunch time sessions at the Cavern:

> They [The Beatles] went "apeshit" [animated] when we started to sing. I can still see George and John racing up to the stage with their mouths stuffed with hot dogs or whatever. The invitation to make our Cavern debut was given as soon as we finished "A Thousand Stars" for them. They insisted we perform that very night. Everything happened completely spontaneously from that point.

He continues,

> The Beatles themselves offered to back us when we told them we'd never worked with a band before. We rehearsed four songs with them and then we ran home to tell all and sundry that we had "made it"! When Brian Epstein [the Beatles' manager] arrived at the Cavern that night he refused to allow the Beatles to back us, but they collectively persuaded him to change his mind—and when he heard us he invited us to appear on many subsequent appearances with them (cited in Harry 2000, p. 252).

This is important history relating to both Black Liverpool and the Beatles as it shows a connection that was based on the respect they had for Black musicians and their local connection to each other. This is relatively lost history in the archives of Beatle folklore, though known within certain circles in Liverpool, outside the city and internationally if you mention the Chants with the Beatles, one will usually get a blank expression of ignorance. Yet this cultural exchange connects Black Liverpool to the most famous band in musical history and it reveals the talent that was prevalent, but not as successful, when the Beatles broke out to become famous worldwide in 1964. What should also be noted is the deep debt the Beatles had to African American musical artists such as Little Richard, Chuck Berry, Barrett Strong, Arthur Alexander, Richard Barrett, and Motown groups—such as Smokey Robinson and the Miracles and the Marvelettes. This again is the transatlantic in motion, cultural exchange, or rather appropriation, and adaptation within the context of Black original talent and its intercultural connection with white musicians.

Alvin Christie, an independent researcher and musician of Liverpool Born Black heritage, whose father was also a WW2 munitions technician, has produced a brilliant interactive presentation of Toxteth/Liverpool 8 and its relationship with the Merseybeat sound (Christie 2018). Essentially, he links the history of Toxteth's Black nightlife with music perfectly. The Merseybeat not only brought together the Chants with the Beatles, but Derry Wilkie and Steve Aldo who were Liverpool Born Black singers and contemporaries of the Beatles. Lord Woodbine (real name: Harold Phillips, 1929–2000) is mentioned, a calypso musician who was often airbrushed out of Beatle history by white editors, even though he was a close friend of Allan Williams, the manager of the Beatles during the Hamburg period in 1960. Derry Wilkie had been wowing the crowds in the German city well before the arrival of the Beatles there. Williams was instrumental in the early formation of managing Liverpool groups to play in Hamburg. In 1960 Lord Woodbine traveled with the Beatles and Allan Williams in a mini-van to Hamburg (Harry 2000, p.1152). We know in hindsight how that all worked out splendidly for the Beatles—but not so much for the numerous Liverpool Black artists.

TRANSATLANTIC MIXING

Liverpool and the Christian family are musically interwoven and it is rather poignant to think of it as a legacy of transatlantic history—yet there is no other cultural way to explain such a construction. Gladstone and Ada came together through the tragic reality of WW2, and they suffered socially due to them falling in love as a racialized mixed couple in a racist society. Their offspring would ordinarily be regarded as Black British of Jamaican heritage. This perspective needs to be unpacked due to the fallacy of concepts such as "biracial" and other more scurrilous terminology such as "half caste" to express the offspring of a racialized mixed union. Those persons born from such partnerships most often have little choice but to socially and culturally align ardently with their Black heritage. This is not rocket science given the appalling consequences of the transatlantic enslavement and colonial eras and the concomitant pseudoscientific racism. Therefore, it should be of little surprise when Black mixed heritage persons tend to consider themselves "Black" and part of the broader, dark-skinned, Black experience (Christian 2000). The topic of mixed racialized heritage is a can of worms to explain because white supremacy as a system over centuries also created colorism. For instance, under the colonial system, the lighter Blacks were often, but not always, given preference in racialized hierarchical societies constructed in South Africa, the entire Caribbean region, along with Latin America. In the United States it took only "one drop of African blood" to be deemed an African American (Broyard 2007; Malcomson 2000). To be sure, it is important to be socially cognizant regarding the deeply rooted experience of Blacks of mixed heritage finding themselves *within* the context of Black experience. To suggest that being of Black mixed heritage is a "best of two worlds" scenario is rather naïve and myopic in a historical and contemporary context (Christian 2008a; Broyard 2007; Malcomson 2000).

Take for example two famous African Americans: Barack Obama and Halle Berry, both born in the 1960s and each having white mothers. Neither of them has ever contemplated being "white" in terms of their social and individual identities. Nor have they denied the reality of their parentage being a man of African heritage and a woman of Euro-American ancestry. Barack Obama describes himself as African American; and so does Halle Berry (Obama 1995; Sanello 2004). Take the seventy-fourth Oscar's ceremony from 2002 when Berry went up to receive her Best Actress award, she teemed with tears exclaiming how happy she was to break through the glass ceiling for other Black women actresses. This was a heartfelt emotional speech in which she stated: "The moment is so much bigger than me, this moment is for Dorothy Dandridge, Lena Horne, [and] Diahann Carroll. It's for the women who stand beside me [her generation of Black women actors]: Jada Pinkett, Angela Bassett, [and] Vivica Fox. And it's for every nameless, faceless, woman of color who now has a chance" (March 24, 2002). There is no doubt that Halle Berry respects herself as a Black woman, regardless of her Black mixed heritage. Indeed, after this rather tearful acceptance speech, she then proceeds to go back to her seat and be congratulated by her white mother! How about that for irony? Yet it is her white mother who raised her to be a proud Black woman, this is a point that many people unfamiliar with Black mixed heritage do not comprehend—white mothers are most often aware of their children's Blackness because they too have experienced the viciousness of racism being with a Black partner.

Just to add a little more spice to Berry's life trajectory, her white mother, Judith Ann Hawkins, was born in Liverpool, England in 1939. She immigrated to the United States at the age of ten with her Liverpudlian parents.

While working as a nurse, she met the father of Halle, Jerome Jessie Berry, an African American. They fell in love, married, and Halle was born in Cleveland, Ohio in 1966. Now, Judith's parents were against the marriage because he was a Black man (Ewey Johnson 2010, p. 2). Significantly, Halle Berry matches the life of many Liverpool Born Black women of mixed heritage. Indeed, she could have fit neatly in the Christian family. Just imagine a world without the talent and beauty of a Halle Berry? The ignorance of her grandparents is not unique but ubiquitous whether it be in Liverpool, England or Cleveland, Ohio. Yet Judith stood strong, and raised her to become the film star Halle Berry is today—she raised a Black woman of beauty and substance. Most white parents of Black children understand that the social world is the major determinant, rightly or wrongly, in how one is treated and accepted.

Similar to Berry, Obama too was raised to accept African American heritage as his primary social identity. Both Berry and Obama have and had loving relationships with white mothers, yet dealt sadly with largely absentee Black fathers. Obama explains his Black mixed heritage and his parents' liaison in socially graphic terms that may explain the pressure encountered by such unions:

> In 1960, the year that my parents were married, *miscegenation* still described a felony in over half the states in the Union. In many parts of the South, my father could have been strung up from a tree for merely looking at my mother the wrong way; in the most sophisticated of northern cities, the hostile stares, the whispers, might have driven a woman in my mother's predicament into a back-alley abortion—or at the very least to a distant convent that could arrange adoption. Their very image together would have been considered lurid and perverse, a handy retort to the handful of softheaded liberals who supported a civil rights agenda (Obama 1995, p. 12).

This citation is a rather poignant reflection on his father and mother's union from Obama, who would be regarded as the first African American president—contemplate Barack Obama having been aborted? It is beyond anguish to contemplate what could have been an unmitigated disaster. Thankfully, his mother, like Berry's, was strong enough to hold on to her dignity and prove to an ignorant world how brilliant her son would eventually become.

Crucially, the social reality of racism has deterred neither Barack Obama nor Halle Berry in understanding their Blackness being the predominant aspect of their social identities. It is only recently that a "multiracial movement" has endeavored to create a third category that is neither Black nor White; but this is rather ridiculous given the nature of white supremacy and its fundamental disavowal of anyone with one drop of African blood in their veins (Christian 2000). It is only in the latter part of the twentieth century that this idea of a multiracial category emerged. For example, consider this, why are individuals such as Frederick Douglass, William Wells Brown, Booker T. Washington, W. E. B. Du Bois, T. Thomas Fortune, Mary Church Terrell, and Anna Julia Cooper, we could add many more, regarded simply as African American historical figures? Their "racial make-up" is rarely questioned even though each had European ancestry in their bloodlines. Their racialized heritage was hardly ever questioned because it did not matter—they were and are regarded as African American. One can beat around the bush but historically there was no interrogation into multiracial heritage for each of them because frankly it did not mean anything to their social standing even if acknowledged. Fast-forward to the twenty-first century and it is largely the same within the broader society. Of course, today one can have an *individual* view that is expansive of one's racialized heritage, but it is the social world that will inevitably determine how you will be considered.

Make note, this does not ignore the fact that colorism or any other manifestation of racist ideology in practice does not operate. Moreover, to suggest that "light to dark skin" is not an issue among transatlantic Black people would also be erroneous. The reality of white dominance has certainly had many negative impacts on people of color—particularly in the Caribbean, Africa, and the Americas. One of the major certainties was to induce an inferiority complex based on darker skin tone. Unfortunately, the colonized world suffered greatly from this malaise and Frantz Fanon, writing from a French-Martinique perspective, dealt with the psychological distress of not wanting dark skin in his book, *Black Skin, White Masks,* published in 1952. Fanon deemed this psychosis as the pursuit of "lactification"—meaning a concerted effort on behalf of specifically colonized women to become white/milky, or at least for their offspring. This is how Fanon explained it:

> For, in a word, the race must be whitened, every woman in Martinique knows this, says it, repeats it. Whiten the race, save the race, but not in the sense that one might think: not "preserve the uniqueness of that part of the world in which they grew up," but make sure that it will be white. . . . The number of sayings, proverbs, petty rules of conduct that govern the choice of a lover in the Antilles is astounding. It is always essential to avoid falling back into the pit of niggerhood, and every woman in the Antilles, whether in a casual flirtation or in a serious affair, is determined to select the least black of the men (Fanon 1986, p. 47).

This is a situation whereby racism and self-hatred has been *internalized* within the culture of the colonized. Though Fanon relates this to his experience under French colonialism, there is more than enough evidence historically to show that this unhealthy pursuit of whiteness was then, and in some ways still is, ubiquitous. In a sense, it could be deemed another aspect of human collateral damage via the colonized experience. Psychologically there is an effort to become as close to the colonizer as is possible—whether that be in a cultural sense or physical. Clearly, there were exceptions to the rule, but it is also fair to suggest that colorism has had a devastating impact on millions in a negative psychological sense. Even the brightest and the best of people of color have to be careful not to buy into the lie of white supremacy. For it has a way of creeping into the psychology of a person and they may not even know it is impacting their outlook on life.

The renowned scholar and cultural theorist Stuart Hall (1932–2014) once shared a poignant story about colorism or pigmentocracy *within* his middle-class Jamaican family. Apparently, as a seventeen-year-old teenager he witnessed the impact of white supremacy and its psychological hold on his parents, particularly his mother who did not favor the darker-skinned in her offspring. Not only that, she marshalled her children to marry "light" and to stay clear of darker Jamaicans. Apart from the obvious tragic psychological trauma in this scenario, the impact on Hall appears to have been profound. It shook him up to the core after his sister suffered undeniably from his mother's misplaced understanding of white supremacy—which unfortunately is still prevalent around the world. Hall explains his family trauma in this manner:

> When I was seventeen, my sister had a major nervous breakdown. She began a relationship with a young student doctor who had come to Jamaica from Barbados. He was middle-class, but black and my family wouldn't allow it. There was a tremendous family row and she, in effect, retreated from the situation into a breakdown. . . . It was a very traumatic experience, because there was little or no psychiatric help available in Jamaica, at that time. My sister went through a series of ECT [electro-convulsion treatment] treatments given by a GP, from which she's never properly recovered. She never left home after that. . . . But it crystallized my feelings about the space I was called into by family. I was not going to stay there. I was not going to be destroyed by it. I had to get out (Hall cited in Farred 1996, p. 33).

The recollection of his sister's experience by Hall deserves unpacking. This was essentially a throwback to what Fanon explained; however, it was the Black mother, not the daughter, who harbored prejudice against the dark-skinned young doctor from Barbados. The Black daughter was in love; we are not sure of her shade of color—we can assume she's lighter. Hall goes on to explain that he was traumatized by his mother for also having a darker complexion. Yet his sister suffered because she effectively lost the love of her life at the hands of parents who had been bought into self-hatred via the colonizer and his cultural barbarism. What is encouraging, if anything, is in the fact that Hall's sister was more than happy to marry her dark-skinned lover—yet her heart was broken, followed by her mind. The tragedy in this event is that it propelled the great scholar to leave Jamaica for Britain in order to find a better life elsewhere—and how he did in becoming a famously renowned cultural theorist.

It should be pointed out, like Hall, Gladstone Christian was a dark-skinned Jamaican too, about the same complexion as Hall, if not darker. Ada did not care for such things as colorism; she had met a handsome Black man from Jamaica, her complexion was sallow, not white-white, and she had deep brown eyes with dark auburn hair—an inheritance probably from the Spanish side of her roots. Nevertheless, it is certain that Gladstone also suffered from the slings and arrows of colorism during his lifetime in Jamaica. He never spoke to his Black British family about such things, but then again, he never spoke much about anything back in Jamaica. That could reveal the actual psychological trauma that he may have encountered. Though Gladstone's mother, also named Ada, was very light skinned, his father was very dark skinned. There were certainly no problems with self-hatred from his father, George Rupert Christian, who had worked with Marcus Garvey and the Universal Negro Improvement Association (UNIA) during the 1920s–1930s. Racial pride was an essential aspect of the UNIA and it is evident that this was relayed to Gladstone and his siblings because he was such a confident man, quiet in disposition but self-assured. If he did keep things to himself in relation to Jamaica, it is doubtful it had anything to do with racialized antipathy for selfhood.

The Christian family in the 1960s and early 1970s were vibrant, showing individual signs of talent, while collectively the siblings were developing various interests in music while endeavoring to eke out a living in an unstable economy. Denny and Roger in the early 1970s gave up the effort to keep the Gems together, a combination in a lack of stick-to-it-tiveness and personality clashes meant that the group imploded. With that they dispersed into various interests mainly to secure a livelihood. The two Christian brothers decided to go and try their luck in London, a more affluent city where it was possible to find work, even if menial. They ended up working in hotels in the laundry rooms, far from ideal for young men of color in their early twenties, but it was a start.

By late 1971 Gladstone reached retirement, at age sixty-five he no longer played cricket but each summer watched the Test Matches between England the West Indies on television with keen interest. Overall, he was not a happy man. Probably due to the impact of old age and still having the burden of thirteen children, the majority of whom were still at school and too rambunctious for his Jamaican sensibility. In his mind life had passed by too rapidly, it seemed like a blink of the eye in how fast time had flown. He recalled his excitement and anxiety while on board the *Jamaica Producer* heading across the precarious transatlantic route during WW2. Anxious to work for the British government during wartime as a skilled technician in a Liverpool munitions factory. How fast the time had disappeared! His cricket exploits, captured in the newspapers, and radio broadcasts carried back to his beloved Jamaica to excite his family and friends back home. Memories—but Gladstone was not content in 1971. Time had taken its toll on him; at sixty-five years of age he was almost fifty-five years older than his youngest son, Mark. Aging for a natural sportsman like him was a cruel experience; no longer could he play a game he once loved. All he had now was reminiscences; no longer did he find peace of mind in the present—it was too noisy and he could see younger, stronger, men sprouting in front of him as his physical prowess diminished. He was aging, retired, reflective, and crestfallen. His mind would wander back to the days of playing cricket with the great Learie Constantine; what seemed like yesterday was now in fact thirty-years in the past. Time had crept up on Gladstone like a thief in the night and he was overwhelmed because he could not help his young family financially. The last ten years of his working life were spent in menial factory work. He did not have the respect he had gained as a skilled technician, and because of the insidious racism in the workplace he was never elevated to a position of management or oversight.

Gladstone had suffered under the experience of Enoch Powell, the far-right Conservative Member of Parliament who early in his career had endorsed the migration of African Caribbean men and women to boost Britain's post-WW2 economy, but suffering from historical amnesia Powell in the late 1960s embarked on an anti-Black immigration platform. This aroused the attention of latent racism in British society. Powell received much support from labor unions, and inevitably this impacted men like Gladstone. He did not deserve such ignorant cruelty, mental abuse, and workplace unfairness. After all, he had come to the rescue of the "mother country" in her hour of need during WW2. Fast-forward thirty-years and amnesia had firmly set in, British society was openly racist, and widespread discrimination endured. Gladstone never shared his feelings openly, but he was morose most often, he gradually kept himself to himself, sometimes there would be a glimmer of humor from him. This was such a shock to our system as young children we would look on in amazement as he displayed a glimpse of his comedic character. But these indications of his once vivacious personality never lasted long, Gladstone withdrew into his room most often—his spirit wilted.

As for Ada, though not the principal breadwinner, she had always been the leader of the household. She was the force, and optimism, the strength, the glue that held the Christian family together. Born July 24, 1922, her star sign was Leo, a lioness. She was a woman who took care of her family at all costs. She led by example, hardworking, determined, and ever present. Ada had taken her fair share of knocks in life by 1971. She was closing in on her fiftieth birthday, and she had been working since 1965 as a store detective in

T. J. Hughes Department Store in Birkenhead, across the Mersey. Ada had no choice; her family needed the extra income and she did her very best to keep the household stable through many setbacks that life offered up. Her first major tragedy was in losing her first born child, Ian, in an awful mishap. He had been playing with a toy wooden train, it was early October 1948, and he swallowed a screw that had come loose from it. Ada took her ailing son by foot and tram car to Alder Hey Hospital in West Derby. In those days mothers could not stay with their children overnight. She left Ian in the care of the doctors and nurses. Apparently, they were able to retrieve the screw lodged in his throat, but when my mother returned the next day, she was told he had died from a "fever" of some sort. She collapsed, had fits, and was in deep traumatic shock. To make matters worse she was then heavily pregnant with her second son, Denny, who would be born December 11, 1948. Ada survived; Ian died October 2, 1948 at three years of age. A tragedy few persons could handle, but she did and moved on in life because there was no other alternative. She had her two-year-old daughter Pam, and now newborn Denny to care for. Though broken-hearted Ada was a person who would always state to her children: "keep going" no matter what challenges you face in life. Ada was mental strength personified. From 1950 to 1962 she had ten more children; on reflection it may well have been a response to the death of her first born that she had as many. Nevertheless, "big" families were also part of her generational experience. Once the "pill" arrived in the 1960s there would be fewer large families. Society rapidly changed as women became more empowered to live their lives as independent breadwinners. Ada was a pioneer, as she both worked *and* raised her large family while under great economic strain. She was a rather private person, family orientated, and not one to gossip or be interested in triviality. Ada kept the Christians moving ahead, come what may, she was a matriarch par excellence.

Her daughters, Pam, Tina, Janet, Rita, and Jenny, were varied versions of herself. Strong-minded, fierce, hardworking, and leaders within their respective worlds. Pam was the lighter-skinned, while Tina and Janet favored Gladstone's darker complexion, though Rita and Jenny could be considered between the lighter and darker hue. Perhaps this sounds ridiculous to the reader, but colorism has been a major problem in the transatlantic experience. As discussed earlier under Fanon and Hall, having light or dark skin can seriously impact how one impacts and is accepted in the social world. As previously pointed out, racialized hierarchy as a system is manifestly to be blame for the manner in which colorism has been an endemic feature within transatlantic communities. Yet, and this is important to note, colorism was never tolerated in the family home, the Christians were never interested in who had the darkest or lightest skin tone among the siblings—even though there was a rainbow of Blackness among the siblings from light to dark brown. It is merely acknowledged here due to the nefarious history of colorism and its ugliness as articulated most effectively by Frantz Fanon and others (Christian 2000; Cross 1991; Farred 1996; Fanon 1986). There can be little empathy of a racialized society that harbors hierarchy based on skin color and racial heritage without comprehending its historical significance.

HISTORICAL CONTOURS OF MIXED AFRICAN AND EUROPEAN RACIALIZATION

The notion of Blackness has always been a complex reality because there has been so much interaction between Africans and Europeans over a period of five hundred or more years. Clearly much of the initial encounters were based on African forced compliance in sexual intercourse from the enslavers and colonizers. The "shades of Blackness" are therefore historical in context, controversial, and can be profoundly disturbing psychologically. These forceful eras in mixed unions would decline largely by the end of the mid-1800s after basic emancipation was achieved. By the 1930s there were more voluntary unions between Black men and white women in Britain—the focus of this study. Blacks of mixed heritage have been a salient feature of Liverpool's history, especially from the 1900s (Costello 2001; Christian 1997a, 2000), due to mainly Black male migration into the city via its transatlantic setting. However, within the broader British context there has been this ebb and flow of interracial history that has occurred without it being highlighted by the dominant cultural sphere.

Of course, there cannot be a specific date one can state as a definitive period whereby mixed racial unions transpired, but the twentieth century is when it was highlighted as a social problem (Fletcher 1930; Christian 2008a). There have always been exceptions to the rule that flouted norms and etiquette in terms of racialized unions between African and European derived humanity. Olaudah Equiano (1745–1797) is a typical example of a man of African heritage who after being enslaved as a child in Africa (of Ibo origin) and taken to North America, then on to the Caribbean, he finally ended up in England as a pioneering abolitionist. He married a white woman, Susannah Cullen (1762–1796), and they had two daughters, Anna Maria (1793–1797) and Joanna (1795–1857). This was an openly consensual marriage between a man of African heritage and a white English woman in the eighteenth century. Equiano's frequent transatlantic travels make him an exception to the rule for his time and place. The horrors of enslavement, the middle passage voyage, and the insights contained in his autobiographical account have had scholars grappling with its complexity for decades. He was an exceptional individual, and his travel accounts relating to the cruelty of transatlantic bondage are preserved (Edwards 1996). The irony of Equiano is he still somehow found a way to live out his life as a free man in England, with a white wife and two daughters of Black mixed heritage before the onset of the 1800s—quite remarkable given the time he existed and his escape from bondage.

Yet, regardless of exceptions, the majority of Black mixed heritage offspring in the eighteenth and nineteenth centuries did not emerge through consensual unions. This phenomenon was more prevalent in the twentieth century and beyond. So many of the men of African heritage who are regarded as Black liberation thinkers had sometime in their lives a white woman as a partner (this theme is covered more profoundly in chapter three). The racialized terminology used for this is "miscegenation," ordinarily defined problematically as two interbreeding humans of at least two racial types. The problem with such a human classification is that it is scientifically flawed within a biological context. Dorothy Roberts has called "race" a fatal invention inculcated with both medical and cultural bias. Her influential book *Fatal Invention: How Science, Politics, and Big Business Re-create Race in the Twenty-First Century* is rather sobering because it means the pseudoscientific racial theories that abounded in the eighteenth and nineteenth centuries that Peter Fryer discussed in chapter seven of his study, *Staying Power: The History of Black People in Britain*, still hold sway even if in diluted form. Crucially, the very idea of "biological races" existing in the past or present among human sapiens is fallacious. This is something shared presently by the majority of the biological scientific community. Indeed, it is racialized prejudice that keeps the pseudoscientific racism alive and kicking into the present day (Sarich and Miele 2005; Roberts 2011). Although Sarich and Miele argue for a more nuanced view of "racialized origins and difference," they still agree on one major relevance, that human sapiens originated from the African continent, as they contend:

> Since 2000 these converging lines of evidence have produced a consistent picture that *Homo sapiens* first arose in Africa only about 50,000 years ago and that no racial divergences predate this time. In short, all living races are very recent and appeared only as ancestral humans migrated out of Africa (2005, p. 6).

Regardless of this scientific consensus in relation to the origins and closeness of the human family, white purity as mythology, with its concomitant racism, has been particularly insuperable and ingrained in Western or Westernized societies—hence persons of Black mixed heritage have most often been a hypodescent group. That is, for the best part of five centuries white heritage has been associated with Africans and their descendants who were subjugated and discriminated in societies created by descendants of Europeans. Whereby whites who shaped *their* "New World" to what can be described as being ensconced in a *pseudo-racialized-superiority* frame of reference—while, paradoxically, the powerbrokers behind it all claimed to be of the Christian faith. Robert Wald Sussman rightly terms this racialized phenomenon as "troubling" and endemic in his book, *The Myth of Race: The Troubling Persistence of an Unscientific Idea*. Sussman succinctly describes the reality of racism in our everyday lives, largely within a Westernized frame of reference:

> Racism is a part of our everyday lives. Where you live, where you go to school, your job, your profession, who you interact with, how people interact with you, your treatment in healthcare and justice systems are all affected by your race. For the past 500 years people have been taught how to interpret and understand racism. We have been told that there are very specific things that relate to race, such as intelligence, sexual behavior, birth rates, infant care, work ethics and abilities, personal restraint, life span, law-abidingness, aggression, altruism, economic and business practices, family cohesion, and even brain size. We have learned that races are structured in a hierarchical order and that some races are better than others. Even if you are not a racist, your life is affected by this ordered structure. We are born into a racist society (Sussman 2014, p. 2).

Clearly, much of what Sussman outlines is the predicament in assuming "race" actually exists when in fact it is an erroneous concept that has little validity scientifically. Nevertheless, the social reality is quite different from the scientific. In point of fact, it was a sociologist, W. I. Thomas, who stated: "If [people] define situations as real, they are real in their social consequences" (Thomas and Thomas 1928, p. 572). Therefore, most individuals raised in racialized societies are socialized to think and act as if they belong to a "race" and this perpetuates the seemingly never-ending cycle of interactions among what really are at best *cultural* groups, certainly not racial. Moreover, these cultural groups are never completely sealed off from one another. Even if a person may think of her- or himself as "white" there are always other factors involved that need to be unpacked regarding such a social identity structure. A reading of Nell Irvin Painter's *The History of White People* allows for a myth-destroying of any vestige in there being *pure* white racial types. Nonetheless, Painter is also adamant that the myth of whiteness has had deep roots in the intellectual development of European thought since at least the Enlightenment—something the philosopher Charles W. Mills agreed with wholeheartedly (Mills 1997, 2017). Painter refers to one of America's greatest writers, Ralph Waldo Emerson, and his myth-making treatise on *English Traits* in North America: " Emerson explicitly excludes the enslaved and skips over native peoples entirely" (2010, p.185). The myth of whiteness is certainly not exclusive to North America, it can be also be related to the British Isles and the mythical notion of English purity.

THE MYTH OF ENGLISH PURITY

Consider Britain and its long history of settlement by various "white" cultural groups over centuries. Too often the ancient settlement of the British Isles is conveniently forgotten when juxtaposed by Black settlement. Instead, there is a racialized myth-making pertaining to a settlement of white purity or cultural sameness, when in fact the British Isles is the personification of a mongrelized nation made up of many cultural groups. Briefly, from say 3000 BC to 1000 BC, this would include from various parts of Europe: Celts, who were farmers, fighters, Stone Age to the Bronze Age. There were rival tribes who fought for their land and chiefdoms, there was hostility and war among the varied Celts whereby they built forts to protect themselves—Maiden Castle in Dorset is one example of such tribal centers. Arguably, it was not until the Roman occupation of Britain, largely England and Wales, from approximately 55 BC through to the end of the fourth century CE, before a more civilized existence in Britain emerged. For example, the Romans introduced currency, law, infrastructure, and modern culture. Yet it did not last, more invasions came to the British Isles as the Roman Empire began to decline. Various "barbarians" largely Angles, Saxons (who would become known as the Anglo-Saxons), Vikings, Jutes, Huns, Vandals, and others attacked, pillaged, and looted the affluent parts of the British Isles. The point here, in short, is that Britain is made up of many "white" cultures going back in history—it is far from a monolithic racialized group of isles. This is not to disparage British history but merely to emphasize the fallacy of any notion of "white purity" in the biological make-up of the white Britons—they are as genetically mixed as any other human group. What is also important to note, as far as existing world scientific history, all roads ultimately lead us back to Africa—the home of human civilization.

The same can be stated in regard to Black persons of mixed heritage; clearly there is complexity in their social identities. However, as emphasized, when it comes to racialized categorization there is usually the "one drop rule" that maintains itself. If there is division and social privilege given to Blacks of mixed heritage this is in relation to the society of specific origin. It is known that the one drop rule is a North American historical manifestation and the majority of African Americans could claim some form of "mixture" in their family trees. Most often there is a white slaveholder or overseer lurking in the historical background. Therefore, definitions of *racial purity* in one's racialized heritage is like looking for gold dust in sand—according to current knowledge there is little to no chance in finding such in human biology (Sussman 2014; Roberts 2011, p. 50). If there is any doubt in the reader's mind about the seriousness of racialized thought in practice she should read

Race in the Mind: Race, IQ, and Other Racisms by Alexander Alland Jr. as it outlines in a uniquely horrible manner how enslaved African Americans were treated when based on Euro-American pseudoscience and experimentation.

It is always useful therefore to share hidden histories concerning racialized fusion in the upper echelon of a given society. There are a number of British royal examples of Black mixed heritage personage leading right up to present-day Meghan Markle who is married to Prince Harry, the son of the late Princess Diana. This is knowledge that may counter the well-known phrase made known by Paul Gilroy, though taken from a racist English Football chant to the Black British player John Barnes in the early 1980s: *There Ain't No Black in the Union Jack*. In point of fact, perhaps the first Black mixed heritage was Queen Philippa of Hainault (1314–1369), who was married to King Edward III, and apparently of African Moorish ancestry. One of their offspring was known as the "Black Prince"—Edward of Woodstock (1330–1376).

Stuart Jeffries wrote an interesting article about the reality of Black British royalty for the *Guardian* (March 11, 2009). Though facetious in part, he offers a point of view that clearly delineates the present royal family having Black mixed heritage blood in their veins. Apart from Queen Philippa and King Edward III, there is Queen Charlotte (1744–1818) who though German came from the Portuguese royal lineage; it is fairly clear that she was the second Black British Queen of mixed heritage. She was the wife of the insane King George III (1738–1820) who reigned Britain from 1760 to 1801, and was the royal who had to deal with the loss of its North American colonies after the Declaration of Independence in 1776. Yet it is both Queen Philippa and Queen Charlotte who bring interest to this specific study due to their Black mixed heritage being in the British royalty—therefore establishing that the present royal family has African ancestry in their blood line is both incredulous and intriguing given the history of racism in Britain.

To bring this up-to-date in royal lineage terms, Queen Charlotte's granddaughter was Queen Victoria I (1819–1901), and the reigning Queen Elizabeth II is therefore the great-great-great-great- granddaughter of Queen Charlotte. By any stretch of the imagination, this is fascinating racialized royal history that is rarely spoken about; most often it is completely ignored by British historians of the royal family. Indeed, just as the history of Thomas Jefferson and Sally Hemings was once dismissed by white American historians, but is now fairly etched across the academic world as historical truth (Lanier 2002), the same needs to transpire with the notion of Black heritage in the British Royal family.

However, historical amnesia has reigned in regard to the racialized past in the history of British royalty. Perhaps this is inevitable given the absurd and fallacious notion of white English purity when it comes to Black British settlement (Fryer 1984; Olusoga 2016, p. 408). What can be stated with historical confidence in the 2020s is that Britain has always been a multiracial society—from ancient times up to the present. Undeniably, though the world is now familiar with Black mixed heritage Meghan Markle's alliance with Prince Harry, there is still the ugliness of British racism that has followed the American princess and the royal prince (Ducey and Feagin 2021). Racism in the British context is as ubiquitous as the corgis in Queen Elizabeth II's Buckingham Palace household—not to be flippant, or to bark it out.

FLETCHER (1930) AND BROWN (2005)—OLD WINE MIXED IN NEW BOTTLES

Two studies in particular relating specifically to Black Liverpool give insight to the problem of stigmatizing Liverpool Born Blacks. The first study was conducted by Muriel Fletcher, *Report on an Investigation into the Color Problem in Liverpool and Other Ports,* known locally as the "Fletcher Report" from 1930. Employing a distinctly pseudoscientific racist methodology, Fletcher imbibed the field of eugenics, particularly leaning on the work of Rachel M. Fleming (1927, 1930) to disparage and problematize Blacks of mixed heritage in the city. This author found the report to be "ingrained" within the cultural white hegemony of Liverpool and therefore decided to dissect it point-by-point in order to expose its pseudoscientific errors, and hopefully banish it to the dustbin of academic scrutiny (Christian 2008a). However, any serious scholar of racialization worth his or her salt *should* still consult and read this report. Those that do not think it is worthy of inspection should rethink such avoidance as it has such importance to the stereotyping of a cultural group. Indeed, as abhorrently obnoxious as the reading of *Mein Kampf* is to any decent human being it still should be read in order to comprehend why millions have absorbed such half-baked political philosophy that came from the mind of a lunatic. The fact remains that the Fletcher Report came out of such pseudoscientific-eugenicist racism that enveloped the mind of Hitler—incidentally *Mein Kampf* is still in print today, unlike the Fletcher Report (Hitler 1993). Therefore, we cannot ignore such racism shrouded in academic guise when it comes to stigmatizing any cultural group with dubious claims to "white superiority"—which is a lie of significant historical proportion. This is how Belchem explains the Fletcher Report of 1930 via the insight of Christian (2008a):

> [The Fletcher Report] has been considered so reprehensible by most scholars as to be unworthy of serious academic scrutiny; however, it has recently been

deconstructed and discredited with meticulous methodological and theoretical rigor by Mark Christian . . . [who] acknowledges, [it] had significant contemporary (and enduring) impact: "it cemented the derogatory term 'half caste' into the social perception of the city, along with previously held stereotypes about Black families and gave them credence via a seemingly 'objective' and unbiased analysis" (Belchem 2014, p. 62).

As pointed out, any academic not responding to the Fletcher Report of 1930 but claiming to know something about Black Liverpool should admit also to the depth of one's intellectual ignorance and limited comprehension of racist ideology in relation to the Liverpool Black experience. To be sure, there are many academic studies prior to and beyond the Fletcher Report era still floating around with similar aspects of pseudoscientific racism in regard to people of color (Fleming 1927, 1930; Davenport and Steggerda 1929; Park 1928, 1931; Reuter 1918)—should we ignore them too? Certainly, again to use *Mein Kampf* as an example, the fact that it can still be purchased *today* more than proves the argument that one cannot ignore such racist studies. To put it another way, one must take these racist studies to task, and break them down for what they are: fraudulent and intellectually unsound (Painter 2010; Smedley 2007). As for the Fletcher Report, future generations now have at their disposal a point-by-point critique of it to comprehend its deceitful methodology, racist posture hidden in an academic guise, and surely this is a good thing for Black Liverpool and the broader society.

Another study which was conducted from the early 1990s and published in 2005 on Black Liverpool and identity is by Jacqueline Nassy Brown. Unlike Fletcher, who was a white woman, Brown is a woman of African American heritage, who received her doctorate in anthropology through her research on Black Liverpool; Brown attended an Ivy League school, Stanford University, in the United States. One cannot describe her book *Dropping Anchor, Setting Sail: Geographies of Race in Black Liverpool* as being overly problematic and racist like the Fletcher Report. Yet it does ultimately express itself as a patronizing postmodernist pastiche blending ahistorical analysis couched in academic verbiage. In the preface, for example, Brown thanks another African American Ivy Leaguer, France Winddance Twine, who had also visited upon the Black Liverpool experience to do research but instead conducted a related study in Leicester (Twine 2011), and states: "in her inimitable way [Twine], bluntly advised therapy" (Brown 2005, p. xii). Well, though this quip implicitly mocks the Black community she entered and was welcomed by, it does not take much to gauge her subconscious reaction to analyzing the Liverpool Black experience. She had imbibed the stereotypes without even knowing it just by sharing that jibe from her close friend Twine. The book by Brown has been dissected and reviewed previously (Christian 2009b);

yet it is important to note here that the stereotyping of the Liverpool Black mixed heritage community did carry weight and it could be psychologically damaging to those who are associated—if one is taken in by such scholarship. Crucially, Brown's study reveals her profound unawareness of Black Liverpool's struggle for a positive Black identity construct more than it does her knowledge of it.

Although Brown does not mention the Charles Wootton College in the acknowledgment section of her study, specifically in it having had a significant role in her settlement into the Liverpool Black community to gain respondents, thankfully there is evidence of her arrival and connection to the institution. In the *Charles Wootton News* (CWN) from December 1992, it celebrated both the status of the Charles Wootton from being a "Centre to a College" and it shared other various community activities of the past year, one of which was the arrival of Jacqueline Nassy Brown to the community to conduct social research for her doctorate studies. This issue of the *Charles Wootton News* also provides a photograph of her standing on the steps of the Charles Wootton College. The write-up about her reads:

> Jackie Brown—Black American Research Scholar . . . originally from Brooklyn, N.Y., was here in 1991 and 1992. She was conducting research on history and identity in the Black community for her Ph.D. in Anthropology. She attends Stanford University, and hopes to graduate in June of 1994. From there she will become a University Lecturer, teaching courses on African Communities in Europe [her university address for contact at Stanford University was also added] (*Charles Wootton News*, December 1992, p. 13).

The preceding citation is an extract from a primary source that gives evidence of Brown's research and presence in Liverpool and of her visiting the Charles Wootton College, but there is no mention of this welcome and support in her book. Overall, she can be deemed as having exploited a historically vulnerable Black community in terms of her depiction of Black mixed heritage identity as an Ivy League anthropologist seeking a unique subject matter for her doctoral studies. It is weak research in terms of its fundamental lack of comprehension in regard to the social history and development of the Liverpool Born Black population. Without careful critique and assessment, this type of research would go undetected among the plethora of postmodernist- analyses of "race," class, and gender. The uniqueness of her study—something one needs to gain a doctorate/Ph.D.—is the topic, but the analysis is typical of many contemporary critiques of Black identity constructs employing a Gilroy-esque hybridity paradigm. It is also ahistorical and poorly referenced in not having an adequate literature review of the Black experience relating to the City of Liverpool. In short, one must ask the question why her peer, Twine, "advised therapy" for Brown after the research foray into the Liverpool Black experience. Indeed, as a writer from the Black British experience, and having spent the last thirty years living and working in the United States, maybe such advice on "therapy" derived from Brown being raised on the opposite side of the transatlantic experience. Because Liverpool compared to Brooklyn is a much safer city and its Black experience, though mired in racialized discrimination, is one to be truly admired for its strength and capacity to endure the many slings and arrows of misfortune. Brown should not have patronized such a Black experience that opened its arms to her—and who had welcomed Frances Winddance Twine before her. From the perspective of an Africana critical studies scholar, these "Black" scholars do only harm to gaining a deeper comprehension of Black British experience—they also give credence to white liberal racists who amply cite and laud such drivel. Brown would have benefited greatly from reading Faye Harrison (1997b), another African American anthropologist who comprehends the "politics of ethnography" more profoundly. That is, there is a significant acknowledgment regarding the historical legacy of anthropology and its racist foundation. It is not in the interest to quibble over the obvious differences found within Black experience, but researchers should be aware not to diminish the political reality of racist ideology that all communities of color have encountered.

BLACK LIVERPOOL MUSIC AND LOVE ACROSS THE COLOR LINE

When Gladstone and Ada met during WW2 it was the coming together in a sense of two British cultures, being the colonial satellite of Jamaica and the colonizer's metropole, Britain. Their offspring would all be born in Liverpool and be supposedly British citizens, nor would they have any direct knowledge of Jamaica other than what popular culture offered and whatever Gladstone revealed to his children through his distinct Jamaican patios and the many idiosyncrasies that emanated from his homeland. As with most large families, there were inevitable ups and downs, tragedies and triumphs, joy and pain. Ada did her best to keep the family steady and did a tremendous job despite the stubborn dearth in household income that came with the early 1970s British economy.

The Christian sisters, Pam, Tina, Janet, and Rita, most often found menial employment, none of them were traditional college students. Pam married an Italian radio operator who worked on merchant navy ships; Tina, having raised three children largely as a single parent, decided to go back to school in her thirties, later graduating as the first woman of color to gain a bachelor's degree in engineering from the University of Liverpool. She would then go on to break through more glass ceilings becoming a head teacher at an elementary school in the city. Janet and Rita were working in factories or going on vocational courses that were offered via government training schemes to help the unemployed of Liverpool—the economy throughout the 1970s was pretty bleak. The youngest of the sisters, Jenny, did not leave school till 1978 at age sixteen and would later become a housing officer.

What they all had in common as Black women of mixed heritage was an uncanny instinct for survival through whatever tribulations they encountered. Though individual in character, they inherited a lot from both Ada and Gladstone who were both strong-minded and pragmatic. The siblings developed a sense of social justice that came from the life experiences of their parents. In short, the Christian sisters were also profoundly interested in doing the right thing for their individual families and for society. Regardless of the usual setbacks in gaining worthwhile employment in a relatively racist city, the main thing was always to bounce back against rejection—to keep going. That spirit of survival came from both Gladstone and Ada, who collectively were special to have endured many slights in their lives together—what sociologists today call microaggressions. As parents they grew stronger, and so did their children. Ada was a true example of survival to everyone at "26" back in the 1970s—clearly her daughters were taking heed.

Liverpool's Black and people of color population have consistently hovered around eight percent to ten percent. Specifically relating to Black and Black of mixed heritage it has been between five and eight pecent. The city's overall population figures according to the Liverpool City Council are just over five hundred thousand; at its peak in the early 1930s the population was over eight hundred thousand. From WW2 to the 2000s there was decline in population but since the millennial there has been a minimal increase. The Black experience, however, continues to be largely "invisible" due to both a lack of opportunities in retail and service industries for Black Liverpudlians. A lack of life-chances largely due to institutional racism is something that has been ubiquitous in relation to the Liverpool Black experience. Discrimination links back to the notorious enslavement era that is inextricably woven into the city's history—and "its horrors should never be forgotten" (Belchem 2014, p. 2). The problem with Belchem's analysis is that he perceives no direct connection between the history of slaving and the twentieth century Liverpool Black experience (p. 2). He has a propensity to offer a linear analysis, with profound gaps, forgetting that the past always impinges on the present. Belchem believes we can wash away the past of Liverpool's slaving history; or can put it away as we look at the present, which is an erroneous standpoint. The inconspicuousness of local Black scholars in the corridors of the University of Liverpool should also be of concern to Belchem who disregards all aspects of institutional racism in his university home in an obtuse manner (Belchem 2014).

In relation to the city presently, what is disquieting relates to the distinct lack of visibility of Black people working *within* the department stores and offices in the city center areas. Something which was highlighted in the 1989 Lord Gifford Inquiry into the city's poor record on race relations, of which recommendation number 26 states:

> Private sector employers must go beyond paper declarations in favour of equal opportunities, and secure a higher representation of Black people in their workforce by a combination of detailed policies (Gifford, Brown, and Bundey 1989, p. 229).

This is particularly pertinent because there have been for decades attractive sounding policy statements in relation to equal opportunities and anti-discriminatory policy to instill practice, yet the conspicuous absence of Black people throughout the city center continues unabated. Obtuse in the manner the anti-racist practices have been implemented; which effectively means there has been no genuine redress to the lack of visible signs of diversity in the workforce. This has been an ongoing feature of the Liverpool Black experience and without positive action being enforced it is likely to continue to be so.

Regardless, the Christian sisters were survivors. When it came to the brothers, Denny passed away tragically in 1975 at the young age of twenty-six years. Roger, Victor, Garry, Russell, and Mark continued in the family tradition in creating harmony as a five-piece vocal group: the Christians. Garry and Russell had been involved in various permutations in bands, gaining invaluable experience. Roger played piano and was the lead tenor, Garry played bass guitar and was second tenor, Victor as well as being a music teacher at John Lennon's former school, Quarry Bank, played piano and sang falsetto. While Russell played piano and saxophone, he was also an occasional lead singer and the group's main harmonizer (giving the key to each singer). Being the youngest of the Christian brothers, I sang baritone/bass and learned to play the acoustic guitar. Overall, the five brothers would sing a cappella together from 1977 until the summer of 1984. In having similar tonality, the siblings had a tight knit melodic and soulful sound. They would practice in public lavatories as the harmonies would echo perfectly; they did not have a manager or anything fancy to break into the professional world of music during this period. Each brother had to earn a living and then find time to practice songs. They had a repertoire of ten songs and would alternate lead singers more or less like the Temptations, but the contents of their songs were essentially replicas of the Persuasions—a famous a cappella vocal group from New York. Their version of the Impressions' "People Get Ready" was copied by the Christian brothers, along with "ABC" and "Chain Gang"—they owed a great deal to the Persuasions, who were basically the idols of the Christian brothers.

Roger could be deemed an R&B musicologist; he would spend many hours looking through record stores for harmony groups from the 1940s to the1970s. He would bring home rare Doo Wop records by artists such as: the Spaniels, the Clovers, the Coasters, the Moonglows, the Orioles, the 5 Royals; along with more established artists like the Drifters. Collectively, these artists brought a soulful harmony to the backdrop of the "26" household. Roger was a force of nature, a powerful personality in the family, and a stylish dresser. He had a real passion for R&B of the past and in his day; his favorite singers whom he tried to emulate were Sam Cooke, Jerry Lawson from the Persuasions, and Johnny Moore and Ben E. King from the Drifters. He would practice songs to get the right tone and the cadence in his voice that would inevitably have an African American timber because he was taking lessons from the phrasing and delivery from them. When listening to him practice in one of the top attic rooms, sometimes Gladstone would complain and there would be tension between the younger son of twenty-something years and the father in his late sixties.

On reflection, one can understand why Gladstone felt overwhelmed with all the young souls he had brought into the world. After all, he had reached retirement age when most of his children had not even finished primary and secondary schooling. It must have been very difficult for an "old man" having to deal with so much youthful energy in the home. Add the pressure of a poor Liverpool economy, all that goes with such societal angst, and it becomes a mixture of home life tension that inevitably spills into interpersonal issues. Roger was a very strong personality, volatile, and given to bouts of unfortunate conflict with his father. Both men were uncompromising in their personalities and the clashes would lead to Roger moving out of the family home in his early twenties. This never stopped him visiting the family home; he was frequently there whenever he had free time from his plastering jobs. Roger loved his younger siblings and it showed in the way he would take his younger brothers for a day at the swimming baths. It was a pastime the Christian brothers always enjoyed during the summer holidays.

Roger's various skills always caught the attention of the family. He had a wonderful singing voice, he could play the piano, and his drawing skills were also eye-catching. Roger was an artist in the truest sense who was not fully able to express it due to the obstacles Blacks in Liverpool encountered across all sectors of society. Singing, however, was something the five brothers enjoyed together, Roger and Garry would take lead vocals, occasionally Russell, with Victor and Mark adding harmonies. We sang the Persuasions' version of Sam Cooke's "Chain Gang," along with "Lonely Man Am I," "So in Love," and the "ABC of Love"—often to rapturous applause whenever we made it on stage. The Christian brothers took to the stage at Walton Hall Park, Liverpool on September 10, 1978 as part of the "Rock Against Racism" (RAR) movement that was taking place to combat the rise of the National Front (far-right Nazi Party) in Britain. There was an audience reported in the local papers stating approximately three thousand turned out to support this antiracist musical event in the city. The following day in a substantial report of the event the *Daily Post* (September 1978, p. 7) partly stated:

> Merseyside rocked against racism yesterday when thousands turned out at Liverpool's Walton Hall Park for a free concert to support the anti-racialist cause.
> The afternoon of music and speeches followed a march by about 500 people through the city, and both events passed off peacefully.
> Afterwards, Mr. Rashid Mufti, chairman of the Merseyside Anti-Racialist Alliance (MARA) stated: "We've demonstrated that thousands of young people—the young, the old, families—on Merseyside care about racialism and want to stand up and be counted that they are against it. It has shown that we don't want racism. We want to kick it out and get rid of it."

The Christian brothers also had a stake in getting "rid of racism" as Liverpool Born Blacks who had encountered it in their individual lives. But the main issue was to prove themselves to the public as a good vocal group—that they did going by the applause received from the audience that day in September 1978. The brothers were not paid to perform that day and most often the reason they volunteered to sing for free was the cause and to gain local publicity. They began to get acknowledged for their tight melodic harmonies and soulful renditions across the city. But there was never enough recognition to think of taking the act to a professional level. Each brother had another life to lead. Roger had a construction business renovating old houses in the late 1970s, I had worked with him directly after leaving school in 1977 aged sixteen years learning paintwork, bricklaying, and being a general laborer. Victor was a school teacher at Quarry Bank, Garry drove a delivery truck, and Russell was a carpenter.

The brothers would practice at various homes, but usually Garry's apartment off Queens Drive in Childwall, Liverpool. They would rehearse to get the songs just right; it was very enjoyable for them to hear and experience such harmony between siblings. Often "harmony" did not translate to the everyday interaction; there would be unnecessary tension between certain members. Sibling rivalry is common in families. Nevertheless, the Christian brothers did their best to enjoy the singing and they auditioned for talent shows and continued to sing at local venues like Larks in the Park, which was held each August in Sefton Park, Liverpool. They did a gig at Quarry Bank School under Victor's organization as he taught music and physical education there. It was a great time for the brothers, as most of the time was spent laughing—there was always great humor and wit among the Christian siblings. Indeed, in 1978 there was an audition in St. Helens, a town on the outskirts of Liverpool, and the gig was to lead to a potential residency spot at a local pub. Well, while getting ready to start Roger was in a nervous state; he would always be tense before singing—even though he was by far the most talented. Stage fright is something some of the best artists suffer from; it is a human condition. This particular evening Roger was a little more nervous and he exclaimed, "Come on! Let's get going!" and this led to Victor giggling, and that then had a ripple effect on all the brothers. Within minutes there was uncontrollable laughter without any pause, and the manager of the pub looked on with a straight face that gave way to bemusement. The audition was, as one can imagine, a great failure, but one of the funniest experiences the brothers collectively had together. It was a time when they laughed and shared a memory that would never be forgotten due to the immense uncontrolled mirth in a serious audition for a music gig.

BRITISH RACISM AND HISTORICAL AMNESIA IN THE 1970s

The middle to late 1970s were difficult years in Britain for people of color. Racism was prominent in political discourse with the newly elected leader of the Conservative Party, Margaret Thatcher. On her march to political stardom as the first female British prime minister to be elected in 1979, she embraced the rhetoric of the National Front and proved to be an insidious white supremacist while in office. Thatcher supported the South African Apartheid regime while Nelson Mandela was imprisoned, and she felt it necessary to defend "white Britain" from being "swamped" by former colonial residents who had made their way to the British Isles. This would include Gladstone Christian and his compatriots who came to the defense of Britain in her time of need. Thatcher was an unabashed supporter of the British Empire and did not care to tone down her outward support for Britain's colonial and imperial past.

The cultural theorist originally from Jamaica, Stuart Hall, was arguably the most insightful Black academic during this era. In London, May 1978, Hall gave a talk arranged by the British Sociological Association (BSA) titled appropriately, "Racism and Reaction" that endeavored to analyze the current malaise of British racism, while indicating its longevity through the history of European enslavement, colonialism, and Empire. Hall was a brilliant thinker and writer, a leftist, who embraced the ideas of Antonio Gramsci and his notion of cultural hegemony among other things. Hall was incisive in his appreciation of how the British powerbrokers often disengaged from past racism while explaining the present. He was particularly cognizant of how the establishment would suffer what he termed "historical amnesia" when it came to the antecedents related to the British Empire. This is how he explained the situation:

> I want to . . . argue that the development of an indigenous British racism in the post-war period begins with the profound historical forgetfulness—what I want to call the loss of historical memory, and kind of historical amnesia, a decisive mental repression—which has overtaken the British people about race and Empire since the 1950s. Paradoxically, it seems to me, the native, home-grown variety of racism begins with this attempt to wipe out and efface every trace of the colonial and imperial past. Clearly, that is one effect of the traumatic adjustment to the very process of bringing Empire to an end. But undoubtedly, it has left an enormous reservoir of guilt and a deep, historical, resentment (Hall 1978, p. 25).

Hall was right, there developed a profound historical amnesia about Britain's long night of racism via its Empire. Its conquest and exploitation of African and Asian peoples, land, and resources, reaching back centuries and involving every conceivable institution in British society. Yet it is a difficult task to erase such a deeply-rooted history from the historical record—it is simply not possible though the power structure tried hard. In relation to Liverpool, there has been a dilution of the immense depth of its involvement in enslavement. The 2006 publication of *Liverpool 800: Culture, Character & History*, edited by John Belchem is a typical example of such a denial of historical fact—particularly the chapter by Jane Longmore titled "Civic Liverpool: 1680–1800" that dilutes, camouflages, and euphemizes the entire history of the city's inextricably interwoven "civic entanglement with enslavement" and its horrors. Hall spoke in London about the macro reality of such history concerning the British Empire and its concomitant racism. But then again there are relevant case studies of cities that grew *directly* out of such history and would not have grown in an economic sense without it. We shall return to this topic more deeply in chapter three.

To emphasize the 1978 perspective of Stuart Hall on historical British racism, consider a speech given by the then Prime Minister Margaret Thatcher ten years later, September 20, 1988 in Bruges, Belgium. The address was titled "The European Family of Nations" and it exemplifies both the arrogance of the right side of British politics and the delusion of grandeur regarding Europe as a "civilizing collective" when it comes to their shared history of conquest and exploitation. However, Thatcher conveniently overlooks the history of warfare that has emanated in two world wars *started by* European nations yet impacting the global population directly or indirectly. Thatcher attempts to play this off by talking about Britain fighting these wars to protect freedom; well, she cannot have it both ways. Either Europe is a civilizing entity or a warmonger and insidious purveyor of social injustice. Crucially, this Janus-faced perspective by Thatcher speaks to Stuart Hall's argument regarding historical amnesia that was apparent in British right-wing political discourse during the turbulent 1970s. She was an avid admirer of the British Empire, much like Winston Churchill before her. This is how Thatcher articulated the European shared history that they should collectively be proud of:

> Too often the history of Europe is described as a series of interminable wars and quarrels [but, actually true historically]. Yet from our perspective today surely what strikes us most is our common experience. For instance, the story of how Europeans explored and colonised and—yes, without apology—civilised much of the world is an extraordinary tale of talent, skill and courage. We British have in a special way contributed to Europe (Thatcher 1996, p. 89).

There is not much leeway here for Thatcher to hide her jingoism for the collective spirit of Europe. It would be good if Gilroy (1993a) could ponder this type of togetherness on the part of European history when breaking apart anything remotely pertaining to African solidarity. Thatcher was defending European colonialism and imperialism with an arrogance only found in the worst of white supremacists. She did not care for people of color or what they had endured and this was made manifest throughout her tenure as prime minister. She was an openly hostile advocate of anything white and British. Thatcher put to her "fellow" Europeans in September 1988 the idea that though there were differences to be acknowledged among our nations we "without apology, civilised much of the world"—but she left out something else she *could have* stated but did not: "during our centuries of conquest, genocide, divide and rule, physical and psychological trauma passed onto Indigenous peoples, we should celebrate this fact as part of our civilizing mission." Of course, Thatcher was being her audacious self while whining about the fear of a united Europe under a centralized system of governance. In retrospection, this did not occur, and with the recent "Brexit" departure from Europe her topic now seems moribund. However, it is still relevant in breaking down the reality of British racism and how its legacy continues to impinge on the present. One should not underestimate the influence of Margaret Thatcher's impact on right-wing political discourse. Yet, her admiration of British colonial history failed to acknowledge the tremendous exploitation inherent in it. As Hall stated facetiously:

> If the blood of the colonial workers has not mingled extensively with the English, then their labour-power has long endured the economic blood-stream of British society. It is in the sugar you stir, it is in the sinews of the famous British "sweet tooth"; it is in the tea-leaves at the bottom of the next "British" cuppa (Hall 1978, p. 25).

Hall was being a tad facetious but it was spot-on analysis in terms of historical truth. It could also be contended that "the blood of the colonial workers *has* mingled extensively with the English" if we consider the Blacks or mixed heritage. There is no denying the premise of Hall's analysis when juxtaposed with that of Thatcher's sweeping "civilizing" thesis relating to a collective Europe and those nations they colonized for centuries. Airbrushed out of the historical consciousness is the immense physical and psychological barbarity at the hands of her "European Family of Nations" speech in Bruges. Thatcher's "first and guiding principle" was to have "active cooperation" between European nations in her pursuit of a European community. But she did not favor outright collectivism—she preferred British *white* nationhood. "Europe will be stronger precisely because it has France as France, Spain as Spain, Britain as Britain, each with its own customs, traditions and identity" (Thatcher 1996, p. 91).

Thatcher went on to use the United States as an example of what *not* to do as a European Union. Claiming it would be "folly to try to fit them [European nations] into some sort of identikit European personality" (p. 91). Thatcher oscillated on what Europe actually meant to her. On the one hand she believed in the common experience, in "civilizing much of the world" together; on the other hand, there is a distinctiveness about what it is to be British, French, German, Spanish, and so on. What Thatcher praises is the European collective subjugation of African, Caribbean and Asian peoples, their lands and resources, under colonialism and imperialism, but emphasizes the *white* Britishness imperative. On the United States specifically, she states, again with a high degree of historical amnesia:

> People went there to get away from intolerance and constraints of life in Europe. They sought liberty and opportunity; and their strong sense of purpose has, over two centuries, helped create a new unity and pride in being American—just as our pride lies in being British or Belgian or Dutch or German (ibid.).

The problem here is in Thatcher conveniently overlooking the genocide of the Indigenous Americans, and the involuntary migration of millions of Africans to Europe's so-called "New World"—in essence it is a white European perspective offered by a British prime minister in 1988. Hall countered Thatcher by providing the point of view from the millions of colonized and their descendants who now reside in the metropole of Britain, as opposed to the satellite. He suggested quite simply to those white politicians who resented the presence of Blacks in Britain, "We are here because you were there." Or to put it another way, Black presence in Britain and other European nations in the twentieth century and beyond is largely to do with the specificity of colonial heritage. It would therefore be dubious to suggest Black and brown peoples did not exist in the formulation of the United States, as Thatcher alludes to her white European family. It is the avoidance of historical truth that is galling when one reads Thatcher or other white political nationalists from an Africana critical studies perspective.

Hall deemed it a paradox in how "home grown" British racism endeavors to erase all vestiges of its colonial and imperial past. Such strategic "forgetfulness" on behalf of white politicians continues to this day. Without coming to terms with the longevity of racialized oppression, one cannot hope to "get rid" of racism from societies mired in unhealthy relations between Black, brown, and white communities. Because at the grassroots level of community relations people tend to know that politicians lie, cajole, and dilute the past in order to sustain power. All things considered, unless the likes of Thatcher and her heirs are challenged on what they stated there can be little progress in eliminating institutional racism. The tempering down of British racist history and its ugliness only serves to increase resentment among Black and brown communities. As it does not foster racialized harmony and reconciliation of differences that would allow different cultural groups to come together—to put down their weapons of mistrust—so to speak. Without a reevaluation of political discourse on racialized relations in Britain, such as that of Thatcher, how is it possible to "move on"? British racism is unconscionable to those whom it has harmed and continues to harm in a variety of subtle and brutal ways.

IT'S A FAMILY AFFAIR

The Christian family represent a sliver of Britain's colonial past and its heritage. Gladstone and Ada created thirteen souls who signify the experience of Black mixed heritage persons growing up and eking out an existence in a rather bleak economy from the 1970s to the1980s. Gladstone transitioned in June of 1978 at the age of seventy-one. Ada mourned again, this time her companion and the family's main breadwinner over thirty-plus years. She had lost her second son, Denny, in 1975, and her mother in 1976. To make matters worse, the family also lost a close friend of Garry's, who would visit "26" regularly, in another tragedy—he was only twenty-three years old. Lastly, in 1976 the family pet dog, Kim, of twelve-plus years also passed away.

It was a difficult period in the mid-1970s for the Christian family. Indeed, it appeared to be a "time of death" for the Christians. It was a particularly rough time for Ada. She was heartbroken with the loss of her favorite son, with whom she had been pregnant when she lost her first born, Ian, in October of 1948, so Denny was more precious to her than anything in the world. It did show itself in the manner of her mourning his untimely death at the age of twenty-six years. The grief lasted a very long time; it seemed like Ada was lost in sorrow for at least a year, which was an eternity to the younger Christian siblings. No one should witness or experience the mourning of a mother for a son lost before his time. She had the unfairness of having experienced this trauma three times in her lifetime. Ada was strong mentally; she had to be otherwise the family would have crumbled. Somehow, she held on, did not break down, and kept the home life moving. Often, she would offer the same advice to all of her children: "You just have to keep going, no matter what challenge life brings." Ada was very wise, grounded, and courageous with an innate intelligence.

The music continued to reverberate around the Christian household. Janet, Rita, and Jenny all had a love for Bob Marley and the Wailers who had recently emerged in Britain from Jamaica under the Island Records label. Rita had all of his albums, starting with *Catch a Fire* from 1973, followed in the same year by *Burnin'*—it was a time of Black cultural rebellion against racism; Rita and Janet were able to see Marley in concert when they visited Britain to promote their first album. Jenny was too young to go, or Ada would not allow her to go with her elder sisters. Yes, the bedrooms of "26" displayed an array of African American musical talent; plastered on the walls were posters of the Jackson 5 and other Motown artists like Marvin Gaye, Smokey Robinson, and the Miracles, and of course the Temptations. Rita and Janet both styled their hair in the Afro, each competed for the biggest and most perfectly rounded. Afros were something to show the world that Black people were in unspoken solidarity with each other. There was an inner pride, after all if the Jackson 5 could look slick with their Afro hairstyles, then it was only natural for millions of Blacks around the globe to follow suit. We should note that the music of African America was a powerful antidote to the racism felt across the globe.

The Christian brothers followed with the Afro style, apart from Garry who for some biological reason began to lose his hair at the tender age of eighteen. I would often tell him to shave it all off and look bald and smooth. In time, the penny would eventually drop and his smooth head helped make him a pop star with a powerful image from 1987 onward. But the sisters' Afros were the very biggest and best kept; they copied the same way the African American activist Angela Davis styled hers. What was happening in the United States in terms of the fight for human and civil rights, along with the Black Power movement, was finding resonance with Black British youth. Both in music and in style, African American culture had a tremendous impact on Black Britain. For example, when Angela Davis was arrested and jailed there was a "Free Angela Davis" campaign in major cities across the United Kingdom—the Christian sisters were part of that struggle in their way too. What impacted Blacks in America was felt by Blacks in Britain—this is not as well known in North America but it is a social fact.

To be sure, the Christian family were essentially followers of Black culture, and this largely came from listening to the music of Black America. The Beatles were, ironically, not played at "26" nor were any other white bands of the 1960s or 1970s. The records bought by family members were largely from the Atlantic Records and Motown labels. Aretha Franklin's "Don't Play That Song for Me" and "Say a Little Prayer" were played so often that they are etched into the soundtrack of the Christian family. There was also the soulful melody of Etta James blasting through the household. Music, in short, was a central feature because all were either listeners or practitioners in the art. However, there is an irony, not one of the Christian sisters would become a singer. Given that there were eight boys and five girls it is odd that not one of the girls had a singing voice. This is made even stranger by the fact that it was Ada, not Gladstone, who had the singing DNA. She would sing while cooking and it is not an exaggeration to state that she sounded like Ella Fitzgerald or Doris Day (who actually modeled herself on Ella) while singing. So melodically in tune and pleasing to the ear, one could often find Ada in the kitchen warbling a hit from the past or something contemporary that was playing hourly on the radio.

Gladstone neither played an instrument nor sang; he was a sportsman, and after his cricket playing days ceased he passed his leisurely time watching cricket or touring around Liverpool and its outskirts during his retirement years. He was not very much into going places in groups—but he would sometimes take two of his younger boys, myself and Kevin out rowing in the local park. Gladstone never shared his Jamaican history with the family, he was a private man not given to passing on advice that would help his children navigate life. He withdrew gradually into his private world after he retired. What is rather poignant to consider in hindsight is in the fact that when he left Kingston, Jamaica in July of 1941 he would never return to his homeland. A few of his siblings came to visit on maybe two occasions, one being his youngest brother known as "Uncle Babe" who was a police officer in Philadelphia. In all those thirty-seven years he never ventured abroad; he stayed in Liverpool with his Black British family. In this sense, it is fair to conclude that Gladstone had the life he may not have expected but that he enjoyed. Indeed, he could have fled back to Jamaica at any time during his stay in England, but he chose to stay with Ada and his children. He never fully expressed his emotion but maybe he did in his actions—he stayed, even though personal struggle with his health made him more reclusive in his behavior.

The following chapter will consider the Liverpool Black experience and life in the 1980s to the 2000s. Focus will continue to intersperse with broader Black British history and the Christian family. Much can be shared in comprehending these decades as formidable social changes took place in the City of Liverpool with grassroots organizations having sprung up to aid Liverpool Born Blacks in the struggle against widespread institutionalized racism. Indeed, British society had to come to terms with Black British children born and raised in cities across the United Kingdom. It was a multicultural Britain that found itself in turmoil.

Chapter 3

Schooling, L8 Community Football, Grassroots Education, and Mainstream Miseducation

The previous chapters have considered the social history of Black presence in Liverpool as it relates to the transatlantic from the eighteenth century roughly up to approximately the 1970s; the focus here will essentially be on the last quarter of the twentieth century. This area, like others, was a struggle for jobs and worthwhile education on behalf of Liverpool Born Blacks. To cover this with a degree of Africana critical studies vigor there will be a need to share local and governmental report findings, particularly relating to education and interrelated life chances encountered by Liverpool Born Blacks. Writings from local Black activists, like Wally Brown (1986, 1983), who can often counter the usual white liberal frame of reference that dominated the social interpretation in academia in the 1980s on Black communities in Liverpool. This is how Brown articulated the depth of socioeconomic invisibility among Liverpool Blacks in the city during the 1980s:

> So, given that there are up to 40,000 black people in the city, have you ever asked the question, "I wonder where they work? They don't work in the city centre, you don't see them down there; they don't work in the factories, where do they?" They do not work anywhere because the situation in this area has meant that they have been completely excluded from jobs. They have never had jobs; the community has never had jobs and never had the advantages that go with jobs, advantages that are normally taken for granted by every person who has a job. The opportunity to be able to choose where you want to live. Those with a job and with a regular wage or salary have got access and can buy a house in a particular bracket. Yet most of this community [Liverpool/Merseyside in relation to its Black population] have got no choice because they have not got the things which are taken for granted, and which I may have also taken for granted if I had not been part of the community (Brown 1983, p. 104).

There was of course a very strong leadership of Black activists who were courageous in the struggle for racialized social justice in the city—this will be a salient feature of the chapter. Significantly, there will also continue to be interspersed throughout the life and times of the Liverpool Black family, the Christians, who add to the social theory a human aspect of growing up in Liverpool during this era. Noting that this study is an insight from a Liverpool Born Black writer sharing his knowledge and bearing witness within the context of education and social history—just as Wally Brown, Eric Lynch, Dorothy Kuya, Maria O'Reilly, Adam Hussein, Joe Farrag, Manneh Brown, Liz Drysdale, and many other Liverpool Born Blacks had done to elucidate the varied experiences of invisibility within the context of a profoundly racialized city.

Education specifically, and relevant qualifications, whether vocational or in the liberal arts, is an area that needs to be highlighted due to its importance within the context of Black Liverpool. As the reader will gauge, the City of Liverpool during this era, and earlier, had a very poor track record in delivering equal opportunities to its Black citizens—this can be traced back as far as the Fletcher Report which did its best to highlight Liverpool Born Blacks as a social problem (Belchem 2014; Christian 2008a; Brown 1986; Law and Henfrey 1981). With the growing Black population in Liverpool during the 1950s to 1960s it was inevitable that racialized discrimination would have to be tackled and a grassroots infrastructure had to be developed. However, community organizations occurred rather haphazardly, if one recalls the 1930s and Pastor Daniels Ekarte's African Churches Mission, based on Hill Street in Liverpool 8, which acted as a communal resource refuge and escape from the horrors of racism and discrimination in the city. It also provided much needed homes for Black children abandoned and/or illegitimate from the liaisons mainly between local white women and African American soldiers, who arrived in the area from 1942 until the war's end in 1945—effectively these were Black mixed heritage children born during wartime in the 1940s in Liverpool of African American and British heritage. Marika Sherwood provides a chapter on this subject matter in her book *Pastor Daniels Ekarte and the African Churches Mission*. She refers to official reports and letters from a number of key individuals of the era, including the noted Pan African writer-activist George Padmore and the renowned scholar St. Clair Drake, who were both interested in this crisis. It was a social catastrophe that amounted to over five hundred illegitimate Black children of mixed heritage being born during WW2 in the Liverpool region (Sherwood 1994, p. 57). To be fair to the African Americans who wanted to share in the lives of their Black mixed heritage children, it was the U.S. government who denied them this obligation (p. 55).

The League of Coloured Peoples (LCP) also got involved, with its Jamaican born leader, Dr. Harold Moody, taking up the cause to advocate for an orphanage, with the supporting activist, Pastor Ekarte (pp. 51–76). According to Sherwood, the pastor always had the education of Black children in Liverpool at the forefront of his mission. As she stated:

> Pastor Daniels was always concerned with the education of Black children, especially as in the 1930s there were hardly any Black children getting into secondary or technical schools. Secondary schools were only for the academically successful or the wealthy as children had to pass a series of competitive examinations for the few scholarships available. Even with a scholarship, parents had to pay for books and uniforms (p. 33).

Clearly, there was a need from the 1930s upwards for proper educational opportunity for Liverpool Black children. This situation, one could argue, did not dissipate greatly in the coming decades. The point to make strongly is in relation to the *structural racism* that was emerging and an erroneous stigma being attached to Black children, particularly of mixed heritage in the city. It was on a continuum between outright racism to condescending paternalism that operated—all the time keeping Black children of mixed heritage firmly in a subordinate social position.

Indeed, this is an area of Black history that deserves deeper research than can be revealed here; one would hope that the children's children of these now elders could give their life histories in order to leave future generations with a record. Again, the scurrilous term "half caste" was repeated during this era in the 1940s and a growing consciousness against this nomenclature developed in the 1960s with the rise in Black consciousness coming via the transatlantic (Christian 1997a, 2000). St. Clair Drake was a sociologist with an interest also in anthropology who conducted some research in 1947 that relates to Liverpool and further afield in Britain to uncover the experience of Blacks in post-war British society. Drake published his findings in a sociological journal in the mid-1950s, and below he makes reference to the African Americans who returned to their homeland while having to leave behind their white partners and many Black children in British towns. Liverpool, as Sherwood revealed, may have had around five hundred such children, known as the "Brown Baby Problem":

> With the close of the War and the return of American troops to their homeland, various groups in Britain began to express concern over the fate of the illegitimate children of coloured American troops (of whom there were some 2,000). This was the Brown Baby Problem. Stories about these children began to appear in the press, sometimes with their numbers greatly exaggerated. In Liverpool, the African Churches Mission and the Negro Welfare Centres (both coloured

institutions) began to formulate plans for raising money to send some of these children to America and to build a Booker T. Washington Children's Home in Britain for others. By 1947, however, responsible British institutions were co-operating with the League of Coloured Peoples in a programme of trying to arrange for some of the children to join their fathers in America, and for others to be placed for adoption or foster care with British families. A policy decision had been made by the Home Office that overseas adoptions were not permissible (Drake 1955, p. 207).

It is interesting that the proposed name of the children's home would be Booker T. Washington (1856–1915), who was also a man of Black mixed heritage due to his mother's interaction, most probably involuntary, with a white American overseer during the era of enslavement. Rather ironic it is that the children in need of a home in Liverpool of the 1940s were largely the offspring of African American GIs and white Liverpool women. Understanding the life of Booker T. Washington would certainly open up a plethora of racialized thought (Christian 2021). Yet within the Liverpool British context, such children in the twentieth century were *still* stigmatized due to the long history of enslavement and colonialism in the British Caribbean, Africa, and the Americas—to forget this historical stigma would be facile as it is a basic aspect of British pseudoscientific racism (Fryer 1984, pp. 133–190). This is important because to think of there being merely *isolated* versions of racialized experiences is rather misrepresentative of the broader historical reality. Of course, there is difference between and within various Black communities, but racism and its concomitant prejudice has had universal outcomes that simply exclude a cultural group or groups while sustaining the hegemony of another—usually designated as white. In short, there are widespread similarities in how the outcome of racism perpetuates social inequality. Liverpool as a city has certain racialized characteristics that can meet with other transatlantic experiences.

SOCIAL AND CULTURAL INFRASTRUCTURE EMERGES 1950s–1970s

The assault on Black Liverpudlians continued into the 1950s and beyond. One has to disagree wholeheartedly with John Belchem and his notion that "Liverpool subsequently emerged as a model of race relations in the 1950s" (Belchem 2014, p. 161). Black Liverpudlians were largely living in slum landlord housing and there was widespread discrimination in employment and education. How can Belchem write such twaddle? Indeed, more appropriately, later he states: "Stanley House Community Centre . . . was beset with conflict over its paternalistic (white) management style" (p. 161). If this is a model for good race relations then it is rather depressing and stifling in comprehension. Certainly, to think that when there is merely no violence against Black people it is a "model of race relations" says more about the writer than it does about the actual reality of Black experience in the Liverpool. Essentially, Stanley House was set up in the early post-war years to cater to the social welfare needs of the Liverpool Black communities, for them to have a place to relax without being harassed by white racism—that is the bottom line. Still, the management was as Belchem notes "paternalistic" and patronizing toward Black Liverpudlians. It was a necessary meeting place for community issues that directly concerned racialized relations and ways to improve them in the city.

One has to also remember that there was a dire need for social clubs and mutual aid societies due to a lack of welfare provisions and the fact that the city centre was a dangerous place for Blacks in Liverpool to visit. Instead, there were local social clubs (sometimes referred to as shebeens) that catered to a de facto segregated nightlife for Liverpool's Black community. Keep in mind, it was akin to a mini-Harlem whereby progressive whites seeking adventure would also frequent the "club scene" in Liverpool 8. Yet, to emphasize, the discrimination in mainstream Liverpool meant that there was little alternative for Liverpool's Black folks but to find ways to entertain themselves. The clubs that sprang up around Toxteth/Liverpool 8 specifically catered to Blacks and nighttime entertainment. To be sure, the 1950s and 1960s was a time of socialized segregation when it came to night life. Moreover, to call this era a time of harmonious racial relations is rather myopic and does not meet with what was actually happening: Black exclusion from mainstream Liverpool. Some of these clubs would become very popular. Alvin Christie has painstakingly put together a list of these clubs that were alive with music and Black culture. Here is just a few of them; the list is not exhaustive: Pink Flamingo, Palm Cove, Dutch Eddies, Silver Sands, The West Indian Club, The Bedford, The Gladray, The Nigerian, The Somali, The Yoruba, The Ibo, and The Embassy Club.

All these, and more, were dotted around the Liverpool 8 community as night life spots. These clubs offered music that filtered into the sound of the Merseybeat (Christie 2018) and it has not been widely acknowledged how important this was to the social welfare of the Blacks in Liverpool. Overall, one can gauge from the names of the social clubs that there was a cultural component to many, giving the name of the African people or Caribbean under the umbrella of the West Indian Club. This gives an indication of the diversity among the Black Liverpudlians born to African and Caribbean migrants and we should not think of *one* Black community but an amalgamation of several—and the offspring of many would then be deemed: Liverpool

Born Blacks or LBBs (Christian 1997b, 2000). It is this cultural group that has had to overcome the social stigma of "half caste" riddled throughout pseudoscientific racist reports. To find a sense of independence and confidence, a collective identity of Liverpool Born Black would clearly overcome any label that denigrated their humanity. It is easy for those outside of this experience to define LBB as problematic (Brown 2005), but in essence it is a shedding of a negative nomenclature pressed onto them that brought about new terminology that was more appealing and relevant to a positively affirming social status.

By the 1970s, the local soul group the Real Thing cemented a sense of pride in being Black and having been born in Liverpool. Their album, *4 from 8* released in 1977 personified their collective spirit in being both born and raised in the Liverpool 8 area—the album is an homage to the area. They had had the summer hit of 1976 with "You to Me Are Everything" and the follow-up "Can't Get by Without You" was another success, which were part of the first album. But it was their second album *4 from 8* that provided Liverpool Born Blacks with a sense of community. The original members formed in 1970 and were: Chris Amoo, Kenny Davis, Ray Lake, and Dave Smith. Kenny was replaced by Chris' brother and former Chants member Eddie Amoo. It was when Eddie joined the Real Thing that they found much success and this gave impetus for other groups in the area to seek similar achievement.

In the mid-1970s Garry and Russell Christian sang with Odie Taylor's combo, but did not find any success beyond local gigs and competitions held in Liverpool. The Christian brothers began singing together from 1977 and they were: Roger, Victor, Garry, Russell, and Mark. This has been covered more deeply in chapter two, but not covered was the development of a group named the Christians. This band developed from the core singers of the Christian brothers in 1985: Roger, Garry, and Russell. Victor and Mark were not part of this due to internal differences within the family. The Christian brothers were initially called "Equal Temperament"—which was an oxymoron given the personality clashes within the group. As Garry Christian explains:

[I started] back in 1974 with a group called Equal Temperament. My brother, [Victor], who is three years older than me, he is a classically trained music teacher. He teaches in schools around Liverpool to this day in fact [Victor retired to live in Spain in 2018]. He is a great musician and he put us together. We called ourselves Equal Temperament. It was the worst name they could have called us really because there was no Equal Temperament at all; family, brothers, siblings, [we] they are always fighting. [We] They are always arguing about something. There we were and we just did the local clubs and stuff and it was mainly a cappella, singing with no music at all and that was great. He taught us how to harmonize really, how to put these [voices] and different tones together, so that was great. That was another learning curve for me, how to harmonize (cited in Leonard and Strachan 2010, p. 100).

Garry is largely correct, the brothers sadly did not get along as a unit due to personality clashes. Apparently, this is common in large families, probably due to a lack of "space" when growing up together in a house that was very active and musical. Nevertheless, it is fair to state that nobody wished the worst for one another in the Christian family. In hindsight, it took a great deal of mental strength as a Black Liverpool family just to survive everyday realities. There can be a lot of subconscious pressure put on the siblings due to a lack of opportunities—only Victor, as Garry stated, was a full-time schoolteacher at Quarry Bank Comprehensive with a professional career. He had done well at school due to the assistance of one teacher from my Comprehensive School providing him with extracurricular piano lessons. Had he not gained support from this kind teacher back in his schooldays he may never have been successful in becoming a music teacher. Victor was one of the first Black teachers in Liverpool, and there were only a handful in the 1970s—he was a pioneer for Liverpool Born Blacks. Individually, the Christians were talented, but not a unified and caring family due primarily to the city and its impact on the lives of its Black citizens. Particularly, the pressure to survive in Liverpool was pretty hard in the 1970s and 1980s—this had an indirect impact on all Black families. Moreover, this kind of external social pressure is often overlooked when Black family interaction is taken into account.

SCHOOL DAYS AND MARK CHRISTIAN

Many writers in the past have shared their school days to explain how they developed character. Take Patrick Chamoiseau's account of childhood in his book aptly titled *School Days,* whereby he captures his intimidating Martinique-French colonial educational experience in elegant prose. But more importantly, there is an insight into what it was like for a young boy of color from Martinique experiencing a classroom that was "familiar and threatening. So was the Teacher" (Chamoiseau 1997, p. 55). Again, whether in the satellite or metropole, or under French, British, or any other colonizer's curriculum, the specter of white supremacy hovers over the educational experience for a Black child.

When I attended primary school aged five years to eleven years in Liverpool, there was that "knowing" feeling that made me feel different. It was difficult being the only Black child in a class at school. At my Primary School in Liverpool there were only a few Black families connected to the school. In September 1970, I was nine years of age and placed in a class temporarily due to my regular class taking a trip to Colomendy—a holiday camp for Liverpool school children based in North Wales. Ada could not afford the school fee for me as we were experiencing difficult times with a poor economy. Therefore, I had to spend a couple of weeks in Mr. Redburn's class. The classroom had a Victorian ambience with school desks that had inkwell holes from an era long passed. There was something inescapably unsettling about this environment to a young boy of Black British heritage. Mr. Redburn was surly and impatient, one of the teachers to avoid, if possible, at primary school. Unfortunately, I could not escape this situation and had to spend two weeks in his company.

On the day I entered Redburn's class for the temporary two-week stay I was given an assignment to write a biographical story on someone famous. With the World Cup football tournament having been won by Brazil in the summer of 1970, I decided to write about the life of the then best footballer on the planet: Pelé. The Brazilian footballer had become an icon to all aspiring children who loved the game of football, what Americans call soccer, and I was a devoted follower of the brilliant Brazilian—who was a dark skinned Brazilian and inescapably part of the transatlantic African Diaspora heritage. I had a football magazine from the summer and had read all about the great footballer on his development. I also had a poster of him on my wall. Hence, I eagerly got to work on the assignment: *Pelé of Brazil*. In covering the master of the football game, I first began with Pelé's playing the game in bare feet due to the poverty he had grown up in; how he got noticed by the local team, Santos FC, and quickly rose through the ranks as a youth player. Pelé was so good he was brought into the national team at the age of seventeen years and played in the 1958 World Cup winning team, scoring crucial goals in the final game—Pelé won his first major world title. By 1970, aged twenty-nine, he retired from the national team as a three-time World Cup winner. He was a man who had overcome poverty and discrimination, due to his dark skin in Brazil being a social impediment to one's life chances in that color hierarchal setting, to become the best footballer the world had seen to date—arguably. Crucially, Pelé played in arguably the best national team that had ever graced the game in 1970. It was an exciting time for anyone who loved football, and I had a passion for the game that showed in my writing of Pelé and his upbringing in Brazil.

I read over the assignment and felt good about it, stood up from my desk, and took it over to Mr. Redburn who sat at the front of the class doodling on a pad while the class worked on their assignments. He looked up begrudgingly as I handed him the paper. Mr. Redburn was wearing reading glasses as he perused; after a lapse of time that seemed like an eternity but was probably a minute, he looked up with his eyes squinting over his glasses and stated: "Go away Christian, you did not write this." I stood there frozen, but managed to smile and respond, "Yes I did, just now in class"—to no avail. Mr. Redburn had returned to his doodling on his pad and never said another word. I returned to my desk perplexed and re-read the assignment on Pelé, smiling inside at his bio-sketch on the greatest footballer of all time. Strangely enough, I shrugged off Mr. Redburn, putting it down to his gruff personality and imperviousness.

Maybe this was a sign of things to come for me in British mainstream education. Without being braggadocio, I was a clever child and absorbed all that I could from my elder siblings. I would watch how they did things and would mimic some styles and reject others from my brothers and sisters. There was a sensitivity in my personality that I most likely inherited from my mother. Ada was a very intelligent woman, and an avid reader. Sadly, I have to admit that I was gradually turned off school largely by the teachers I had encountered in both primary and secondary schooling. In England there is "Primary" (aged five to eleven years) and "Secondary" (aged eleven to sixteen years, with a possible two years more). By age eleven years, I was not "tuned in" to the hidden curriculum of what school is for Black working-class children in Liverpool. That is, to merely obey rules and authority, imbibe white domination, and be prepared for menial work, if it was available. There was not much to inspire me as a young boy who had much untapped potential like many other school children from less affluent social backgrounds. Indeed, the education system was not designed to support working-class children as it did the middle and upper in Britain—particularly Black children.

Sociologically speaking, this type of education was revealed by Paul Willis in his book *Learning to Labour: How Working-Class Kids Get Working-Class Jobs*. His study was conducted employing a qualitative methodological approach under participant observation from 1972 to 1975, and was published in 1977. Ironically, this study from its inception to publication covered the years I attended Comprehensive School. Therefore, it resonates with my experience. However, Willis' study was based in Birmingham in the Midlands, not Liverpool in the northwest of England. Moreover, it only studied the experiences of white British working-class children. Willis found that the school system did not inculcate a love of education, but actually groomed the students for factory jobs that did not demand too much imagination. His research ultimately found that the children were uninterested in learning and had expected a life that did not involve having to think too deeply. In other words, the school system he researched produced "working-class kids for working-class jobs" (Willis 2017).

Though it is a useful starting point, a major problem with Willis' research is in it failing completely to consider Black British children, yet this was the normative with much of white sociology in the 1970s—it failed to comprehend the reality of Black life in British schools. Indeed, how does one explain a Mr. Redburn? This experience of mine has never been revealed until now, but how many Black children had suffered the same dismissiveness from a teacher? We only have to consider Malcolm X's experience when he was doing so well at school until asked by a white teacher what his aspiration in life was. Malcolm replied, "I want to be a lawyer" and the teacher said to him it was not a realistic goal for a "Nigger"—Malcolm drifted away from taking education seriously (Malcolm X 1987, pp. 117–118). Like Malcolm, I was the only Black child in the classroom, but Mr. Redburn never even considered my aspirations in life, in fact he blatantly refused to accept I even had potential. Malcolm and I were a generation and a transatlantic distance apart, but still experiencing the same kind of ignorance from a white educator—not being taken seriously. White researchers cannot easily comprehend these microaggressions that are encountered by Black children in schools everyday whereby they are in a cultural minority setting.

The experience of Black British children in the education system in 1970s Britain was famously captured by Bernard Coard in his 1971 study, *How the West Indian Child Is Made Educationally Sub-normal in the British School System.* What is significant about this pamphlet is in it being accessible to all readership levels, from school administrations to grassroots community activists. Therefore, it would become very popular and read widely among Black communities across Britain. Herman Ouseley, in the preface to the 1991 edition, succinctly expresses the importance of Coard's study:

> Bernard Coard's work has withstood the test of time because the problems facing African-Caribbean parents and their children have fundamentally remained the same; racism, race prejudice and social inequalities are crucial factors in the perpetuation of educational policies and practices which cause the system to fail the African-Caribbean community. These will prevail even though there have been some changes and new developments in the intervening 20 year period (Ouseley 1991, p. 9).

Coard's analysis and indictment of the British education system's racism toward to the African Caribbean child is now over fifty years ago, and Ouseley's response is now thirty-plus years ago; this is concerning because racism in British society has not waned significantly since (Ducey and Feagin 2021). Moreover, the longevity of Black British participants suffering miseducation or being subjected to racism and exclusion has been perpetuated mainly on young Black boys in the British education system (Christian

2005b). What is uneasy to comprehend relates to the insuperable disregard white power structures reveal for they never appear to grasp the consequence of the racialized dilemma. That is, the depth of white supremacist thought that is ingrained, directly or indirectly, in the student and the teacher. Basically, the Black student can feel very uncomfortable in the presence of white authoritative figures, like schoolteachers, and the teachers often have subconscious bias against Black children. As Coard contended in 1971:

> In Britain, Peter Watson, a white Educational Psychologist, went to a secondary school in East London where there are many West Indian pupils. He took with him a Black assistant. The two of them tested groups of West Indian children separately. The group of West Indian children tested by the Black examiner did considerably better than the group tested by Peter Watson, the white examiner. In other words, they did much *worse* under the white examiner than the Black one (Coard 1991, pp. 28–29).

Therefore, the problem of Black underachievement can occur simply by having a white examiner in charge over his or her educational experience. Just as Mr. Redburn made me feel worthless in regard to my academic effort, the same thing can happen *within* the psychological make-up of the Black child who has to be tested via the white gaze. This is not an insignificant issue and is fraught with psychological complexity because it is more than just the teaching process, the pedagogy, it has something to do with the historical nature of Black and white interaction. Even the most well-meaning of white teachers can cause great damage to the confidence of Black children simply by his or her presence in a classroom. Indeed, when I entered Comprehensive School in September of 1972, I was one of only four or five Black children in the entire school of maybe six hundred pupils. There was not one Black schoolteacher in my entire school experience in Liverpool from 1966 to 1977. I did, however, learn to read and write, I learned arithmetic, white English literature, and its related history. So, to suggest I was ever "educationally sub-normal" would be erroneous. I suppose it would be apt to be described as unique—because I had been home schooled indirectly by my elder siblings. British schooling allowed me to learn to read and write, gain mental arithmetic skills, and general social interaction that were all transferable to the broader society. What they did not allow me was "certification" that endorses ability. Again, no different to many others who leave school early due to unforeseen circumstances, or due to outright discrimination that occurs frequently.

As mentioned earlier, my brother Victor had gone on to be a schoolteacher himself, breaking through numerous barriers. He is almost a decade older than I, and extremely accomplished in both classical and jazz music. Moreover,

Victor was teaching in a Liverpool school when I was still at school, and there were teachers at my Comprehensive School who actually knew Victor from his time there. Therefore, it cannot be stated that there was anything about myself that could deem me incapable of succeeding in school. But I never did succeed in gaining qualifications because I was never encouraged to do so. Unfortunately for me, Mr. Fred Ahearn had passed on, literally, and there was no teacher who believed in me in the manner he had done with Victor. This is very important, because it only takes *one* good teacher to change the trajectory of a life, and when it comes to Black children in predominantly white controlled schools it can be a rather difficult terrain for the Black child to navigate the day-to-day harsh realities of white interaction and its understated racism. Whether subtle or brutal, racism has a way of stifling Black achievement in British schools. Coard was correct in the sense that the British education system was actually failing its Black British citizens through a labyrinth of racialized ignorance and dismissiveness.

For myself, it was both the curriculum and the insipid teachers that took my mind elsewhere when listening to a lesson in a classroom. One history teacher was particularly drenched in British colonial history and would literally play with toy soldiers on his desk. Like Mr. Redburn at my Primary School, a history teacher at my Comprehensive School, Mr. Rimmer, showed no interest whatsoever in the academic ability I could offer. Actually, he did not even regard me as having any potential—I was invisible to him. There was an aloof coldness about Mr. Rimmer that made me shudder in his presence. I readily concluded there was nothing of substance to be learned in his British jingoistic history class. Therefore, my mind drifted into what I would be doing once the school bell rang. It was simply a waste of my time being there listening to this advocate of British Imperialism explain the Boer War and how the British won it. It was jingoism and uninteresting to me; I was by then listening to Marvin Gaye's *What's Going On* album in my bedroom at home after school. I certainly had no interest in the British Empire and how it had conquered parts of the world to spread its divide and rule "democracies" throughout the Caribbean and a good part of the African continent to "civilize" the natives. No, my young mind was too fertile for Black perspectives though I did not know it at the time. But I was absorbing all that my elder siblings were sharing about Black music and its history. The Temptations' *Puzzle People* album from 1969 was a staple item on the stereo player at "26" and I absorbed the empowering lyrics and soulful harmonies. Songs like "Don't Let the Joneses Get You Down" and "Message from a Black Man" were educational and an antidote to the ethnocentric education I was receiving from my teachers during my school days.

Overall, my Comprehensive School experience was not particularly helpful in terms of gaining the standard academic qualifications, but I left with a school reference that is very interesting to unpack due to its economy of truth. It is dated February 28, 1977:

> Mark Christian joined the school in September 1972.
>
> He is a boy whose appearance has always been good and I have always found him honest.
>
> He has been educated to C.S.E. level and the standard of his English is particularly good.
>
> It is in sport that most of his interests in school have shown themselves. He has always been keen on football, athletics and swimming and has reached a competent standard in them.
>
> Signed by the Deputy Headmaster.

Well, the problem with the above school reference is twofold. First, I was at a higher standard of education but was not allowed to show it due to not being entered for any examinations. Second, I was competent in arithmetic but this is not mentioned. Yet, and this is the kicker, the deputy headmaster is fine elaborating on *sport*. It is true that I was a keen footballer, winning intramural awards three years in a row for football with my classmates. However, I never once entered an athletics program that the school was involved with, nor did I or my classmates ever go to a swimming bath with my Comprehensive School from 1972 to 1977. The point here is that the deputy headmaster was willing to be mendacious with sport related activities, but *not* with my academics. This reflects the subconscious bias to be found in education administrators who lack cultural proficiency (Welborn et al., 2022).

Importantly, I left my Comprehensive School with no formal qualifications. I would return to gain the necessary diplomas in due course via a Liverpool Black grassroots education establishment. The school experiences were not unique to me alone; most of my talented siblings suffered the same fate, and most of my Black friends had similar stories to tell about their schooling in Liverpool. As Bernard Coard argued, " More than likely he [the Black child] has encountered a racist teacher in the past; he has certainly been called 'Black bastard' or 'Wog' " (1991, p. 29). Yes, the racist teacher was there in my past, and the name-calling, but this did not deter me because of the grounding I received at home from my family. The Christians were a good-looking family and racism could not stifle us completely. Yes, discrimination may have been able to stop members of the family doing well in school, but it could not stop us pushing ahead and succeeding come what may. This is an important aspect of life; regardless of obstacles and setbacks, there is often a way to still succeed if one has the perseverance. There is too much emphasis put on "formal qualification" and a diploma that states "one is educated" when in fact one can be truly "miseducated" if a person of color has imbibed the hidden curriculum evident in a school (Willis 2017; Christian 2005b)

PROBLEMATIC PEDAGOGY

As exemplified by Paul Willis and Bernard Coard earlier, the British education system can often stifle the creative juices from flowing out of the child. There are many talented children that do not get to express their individual talents, regardless of one's cultural background. The British system of education has not fundamentally changed much in over eighty years. It merely expanded to include more working-class communities from the 1960s due to the economic infrastructure requiring a greater educated and skilled workforce. But the actual structure of British elitism has largely remained whereby most of British society's privileged are educated in highly coveted schools that have an elaborate way in producing the same class structure in Britain.

A white educator, Ken Robinson, who was born and raised in Liverpool from humble origins, rose to become a noted international educationalist offering greater insight into the process of education and the child. He tapped into an aspect of education that is often obliterated when the child goes through the school system in Britain, and frankly in most other nations. That is, the innate talent and ability of individuals is often suppressed and not allowed to manifest itself unless one is from a richly resourced school. Yet the majority of public schools in Britain are far from being richly resourced. If one learns to read and write at a decent level, has mental arithmetic skills, then he or she has done very well. This is not being facetious, there are many children who actually leave school unable to properly read and write. In his book published in 2009, *The Element: How Finding Your Passion Changes Everything*, Robinson argued:

> Most students never get to explore the full range of their abilities and interests. Those students whose minds work differently—and we're talking about many students here; perhaps even the majority of them—can feel alienated from the whole culture of education. This is exactly why some of the most successful people you'll ever meet didn't do well at school. Education is the system that's supposed to develop our natural abilities and enable us to make our way in the world. Instead, it is stifling the individual talents and abilities of too many students and killing their motivation to learn (p.16).

Robinson is correct, the public schools like those attended by myself and other members of my family in Liverpool were not designed to produce the talent and abilities of the students. They are primarily designed to introduce conformity and the curriculum has a hierarchy of subjects that favor the economy: mathematics and science. The arts are on the lower end of the scale in the curriculum. Now, this is a general acknowledgment, there are always in the human experience exceptions to the rule. Victor Christian happened to have a teacher who took the time out to develop his music skills via the piano. Alternatively, I did not even have a teacher who encouraged my academic skills in English writing and in football. So, there is an element of fortune involved for those who succeed in developing *their* innate abilities and creativity. What Robinson had tapped into explores the deficiency in the education systems that actually dumbs down the student and fails to allow true creative expression.

He used the example of Paul McCartney to emphasize his point of teachers failing to see the talent in their students. Paul McCartney and George Harrison, of the Beatles, went to the same school: Liverpool Institute. Clearly, anybody studying the life and times of these two Liverpudlians know that they possessed a great deal of creative talent and energy. Yet according to Robinson, McCartney spent most of his time at school "fooling around" and focused largely on listening to rock n roll music (Robinson 2009, pp. 10–11). Meaning, he focused on what was right for *his* creative expression, and not what the school was offering. For example, the music teacher at his school did not even recognize McCartney's musical talent, which sounds preposterous given the immense reservoir of creativity he has produced since his school days. What is particularly ironic, McCartney and Harrison's school became derelict in the 1980s, was brought back to life by the former Beatle, and is now a prestigious performing arts school. Robinson attended an equivalent school to McCartney called Liverpool Collegiate, which ended up as a luxury set of apartments. The point here is, McCartney had enough influence to turn his creativity into reforming his old school into a performing arts institution. Had he attended Liverpool Collegiate that school would most probably be the performing arts school and the former Liverpool Institute would no doubt be the luxury set of flats. It is simply a matter of fortune—but the schooling experience that Robinson explains is paramount in understanding the involvement of school children who do not fit into the tight mold of curriculum uniformity.

Although Ken Robinson is profoundly insightful, in comprehending the stifling nature of the British education system, he missed one crucial *element* (pardon the pun): racialization. In other words, for all his pedagogical analysis there is no focus on antiracism and improving the education systems that produce generation after generation of white privilege. Also, as important as it is to consider the *individual* experience in schools, it is equally important to consider *community* too. Keep in mind, for example, McCartney and Harrison, and Robinson, are all white men and actually attended *very good* schools in Liverpool. Now, if they can have an experience whereby their talents are not tapped into, what chance then does the average Black child have attending a working-class comprehensive school? Because Liverpool Institute and Liverpool Collegiate were two of the prestigious schools to attend in the city during the 1950s. So, not to dismiss Robinson's importance in how individualized talent should be mined from each child, there is an imperative to counter the institutionalized inequality that manifests in a number of salient ways: monolithic curriculum that extols white history and achievement; social stratification endorsement in keeping working-class persons in working-class occupations; targeting of Black boys as both delinquent and deleterious to white society (Christian 2005b; Coard 1991; Saakana and Pearse 1986).

There are more ways to impact and reinforce a negative outlook for Black children and that is well documented, and this aspect of the education system is unfortunately not considered by Robinson. The point is, though McCartney spent a great deal of his time at school messing around, he was never excluded. He was still a choir boy, and he continued to develop positively and confidently in society as it implicitly endorsed him as a white boy who would become one of the most famous humans on planet Earth in due course. For Black children who "mess around" in school the punishment has most often meant permanent exclusion, particularly in relation to Black boys. In Liverpool, the history of Black underachievement has followed the entire history of British education, and this is probably of no surprise to the reader. Later, there will be a consideration of education reports that emerged in the 1980s. Whereas education is a salient aspect in determining life chances, it does not necessarily guarantee success if one "does well" at school. Nor, has institutionalized education been the paramount way to achieve in society for Blacks. Most often it has been sport or music that produced the successful individuals, and it could be contended this only happens because white society has opened up to Black competitiveness in sports. As for music, the talent of Black folks has never been able to be curtailed, though it has been extremely appropriated.

RACISM IN FOOTBALL AND LIVERPOOL—1970s TO 1980s

Besides the Beatles, perhaps the most famous cultural aspect of the City of Liverpool in the twentieth and twenty-first centuries is in its two major football teams: Everton Football Club (EFC) and Liverpool Football Club (LFC). In the early 1970s both teams in the city were chasing honors, but it was LFC who would dominate the decade as the best team in the land and much of Europe led by the great and late Bill Shankly (1913–1981). Originally from Scotland and a former professional footballer, he became the manager of LFC in 1959. He immediately began to transform the club into a winning enterprise. Shankly had risen from humble beginnings and was the epitome of being called "a man of the people" in Liverpool. If an academic can speak of "class" in a social stratification sense, then Shankly was a diehard working-class hero, a great human being who disliked "greedy buggers" who fleeced the ordinary working man and woman. Well, this ethos of his was delivered in kind via his football teams who played with passion and enthusiasm. The team embodied the spirit of Shankly and this philosophy transferred to the fans. Unfortunately, and this could not be attributed directly to him, racist chants emanating from many of the Liverpool supporters who watched the games were a ubiquitous feature at games in the 1970s and 1980s in Britain.

By all accounts, and in public, Shankly was not a racist; he seemed far too human for such a small-minded attribute. Moreover, it would be unlikely given Shankly's grounding in life and experience of coalmines—it is not being facetious to note that coalminers often comprehend the experience of Black people. They understand the visceral nature of Blackness due to spending their lives in coalmines. Yes, they can wash the black coal off come the end of a shift, but there is something about the miners that speaks to broader humanity. They understand hard graft and the difficult living conditions endured only serve to allow for greater empathy for others. This is not idealism; there is something about the miners that gives them a sense of humanity not found in other working life.

Take, for instance, how the Welsh miners embraced the great African American artist Paul Robeson (1898–1976), who wrote: "I have an invitation from the South Wales Miners to sing at the Miners' Singing Festival on October 6, 1956, and in a series of concerts in the mining valley thereafter" (Robeson 1978, p. 435). The year 1956 was during the civil rights fight against segregation and racism in America, and for the Welsh miners to openly embrace Robeson, an outspoken advocate for equality, was also an indication of their outright support—a humanity that Shankly also shared for the oppressed. Indeed, Shankly opens up his autobiography with the words:

"I was born in a little coal-mining village called Glenbuck, about a mile from the Ayrshire-Lanarkshire border " (Shankly 2009, p. 31). There was an honesty about Shankly that was infectious—he was an ordinary soul who had an extraordinary personality—a man of vision, pride, salt of the earth, who gave strength to anyone who met him.

I recall meeting Shankly one Liverpool spring day in 1977. He had parked his purple Ford Capri in Osborne Road, where I lived at that time, and he was heading toward the NatWest Bank on its corner with West Derby Road. As Shankly came walking toward the bank, with a swagger like the 1940s film star James Cagney, I was heading in the opposite direction with a pair of trousers over my shoulder that I had just picked up from Johnson's the cleaners. Shankly in his deep Scottish accent uttered with a smile, "Hello son!" . . . in shock and awe, I replied, as any other starstruck sixteen-year-old would, "Arrright Bill!"—and that was that. Shankly disappeared into the bank to deal with his personal business. Yet that serendipitous meeting left a deep impression on me. I had met the great Bill Shankly and he had recognized me as a fellow human being to bid him a greeting too. I recall having a grin from cheek-to-cheek all the way home. Then, of course, I spent the rest of the day trying to tell anyone who would listen in the family what had happened at the top of "our road" today. By this time, however, Shankly had retired as the manager of LFC by about three years, and the club would go on to win the European Cup that same year for the very first time in May 1977.

I attended my first LFC match at Anfield in the fall of 1972, aged eleven years, whereby I entered the ground once the doors had been opened during the latter part of the second half period to allow fans to leave the stadium, this would permit about twenty minutes of spectating. I was always a fan of the team but it developed more rapidly with my forays to Anfield to watch them play. I grew up watching players such as Kevin Keegan, John Toshack, Emlyn Hughes, Ray Clemence, and later Kenny Dalglish, Howard Gayle, and John Barnes. The latter two players, Gayle and Barnes, relate specifically to the Liverpool Black experience. Howard Gayle, a teenage friend of mine, was the first Black player to play for LFC. He only played five times for the first team but it was a major breakthrough for Liverpool Born Blacks as he played often for the Liverpool reserve team. In hindsight, had Howard been a white player he would undoubtedly have played more games for the team because he had lightning speed. He was very strong; one time he played with our friends in Sefton Park, and I was in the opposing team. What we call a "kick about game" and I came up against Howard—it was like hitting iron, his strength was impressive. From 1977 to 1983 he was with LFC before leaving for another British team.

Regardless of the shenanigans that forced him to leave for other pastures, he broke through a major barrier because LFC was known as a "white club" until Howard Gayle gave them some color. He had to deal with racism from *within* the club at the time. It is hoped that Shankly would have stamped out that ignorance had he still been the manager, but it was Bob Paisley in charge. Howard recalls his meeting with Shankly, again in 1977 but at Melwood, the LFC training facility. Shankly would visit on occasion as he loved to be involved with the game even in retirement. Gayle states:

> He placed his arm around my shoulder and said, "You've got so much pace, nobody will catch you, son. And you could catch pigeons! All you need to do is knock it into space and get after it . . . " I looked around, to my left and to the right. "Bloody hell," I thought, "Bill Shankly just spoke . . . to me!" (Gayle 2016, p. 90).

This explains why it is easy to suggest Shankly harbored no racial ignorance. Howard was a young reserve team player at LFC, and there is the great socialist, Bill Shankly, giving him words of encouragement that made him feel two inches taller. That is exactly how I too felt meeting Shankly by accident in Tuebrook on that spring day in 1977, actually, not far from where Howard Gayle grew up in Norris Green. It seems that the Scottish man of grit had the same feeling on all who met him and had the fortune to learn from him. Sadly, this cannot be stated about a so-called LFC legend, Tommy Smith, who gave young Gayle a hard time calling him the usual negative epithets that ignorant whites call Black persons. As Gayle recalls, Smith represented his "biggest problem at Liverpool" and he did this trying to "distract me by making nasty comments related to the colour of my skin" (Gayle 2016, pp. 95–96). Smith was the antithesis to Shankly, and this is strange because he worshiped the man. As Gayle contended, Smith was a diehard racist and a bully but young Gayle eventually stood up to him, as he was no pushover. In fact, if Smith had ever decided to go beyond name-calling, it is highly likely he would not have survived a fist-fight with the young lean and tough Howard Gayle—it would have been over and done rather rapidly—after all, bullies tend to be cowards when actually confronted head-on.

Football and racism are often interwoven, and it is something that still impacts the 2020s; one only has to Google "Football and Racism" to find almost 180 million hits. However, back in the 1970s to 1980s racism was much worse in British society. What Howard Gayle encountered came from *within* and outside of LFC. He broke through a racialized barrier in order to allow the first Black football superstar to emerge in John Barnes, who joined LFC in 1987. There was a tremendous "anti-John Barnes" feeling when he first joined Liverpool; today there is again some kind of historical amnesia to this fact because John Barnes would eventually become a legend in the ranks of LFC folklore. In a cup-tie game that took place in October 1987 against the local rivals EFC, their fans chanted, "Niggerpool, Niggerpool, Niggerpool!" and "Everton are White, Everton are White, Hello!" This was in relation to John Barnes being in the LFC team. It was an awful indictment of English professional football and on the City of Liverpool. If truth be told, there were literally thousands of LFC supporters too who did not want John Barnes in their team initially. This may sound rather prehistoric given the number of Black and brown players who wear the LFC shirt today, but we are considering something that is not more that thirty-five years ago. In a sense, times have changed in terms of the participation of Black players on the field of play, but one could argue still for a greater need to end racism off the field. On reflection of John Barnes' experience, Dave Hill wrote in his book *Out of His Skin: The John Barnes Phenomenon* regarding that specific game:

> The blue choir [EFC fans chanting obscenities] made their feelings known, and it was a symbolic demonstration. Liverpool versus Everton in the Littlewoods Cup was not just a football match. It was a night when all the [racist] skeletons in Merseyside football's closet stepped ghoulishly into the spotlight. Despite the failure of LWT's [London Weekend Television] match commentator and programme presenter to draw attention to it, the brutal undertow to prejudice to which Barnes's mere presence was provocation could no longer be ignored (Hill 2001, p.184).

The fact is simple, John Barnes was a brilliant Black footballer of Jamaican British heritage who had to deal with outward racism playing for an all-white team at LFC. EFC supporters were the fierce local rivals, who did not currently have any Black players in their team, and a significant group of them were chanting the vilest of racial obscenities in relation to John Barnes' presence that night. All the while, the commentator, Martin Tyler, ignored it. According to Hill there was some condemnation the next day on a local radio program in Liverpool. Yet, overall, the newspapers failed to mention the appalling behavior from the racist element of EFC fans, which not only involved abusive chanting but also the throwing of bananas onto the pitch. What happened to John Barnes that night was not particularly unique; all Black British footballers received racial abuse in the 1970s and 1980s. Racism in football continues to be a problem in Britain and across Europe—one wonders if it shall ever be obliterated.

Even when John Barnes was playing for England a chant from a section of racist supporters sang in unison: "There Ain't No Black in the Union Jack, Johnny Barnes, Johnny Barnes!"—which effectively meant to those chanting that they did not want him in the England team. Other Black players have articulated what they went through during this era. In a book titled *Racism and Antiracism in Football* the authors cite Cyrille Regis, a Black British player who played for West Bromwich Albion in the middle to late 1970s, who stated:

> Racism came in the form of letters, chanting from the crowds, banana throwing, monkey chanting, songs, and not just one or two but thousands singing racial abuse, chants, that kind of stuff, and letters through the post. I remember one time I got picked to play for England for the first time, and I got a letter saying that if I actually stepped onto Wembley Park I would get a bullet through the knees, and there was a bullet in the letter as well, wrapped up in cotton wool (cited in Garland and Rowe 2001, p. 1).

The only good thing that came out of the appalling chant from the England fans to John Barnes is that it became an award-winning book title for Paul Gilroy's 1987 *There Ain't No Black in the Union Jack.* The intimidation that Cyrille Regis received is difficult to conceive in the 2020s. However, if one considers social media and the racial abuse of Black British players then it has certainly not gone away, it has merely morphed into other forms of articulation via social media. Simply put, the players of the past may have received more graphic displays of racism in football, with unsavory abuse, but it would be rather naïve to think that it is something that remains in the past given the vile racism that emanates from social media.

In relation to EFC and LFC they have a large percentage share of Black players in both teams in the 2020s. This is clearly a sign of progress in the professional game; yet there is still a long way to go in the game itself due to a distinct lack of Black football coaches and managers. Moreover, perhaps it is too sanguine to expect racism to disappear from all areas of social life when it has been so firmly ingrained into the fabric of society. It is not enough to silence the racists, but it is necessary to root out what allows it to fester. Showing zero tolerance signs from the football community may merely take the racists underground—maybe if the football authorities actually went further by creating spaces for proper dialogue instead of avoidance of such verbal and physical violence. There can only be true progress when the present generation learn from the past. Indeed, reading the accounts of former Black footballers like Howard Gayle, John Barnes, and Cyrille Regis can certainly give warning to what can occur if outright racism is allowed to fester while enjoying the game of professional football.

LIVERPOOL 8 AMATEUR FOOTBALL 1970s–1980s

Many football teams developed in the 1970s and 1980s (Gayle 2016). Along with my brother Garry Christian, we played for the Caribbean Football Club in 1978 based on Upper Parliament Street and Grove Street in Liverpool 8. Garry is a tall six foot and four inches, but he did not last long playing football because he did not have the skills to survive. He was more orientated toward singing and music and proved that by becoming a "soul-pop-star" in the late 1980s onward. However, I stayed with the Caribbean FC for three seasons, winning a major amateur cup in 1980. I do recall having an awful game in the cup final as a center forward, but the team still won 2–0 and that is all that counts. The Caribbean FC could not win the league due to another Liverpool 8 team, the Stanley House Football Club, having more experience and better players. Nevertheless, we had some good games against them, these were "derby games" that brought out a large crowd from the community to Sefton Park—football was in fact a great community activity and allowed for friendship to flourish among Liverpool Born Blacks and their friends. The teams were made up of majority Black players, with maybe one or two white players, which was an interesting scenario as in this one cultural activity the tables were turned on white society in Liverpool—Blacks were actually in the majority.

Some of the players in the Caribbean FC were hardcore community activists who often organized marches to protest various forms of racism. Men like Dave Clay and Joey Joel were experienced players in amateur football and acted as de facto role models for myself and other younger Black players. They were also articulate and determined Black activists and one could learn from them how they carried themselves with confidence and humor. Dave Smith was our trainer and he would have the team running into the city center when the team went on a run for exercise. He was a true larger-than-life character, a great man to be around because he did not give any thought to racists—he was tough and I developed much respect for him. In those days, 1978 to 1981, I was a quiet soul who was the youngest player in the Caribbean FC team. Therefore, I was wise enough to listen and learn from the elders who had up to ten years or more experience than I had in football and life generally. In hindsight, it was a period in my life whereby I soaked up all that was possible culturally from playing in this largely Black Liverpudlian team. My best friend during this period was Chris Oye, a chef, who was always somehow employed due to his brilliance; he was strong and courageous in his game too. Another player who went on to be a skilled Black British academic was also part of the Caribbean FC set-up in the late 1970s—Barnor Hesse. Overall, there was something very special about playing with a Liverpool 8 based football team because it involved both community activism and sport.

Playing football in Liverpool was a great escape for me. Along with singing a cappella with my brothers, from age seventeen to twenty-seven years I played football regularly. During this period I made a number of close friends and would spend time socializing in the various nightclubs that allowed for

Black Liverpudlians. Quinns and Kirklands were my favorite hang-outs on Friday and Saturday nights with friends, and often family. These were great times because youthfulness allows for confidence and intellectual growth. Playing football in a winning team also gives extra self-confidence. Moreover, it keeps your body fit and healthy too; if you wanted to play well and keep your place in the team one had to stay fit. You had to prove to your teammates that they could rely on you during a game, and Liverpool 8 teams came up against difficult circumstances playing in areas where Blacks were not welcome. That was certainly a challenge to your courage because it was not just football, it was about having the right attitude to deal with the name-calling and racial epithets hurled at the team from the opposition support. Some players lost their tempers under the heat of racial abuse and would fight, get sent off, and this would only be detrimental to the team. So, having a cool head in tricky situations encountering white racism was a key factor in being a successful Black player in Liverpool in the 1980s.

I joined Saana FC in the summer of 1982. The sponsor of the team was originally from Yemen, Mr. Ahmed—but "Kojak" was the pseudonym he was known by. Kojack owned a local grocery store on North Hill Street, Liverpool 8, that sold alcohol and other beverages. His favorite football teams were Argentina and Brazil, so he got the team Argentina shirts in the first season in the Huyton and Sunday District League. Saana FC won the League and two cups in the first season of competitive play in 1982–1983. By then I played in my favorite position—center midfield, right side. Here I excelled, scoring on average ten to fifteen goals a season. I scored a number of crucial goals that won games for the team, and my confidence grew with the team because we rarely suffered defeat. It was arguably the best time I had experienced in life, being twenty-one years old, playing in a successful amateur football team, and making odd appearances in local events singing with my brothers. Life could not be better during this period, apart from the continued experience of racism in the city, even while playing amateur football (Burdsey 2011; Christian 2011; Gayle 2016).

In the fall of 1983, Kojack arranged for the team to visit Yemen for a football tournament. Here is an example of the absurdity of racialized classification. The majority of the team had African or African Caribbean fathers, only one player on the team had heritage that could be deemed part Yemeni. Yet, the team was going out to Yemen as representatives of their immigrant diaspora. Many of the team actually changed their names for their passports, but I refused to do that. I would travel with my birth name as "Mark Christian" or not go at all. With a name like "Christian" I wondered if it was even possible in a Muslim nation, but it was and I joined my teammates for the trip of a lifetime aged twenty-two years. The irony of racial identity is that the team of essentially Liverpool Born Blacks were "faking" a Yemeni identity.

It was an interesting experience in Saana because the team were treated like superstars in the town. There was no war conflict at this time, President Ali Abdullah Saleh actually proved to be a great host, and Saana FC even walked in a procession to celebrate their civil war from 1962 that created the Yemen Republic. It was a surreal experience for all the young Black Liverpudlians; in fact it would have made for a unique film because fiction could not create such a scenario. On top of everything, Saana FC won the tournament and would become heroes to the Yemeni people during the three-week sojourn. I recall distinctly that the people of Yemen were a wonderful people to meet, there was no animosity, just smiles and friendliness from the locals. It was my first experience in an Arab nation; they were a brown people and looked very much like the average Black Liverpudlian. It was an experience that gave me an added insight into a different culture, and way of life. One of the trickiest aspects was going to the toilet! A hole in the floor and a crouching that contorted the sinews. Thankfully, I was wise enough to bring a roll of toilet paper for the trip. Cultures differ, and Yemen taught me how to adapt and respect other peoples' norms and values without judgment. It was one of the best times I have had in life; sharing those three weeks with a group of Black Liverpudlians in Yemen was definitely a unique and rewarding experience.

On leaving Yemen, as we embarked the coach that would eventually take us to the airport, for some odd reason Yemen soldiers held the team up and commenced to have a conversation with the driver. There was an exchange with the soldiers, driver, and our interpreters. We had the winning cup on board the coach, and most of the Black Liverpudlians were perplexed about what was happening, but after about ten minutes the soldiers suddenly left just as quickly as they had arrived. It was a little scary as the team had no idea what it was all about, and to this day it has never been fully explained—the incident remains a mystery. Crucially, the team "escaped" to the airport and traveled back home to England as tournament winners on foreign soil. Indeed, it was the trip of a lifetime for those young Black men from Liverpool, many of whom had never traveled so far by plane. Travel opens the mind, and what happened to that group of young men during the tournament gave them an insight into what it takes to stick together and enjoy each other's company outside of Liverpool. They had relied on one another, and had learned to respect another culture; and they grew from having to spend a long time away from the city where they were born and raised. This was a football trip that would go down in folklore history in Liverpool 8, and the Saana FC team of 1983 was also one of the best the community had ever produced. To be frank, a number of the players could have turned professional if there was greater opportunity for such Black talent. The opportunities continued to be few and far between for Black players to break through to the ranks of professional football in the early 1980s.

GRASSROOTS EDUCATION AND THE CHARLES WOOTTON CENTRE/COLLEGE

If football was an important aspect of community welfare for Black Liverpudlians, then grassroots education would be just as vital to the prospects of many young men and women wanting to get ahead in life. As mentioned earlier, mainstream education for Black British children was pretty dismal in the 1970s and 1980s. Too many children were failing in the school system and this brought about more social problems due to many unqualified youths not being able to find adequate employment. To add to this difficulty there were the usual problems with institutional racism. In the early 1980s there was a lack of jobs in the city for the majority white population, and this being the situation it would then be double the rate of unemployment for Liverpool Born Blacks (Brown 1979, 1986). There had to be something done about the appalling number of young Black men and women who were leaving school without adequate qualifications in the city.

A government description of education for British minority cultures was documented in what is now referred to as the Swann Report (1985). This was a report covering the problems of immigrant communities having difficulties adjusting to the British education system. Rather incongruous is chapter fifteen being titled "The Educational Needs of 'Liverpool Blacks'" because it is a report that largely related to language difficulties; yet this cultural group were born going back two, three, and more generations of Black British heritage. In other words, Liverpool Blacks were fully acclimated to the British way of life—so to speak. Moreover, this Black British cultural group did not have any problems with language or having been born in another nation. They were no different, other than skin color and the racism they encountered, to the majority of white British citizens. Yet they were having great difficulty in the Liverpool schools gaining academic success in terms of receiving qualifications. This was something to do with how young Blacks in Liverpool were treated by the education system itself, a structural and white cultural problem manifesting from ingrained racism. In the foreword of the report, the then British Member of Parliament Sir Keith Joseph wrote:

> The government is firmly committed to the principle that all children, irrespective of race, colour or ethnic origin, should have a good education which develops their abilities and aptitudes to the full and brings about a true sense of belonging to Britain (Swann Report 1985, p. ii).

These were pretty sounding words from a British government representative that had little substance in the average experience of Liverpool Born Blacks. "Race" has certainly denied many from achieving their full potential in schools that actually failed them. Victor Christian was one of the lucky Liverpool Blacks to achieve in mainstream secondary education due to a forward-looking educationalist. Indeed, this has been claimed to have been due primarily to the kindness of one schoolteacher, Mr. Ahearn, during his time in Comprehensive School. Clearly, given the evidence from the Swann Report of 1985, there were not many "kind teachers" in Liverpool schools if many Black children were failing to get the qualifications on paper needed to succeed in society. In the 1980s it was an institutional issue that needed to be solved if things were to turn around for future generations. There developed a greater interest in education due to the 1981 uprisings and with that concerned community leaders were ready to address the problem.

Because of the problems in mainstream education at the secondary school level, Wally Brown argued that it was "normal" for young Black adults in Liverpool to return to school for the basic qualifications they did not receive in the schooling system. He argued this in his master's thesis (Brown 1986), and he knew very well the terrain because he too was a mature student taking a degree later in life. Basically, he argued that Liverpool Blacks were actually being set up for failure and that is the reason it was necessary to have an alternative educational grassroots community structure in place as a way to get talented individuals back on a successful education track if they indeed wanted to pursue a professional career.

Chapter fifteen, point one, of the Swann Report reveals an insightful British cultural observation of this seemingly unique Liverpool Black experience:

> We have included "Liverpool Blacks" in our report for two reasons. Firstly, this group has probably, we believe, fared worse than any other we have described, with the exception of travellers [Gypsies], in its educational and career achievements, and therefore has a particularly strong claim to the consideration and positive action which we hope will arise out of our findings. Secondly, and paradoxically, this group appears to be more closely assimilated with the "majority" by ancestry, language, culture, and length of residence than any of the others [cultural minority populations] we have looked at. Its experiences therefore lead us to ask new questions, both about this particular group itself and about many of the accepted assumptions concerning ethnicity (Swann Report 1985, p. 733).

There it is, a government report acknowledging the in-depth discriminatory practices and outcomes against the Liverpool Born Black population. Indeed, there had to be something awry in the education system for Black school children to, overall, fair so badly at the secondary level. What is important about this fact being acknowledged is because it emanates from an authoritative study of racialized relations in education. It baffled the investigators that a Black British born population group could have such a negative outcome. No doubt the racists would have argued that this was due to biological inferiority because most of the Liverpool Black population had Black mixed heritage. The stereotypes do not often match the reality as Blacks of "mixed heritage" are allegedly supposed to be more intelligent than their "full Black" counterparts in racist folklore. This of course is a ridiculous notion but it has long lived in the annals of pseudoscientific racism and sociological circles from the past and present.

Take the noted sociologist Robert E. Park, for example, who wrote extensively on racist mumbo jumbo relating to "hybrid humans" (Park 1928, 1931). His work on "human hybridity" should be consigned to an academic dustbin but sadly it is still being recycled into modern sociological discourse. Certainly, a recent scholar revisited Park's "marginal man" which is an extension of the "human hybrid" and is just as problematic in essence. Goldberg writes in 2012 lauding the contemporary importance of Park:

> Who now reads Robert Park? The answer, it turns out, is that many still do, and with good reason. Robert Ezra Park (1864–1944) was one of the leading figures in what has come to be known as the Chicago school of sociology, which played a central and formative role in American sociology as a whole, especially from 1914 to 1933 when he taught at the University of Chicago (Goldberg 2012, p. 199).

Too often there is no accountability in the manner racialized sociology from a white perspective is retrieved from the past and fed to contemporary graduate students who will then go on to teach the same twaddle to a new generation of students—this is rather dangerous but it has occurred for centuries. Therefore, let us consider the Liverpool Born Black experience in relation to Park's theory on human hybridity because it reveals a glaringly methodological flaw in his assessment. For example, Park frames his analysis in deeply problematic pseudoscientific racist terms, firmly establishing "biologically superior and inferior races" in his sociological analysis that today should summarily be dismissed as bogus. But Goldberg (2012) has acclaimed Park to be worthy of sociological eminence in the twenty-first century. It is in the interest of the contemporary reader to consider the actual words of Robert E. Park. Writing in 1931 in an article titled "The Mentality of Racial Hybrids" he sets out his theoretical grounding in this manner:

> Racial hybrids are one of the natural and inevitable results of migration [voluntary and involuntary] and the consequent mingling of divergent racial stocks. The motives bringing peoples of divergent races and cultures together are, in the first instance, economic. In the long run, economic intercourse enforces more intimate personal and cultural relations, and eventually amalgamation takes place. When peoples involved are widely different in culture and in racial

characteristics, and particularly when they are distinguished by racial marks, assimilation and amalgamation takes place very slowly. . . . The *mixed blood tend everywhere to be*, as compared with the full bloods with whom they are identified, an intellectual and professional. The most obvious and generally accepted explanation of the superiority of the mixed bloods is that the former are the products of two races, one of which is biologically inferior [African/African Caribbean heritage] and the other biologically superior [any of the white mongrelized European heritage] [Italics my emphasis] (Park 1931, p. 534).

There are so many problems with Park's analysis that it is difficult to know where to start a critique. Perhaps in relation to Liverpool Born Blacks one can state he is clearly mistaken in his assumption that Black mixed heritage yields social mobility. The Swann Report from 1985, more than fifty years beyond Park's theory, makes a mockery of such a suggestion. Nevertheless, this stereotype has longevity regarding Blacks of mixed heritage getting some form of social privilege. This may be the case in the certain regions of the transatlantic paradigm, but it is *not* the case when it comes to a sociological analysis of the Liverpool Born Black experience. Liverpool Blacks have suffered consistent social discrimination in regard to their collective history in the City of Liverpool (Brown 1979, 1986; Christian 1995b, 2000, 2008a; Murphy 1995; Nelson 2000; Swann Report 1985). To be sure, what Park pontificated was merely static pseudoscientific verbiage. It may hold sway within the context of mainstream (read "white") sociological discourse, but it does not measure up under closer scrutiny as a universal law. Liverpool Blacks of mixed heritage clearly indicate that their experience is an anomaly compared to other Black settlements in predominately white space (Small 1991). Without exaggeration, there is a genuine racialized inheritance of discriminatory practice in Liverpool's Black history.

Of course, as Park elevated such, in every stereotype there is a kernel of truth that can be extrapolated in order to make it seem worthy. For example, Park mentions that migration inevitably creates mixed unions, whether they be human or cultural. This is not rocket science, any person comprehending the movement of peoples around the globe can gauge quite easily that they will unavoidably come into contact with the majority culture and its people. Some will remain close to their cultural foundation, but often there is a crossing of cultural boundaries. Yet to suggest as Park did that some humans, Black or brown, are biologically inferior and the other humans, of white heritage, are superior is just plainly and categorically fallacious. One cannot by rational-biology measure the intellectual and cultural worth of one human to another based on racialized characteristics—racism is the only thing that does that erroneously.

Therefore, when a scholar like Goldberg (2012) exalts the work of Robert E. Park he should be aware of his writings that clearly prove an openly racist and ethnocentric content. Significantly, Park should be read with caution and not paraded as a sociological guru because it is dangerous to elevate this kind of racialized thinking as Goldberg, maybe unwittingly, did. This does not mean one should not engage intellectually with the likes of Park; on the contrary, he should be thoroughly examined. The problem is that most white sociologists leave out the racist element of the past—or dilute it for a contemporary palate of a more "sophisticated" generation when it comes to racialized matters. The problem with Goldberg (2012) and this scenario is that the social theory of Park is far from being sophisticated. Moreover, racism is rampant in the 2020s British and United States context. White nationalist jingoism was evident in the Brexit issue in Britain, and Trumpism in the United States. One could rightly ask, what role has higher education and its "university presses" played in disseminating such racist ideas that emanate from renowned scholars such as Park? It is in the interest of the community, and scholars in academia, to engage unreservedly with racist literature in a deeper philosophical manner. Particularly in the area of philosophy as there is much to be done before we can consider it antiracist (Mills 2017, 1997). For Africana critical studies it is imperative to critique anything that undermines African humanity (Asante and Dove 2021).

When I left secondary school in 1977, aged sixteen years, I decided to do painting on a government "Job Creation" scheme for teenagers. This only lasted twelve months and I would continue to learn about life working with my elder brother Roger in construction. Along with playing football on the weekends and singing a cappella, I learned how to drive and got my full license at eighteen years of age. I had also left "26"—the family home—to branch out as an independent adult. However, I was itching to get back into education. The opportunity came when my elder sister Rita talked to me about her time at the Charles Wootton Centre in Liverpool 8 from 1979 to 1980. She was on the course with her Black girlfriends and explained to me that there were Black teachers and that they offered classes in English, Black history, math, and other disciplines. Intrigued, I signed up for the course that started in the fall of 1980. I was nineteen years of age, I had a car, a studio apartment in Kelvin Grove, Liverpool 8, and a nice Afro that I groomed with artistic perfection to be round and bold.

In 1980, the director of the Charles Wootton Centre, which was known colloquially as the "Charlie," was Ms. Janet Barrett, a dark-skinned attractive woman with a short neat Afro. She was not from Liverpool originally, like other Black employees at the time. But one could surmise she was a Black and proud woman who was endeavoring to empower the Liverpool Black community through grassroots education. All of my teachers in the class of

1980–1981 were Black and this was like a dream for me to experience. My math teacher was Ben Agwuna (Chief Ben) from the Ibo people of Nigeria. It is widely known among Africana peoples that the Ibos are excellent in math; they have a natural gift and only the creator can explain such a phenomenon. Now, consider how math for African heritage peoples in the African Diaspora has been de-culturalized out of the average Black person. The skill has effectively been denied by generations of white teachers who have suppressed the intellect of millions of Black children over centuries. Math now to the average child is a horrible experience. This is what I endured in my secondary school years in the British education system. However, at the age of six years I was awarded a gold star for math from my primary school headmistress, Ms. Wilkes. Whatever happened to that potential I had in math is probably again due to poor teaching, but I never developed an aptitude for pure math as time progressed. However, when I started the Charles Wootton Centre the apprehension began to disappear with the prompting of Chief Ben, who developed a relationship with me that was based on a respect for one another. Quite frankly, I was in awe of all these teachers of African heritage who were there to put back what the mainstream education system had taken: confidence in one's academic abilities.

For those readers skeptical of African intellectual virtuosity, one should take time out to read a book by the noted writer Basil Davidson. A white British writer who must go down in history as one of the most honest and fair-minded who never pandered to the folly of white supremacist balderdash. He even gained the academic respect of the African American educator and scholar John Henrik Clarke for his work on African history. This particular book is rather rare and first published in 1969: *The African Genius: An Introduction to African Social and Cultural History*. For a book that is surprisingly over half a century old, it bears the resemblance of a useful introduction into how Africa was denied its place on the historical plain of human evolution and civilization. Davidson had a deep respect for African history and found it "strange" how some of his fellow white historians had maligned the continent. Maybe he was ahistorical and apolitical, but most scholars in Africana critical studies are fully cognizant as to why Africa and its history has been abused by European writers and it all basically goes back to enslavement, colonialism, and imperialism. The conquering of the African continent is a reason why the ancient history has been distorted by European writers— again this is not that complicated to consider (Asante 2007a). Another book worth reading by Basil Davidson is titled *The Lost Cities of Africa* whereby he traces many affluent kingdoms that thrived on the continent more than fifteen hundred years before European vessels first arrived on African shores.

In considering Chief Ben at the Charlie, as an Ibo/African he was very proud of Africa and always possessed a sense of confidence in his people. Davidson explains the vitality of the Ibo in this manner:

> The flexibility [of Ibo culture] was perhaps a function of the natural fertility and farming wealth of Iboland. . . . By the sixteenth century, and probably much earlier, simple forms of subsistence economy flanked by a minimal exchange of manufactures, locally produced, had given way to more complex economies in which a division of labour was able to support markets every four days or eight days (Davidson 1969, p. 93).

Perhaps, in attending the Charlie, my most optimal experience was joining Black studies classes with my fellow Liverpool Born Blacks. Actually, there were also two elders from Somali in the class who also attended, former sailors who had settled in Liverpool. They were endeavoring to improve their life skills like the rest of the classmates. The Black studies teacher was Ron "Babatunde" Phillips, who was the elder sibling of two prominent Black British writers and journalists: Mike and Trevor Phillips. Apparently, they had arrived in Britain as young boys in the 1950s from Guyana. Though they had not much wherewithal, they rose to become famous and have received recognition in British society. Trevor has worked for the BBC and other British broadcasting outlets—he is a renowned journalist.

However, Babatunde was less appealing to mainstream Britain because he was a Pan Africanist thinker and activist, whereas his younger brothers did what they could to improve themselves by being less political in their pursuit of success. This is the price of the ticket—so to speak—when it comes to individual success in a predominantly white society for people of color. One is faced with the question: Does one assimilate or stay within one's cultural boundaries? Most often there is no choice for a person of color as a society based on racialized hierarchy will not open up life opportunities if one is deemed an outsider. Therefore, the more one assimilates toward the dominant cultural norms and shows no response to racist microaggressions, the more likely is her or his success in British society.

Babatunde taught with passion and knowledge, and he wrote a children's book that he shared with the class. In hindsight, it revealed a story about a little Black girl who developed a positive consciousness based on her heritage. The book is called *Ndidi's Story* and the author is simply "Babatunde"—the pseudonym for Ron I. Phillips with the copyright symbol. In the publication data it states: "First published in 1980 by the Pan-African Publishing Co-operative" and it has a citation from Amilcar Cabral that states: " The children are our flowers and the principal reason for our fight" (Phillips 1980, p. 1). Importantly, I and my fellow classmates had a brilliant Black studies teacher who was grounded in his people. Babatunde only wanted the best for those Black Liverpudlians based in an urban setting and endeavoring to get knowledge that would empower our lives. In the copy of Babatunde's book, the inscription reads: "To my brother Mark as a small beginning of your own writing in the future. Forward youth—Babatunde." The inscription has stayed with me throughout my life; I felt the confidence that Babatunde had in me running through my veins because no one had ever described me before as having the potential to be a writer. Indeed, I recalled the day Mr. Redburn from my Primary School had scorned me when I gave him the biographical sketch of Pelé: "Go away Christian, you didn't write this." Yet there at the Charlie, ten years later, I was being praised for my budding prosperity as a writer in the future.

The reason Babatunde had written those words to me was in relation to the poetry I had produced as part of a class project. All of the poems were to be experiences of the Liverpool Black experience, from students who had taken courses at the Charlie. Babatunde organized and collected poems from those who wanted to write from the "Class of 1981"—I produced three poems. The title of the poetry publication is *Speaking for Themselves: Poems from the Charles Wootton Centre*. It is interesting to note that the poems were published in June of 1981, and in the following month the infamous Toxteth/Liverpool 8 uprising took place after a young Black man, Leroy Cooper, was harassed and arrested July 3rd on Granby Street, in the heart of Liverpool 8. The publication date is interesting because some of the poetry foretold such an event would occur because the outright discrimination against Liverpool Born Blacks in the city by police and other institutions was rife and reaching the boiling point. Take this poem by Jennifer Baker, who wrote it with a tinge of Jamaican patois, titled "Black and White Unite—Don't Fight":

> Why can't we all unite?
> Why we all have to fight?

(Class of 1981, p. 10)

Poems that spoke to the harsh social realities of life in Liverpool for Black persons are evident in this collection, and considering they represent such a poignant time in Liverpool's history it is strikingly sad how such poetry has not become nationally and internationally known. Another poem called "Playing" from Ahmed Y. Mohammed, is by one of the African elders in the class at the time. To paraphrase, his poetry spoke of how time passed so quickly, and how when he arrived in this "cold land" he could not speak English. It is a rather poignant poem from an African elder looking back at his life, and implicitly stating how the British school system was essentially able to allow him to fail in his studies.

So many, young and old, had lost out on a formal education because the system did not care for them to have one. There is no other way to explain this cultural reality. Black people were most often denied a decent education due to the institutional setting they entered. At the Charlie it is clear from the poetry produced that the students were free to express themselves, to be vulnerable and to share their sensitivity because Babatunde encouraged the class of 1981 to express inner feelings. In this sense, I had a formidable interest in Dr. Martin Luther King Jr., though I had not yet directly been exposed to Malcolm X at that time. I had, however, followed Muhammad Ali with great interest and respect since a young boy. In fact, I found him to be a great inspiration in terms of Black pride and keeping one's physical body in shape. But Dr. King was someone whom I had admired from whatever news I had absorbed and learned through documentaries and readings. I specifically admired his sense of humanity and his desire to reach out to all communities for peace. Yes, it was a tad naïve to think racists could ever become noble citizens of the world, but this is not the main point. Instead, it is the human spirit that should desire the best even if the worst in humanity exists. I wrote a poem titled "Remember Martin" which is basic but heartfelt, and I think in line with what Dr. King actually lived for during his lifetime:

> Please gather together
> For the message I do bring
> Is always to remember
> Martin Luther King
> The man who lived for freedom
> The man who had a dream
> To make us stand together
> As one and in a league
> To conquer hate and prejudice
> A source of evil means
> An end to segregation
> For him this was his dream
> Although he has passed on now
> His work will carry on
> To help us gain our freedom
> So as Blacks we must endeavour
> Never to be restrained
> To praise and sing of the man
> Martin Luther King

(Class of 1981, p. 10)

To put the Dr. Martin Luther King Jr. poem in greater context, it was derived from a teenager who had left the British school system without formal qualifications. But as educators have argued (Robinson 2009), often schools fail to bring out any form of talent possessed by creative individuals. This may not be the poetry of a seasoned poet, but it is rather profound for a Black Liverpool teenager studying in a poverty-stricken community with little resources for arts and culture. With this in mind, the class of 1981 of the Charles Wootton Centre, under the guidance of a master teacher in Babatunde, were able to express themselves within the setting of Black Liverpool. How I knew so much about Martin Luther King Jr. at such a young age baffles me to this day—there is something spiritual about this that cannot be fully explained.

I, for example, recall being in an art class at my Comprehensive School, and there was a blackboard with chalk. In art class one day I began to write a "Martin Luther King Jr. Speech" using phrases that came from my mind that Dr. King may have uttered. I wrote from the top to bottom on the blackboard and it gained the attention of the art teacher. He stood there reading what I had written, and then left the classroom. He returned shortly with a colleague to have him read the "speech" and they then looked at each other in astonishment. However, when his colleague left the room the art teacher said nothing to me directly to indicate whether it was good writing, but I surmised that it must have been good enough because he had left the room to get a colleague to read it. I was not punished or reprimanded for writing on the blackboard, therefore there was no profanity in what I had written. I was fifteen years old at the time, and it is another example of me being ignored for having written something of merit straight from my mind. At age fifteen, I wore an Afro hairstyle, and in the school report I received from this art teacher it reads: "When not worrying about the state of his dress he managed the odd piece of work" (Comprehensive School Report dated November 25, 1976). This is a rather unfair report given the dust that emanates from an art pottery class, whereby there were no overalls to wear to protect one's clothing from the clay and debris. I only had two pairs of trousers to use for school, and yes, I did always try to look clean and tidy. To use the fact that I wanted to keep clean against me was rather unsporting of the art teacher.

However, in comparison to mainstream schooling, I excelled in *all* of my classes at the Charlie. The difference was simple, I was recognized by the Black teachers and given confidence to improve my academic abilities. I was not someone who disregarded school work, but I was a Black youth who disregarded the attitude of white teachers. Especially those that appeared to have no interest in my potential, and if they did, they certainly kept it to themselves. The difference between my secondary school experience and the time spent at the Charlie was as varied as chalk and cheese. I was in "heaven" rather than "hell" in terms of my educational growth. Babatunde introduced the class of 1981 to the history of Marcus Garvey and the Universal Negro Improvement Association (UNIA). At this time, I had no idea who Garvey was and that my very *own* grandfather from Jamaica had worked with the UNIA while in Columbus, Ohio and Jamaica. It would be a further twenty-plus years before this family history would be revealed to me.

Overall, my time at the Charlie was replete with knowledge of Black history, various educational experiences, and social interaction with fellow Black students who were all working toward improving their life chances in a city that stifled them. The thing also unique about the Charlie was its location, it was based in one of the old merchant stately homes located on 248 Upper Parliament Street on the corner of Kingsley Road in Liverpool 8. It had a large basement and three upper floors. Originally, these houses were occupied by merchant traders once involved in the transatlantic slavery enterprise and beyond. It is ironic to think that in the latter part of the twentieth century young Black Liverpudlians were now benefiting from the building being employed as an educational establishment for mainly Liverpool's Black population. Indeed, music classes were taught during the evening and Victor Christian was one of the tutors—working in the community after he had completed his regular teaching role at Quarry Bank School—John Lennon's former school in Allerton.

The cook at the Charlie was named Hessie; she was a strong African Caribbean woman who made various Jamaican dishes with rice and peas, curry goat, chicken, fish, and her cabbage was delicious—I found her to be a wonderful human being. We could smell the food coming from her kitchen area on the second floor and we would race to get in line to order a plate of her scrumptious food. I made a lot of friends while at the Charlie, all Black Liverpudlians. There was Michael Greenidge and Joy Rogers whom I spent a lot of time with. Michael was very smart and had a political insight into Black issues that were impacting the community; he would often speak about the need for economic empowerment to develop among Black Liverpudlians. As for Joy, she needed help when it came to figuring out algebra equations given in Chief Ben's math class. I sat next to her in the math class and we would talk about our ambitions in life while working out equations together. It was a camaraderie we had never experienced before as we were an all-Black class. We were learning without a concern for our Black heritage being an impediment, in a classroom setting with an African mathematician—how could we fail? We did not; we all entered the exams and gained certificates in English, math, history, and other subjects. There were also trips to museums and the class would have recreation on Friday afternoons by attending a local gymnasium to play badminton, and Kwanzaa was celebrated in the December of 1980. Although Dr. Maulana Karenga created this holiday for African

Americans, it is also regarded as a Pan African holiday in many Black communities across the globe. This all took place in one short year from 1980 to 1981. Indeed, much happened at the Charlie in 1981 that needs to be covered in the following chapter, along with its importance as a key community organization in Liverpool 8. Crucially, on a journey to knowledge in Black history and culture, it was the best educational experience I had experienced in my short life. We shall return to the Charlie and its history again in chapter four.

ACCESS TO HIGHER EDUCATION IN LIVERPOOL 8

The educational qualifications attained at the Charles Wootton Centre were the equivalent to the American version of the General Educational Development (GED). There were some vocational qualifications one could receive if wanting to get into secretarial and receptionist work. But for those Black Liverpudlians wanting to get a degree in a university setting without formal "A-Levels" one needed to take a Mature Matriculation exam, and this was not available at the Charlie. Therefore, the Access to Higher Education located on Grove Street in Liverpool 8 emerged in the early 1980s, as a way to combat the dire lack of Black Liverpudlians getting into higher education. It was set up after the Toxteth/Liverpool 8 uprising in the community in 1981 (see chapter four) as a way to ameliorate this glaring social problem. In other words, there was clearly a need to arrest the continuing significance of racism in the mainstream education system that was stifling Black Liverpudlian progress. The Charlie could only do so much, the number of students it could handle a year was around sixty and that was capacity. The need for greater educational opportunities was obvious to all involved and grassroots community organizers in consultation with the Liverpool City College set up what came to be known locally as the "L8 Access to H/E" which secured university entry level classes.

The course was offered either full-time for a one-year duration, or part-time over two years. The level of education was the equivalent to A-Level standard and among the subjects were English, Math, geography, sociology, Black history, and global studies. It was intense for those who participated, and it meant a significant amount of study time as it entailed a Monday to Friday schedule like the Charlie. Quite a number of the Black community persons benefited from this course and it led to them gaining professional careers in various fields such as social work, probationary officers, and as housing officers. It was a worthwhile development and necessary for the Liverpool 8 and surrounding areas to progress positively. As Wally Brown had argued vociferously, "Liverpool Blacks had been underdeveloped for decades" (Brown 1979), and though many came into higher education a little later than their white counterparts, because of a more mature outlook they often surpassed the average white student due to sheer determination and focus while at university.

After I left the Charles Wootton Centre/College, and against the wishes of my teachers, I tried out on another government scheme—this time outside of Liverpool near Manchester—for bricklaying. I learned how to lay bricks and it was something I really enjoyed. However, I was too slow in laying the bricks to ever make it as a professional bricklayer. Nevertheless, I did use the bricklaying skill to do jobs for myself, family members, and friends. In hindsight, I learned early to use my "head and hands" just as Booker T. Washington had taught his students at Tuskegee Institute in the nineteenth and early twentieth centuries (Christian 2021). Moreover, I later earned a living as a taxicab driver and again this gave me a profound insight into different types of people one can meet in the city. What better way is there to learn sociology other than by actually meeting and talking to different people all day? I was in my mid-twenties when the urge to "go back to school" set in and I decided to enroll on the access to higher education course in Liverpool 8.

However, it was a continuing interest in Black history that sparked my imagination for greater education. Even at the L8 Access to H/E there was a teacher who introduced Black British history and he was a very good teacher, a Liverpool Born Black, Brian Khader. The class of 1989 was predominately Liverpool Born Black and from the city. The book we were given to read is by Peter Fryer titled *Staying Power: The History of Black People in Britain*. It is an insightful read, rich in the history of Black settlement and struggle within the British context, and his perception into Liverpool's involvement in the transatlantic enslavement system is eye-opening. There are a number of white British writers who have provided honest and scholarly studies on Black history, but the best of these have to be Peter Fryer, Basil Davidson, and James Walvin. Their collective works have provided a profound foundation to the understanding of British enslavement, its dissemination, and colonialism under what came to be known as the British Empire.

What is galling to those scholars in Africana critical studies is how contemporary scholars, such as David Olusoga in his *Black and British: A Forgotten History* (2016), fail to fully acknowledge the debt of previous scholars. Even the title of Olusoga's book reveals an arrogance that needs to be discussed. For example, there has been far too much Black British scholarship for it to be "a forgotten history"—it would be more relevant to have deemed it "an ignored history." Indeed, Olusoga is clearly aware of scholars from Black Liverpool who have written extensively on Black presence yet he openly failed to cite any of them. He is aware mainly because he received a degree in history, studying the history of slavery, from the University of Liverpool in the early 1990s. Olusoga was born in Lagos, Nigeria to a white British mother and Nigerian father; they migrated to England when he was five years old and he was raised in Gateshead, Town, and Wear in the north east of England. He has become a rare success as a Black Briton of mixed heritage—being awarded and receiving an Order of the British Empire (OBE) as a historian. This is troubling because it shows his work has been accepted by the establishment and it is anything but counter-hegemonic in analysis. The fact that he was educated at the University of Liverpool is also significant because that institution has done little if anything for the Black empowerment of Liverpool Born Blacks.

Often "outsiders" like Olusoga get the kudos from the mainstream for work that was produced long before they established themselves as historians. For example, Peter Fryer's *Staying Power: The History of Black People in Britain* was published thirty-two years before Olusoga's *Black and British: A Forgotten History*. This is important in relation to this study because the marginalization of Black Liverpool scholars, specifically, has been a key feature of their experience in the city. Someone has to be bold enough to set the historical record straight: David Olusoga as a Black British historian has been disingenuous in regard to the historical literature on cities like Liverpool. His study is also bereft of political insight into the social exclusion of Liverpool Born Blacks. What is particularly frustrating is his exploitation of Charles Wootton and his story (covered in depth in chapter four), while disregarding the legacy of the Charles Wootton Centre/College that kept his name alive in the city for a quarter of a century. This is unacceptable historiography as it further cements the "invisibility" of Black Liverpool souls who came before him, who worked against a tide of vicious institutional racism, so that the likes of him could be freer to write and prosper in mainstream circles. One of the key themes in their collective work is to keep local Black perspectives outside the reach of mainstream academia, and to dilute the history of Liverpool in relation to the enslavement era—John Belchem's *Liverpool 800* published in 2006 personifies this point.

On the other hand, grassroots education in Liverpool 8 such as the Charles Wootton and the L8 Access to H/E provided potential young scholars like myself with the impetus to write a history of Black Liverpool from the perspective of the community. This was ingrained in my comprehension of its history due to the longevity of social exclusion local Blacks had endured. Without grassroots education many Liverpool Born Blacks would have suffered continued exploitation of their collective history and future generations would only have the diluted version of Black history in Liverpool that emanates from mainstream historians such as John Belchem (2006a, 2014) and David Olusoga (2016). For example, a reading of Wally Brown (1979, 1986), Stephen Small (1991), and Mark Christian (1995, 1997b, 1998a, 1998b, 2000, 2007, 2008a) would clearly make evident the omissions in the studies by Belchem (2006a, 2014) and Olusoga (2016) on Black historical context in Liverpool. This is certainly not a trivial matter; on the contrary, to overlook scholars who have completed studies on Black Liverpool because they are more counter-hegemonic to mainstream historical versions is not fair in terms of twenty-first century scholarship. Indeed, all voices should be allowed to be heard, especially if such research has been legitimated in quality academic outlets as those of employed by Christian (1998a, 2000, 2008a) and Small (1991).

The L8 Access to H/E was, like the Charles Wootton Centre/College, borne out of social protest and struggle. Those who attended these grassroots institutions understood they were receiving opportunities that mainstream education institutions were not providing. Wally Brown, a Liverpool Born Black and grassroots leader, emerged from the 1981 uprising to become a prominent leader in the city for articulating the grievances of Black Liverpudlians. The 1919 and 1948 anti-Black riots in the city's history and the 1981 rebellion in Toxteth/Liverpool 8 will be covered in chapter four. But in terms of education opportunity, it is important to note that mainstream Liverpool further and higher education was regarded as "white" and unwelcoming to the average Liverpool Black individual (Brown 1986). Therefore, Liverpool Blacks had little choice but to develop alternative approaches in providing educational opportunities. Specifically, there had to be an emphasis on Black history and culture being taught because of the dire need to uplift the self-perception of Blacks in Liverpool. For instance, when Wally Brown was a community leader from the 1970s through to the early 1980s at the Methodist Centre in Liverpool 8, he organized a library facility for local teenagers to learn about Black history. He called it the "Elimu Wa Nane" (which means in Swahili: Education for Eight, referencing Liverpool 8). This then represented an after-school program to get the Black youth involved in education. It was the initiative of one dedicated community man who was thinking about the schooling and life chances of Black youth.

Later in the early 1990s that library resource would become a full-fledged school for young Black children struggling in the education system—who had often been excluded from the mainstream. Gloria Hyatt, a Liverpool Born Black woman and an L8 Access to H/E classmate of Mark Christian from 1988 to 1989, went on to gain a bachelor's degree in education (B.Ed.). Again, this shows the creative potential of young women and men who would ordinarily have been "lost" had it not been for grassroots opportunities in education. Gloria would eventually receive the Member of the British Empire (MBE) award for her work at the Elimu Academy. I, on the other hand, would find it the height of hypocrisy for a Liverpool Born Black person to accept such an award that basically extols the virtues of the British Empire—the actual source of misery for millions.

Nevertheless, I would also later teach, in a part-time capacity, Black studies at Elimu to teenage children in the afterschool program from 1993 to 1994. This was after returning from the Ohio State University where I had read for a master's degree in Black studies. These achievements of Gloria and I would not have been possible without the grassroots education community organization and the fight that Wally Brown and others put in to secure opportunities for Liverpool Born Blacks. Crucially, many local Blacks proved with certainty that if given the right opportunity to learn they could not only go on to achieve in education but also make profound contributions to their community. Seeing is believing it is often stated, and persons who gained top educational qualifications would then inspire other Black Liverpudlians to do the same. It can be deemed a snowball effect whereby the impetus for educational achievement is created that then inspires others to follow the same course of action—"if he or she can do it, so can I" is a sentiment that carries weight in Liverpool and elsewhere. If there is no progress for Blacks in education this can impact an entire community.

Once I completed the access to higher education course, I then went on to read for a degree at a mainstream higher education institution in Liverpool. I was in my mid-twenties when I had applied to the access course, with life and work experience, and I was educated in Black history within the context of Black grassroots struggle in Liverpool. Therefore, when I entered the university there was a conscious resilience in me that would not dissipate when faced with the reality of a predominantly white curriculum. I knew that to achieve my goals there had to be very hard work ahead. To learn what the institution had to offer, and then to take the bachelor degree qualification and marry it with my grassroots education. I was sure to never miss a lecture in the three years spent studying for a double major in American studies and sociology. Had there been a Black studies major on offer I would have taken it but it was not available there, nor in any other university in Britain at the time. On entry to the university, however, there was a difficult experience I encountered during the interview stage.

When I applied for the American studies program, I had driven up to the institution with a group of L8 Access to H/E students. I was the most knowledgeable among the group about general American history due to my avid interest in African American music, so questions about the United States were asked by my peers, and I answered them with aplomb. But when it got to the interview stage to get entry into the American studies program, every one of my peers were allowed entry into the course but I was rejected by the program's lecturers. During the interview I was asked what American writers I had read, and in reply I stated that I was familiar with Richard Wright, James Baldwin, and other Black writers, and that I had read Malcolm X's autobiography. Moreover, that I followed Muhammad Ali keenly and had a passion for African American music. I also mentioned having an interest in Frank Sinatra as a singer. In hindsight, the American studies lecturers were looking for answers such as Mark Twain's *Huckleberry Finn* and writers like Ernest Hemingway—my responses were clearly "too Black" for the interviewers who maintained the boundaries of white America within the context of the program at the mainstream Liverpool university.

    This rejection that I encountered inevitably caused friction with the L8 Access to H/E teachers because they were aware of my academic abilities as I had performed immeasurably well during the course. The decision was therefore protested and the program coordinator of the American studies program visited the L8 Access to H/E course; his name was Dr. Mullard. He offered me a place on the program during the meeting. In turn, I had received a letter of apology from the institutional hierarchy for the "offhand manner" in which I had been treated by the American studies interviewers. I accepted the apology, even though it was politically based, and set my mind on proving my rejecters wrong. I was galvanized by what can now be deemed a Black perspective in education and felt that I was representing Liverpool Born Blacks in my pursuit of a bachelor's degree. But let it be known, the only reason I was "reinstated" to the American studies program was because of the political climate in the city. There was an emphasis on creating greater access for Black Liverpudlians to enter such institutions of higher education. Had it been another era, whereby the government was not taking a closer look at racialized relations, I may never have received such an apology from an institution of higher education in Liverpool for blocking my life chances. It must also be stated that without the advocacy of the L8 Access to H/E staff I may never have gained entry. Make no mistake, this was not an act of affirmative action, it was an act of social justice. Moreover, the entire unsavory episode proved the efficacy for a grassroots educational infrastructure in Liverpool 8.

    I was not embittered due to being fully conscious of the challenge before me and in the thought of breaking through barriers for other Black Liverpudlians who followed. It was about being determined to prove those folks wrong who had endeavored to stifle my education. While there, I never missed a lecture, I devoured everything of interest from a Black perspective in the library. It took great effort to learn how to write the papers at university level. I would read the A grade papers from my peers who were not from Liverpool, who were "traditional" students: eighteen to twenty-four years of age. Well, once I got the rhythm of lectures and had spent so many hours studying in the library it became very easy. Indeed, whenever someone asked about my whereabouts the reply would normally be: "he's in the library." This did not come naturally; at first libraries struck me as intimidating and colossal in scope. But to combat such anxiety I decided to conquer it by going to the library early in the morning. I found a comfortable table and settled down to read. The university was a very comfortable and aesthetically appealing environment to read and write papers. Yet there was always looming over me the ghost of white supremacy. Perhaps it was the psychological pressure to prove that I was more than good enough to be there, that I could survive against the odds and repel the "chilly winds" of exclusion encountered from a number of the lecturers. I knew that I was labeled by them as a "Liverpool Born Black" who was from the L8 Access to H/E course, and therefore a curiosity at best, and an impediment to their privileged world at worst.

I made sure to keep in touch with the Charles Wootton Centre/College. Chief Ben had been promoted as the director, so I volunteered to make sure the link between the community and the university was cemented. I would go back to the Charlie for psychological sustenance whenever I experienced a particularly "cold day" on the predominantly white campus. Only people of color can comprehend what it is like to survive in a majority white British higher educational environment. I was particularly aware of how to cope with this scenario because I had studied Black history for a number of years before entering a mainstream Liverpool university. One cannot emphasize the importance of being grounded in one's cultural heritage as a Black person, or person of color, surviving in white spaces. The day-to-day realities can be rather difficult if you are an isolated and unwelcome entity in majority white surroundings. Microaggressions can eventually wear down a person, but if grounded in one's cultural heritage they are far less able to penetrate—you can survive regardless if there is the presence of negative forces.

A small section of the American studies program focused on the "Black American experience" and that involved history. In other words, they allowed three weeks' focus out of the entire semester on African American history and culture. I recall a lecturer starting his history of slavery with the words: "I start after the 1830s because whites would never treat whites like they did African Americans"—at the time I found this such a puzzling way to open up a course of study, but in time as I developed my knowledge it was fully understood the historical evasion he had performed. To be sure, up to the 1830s there had been a system that involved European indentured servants. These were basically men who had to serve a sentence of approximately seven years before they could be freed. The system of indentured labor was akin to enslavement and just as dehumanizing in its barbarity. The white American studies lecturer simply "cut out" that part of history and hence his opening sentence that obscured young minds from the broader aspect of white indentured servantry. This was another example of higher education misrepresenting the veracity about enslavement and oppression—and hiding historical knowledge from unsuspecting minds. It was in actuality a form of miseducation.

The American studies lecturer did his best to indirectly inform me that he was not there to educate properly. In turn, I made sure to sit on the front row and to never miss one of his misrepresentations of history sessions. While listening to his ethnocentric analysis of American slavery and the buildup to the Civil War being essentially about "States' Rights" and not the issue of enslavement, I knew this was basically another form of miseducation and untruthfulness. Certainly, I was now grounded enough in Black history to know that lies were something common emanating from the mouths of white lecturers and teachers in the British education system. My experiences at my Primary School with Mr. Redburn's cruel dismissal of an assignment, and later my indifferent experience at my Comprehensive School, had made me very wary of white educators. As I listened carefully to the American studies lecturer, I could sense the economy of truth springing from his knowledge base. The writer James Baldwin once expounded: "American history is longer, larger, more various, more beautiful, and more terrible than anything anyone has ever said about it" (cited in Loewen 1996, p. 11). What was being revealed to me at the university via the American slavery class was merely a reflection of a white man's delusional attempt to misinform and miseducate a generation of undergraduates. Fortunately for myself, it was now impossible to obfuscate historical realities because I had spent so much time learning African American history in a self-taught manner. I also developed a mantra: *whatever I do not know today, I shall learn tomorrow.* Without having a grounding in grassroots education from Liverpool 8 it is very likely I would not have survived higher education at the university.

Ironically, on November 6, 1997, the year I received my doctorate in sociology from a university in another British city, my alma mater university in Liverpool held a conference titled: "Raising Achievement and Promoting Equality within Education." Among the speakers that day were Stephen Small, a Black Liverpudlian, and Gus John, the latter being from outside the city but extremely familiar with inequalities in British education. Small's keynote address was revealing in the sense that he covered the nuances of racialized problems in education associated with Liverpool Born Blacks nearing the close of the twentieth century. He echoed the perspective of Wally Brown, whose citation opened up this chapter concerning the dire employment prospects and related issues for Blacks in the city. In a sense, Small is himself an anomaly, whereby he went through the education system as a traditional white person would, completing his education at Liverpool Collegiate—a fairly prestigious school to attend, even in the 1970s, in fact, the same school that the famous educator Ken Robinson, discussed earlier, attended. It was a school once favored by the most affluent of Liverpool children. Then in the late 1960s it endeavored to offer opportunity to the "the best and brightest" of the working class to savor an elite education. So those who attended Liverpool Collegiate were fairly fortunate and privileged. However, as Small (1998) recalls, gaining the best qualifications from a prestigious former grammar school, and going on to university straight after within the traditional time period of whites, did not allow him to avoid the discrimination associated with being a Liverpool Black person of mixed heritage:

> I had the best education that the West has to offer, the best formal education—O Levels, A Levels, Bachelor of Arts, Master of Science, Doctor of Philosophy, and yet my memories of education are some of the most painful, hurtful memories that I have. In the books that I have read there were savages from Africa, Heathens and idol worshippers from India, black women running naked in the jungle, and Tarzan swinging around saving everyone (1998, p. 10).

Small continued to explain the uniqueness of the city in terms of the dire lack of Black representation in the city compared to other cities across Britain. Wally Brown had stated similar things regarding the conspicuous absence of Black Liverpudlians in the service sector. Indeed, there is something rather odd about Liverpool in this sense. It has an unwelcoming vibe if you are seeking a genuine cosmopolitan feel visually in the city center. That is why the perspective of Belchem (2006b) is a fallacy when it comes to pontificating about Liverpool's "cosmopolitan character" because Black Liverpudlians rarely see a reflection of themselves in Liverpool's main shopping area. Small again articulates this paradox in the distinctiveness that the city possesses:

> I wanted to say some things about the uniqueness of Liverpool, but you know yourselves in terms of residential segregation, in terms of employment segregation, in terms of the constraints on black peoples' movements around this City. It is amazing that black people who leave this City to go to Manchester, Birmingham, London see black faces in the stores, this is what is unique about Liverpool and the fact that the indigenous population, black, [is not visible even though] . . . the majority of us who are Black and Asian were born here and we are still treated as if we are immigrants (Small 1998, p. 12).

Stephen Small's point of view brings us right back to the Swann Report (1985) that stated that the uniqueness of the Liverpool Blacks is in them being born and raised in the city going back many generations. Yet discrimination has persisted, particularly in education and employment. Nevertheless, what does not kill you makes you stronger is the wisdom of those who fight on for a better life regardless, and in spite of racialized oppression. This is another aspect of Liverpool Born Blacks that often gets understated: *their capacity to survive and often prosper against the odds*. Those Liverpool Blacks who knuckled down and focused on achieving their goals would have to ignore the slights and underhanded contempt from those who scorned and abused them in authority positions.

Indeed, when it comes to myself and others from the Liverpool Black experience, we simply bear witness to the possibility of success even if social barriers were erected to exclude us. I among many others derive from a city that should have openly embraced my talent, and the abilities of many other Liverpool Born Blacks, but it failed to do so on many occasions—particularly in mainstream education. It took grassroots education, my family background in music, the amateur football in the Liverpool 8 community, and Black history and culture to consolidate my humanity. There is no room for obtuse educators who do not listen or empathize with those who suffer from the indignities of racialized oppression. Nobody should have to fight every inch of their lives in order to achieve social justice. Liverpool is certainly a unique city, but it has also been aptly described as "uniquely horrific" when it comes to institutionalized racism (Gifford, Brown, and Bundey 1989). The next chapter will cover the history of anti-Black racism and the demise of the Liverpool Black organizational infrastructure largely at the hands of the Liverpool City Council.

Chapter 4

Anti-Black Riots, Resistance, and Black Organization Demise 1919–2000s

The legacy of enslavement, colonialism, and racialized discrimination was once explained by Eric Lynch, a local historian and activist, within the context of late twentieth- century Liverpool, England. He spent his life fighting for social justice for Liverpool Born Blacks, and others who suffered such treatment in the city. There was no sugarcoating the issue for him; he did not care for fools who would deny the veracity of racism in the lives of his people. Eric Lynch was a man of the Liverpool Black experience, a proud and confident man who led the fight against racism with great courage. He was well known in the community of Liverpool 8 and beyond, and was well respected by all who worked with him in the struggle for a social justice. His passing in November of 2021 at the age of ninety years was as mournful as any transition of a respected elder from the Liverpool Black experience. But more than this, his life should be celebrated because for a man of color in Liverpool it was a minor miracle that he reached such a grand age—his longevity speaks to the strength of his spirit. The loss of his presence will be felt, but his legacy is enshrined in the city and in the history of Liverpool Born Black heritage. Eric Lynch spoke for generations of unborn Liverpool Blacks and for unborn whites who we hope will be free of delusions of grandeur and comprehend the essence of all humanity—not the racialism of their forebears. Below is how he rallied for a Liverpool Black consciousness:

> The time has come when we, Liverpool Born Blacks, can no longer tolerate the situation that we are forced to live in. The time is coming, in fact the time is very close, when more and more of us realise, and through the realisation act collectively to take that which is rightfully ours into our own hands. By that I mean, to ensure that our children are educated in the way that we the Liverpool Born Blacks want our children to be educated . . .

> We who are born outside of Africa, we Black children of Africa, who now call ourselves Liverpool Born Black, we have not iron chains around our legs. We have no longer to wear the iron collars around our necks, and yet, we bear the chains of slavery mentally because through the lack of understanding, through the lack of education, through bigotry and racism which is handed to us and is fed to us by the White society in which we live, we are shackled and have been shackled since the first Black man or woman was so called freed of slavery, and told that now at least in this country of England he or she was free (cited in Gifford, Brown, and Bundey 1989, pp. 247–248).

Therefore, this chapter will focus on key aspects of Black Liverpudlian history that galvanized local resistance, particularly through grassroots organizations and strategy, to combat both individual and institutional acts of racism. First, a consideration of anti-Black riots and acts of violence encountered such as the murder of Charles Wootton (at times spelled Wootten) in 1919 and the wanton violence in 1948 against Black communities. There will be a consideration of how Liverpool Black culture was represented in the 1960s to 1970s. Then in regard to the 1981 Liverpool 8/Toxteth uprising, though essentially a Black protest against police brutality, it was more complicated in a racialized sense because it also involved a minority of working-class whites on the side of Blacks because they often shared urban poverty conditions. There will be a consideration of the Liverpool Black organizations versus a militant far-left political Liverpool City Council in the early 1980s to approximately 1987. An analysis of the role played by the Charles Wootton Centre/College during the 1980s to 2000, in terms of its centrality in grassroots community infrastructure will be assessed.

The Charles Wootton Centre/College, along with being a key institution for education, also played a pivotal role in the organizational set-up of the broader grassroots community in Liverpool 8. This has too often been underplayed or dismissed by scholars based at local universities (Belchem 2006a, 2014; Frost and Phillips 2011). It is therefore imperative to situate the historical context of the Charles Wootton College in Liverpool 8 because of the profound historical amnesia surrounding its history. This is apparent in what can be deemed "academic misrepresentation" or "non-representation" in regard to Black expression of resistance to white cultural hegemony in the city, particularly, in terms of the essential role Africana/Black studies played in lifting the consciousness of Blacks in Liverpool. It will be argued that the demise of the Charles Wootton College in 2000 had a domino effect on other Black organizations. Meaning it was rather cynical on behalf of the Liverpool City Council to withdraw funding and support for grassroots organizations that tackled social inequality and racism—this occurred most evidently in the late 1990s and into the early 2000s.

Who is ultimately responsible for the collapse of these important grassroots establishments? The Liverpool 8 city councilor and self-styled community advocate, while steering local research as a lecturer at a university, Gideon Ben-Tovim, requires some attention due to his profound connection to racialized issues in Liverpool 8. His relationship with two prominent Liverpool Born Blacks, Wally Brown and Dave Clay, for example, meant he had great influence on how the community shaped and organized resistance to racialized discrimination. To be sure, it is doubtful given the inevitable outcome in defunding of many grassroots organizations, particularly the Charles Wootton College and Liverpool 8 Law Centre, that Ben-Tovim did not have a significant role in the process due to his influence in the corridors of power as a labor councilor and chair of the Education Committee, specifically regarding educational funding and policy toward grassroots infrastructure in Liverpool 8. Crucially, there ought to be further research into the manner in which the Liverpool City Council defunded Black organizations in Liverpool 8 during the late 1990s and into the early 2000s. This chapter closes with reference to the official Slave Trade Apology from the Liverpool City Council in December of 1999—and its subsequent betrayal of the significant promises it made in writing to work steadfastly with Liverpool's Black communities to ameliorate institutional racism in the city.

RACIALIZED VIOLENCE IN LIVERPOOL

There have been recorded historically some major disturbances in the city involving anti-Black sentiment emanating from the broader white community. Although 1919 is often regarded as a starting point in racialized violence in Liverpool, a keen researcher found an interesting fact that is rarely revealed. In December 1918 there was a racially motivated disturbance in the city which related to Black soldiers being attacked in their uniforms. The Black soldiers had volunteered to help the "mother country" in her hour of need, only to be abused by a mob of native white Liverpudlian and other British soldiers. Much of this is hidden history in regard to Black participation in British wars. Nevertheless, if one is dedicated to finding the historical truth there are scholars who have delved into this underbelly of British mainstream history to find much evidence of participation (Costello 2015; Fryer 1984; Marke 1975; Murphy 1995). Again, it is a common aspect of mainstream historical record to place what is central to Liverpool Black history on the margins of analysis. Without careful archival work the veracity of Black historical presence would be unknown. As Andrea Murphy notes in her important study *From the Empire to the Rialto: Racism and Reaction in Liverpool, 1918–1948*:

[Anti-Black] hostility in Liverpool occurred in December 1918 when fifty Black soldiers were attacked by four to five hundred White soldiers at Belmont Road Military Auxiliary Hospital. The Black soldiers belonged to the British West Indies Regiment, a volunteer body, and some of their attackers had returned from service in South Africa, were Pass Laws already segregated Black and White people. White troops at the hospital became abusive to the Black soldiers and banned them from the concert room. When one of them appeared to be about to question this exclusion, he was struck by a guard (Murphy 1995, p. 13).

To reflect on this incident at a hospital for WW1 British soldiers, Black and white, it is unutterably sad to consider them at odds because of the difference in skin color. The real enemy in their lives had been the Germans whom they collectively were at war with between 1914 and 1918. Yet this is also the absurdity of racism; it overrides logic and rationality so often to the detriment of humanity. Those Black soldiers, from various African Caribbean islands under British colonialism had volunteered to protect and fight for Britain during one of the most dreadful wars that humankind has ever witnessed. Murphy goes on to explain that many of the Black men in that hospital in Liverpool had been crippled via their participation in the war to defend Britain. It is incredulous to contemplate what they were going through while being attacked by their fellow British subjects due to their color—ultimately.

Murphy recalls another incident in April of 1919 whereby two Jamaican soldiers were harassed by police and taken to Bridewell Station in the city center by tram to avoid a "menacing" reaction from fellow agitated Blacks who witnessed the injustice on Oxford Street. The two men, Francis Henchard and Josiah Williams, were fined and imprisoned yet pleaded they had been unfairly treated to no avail. Henchard stated at the time, "I am as good as any white man. My blood is just the same: it isn't black and I've done my bit [served in WW1 for Britain] just as Lloyd George for King and country" (cited in Murphy 1995, p.14). This was commonplace treatment of Black soldiers who had fought for British ideals in wartime. On the streets of Liverpool, it could be very dangerous, maybe just as perilous as being in a war zone. The catastrophe of such is that this anti-Black sentiment was deeply ingrained into the white working-class psyche. There was a viciousness that stemmed from a visceral reaction to Black and brown skin—one can try to comprehend the mind of a racist but it is difficult to fathom if one does not hold such enmity. Not all whites held this kind of feeling toward Black presence in Liverpool during 1919, but it was popular enough to draw hundreds of whites onto the streets to hurt Black bodies and destroy their homes and property.

In his book *Staying Power: The History of Black People in Britain*, Peter Fryer aptly designates 1919 "racism as riot" and describes there being lynch mobs in Liverpool, and in another seaport, Cardiff in Wales. The fact of racialized hostility was due to the postwar climate and the lack of labor required—especially the need for Black labor. Fryer opens up his discussion in the following manner relating to the precariousness of Black seaman after WW1 had ceased:

> When armistice was signalled on 11 November 1918, the war-time boom for black labour fizzled out as quickly as it had begun. Once again shipping companies chose to sign on white foreign seamen rather than black British seamen. The National Sailors' and Firemen's Union and National Union of Ships' Stewards, Cooks, Butchers and Bakers, the two forerunners of the National Union of Seamen, were implacably opposed to the employment of black seamen when white crews where available (Fryer 1984, p. 298).

The fact that unions, representing white working-class workers, were adamantly opposed to Black labor is something that needs to be understood in relation to Liverpool. It is renowned as a working-class city, but it is not renowned for working-class solidarity with Black Liverpudlians. There is also a religious sectarianism that goes back centuries, but this is something among white Protestants and Catholics (Belchem 2006a, pp. 326–328). Yet, regardless of the broad diversity among white cultural groups, when it came to work and exclusionary tactics, they were most often "all for one, and one for all" against Black labor competition. White unionism has a long history of discriminating against Black workers; even when one considers the 1848 *Communist Manifesto* by Karl Marx and Frederick Engels there is nothing in that document that speaks to the freedom of African labor, much of which was still enslaved. When we fast-forward to the twentieth century, the ghosts of Marx and Engels are alive in the brains of the white working classes of England in regard to their Black working-class counterparts. Certainly, it is baffling why so many Black thinkers have embraced Marx's philosophy when in fact it had little to do with the liberation of Black men and women in his day, nor could it be seen in twentieth century Liverpool of 1919 and beyond.

If capitalism has its own "seeds of destruction" then white cultural hegemony would still find a way to maintain itself. Black soldiers and seamen were excluded from white unions systematically and ruthlessly—let this not be forgotten in the books written by so-called socialists and communists. In retrospection, the anti-Black sentiment found in white Liverpudlians was an ingrained delusion of grandeur, many of whom were no better off than the Blacks they despised and/or envied as a threat to them. Yet they drenched themselves in the mantra: "I maybe poor, but at least I'm white"—if it was not so pathetic one could sympathize with such "false consciousness" among whites who harbored false notions of human superiority over people of color.

It is this grand lie that has endured to stifle the best of humanity and human diversity to flourish and prosper based on class (Isenberg 2016).

Jacqueline Jenkinson's study, *Black 1919: Riots, Racism and Resistance in Imperial Britain*, first published in 2009, covers various racialized disturbances that broke out in British port cities, including Liverpool, that were a reflection of the unrest among whites and people of color and it certainly related to transatlantic history. Jenkinson, as with other scholars before her, noted that mobs of working-class whites targeted Blacks, their families, along with any Black businesses they could loot and ransack. Again, the key factor was the competition that people of color manifested as workers. The entire white union structure, along with local authorities, deemed Black presence in post WW1 as a nuisance. It is important to unpack this entire racialized prejudice for what it was, ignorance and prejudice based on miseducation via popularized culture. Moreover, the stereotypes embedded within British colonialism subjugated colonized peoples and later their offspring would encounter its manifold legacy. One must keep in the mind that the British racialized stereotypes in regard to people of color during WW1 and beyond were carefully crafted over centuries of exploitation and domination. Jenkinson explains it this way:

> British feelings of superiority over subject peoples were already well established by the time of the 1919 seaport riots. However, the recent experiences of the First World War brought many native white people into first or extended contact with black colonial British subjects, who came to Britain in their many thousands as workers, soldiers and sailors. The presence of black British troops and workers failed to alter popular one-dimensional perceptions of Britishness. A study conducted in 1918 revealed strong "race" prejudice within wartime British society. This prejudice was not based on hostility as a result of personal contact with black British colonial subjects but on the broad process of imperialism, which brought the prejudices of colonial administrators and travellers back to the metropole (2019, p. 5).

There is much to unravel from Jenkinson's perspective as it does encapsulate the essence of British racism. As she notes "feelings of superiority over subject peoples" were already established long before 1919. It had been ingrained consistently through popular culture and the myth of the "white man's burden" to civilize the world. Yet much of what was done in the name of "civilization" was tantamount to barbarism. That aside, white working-class enmity was something that had been inculcated into their minds long before contact was made with Black and brown colonial subjects. Those colonized subjects who volunteered to aid white Britain to "save democracy" during WW1 did so in fact to save it from another white nation—Germany. The irony is overwhelming but it is social reality, not fiction. What was meted out to those

Black British servicemen at that Liverpool hospital in December 1918 was inhumane, though this was not how it was reported in the local press. Most often the blame for anti-Black feeling and violence was merely put down to the presence of Black and brown men; "they got what they deserved" was the underlying retort from white journalists and the established authority spokespersons.

THE MURDER OF CHARLES WOOTTON IN LIVERPOOL ON JUNE 5, 1919

The first full account of Charles Wootton was written by a Liverpool Born Black man, Louis Julienne. He published the account as a pamphlet to raise funds for the fledging Charles Wootton Centre in 1979. Again, this fact is overlooked by the mainstream historian John Belchem and those researchers he has supported, such as Diane Frost from the University of Liverpool. Indeed, white researchers have in general underplayed the significance of the Charles Wootton Centre—especially in relation to its importance in the functioning of Black grassroots community survival from the 1970s to 2000. Julienne described in detail the events that led to the death of Charles Wootton, a twenty-four-year-old Bermudan seaman employed by the Royal Navy during WW1. He lived in 18 Upper Pitt Street in Liverpool 1, which was the first area where most Blacks and people of color resided back then before largely, not all, moved to the Liverpool 8 and surrounding area. Liverpool's Chinatown is in close proximity to the Upper Pitt Street area (Julienne 1979).

On June 5, 1919 there had been an altercation between some Black seamen and Scandinavians, and tension had been simmering throughout the spring due to Black men being "attacked again and again" walking peacefully on the streets (Fryer 1984, p. 300). On one occasion an African Caribbean was stabbed by two Scandinavians, which led to a reprisal assault the following evening with an all-out brawl taking place and police being called. During the melee a police officer was allegedly hurt. There was then a mob of up to three hundred whites who went looking for Blacks who resided in hostels in the Upper Pitt Street area; they ransacked the homes and burned furniture. It is during this melee that Charles Wootton was chased from his home to the Queens Dock about half a mile away whereby he was arrested by the police. But the lynch mob pulled him away from the police and threw him into the water, pelting him with bricks. Fryer states the cries from the whites were, "Let him drown!" (p. 300). Charles Wootton after a long struggle eventually succumbed and drowned. He was pulled from the water—no arrests were made even with police present at the scene who witnessed the bricks being hurled at the dying man.

The anti-Black rage did not cease after the murder of the young African Caribbean sailor. There would be another long five nights of terror heaped on the Black community in Liverpool whereby more property was vandalized and numerous physical attacks occurred. Indeed, any person of color could be assaulted who happened to be in the wrong place at the wrong time. The white mobs were in a frenzied state and viewed any Black person as a target for a severe beating. This was British terrorism at home against those who had put their lives on the line for "King and country" only months earlier. It was a nadir for Blacks in Liverpool and a stark indication of the harshness to be confronted by those who did not fit into Britishness as whites claimed it to be—white and native. At this time, it was estimated that Liverpool's Black population was around five thousand in number—this is not a definite figure due to the nature of a seaport that had fluid movement and multiple home occupancies for those who sailed the transatlantic pathway. Even so, five thousand souls at least concentrated in a designated area of the city who were an easy target for both police and thugs—it was difficult to distinguish between the police and thug in terms of the brutality meted out to people of color in the city. It was vicious from both the thugs and the police—the latter would also fabricate charges to convict Black souls who were most often trying to go about their business in a profoundly racist environment. In summarizing his essay on Charles Wootton, Julienne states:

> Historically, Liverpool 8 [and other areas] has been the scene of continuous battles and struggles, pain and wretchedness which have had as their root cause racial discrimination. Charles Wootton, we think, epitomised this—he died the victim of racial discrimination. A violent death but not a vain one (1979, p. 15).

It is difficult to deny the detrimental impact such an unnecessary loss of life has on a community suffering from the long night of oppression. Charles Wootton himself merely symbolizes the tip of the iceberg when it comes to racialized violence in Liverpool. Though physical and inhumane as it was, there were thousands of Black children in the city not having decent education, housing, or social welfare amenities on the basis of their Black heritage. That too was a form of violent conduct against a community of vulnerable persons. It was institutional racism in action and an open failure to cease the perpetuation of discrimination.

Assessing the history of Black presence, and linking Charles Wootton's murder, too many studies have tended to whitewash (pardon the pun) over the ugliness of institutional racism in Liverpool—Belchem (2006a) is one such study. Another phrase often used by white commentators like Gideon

Ben-Tovim is in relation to the Liverpool education system, "[Black children] are given every support in achieving their all-round potential. But . . . there is still a long way to go" (1998, p. 3). Well, such statements reveal cognitive dissonance because a Black child in Liverpool could not be "given *every* support in achieving" while there is *still* a "long way to go"—the statement is incongruent. The same goes for the teaching of Black historical reality. Too many white commentators control the interpretation of Black experiences and write historiography that meets with the status quo in maintaining a white cultural hegemony in the city rather than fairness of historical fact. Crucially, whether it be educators or historical chroniclers, the murder of Charles Wootton should never be understated or forgotten. It was a blatant lynching that occurred on June 5, 1919. It was witnessed by the police and this incident advanced a general disregard for Black humanity in Liverpool that was unjust and uncivilized.

OLD MAN TROUBLE IN 1919 AND UNDERCOVER POLICE BRUTALITY

A man who not only suffered for King and country during WW1, but nearly lost his life to crazed white mobs has been documented. Ernest Marke believed the cause of the anti-Black riots was essentially due to unemployment rather than pure hatred toward Black people. He lived through the experience therefore it is important to take on board this point. The fact is when there is a lack of jobs a scapegoat often emerges to take the angst of the majority population. During this post-WW1 era the world economy was in bad shape; there had recently been a Russian revolution (1917), so the capitalists were concerned for such not to happen in British society. It could be argued that the authorities' lackadaisical attitude and the blaming of Black presence for the anti-Black sentiment was a Machiavellian move to divert attention away from the poor economy. It should be noted that the Nazis in the 1930s scapegoated Jewish people for the demise of the German economy. Scapegoating has been proved to be useful for the majority elite, but devastating for those on the end of it.

Two Liverpool Born Black women, Madeline Heneghan and Emy Onuora, have recently researched archives of the era that took the life of Charles Wootton. Their book is titled *Great War to Race Riots: Black Experience in Post-WWI Liverpool* (2019). It is informative due to drawing directly from primary documents that give evidence to the tremendous strain Black people were under in Liverpool during this period. Indeed, this was a time that was insecure for all concerned but if whites suffered then one can be sure Black lives suffered at least three times harder. The following analogy is apt in relation to a poor economy and its impact on communities, "If whites catch a cold, then people of color usually get pneumonia" in a bad economic slump. Heneghan and Onuora offer firsthand proof that provides knowledge of the dire condition demobilized servicemen and auxiliary factory workers found themselves in after the WW1. More "unheard voices" are emerging because of newfound archive material that speaks to the Liverpool Black experience. This will further give credence to the research of Louis Julienne and other pioneers of Liverpool Black history that went unnoticed for decades.

In his autobiography, Ernest Marke, an African serviceman who settled in Britain, recalled being on board the *SS Adansi* from Sierra Leone to Liverpool when a German torpedo hit the ship—this was May 6, 1917 during WW1. He was a fourteen-year-old boy and miraculously survived after being pulled unconscious from the sea. If only that incident was to be his major catastrophe in life it would be horrendous enough for the average human being to endure, but it was not. As an African born in Sierra Leone in 1902 with a good soul and disposition, he would face further perilous situations in life: poverty, discrimination, and racialized violence would follow later in Liverpool. His autobiography is aptly titled *Old Man Trouble* because everywhere he went in life "trouble" ensued. Being a teenager when he was on the *SS Adansi* that sunk, he could not swim but somehow was saved that haunting day in the cold Atlantic Ocean. Yet, he survived WW1 only to find more trouble and strife in Liverpool as he strived for a better life. When in that life and death moment of nearly drowning his mind wandered to the many sights and places he had read about that he wanted to see if he ever made it to England. As he stated:

> Everything was racing through my mind. So this is the end I thought. I'd always longed to see Great Britain: London, Buckingham Palace, the Houses of Parliament, the Bloody Tower [Tower of London] and all those other places I'd read about; now I was never going to see them (Marke 1975, p. 10).

Fortunately, Ernest was saved that treacherous day and lived to tell his story to future generations. He eventually made it to Liverpool and stayed in the home of the chief steward, where he recovered from injuries to his feet. While in Liverpool he attended a local Roman Catholic Church as his family had been converted in Africa by missionaries. He recalled as he served at the altar, as a church volunteer, a woman fainting at the very sight of him. When she recovered from the collapse people around her stated she had "seen the devil at the altar"—the devil to that white Liverpudlian woman was Ernest Marke (p. 14). He surmised it as being the first time the woman had ever seen a Black man in person. Though he wondered why she represented him as the devil. Why could she not have seen an angel at the altar? This again is indicative of the type of cultural ignorance that had been imbibed not only by that

Liverpool woman but millions of Britons. Popular culture in particular had disseminated such misrepresentations of African peoples, specifically during the Victorian era and the notion of "darkest Africa" in colonial featured magazines (Bolt 1971). Therefore, who can be blamed for such unfamiliarity? Certainly not the woman who had fainted on the sight of an African man serving at the altar. The responsibility lay with the then British media and its system of education, and more importantly, with the colonial authorities who had the power to disseminate stereotypes and falsehoods. The reason for these misrepresentations is self-explanatory—those who had the power to do so created misinformation that was devoured by an uncritical mass. Western popular culture that emerged during the Victorian times and beyond was rife with colonial racist stereotypes that still hold sway to this day (Bolt 1971).

The life and times of Ernest Marke did not get any easier, and his autobiography is replete with tales of woe and anguish as an African seaman in Liverpool and other parts of Britain. Though the 1919 anti-Black rioting had passed, in 1921 he recalls there still being great racialized tension in the city. While walking home near Hope Street he was accosted by three undercover police officers, who had first asked him for a light to a cigarette. He replied that he did not possess any matches but was then punched in the stomach by one of the three, and then all began to kick him. He managed to fight back in his defense but was overwhelmed. Briefly, he was dragged to the station and charged with attempted murder of a police officer (p. 52). Of course, this was all fabricated and eventually after spending time in jail and going through a trial, whereby he defended himself, he was freed by the judge and jury. What is rather incredulous is the intelligence and humanity of Ernest Marke that runs right through his autobiography. The manner in which he defended himself is accounted for in chapter three, "A Brush with the Law," and it should be widely read and broken down for its depth of logic and brilliance in defense of his life. He was in a white court of law, in a foreign land, up against the testimony of three policemen and his defense was quite stunning. If there is a record of this trial that exists future researchers need to excavate it as a response to the delusion of white intellectual superiority. Clearly, he was an extremely intelligent African seaman who was worldly wise and had the spirit of his ancestors with him through his trials and tribulations.

Sadly, he earlier recalled the anti-Black rioting of 1919 whereby he and a roommate were chased. They were caught and beaten to an inch of their lives by a rampaging mob of whites looking for Black men—anyone with a darker skin than white. Had it not been for some white women leaving a factory for their lunch break, who intervened, he recalled that they would probably have died that day. This is how he remembered the painful episode that occurred on the streets of Liverpool in June 1919:

> I went out with my room-mate to the grocer's shop around the corner. From nowhere a mob appeared. We started to run back—only to find another mob facing us. We were trapped, and though we fought hard for our lives there was nothing we could do against so many. They beat us up mercilessly. Had it not been for some working women coming out of a nearby factory for their lunch hour, I would not have lived to write this story. The women rushed at the mob, shouting and screaming madly. Their screams and shouts probably frightened the mob away. We were both laid up for three weeks (p. 31).

White researchers who cite Ernest Marke's autobiography fail to mention both the police brutality and his life-threatening escape (Jenkinson 2019; Belchem 2014), and it is this type of diluted interpretation that masks the depth of enmity met by men like Ernest, who merely had ambition to see the world, the sites, and grow as any other human being who endeavors to get the most out of life. Importantly, white historians on Liverpool particularly have tempered the ferocity of white violence in their writings and this is why it is imperative for Africana studies scholars to revisit autobiographies like Ernest Marke's to share extracts that have largely been ignored—particularly regarding the viciousness of white violence. Moreover, there still can always be found the humanity among whites, such as the white women who came to the rescue of Ernest and his roommate that fateful day they were beaten to an inch of their lives in Liverpool. Also, when Ernest was leaving the court a free man after police had fabricated an attempted murder charge, two old white ladies wished him well and gave him five pounds sterling (p. 61). In other words, there is no need to dilute the historical record as many white historians have done because there are most often within these terrible realities displays of humanity from those on the oppressors' side. This indeed is something we can feel hopeful about—even if these acts of humanity were few.

ANTI-BLACK RIOTS IN 1948

Another historical anti-Black riot in Liverpool of note is the one that took place during the British August Bank Holiday of 1948. Africana critical studies should be grateful, again, to the research and analysis of Peter Fryer's *Staying Power: The History of Black People in Britain* because of his scholarly depth and scrupulousness in rescuing it from the usual British historical amnesia when it comes to Black settlement. There was racial tension in the city largely due to WW2-postwar unemployment—principally in relation to the docks and shipping lines. The racial tension took place in and around the Upper Stanhope Street and Upper Parliament Street area, where the businesses owned by local Africans and Arabs would be the scene of violence (Belchem 2014, p. 140).

Barnor Hesse, a well-established Black British scholar, has been critical of how the postwar settlement of Blacks in Britain tends to start with the arrival of the 1948 *SS Empire Windrush*, which brought nearly five hundred Jamaican souls to work in the flagging British economy. There exist newsreels of the arrival as the ship traveled up the Thames to Tilbury Dock in London, adding to the myth in the starting point of "multiracial Britain." The legend was captured fifty years later by Mike and Trevor Phillips in their 1998 book, *Windrush: The Irresistible Rise of Multiracial Britain*—adding another bout of historical amnesia to the confusion in the origins of Black Britain. Hesse relates to this incongruity in this manner:

> What "1948" fails to signify, interestingly enough in this recuperation of settlement chronology, that is within the narrative, are the "racist riots" which erupted in August in Liverpool where Black settlement was so to speak, already in place ... by this time there were about 8,000 Black people in Liverpool.... Yet though this event was regionally, it somehow manages to evade inclusion in the national political narrative of "race" as settlement.... The usual periodization of postwar [Black] settlement (1948–58) from Windrush to Notting Hill and Nottingham simply leaves this out (Hesse 2000, p. 79).

Hesse touches on an important aspect of Black British historiography that is largely "London-centric" in its starting and ending points—especially in relation to post-WW2 Black settlement. As reflected in chapter one, the writings of Stuart Hall and Paul Gilroy make no mention of Liverpool and its longevity of Black settlement. Hall and Gilroy are akin to "father and son" in British academia, sharing similar academic DNA that has rippled across the transatlantic to find homes in the elite universities. To know anything about Black Britain one has to consult Hall, Gilroy, and their acolytes—of which there are many. That stated, this is problematic because it essentially omits much of Black history and fails to consider how British racism has impacted cities like Liverpool. Hesse is correct in his assessment of Stuart Hall and his incorrect notion that "the first signs of an open and emergent racism of a specifically Indigenous type appears in the race riots of Notting Hill and Nottingham in 1958" (p. 79). Clearly, Hall did not take the time to study 1919 and the British ports of Liverpool and Cardiff, which should have been "historically specific" to the guru of racialized relations. Perhaps, Hall, Gilroy, and others suffered from being closed off to other aspects of Black Britain being firmly fixed intellectually in cosmopolitan London.

Like Barnor Hesse, though a white British academic, Michael Keith has analyzed the 1948 anti-Black riots in Liverpool. The problem with his account is in the manner he endeavors to fragment Blackness due to the obvious diversity of the Black heritage in the city. Claiming nothing particularly novel in the fact that Black Liverpudlians and Black migrants are made up of a blending of cultural heritages: African, of many cultural groups from the continent, along with Arabs. He further acknowledges that there was more than antagonism over Black seamen and the National Union of Seamen, that it was a mixture of a fight to exclude Blacks from labor, and that any Black person was targeted for assault by white mobs. Again, there is nothing particularly new in the analysis of the 1948 anti-Black riots in the city. The fact that Africans and African Caribbean men were arrested who were not seafarers, along with Blacks born in the city, shows it was not merely a white versus Black seamen issue. Racialized antagonism was deeply rooted as far back as 1919 and it did not cease; the city was difficult and dangerous for Black and brown persons consistently beyond WW1. To be sure, Blacks in the 1960s to 1980s were in danger of their lives if they ventured too far into areas where whites lived predominantly. This social fact of de facto segregation was ingrained into the racist culture of the city.

Michael Keith seems a tad confused analytically in regard to the reality of how racism operated on the ground, in real social experiences, and focused on theorizing the conundrum in the concept of "race" itself. To further explain, when Malcolm X clarified how white racism operated, he would often argue, paraphrased, that Black people are not attacked because they are Christian, or Muslim, rich or poor, lighter or darker in skin tone, but they are assaulted due to their collective Blackness or Black heritages. That is why Black people have to stay together and fight this issue of racism in solidarity—while leaving any cultural differences at home, in the closet. If there is to be an end to police brutality and vicious racist mobs, Black people in all their complexity need to be as one to conquer the same enemy that is attacking their humanity. However, Keith would write in academic verbosity:

> It is suggested here that rather than employ the concept of race to explain violent conflict it is necessary to analyse the conflict in order to understand the use of the concept of race. . . . In this inversion racial groupings are seen to emerge from the crucible of social interaction moulded by ideologies of racism. Race is a contingent, not a universal analytical, category. Consequently, popular mobilization of racially structured grassroots movements depend on the meaning of race at particular times and places. The coalescence of racial formations is itself problematic (Keith 1992, p. 8).

What appears to be rather overblown, conceptual, academic hyperbole can be broken down rather simply: *"race" does not exist as a biological concept when thinking of racial types, but Blacks in their diverse heritages are often required to mobilize as "one" in social movements to secure their human and civil rights as "people of color" due to the white racism they encounter.* Now, keep in mind, Keith not once in his account of the 1948 anti-Black racial disturbance broke down who and what represents "white people" and their immense diversity. Who, for example, are the white seamen? Were they born in Liverpool of Irish, Scottish, Welsh, or English origin? Or were they foreign born whites like Scandinavian, Polish, or some other white ethnic group from Europe? This is not considered by Keith in his sociological analysis of "race" but Black people are broken down into "fractions" for a theoretical analysis of a problematic conceptualization of racialized violence. This is academic posturing to explain the varied Black communities existing, within the context of Liverpool in 1948, being assaulted. It simply amounts to another mainstream perspective from an academic who does not even consider the reality of *his* whiteness in the role of a scholar. This could well be a case of unwitting privilege playing out without his conscious knowledge because it was a taken-for-granted aspect of Michael Keith's world in a white-dominated field of sociological discourse in the 1990s.

The problem here is in how a mainstream sociologist would employ real life historical trauma of a Black experience merely for a theoretical framework within the context of racialized relations. Keith acknowledged his obscure analysis by endeavoring to bring it to the fore in an attempt to cover his dubious theoretical tracks:

> Superficially it may appear pedantic to distinguish between a putative coloured community existing as a natural social unit and an amalgam of disparate cultures and nationalities that exists as a coloured community principally in the *perception* of those outside of it, yet it is an issue of political, theoretical and empirical significance (Keith 1992, p. 23).

Keith goes on to explain the obvious: a disparate group of Blacks living under the threat of violence in Liverpool, being attacked in the streets because they were simply darker in hue than white, come together as a community to fight the violent racists. It is *known* historically and contemporaneously that Black Liverpudlians are an amalgam of African, African Caribbean, African American, and European heritage. This could also be stated for African Americans themselves and many other African derived communities in the Diaspora. One could add to the blending of these disparate Black cultures Arab and Asians in some cases. Human interaction in seaports has a long history and it should not be a surprise when one meets an individual who is, for example, "Black" with some oriental phenotype. Yet, in the encounter with white racism at its ugliest, given the 1948 racial attacks, people of color would clearly come together and put aside any cultural differences for the sake of their collective safety.

It is rather ironic, but probably done purposely, that Keith chooses to end his analysis of the anti-Black riots in Liverpool with a citation from Stephen Small, a Black Liverpudlian academic who had also imbibed the sociological jargon of "race" to a large extent when he wrote on Black Liverpool being an "anomaly" and "harbinger" for other parts of Black Britain due to the longevity of Black presence in the city—the aspect of Black British history that was disregarded by Stuart Hall and Paul Gilroy in their comprehension of Black settlement. However, Keith chooses the most obtuse aspect of Small's article which makes little sense to the overall anti-Black violent reality that took place in Liverpool over the August Bank Holiday in 1948. The obvious is often obscured by British sociological analysis of racialized relations. This could well be a manifestation of the discipline of sociology itself, with its jargon-layered prose posing as intellectual vigor. Indeed, one can get lost in the fog of sociological discourse when there is no necessity. As Keith ends his piece, leaning on Small's sociological prose:

> At the heart of such matters will be found the key to theoretical understanding, the maximum benefits for empirical analysis, the best means to policy formulation and the best foundation for political action (Small 1991, cited in Keith 1992, p. 27).

Significantly, Michael Keith was aware that the varied Black cultures of Liverpool were in solidarity for cultural unity and safety, what one could deem a "Pan African" camaraderie, based on the reality of violent white racism. The problem with his perspective on the diversity of Blackness is that he fails to consider the same situation for whiteness in Liverpool, which is far from uniform. Had he looked more closely at *his* cultural baggage perhaps there would have been a greater balance in his theoretical verbosity on the complexity of "race" as a concept. As Barnor Hesse has correctly contended, time and place are significant factors in the analysis of Black British experience, and it would be useful not to be so rigid in articulating such in static terms for theoretical license without carefully comprehending the immense violence involved in racialized histories. Significantly, one should not dismiss Black solidarity because the components of it are blended in cultural formation, especially while not even considering the profound amalgamation of whiteness. This type of theoretical incongruity only confuses, it does not clarify the manifold nature of white racism that involves: fear of status, livelihood competition, sexual envy, and sheer violence for violence's sake.

It is therefore apt to conclude the analysis of the 1948 anti-Black riots with greater clarity, and that is again offered by Peter Fryer, who revealed:

There was little that black people could do [in 1948 Liverpool] to defend themselves against this attack on their livelihood. When they dared to defend themselves against the physical attacks that the NUS [National Union of Seamen—white seamen] policy could not but stimulate and encourage, the Liverpool police retaliated with what one commentator has called "a singular lack of discrimination." Except, of course, racial discrimination (Fryer 1984, p. 367).

What Fryer explains above, implicitly and explicitly, is the fact that it was both institutional racism on behalf of the National Union of [white] Seamen, and the Liverpool Police Force that ultimately crushed Blacks in Liverpool during the August Bank Holiday of 1948. The dispute was about the threat Black seamen posed to white livelihood when employment was scarce. This then snowballed to an outright attack on *all* Blacks in Liverpool on the streets, and in the wrong place at the wrong time. Businesses owned and frequented by Liverpool Black communities were targets for racialized violence, and anyone with a dark skin could be victimized by frenzied white mobs seeking to hurt or kill during these three nights of unrest. In one incident a crowd of two thousand whites attacked Colsea House, a hostel for Black seamen based on Upper Stanhope Street. The occupants had to barricade themselves inside while the mob pounded on the door; the police eventually restored order, but those arrested were majority Black for defending their lives and community (Fryer 1984, pp. 368–372). The specter of white racism was ugly, vicious, and vituperative on the side of its citizenry and authorities—Blacks in Liverpool were under constant assault and this was a social reality that was most often explained as the problem of Black presence, not white racism. This then is the more authentic analysis that is devoid of sociological jargon and the obscuring of what happened to people of color in Liverpool during what should have been a holiday break in the summer of 1948. Instead, it would turn out to be a festival of fear and hatred on behalf of white racism.

NEW RACISM, NEW SAVAGES, AND RACIALIZED TENSIONS: 1970s

A Liverpool Born Black man, Dave Clay, has a long history of local activism on behalf of the Black experience. He recently published in 2020, with support from the local activists, organizations, and the Liverpool City Council, a book titled *A Liverpool Black History—100 Years: 1919–2019*. It is very descriptive and offers a visual insight into key aspects of history and culture surrounding Black presence in the city. Along with the trials and tribulations there is great cultural depth with rare photographs that prove the viability of Black youth presence—particularly from the 1960s to 1990s. There are many areas of hidden history that Clay considers white academics have failed to consider because they do not offer a Black perspective in whatever they write on Black issues concerning Liverpool. For white social researchers it is merely a case of considering urban decline and deprivation—and though important there is no analysis of how Black people have continued to survive against tremendous odds.

What is particularly encouraging about Clay's research is in the fact he documents many areas that have been overlooked, like the "Blackie" based on the intersection of Nelson Street and Great George Street in Liverpool 1. Originally a Congressional Church built in 1811 and now listed as a Grade II building by the National Heritage Trust, in the 1960s it would become an arts center frequented by the Liverpool Born Black community. The leader of the Blackie was Bill Harpe, an arts organizer and white hippie styled leader. Clay recalled taking a trip to the Blackie would involve "risk" due to white gangs looking to attack any Black person who ventured outside of Liverpool 8, and with it being located just outside the designated Liverpool 8 area there was an element of danger in going there to enjoy oneself (Clay 2020, p. 43). Nevertheless, Black teenagers would congregate at the Blackie, and there would be African American groups like the a cappella group the Persuasions, who took up a one-week residency in 1972 to provide workshops in singing for local Blacks—members of the Christian brothers attended these workshops and were clearly inspired by these great singers. The Blackie also engaged the Last Poets for a week's residency, who were a radical African American poetry-music group formed in the mid-1960s after the assassination of Malcolm X. Clay has documented this era with graphics and careful commentary that gives real insight into the lives of Liverpool Black youth of this era.

Moreover, Clay (2020) covers a racialized confrontation that took place on the notorious Falkner estate in 1972. This was a period when skinheads were popular and were picking on vulnerable Black residents, using intimidation tactics, including smashing the windows of homes and throwing bricks at vulnerable persons going about their daily business. Black youth in the area came to prevent these skinhead thugs hurting Black families by barricading the entrances to the estate. The police refused to accept that there was racial oppression being meted out and removed the barricades by force only for them to be erected again by Black youth in order to keep the skinheads from having free access to intimidate the residents. In a sense, this was a clash between white and Black working classes. The white youth were the assailants and the Black youth were protecting the property of the defenseless Black families. This is why the talk of Marxists often irks the sensibilities of Africana studies scholars. Too often the idea of "class" overrides the reality of racism and fails to capture the ignorance of white racism in union membership and on the grassroots level whereby Black residents live in the fear of their homes being attacked by white hooligans. The Marxist will speak of "false consciousness" in the white working class in regard to capitalist exploitation, yet rarely do they explain in layman terms the reality of white working-class racism.

The racist attack on Black homes in the Falkner Estate occurred in the month of August 1972 and was captured in a documentary by a famous white British liberal journalist, Jonathan Dimbleby, in an episode of *This Week*. Belchem (2014, p. 215) explains that the racialized tension lasted four nights. The national attention brought to a head a profound mistrust between Black and white youths who did not live too far from each other. Overall, the reality of racism was inextricably linked to urban poverty. Whites were living in poor housing, therefore angry and bitter, and Black Liverpudlians suffered from poverty and racism in most situations. They were twice or more likely to be unemployed and with it being summer the racialized tension grew stronger before boiling over. What can be revealed from 1972 is there was a dire need for recreational facilities for both Black and white youths who were caught in racial enmity and antagonism toward each other. Sadly, this scenario had deep roots in the city but what was emerging in light of all these *class-clashes* revealed a distinctly important problem: Liverpool poverty. When people are impoverished with few resources it is inevitable that antagonism will rise and tension will spill over into unnecessary violence. These white and Black youths had far more in common than in difference, though neither side understood this reality. The only variance was in skin color, and maybe some aspects of culture, because the manner in which they lived was in very similar housing and environment conditions.

A writer, Timeri Murari, originally from India but working as a journalist with aspiration to be a novelist, made use of gang warfare between Black Liverpudlians and whites in and around the tenements of Upper Pitt Street and Henry Street, taking in Great George Street and St. James Place, effectively Liverpool 1; with other "action" taking place in and around Princes Road, Berkeley Street, Upper Parliament Street, and Granby Street. Murari's book was based on his participant observation in how these gangs interacted and operated on these streets. He certainly integrates his "non-fiction" with some embellishment, *but* in reading the account of the Falkner Estate racial strife from 1972, more or less the same time period of Murari's book, he is not far off the mark in his depiction of how Black and white youth battled for turf dominance in early-to-mid-1970s. Murari published his evocative novel titled *The New Savages* in 1975. It is a book certainly worth reading if one wants to comprehend racialized relations among youth during this era. As noted earlier, we are considering working-class teenagers who practically share the same urban poverty experience in their lives, but it is "race" that separates them based on age-worn stereotypes and ignorance. There is the pot smoking, women beating, calling police pigs, and a range of ugly racist epithets surrounding Liverpool Born Blacks that indicates Murari had done his research in the area before writing his account. In all fair estimation, Murari's depiction of the gang culture of Blacks and whites in the early 1970s appears more feasible than fictitious. Clay may not have read the book, as he does not mention Murari in his account, but he does reference the dangers related to gangs based on racialized issues back in the 1960s and 1970s. Reflecting on how taking a trip to the Blackie on Great George Street could be perilous, Clay writes:

> A trip downhill (Duke Street) to the Blackie was a trip outside L8 to the former "coloured quarter." Numerous confrontations occurred with white gangs, the skins (heads), or John Bulls (JBs) as we called them. I won't mention what they called us! So why would young Black lads and girls "risk" the walk? (Clay 2020, p. 43).

The question Clay asks can be answered simply, the fun at the Blackie was worth the risk in terms of a confrontation with aggressive white youth. Crucially, Murari did his research on certain aspects of the Liverpool Black experience in the early 1970s that revealed a tension between Black and white youth in certain areas of the city. *The New Savages* could be considered a British version of *Tally's Corner: A Study of Negro Streetcorner Men* first published in 1967 by Elliot Liebow—similar in terms of exploring inner city behavior of youth. Like Liebow did with an urban group of African Americans, Murari certainly got close to some urban Liverpool Born Blacks. It also seems from reading Clay (2020), and his insights into Black youth culture from an insider's point of view, that Murari did actually visit the Blackie and watch the Black youth in their everyday interactions, along with the youth workers. There is a passage where the narrator in *The New Savages* explains how Bill Harpe from the Blackie employed two Black youth workers because his white middle-class co-workers could not identify with the Black Liverpudlians. But Murari also explains how the female white middle-class youth worker would rather work with the Black youth of the area than the white working-class youth. The narrator gives her account of working in the Blackie at this time:

> I prefer the black kids. When the Blackie was being used by the Skins [skinheads], it was awful. The white kids were just crude. They weren't able to appreciate anything you did for them and they'd be so destructive. The black kids are gentler. They have a culture—their music, their dances, the way they

dress—which the white kids just don't have. In a way, I feel far sorrier for the white kids. They really do have nothing (Murari 1975, p. 65).

This is very perceptive because Black youth in Liverpool did have a style, a fashion, in the 1970s with their Afros, clothing, and a way about them that was drawn from the culture of their transatlantic African American cousins in the United States, with a unique twist of being Black from Liverpool. There was a Black man too from the Blackie, a poet, a thinker, an artist, who personified the transatlantic links between Black Liverpool and Black America—Bobby Nyahoe (1946–1991). He was a Liverpool Born Black, and someone who had studied the Black Panthers, and he was also involved in Stanley House, the multiracial community center based on Upper Parliament Street. According to Clay, Bobby was a "respected Liverpool-born Black activist" who "forged a close relationship with the youth" (2020, p. 47). In thinking about Bobby Nyahoe and his presence at that time in Liverpool, it would be fair to suggest he was akin to Amiri Baraka (formerly Leroi Jones) from Black America. Murari clearly had met and observed Bobby and another prominent youth worker based at the Blackie, Peter Eyo—who was the man who pushed the idea to bring over the Persuasions to do singing workshops at the Blackie. Clearly, Bobby and Peter were conscious young Black men from Liverpool who knew something about Black empowerment. This goes back to "style" and "culture" that the Liverpool Black youth experience possessed that white culture did not, explained by the white youth worker to Murari at the Blackie.

Moreover, few historians have ever noted the Liverpool Born Black youth group who called themselves the "Green Jackets"—again it was another form of "styling" and bringing forth creative expression in the Black experience of the early 1970s. There were the "Young Black Panthers" who again exemplified what was going on in the United States at the time, especially with the "Free Angela Davis" campaign (Clay 2020, p. 46). Overall, in combining *The New Savages* (1975) and *A Liverpool Black History* (2020), while reading between the two texts, though separated by almost half of a century, there is much veracity to be gleaned concerning what was taking place in Liverpool 8 and the surrounding areas for Black and white working-class youth. There was great tension with racialized violence, urban poverty with a heavy, often brutal policing of this festering social crisis in the 1970s.

A book published in 1972 by Derek Humphry, with commentary by Gus John, titled *Police Power and Black People*, epitomised the problem of tension escalating between Black communities and policing. The very first chapter deals with "'Agriculture' in Liverpool" whereby the police were actually found to be "planting" drugs on Black persons they had arrested in order to secure a conviction. Humphry provided a whistleblower account from a police officer who had witnessed harassment and the planting of evidence firsthand, and this is part of a statement recorded and aired on a radio program: "In certain police stations, particularly in the city centre, brutality and drug planting and the harassing of minority groups takes place regularly" (Humphry 1972, p. 18). To suggest that racism in policing of Black communities did not exist would be tantamount to mendacity—it was rife. But the planting of drugs to convict Black persons of a crime not committed was a pretty low point in relations between the police and community in Liverpool.

In terms of Murari's novel based on Black youth in Liverpool, one could argue that he should have used a more humane title than *The New Savages*. But on reflection the police at the time largely viewed Liverpool Blacks as "savages"—nor did they think too highly of working-class white youth. What occurred on the Falkner Estate in 1972 with racialized violence was a warning for the authorities to take heed in relation to urban decline. The establishment failed to do so and once Margaret Thatcher emerged as the leader of the Conservative Party in 1975 it was the beginning of much greater austerity and urban unrest in Liverpool and other inner cities across Britain. There was, for example, the "winter of discontent" from late 1978 to 1979 that caused widespread disruption due to the pay demands from unions representing mainly white workers. The demands for better pay and working conditions led to ubiquitous strikes and unrest culminating with the defeat of the Labour Party and the rise of Prime Minister Margaret Thatcher, also known as the "Iron Lady" who would dominate British politics for over a decade—taking on trade unions, specifically the miners, and anyone else who did not fit in with her conservative, far-right, policies.

THE 1981 UPRISING IN LIVERPOOL 8—
BEARING WITNESS NOT FICTION

Unlike 1919 and 1948, one could not deem the July 1981 uprising in Liverpool 8 an anti-Black disturbance, yet it had strong racialized elements to it that have been accounted for in the 1989 *Loosen the Shackles: First Report of the Liverpool 8 Inquiry into Race Relations in Liverpool*—also known as the Gifford Inquiry. Clearly, urban poverty breeds discontent among all who live within its grasp. What sociologists have considered a "cycle of cultural poverty" whereby generations of families endure the same lifestyle and only the tenacious few break away to eke out a better life. For the majority there is the stifling reality of living and surviving with poor job prospects, which creates poor housing, which then creates poor health, which leads to poor education, and often prison for those youth unable to navigate the harshness of it all. This cycle of cultural poverty can be found in most urban areas, but in Liverpool 8/Toxteth there was all the above plus a rather heavy-handed policing policy that was meted out to Black youth in Liverpool.

The spark that ignited the 1981 uprising of Black youth initially, with many white youths joining in later, was due to the arrest of a young man on a motorcycle, Leroy Cooper, on Selbourne Street, close to Granby Street on July 3, 1981. The police at this time had a very bad reputation for "stop and search" tactics of Black youths. Tension was rife and an irritated group of Black youths had taken enough discrimination; they responded by throwing missiles at the police and within hours there was a full-blown uprising against the police raging on Upper Parliament Street. Moreover, one must comprehend that this was 1981, unemployment across Britain was at a fifty-year high, Thatcher's policies as the prime minister were draconian and brought great strain on Merseyside as a whole, but Liverpool 8 suffered greater austerity due to the decades of racialized oppression. The chief constable of the area at this time was Kenneth Oxford, a rather supercilious fellow who had been shaped by delusions of grandeur and white superiority via his background in the Royal Air Force. He was a man who did not care for Black people in Liverpool and had the worst instinct for improving racialized harmony in the area. Police tactics were imposed by a Special Patrol Group that specifically targeted Black youth with impunity—it was pretty horrendous. As noted earlier, police were found to be fabricating crime on Black youth in order to get a conviction, underhanded policing was commonplace in Liverpool 8. Oxford's tenure as the chief constable on Merseyside reigned from 1976 to 1989. In that period, he also refused to cooperate with the Gifford Inquiry (Gifford, Brown, and Bundey 1989, p. 159). Oxford was obstinate, arrogant, and rather dismissive of the social problems his leadership encouraged in terms of heavy-handed policing and the targeting of Black youth.

It was certainly a combination of social factors that led to this tinderbox being ready to explode and it did on that fateful Friday evening in July 1981. Though it was an apparent shock to Prime Minister Thatcher and her cabinet, those on the inside of Liverpool, like Margaret Simey, a staunch advocate for the poor and Black Liverpudlians in her Granby/Toxteth Ward as councilor. In her book *Democracy Rediscovered: A Study in Police Accountability* she gives her forthright views on how Blacks born and raised in the city were not "immigrants" but bona fide British citizens who had a right to express their grievances against police brutality. She was a brave soul to stand up for the rights of the oppressed. As a social researcher in November 1995, I spent time at her home in Blackburn Terrace Liverpool 8, interviewing her about the Fletcher Report of 1930. I recall the "old lady" being a gracious host and friendly during our two hours' discussion. She spoke about her husband being a colonial administrator in Jamaica and how she was a classmate of the notorious Muriel Fletcher. She explained to me that Fletcher was actually chased out of town due to the racism embedded in her report. Simey was clearly a rich source of information regarding the Liverpool Black experience, particularly regarding a white liberal political perspective.

At the time, being a young scholar working on a Doctor of Philosophy degree in sociological studies at the University of Sheffield, I was rather skeptical at the thought of interviewing Margaret Simey. I mentioned to her that I had completed my master's degree in Black studies at Ohio State University between 1992 and 1993, and that I was now trying to promote such education in the Liverpool higher education establishments with great difficulty due to the cultural hegemony of mainstream academics in the city. I did not mention to her that I had met with Rosa Parks and many of the key Civil Rights Movement leaders while in the United States. Indeed, I had a photograph of myself holding the hand of Ms. Parks—I do regret not sharing it with Margaret Simey the day I interviewed her. I suppose it was because I did not feel it was a comfortable enough setting due to my questioning her specifically about Muriel Fletcher.

Nor had my overall experience with white liberals been one of equal exchange as the "ghost of white supremacy" tended to most often intervene in any relationship between myself and a typical white liberal—one who felt he or she was "helping" Black people in their struggles. Yet in hindsight, she was at least fifty-five years my senior, and her track record as a white liberal was impeccable in terms of advocating for the rights of Black Liverpudlians. She was cordial, clearly a little old-fashioned in manner and style, but full of vivacious energy when she spoke about her fight for social justice in the city. In point of fact, after completing my doctoral studies in 1997, I published my first solo book in 2000, *Multiracial Identity: An International Perspective* by Macmillan Press, and part of its content relates to the November 1995 interview with Simey. She clearly did help me understand who Muriel Fletcher was as a person; and without her insight into 1930 I would not have gained such in-depth knowledge on the subject matter. After all, it was essentially a Liverpool Born Black research project by Fletcher that did much to stigmatize Black families of mixed heritage in the city (Christian 2008a). Moreover, the stereotypes contained in Fletcher's report would later be manifested in the articulation of the Merseyside chief constable in the 1970s to 1980s—Kenneth Oxford.

Margaret Simey was indeed a firm critic of the chief constable. She felt strongly that Oxford should have been made accountable for the manner in which policing was so draconian in Liverpool 8. He was also responsible for the decline in social club licenses in the area where Black youth went to blow off steam. Indeed, it was still perilous for Black Liverpudlians to venture outside of Liverpool 8 to socialize, so the closing of social clubs was a rather mean-spirited action on his behalf. In this sense, Oxford was a problematic

Merseyside chief of police, and Margaret Simey was his main critic—though ultimately the British establishment sided with Oxford not Simey. Thatcher and her cronies in the 1980s would suppress dissent and make the police force throughout Britain stronger, more violent, and heavy-handed in its operations. Thatcher's Britain was "white and proud" and she did all in her power to maintain right-wing policing throughout the nation. Therefore, her outright support for the chief constable was not surprising, and he in turn must have gained greater confidence to enhance his policies that maintained a firm grip on law and order. Here is how Simey explained the decline in democratic politics and the situation in Liverpool during the turbulent 1980s:

> In the context of Liverpool in the 1980s it is difficult to do other than despair. The unseemly abuse of power in recent years by the Militants, the abolition of the Merseyside County Council and with it the Police Authority, the deepening despondency in the inner city as the walls of the ghetto of deprivation become ever more tangible, are witness to the decay of the entire system of government as I have known it. I hate to think that in my five years as Chairman of the Merseyside Police Authority I should have presided over a decline in democratic practice such as I never have thought possible in so short a time (Simey 1988, p. 1).

Basically, the response of the established order to Margaret Simey's criticisms of the police were met with disdain and eventually they took away her power to make the Merseyside Police accountable in the day-to-day policing of Black communities. This was a slap in the face for those who fought for positive social change in Liverpool and it made life very difficult for all those involved in improving the dire social conditions. In terms of the actual uprising, Simey explains in chapter three of her book *Democracy Rediscovered* something that is important and often gets lost in the implicit racism and sociological interpretation of Black protest. Though Black and white Liverpudlians fought the police during the uprising in Liverpool 8, the looting of shops on Lodge Lane and other areas was conducted mainly by whites from *outside* the area. This social fact largely gets disregarded by white commentators, which is why Margaret Simey has a special place in the hearts of the majority of Black Liverpudlian thinkers. She was a very honest and forthright woman who had her own struggle for women's rights, and therefore could possibly appreciate the disempowering impact of racism and discrimination.

The uprising lasted about nine days in Liverpool 8 and was accounted for as the worst witnessed on British soil. Yet these disturbances had effectively been building up for decades. There was the consistent criminalization of Black youth that rankled any decent citizen. Dire poverty-ridden housing in urban areas, and outright racism in the policing of Liverpool 8 that could not be condoned in a so-called democratic state. The statistics state that nearly one thousand police officers were injured, and that the use of C.S. gas grenades on the homeland occurred for the first time when they were fired at the protestors on July 6, 1981 on Upper Parliament Street. The Gifford Report cites Lord Scarman's inquiry into the Brixton disorders that occurred in April 1981, three months prior to the Liverpool 8 uprising. Though Scarman did visit Liverpool after the disturbances had cooled down, his report related specifically to Brixton in London. Nevertheless, Scarman's overall evaluation was quite forthright:

> All the evidence I have received, on the subject of racial disadvantage and more generally, suggests that racialism and discrimination against Black people—often hidden, sometimes unconscious—remain a major source of social tension and conflict (cited in Gifford, Brown, and Bundey 1989, pp. 50–51).

Regardless of those in power who acknowledged the obvious, like Simey and Scarman noting racialized discrimination and poverty as foremost problems in British inner cities, Prime Minister Margaret Thatcher, who was at best an implicit racist, and at worst an overt one, did little to improve things for the Liverpool Black experience. In fact, she was rather dismissive and contemptuous in her response to the urban disturbances, refusing at every political turn to suggest the root causes were due to police brutality and poverty. "Poverty is no excuse for violence and looting" was the political mantra. However, Thatcher did send "Tarzan" to Liverpool or Michael Heseltine as he was also known for a few weeks' sojourn in the city. While in Liverpool he meandered around, often aimlessly, looking chirpy against the backdrop of dire social deprivation. His remit was to find out what could be done to improve the situation, and try to improve the entrepreneurial spirit of the city. He also stated he was prepared to "listen" to the profound grievances of Liverpool's Black communities. Perhaps he meant well, but Liverpudlians were skeptical of men like Heseltine who were from affluent backgrounds and ultimately had nothing in common with the common man and woman.

In his autobiography published in 2000, aptly titled *Life in the Jungle: My Autobiography,* he exposed his true intention during a camera-optic visit to Merseyside. He shared some rather fallacious stories about Liverpool 8 that come right out of the playbook of many stereotypes that float around regarding the people of Liverpool. It is important to share Heseltine's own words, not paraphrased so the reader can gauge the implicit insincerity of the man, and his links with journalists, who are supposed to be free of political bias when reporting on social crisis:

On the evening of 20 July [1981], my first night there, I organised a meeting of the local community groups in Toxteth [Liverpool 8]. I arrived at the venue, the local YMCA. A small group of journalists and a television camera were waiting at the door. One of the journalists whispered to me: "They're going to walk out." I saw at once the next day's headline: "Heseltine snubbed in Liverpool." That would be the story. The journalist had not specified who "they" were. It wasn't long before I found out (Heseltine 2000, p. 219).

One can gauge from the extract of Heseltine's account that his main concern was in how he would be perceived by the press the following day. The man was all about ego and he had no genuine interest in the social welfare of those to whom he was supposed to convey the government's sincere concerns and strategies for restoring the health and vitality of a broken community. Fundamentally, Heseltine was in Liverpool to boost his ratings and to shine in the spotlight as a "Tarzan" who visited the "Jungle" to tame feral unrest among the "natives" who were spoiling the tranquility of the "British way of life" for the majority. He was akin to a colonial administrator coming in from the metropole to assess the colonized and to dampen down the possibility of more conflict arising. Moreover, he had no understanding of the Liverpool Born Black experience, calling the spokespersons for the community "largely Afro-Caribbean" when in fact the majority of the Liverpool 8 Defense Committee, as they were called, had been born and raised in Liverpool from several generations of presence. The ignorance in Heseltine's autobiography is illuminating. The problem with books like his is in the fact that so few persons take the time to read the twaddle therein. He does acknowledge Toxteth as an "isolated community" with an "atmosphere of hopelessness" that was representative "proof of the long-term decline of the wider city" and the overall degeneration of Liverpool itself.

Moreover, Heseltine did not view the core problem in Liverpool being a racialized issue. He viewed the situation purely in structural economic terms. Therefore, if the city was vibrant and had a strong economic base the issue of "race" discrimination would not be a factor. Well, again Heseltine proved how little he comprehended the depth of British racism. One could simply retort, if his analysis had any modicum of veracity, why then had there been riots in Brixton, London, and other fairly affluent areas of the United Kingdom? His assessment was poor, ill-informed, and way out of line with the social reality of institutionalized racism in British society. Indeed, the racism in Liverpool was clearly deep-rooted, and the local analysis, *still to this day*, is "where are the Black people in the city center, the banks, the shops, and the service sector?" That is a viable starting point for any visitor to the city; keep in mind that Liverpool has arguably the longest presence of Black settlement in Britain (Costello 2001). Yet the invisibility of Black presence in the city center has been a mainstay for literally hundreds of years.

Obviously, the economic decline is relevant and one cannot deny this, but it does not explain the overall institutional bigotry that has beset this transatlantic Black experience. Heseltine in 1981 was determined to avoid any issue regarding racism in the British society at the hands of those who wielded power. He was wary of such questions from the press, because it was clear to most fair-minded commentators that racialized discrimination was a structural issue in regard to the 1981 uprising—though it was also class-based with the participation of some white actors. It is interesting how Heseltine is at ease explaining his ideas some twenty years on from the worst disturbances Britain has faced on its mainland. In regard to questions from the press in July of 1981, Heseltine writes:

> I knew only questions that mattered would concentrate on my reaction to the race issue. This was perceived to be the root cause of Liverpool's problems. It wasn't, of course. It was a violent and dramatic symptom, not the problem itself, which stemmed from the long-term structural and economic decline of the city under local [white] leadership quite unable to rise to the challenge of events (p. 219).

Heseltine is somewhat evasive; putting the culpability on the Liverpool City Council leadership was a political ploy as they then represented the Labour Party. Yes, the council were problematic, but at the heart of it was racism and policing, not purely economic decline. Black Liverpudlians were kept out of jobs, denied union representation, as discussed earlier with the example of the National Union of [white] Seamen from the 1948 anti-Black riots in the city. So, Heseltine was avoiding the "race issue" yet Liverpool Blacks were twice more likely to be unemployed compared to their white counterparts. It was ridiculous to avoid the deeply-rooted reality of racism in the city, but this is what Heseltine did, and it is now expressed openly in his autobiographical account.

Tarzan brought nothing to Liverpool 8 but some trees planted along Princes Road. To be fair, trees are beautiful, nature is important to any environment, but as the old saying goes: "money does not grow on trees"—and Liverpool Born Blacks required jobs and opportunities for self-development. The schooling system was defunct, and few opportunities existed in the workplace—is it any wonder there would be social problems that led to an uprising? Add to this the heavy-handed policing and society becomes a ticking time-bomb just waiting to explode. No community can exist in harmony if a specific cultural group is denied equal access to the fruits of labor and enterprise. But more than that, there has to be an end to racialized exclusion that takes place on every level of social interaction—even for those well qualified within education from Liverpool's Black communities. This seems incongruous, but racism was more subtle in 1981 than it appeared back in 1919 and 1948. Yet the outcome of systemic exclusion of Black Liverpudlians in the 1980s remained palpable and enduring.

Heseltine, also known as "Tarzan" which is problematic in itself, came to Liverpool 8 a skeptic, and left by all accounts a bigger one. Having been born and raised in the city, I am no different than a James Baldwin leaving his exiled home in Paris to revisit the city where he was born to write about it—Harlem. That stated, reading Heseltine's ignorant account of the urban uprising, and his stereotyped version of Liverpool 8, is difficult to endure. To add further insult, he adopts the simplest means to destroy Toxteth's reputation by using a criminal minority to speak for an entire community. As he contended:

> Toxteth was the centre of numerous criminal activities. Many of the most powerful people in the area at the time were deep into drugs, prostitution and protection rackets. All of this was the real world of Toxteth. This was the world with which I had come face to face (p. 220).

So, Tarzan comes face-to-face with criminal Toxteth—this is how he depicts the Liverpool 8 Defense Committee. It is an easy way out for Heseltine writing his memoir in the comfort of luxury as an acknowledged wealthy Briton (Heseltine 2000), but the fact remains that the Liverpool 8 Defense Committee were made up of Liverpool Born Blacks who were community activists, grassroots intellectuals, who had the best interests of the people in mind. Maria O'Reilly, Manneh Brown, Dave Smith, Peter Bassey, Dave Clay, Joe Joel, Liz Drysdale, Adam Hussein, and others were not criminals; they may have been criminalized one time or another in their lives, but they were Black Liverpudlians who wanted only the best for the community. Liz Drysdale, for example, went on to take Margaret Simey's seat on the council in 1987 after she retired, breaking barriers as a local Black woman to serve in the Liverpool City Council. Others from the Liverpool 8 Defense Committee went on to establish the L8 Law Centre in 1982 that helped protect vulnerable people from police harassment. Adam Hussein started up an invaluable bookstore that served Black history and culture in Myrtle Parade L8. Adam is a profound Black intellectual who was as close to being a criminal as Mother Teresa—he was a thoroughly good man with sound intellect back in the throes of community activism. To be sure, these were men and women indirectly defamed by Heseltine in his autobiography. The fact is he failed in his visit to Toxteth in 1981; and on reflection his memoir merely points out old worn-out stereotypes that have no substance to the reality of an entire community. If one reads his autobiographical account from the perspective of

Africana critical studies then it is a problematic account of Liverpool Black experience.

Of course, in *any* inner city with high unemployment and poor housing, health, and education there will be crime—that is sociology and criminology 101. But to paint an entire community with the same brush is indefensible and cowardly. Liverpool has had its share of high-profile criminals, who have served their time for crime related activity. Some have written books and exposed themselves to the public. The most recent of these would be the story of Stephen French depicted by the writer Graham Johnson in *The Devil: Britain's Most Feared Underworld Taxman* (2009). Though sensationalized and graphic, what should also be stated is that French received a degree from the University of Liverpool. Maybe had there been other viable opportunities to encourage his entrepreneurial skills he would not have turned to criminal activity? Liverpool to this day offers very little opportunity for Liverpool Born Blacks to prosper. However, I cannot condone anything criminal in the life that French chose. But in a sociological sense, it could be argued that had there been legitimate opportunity he may well have turned to such activity—this is simply playing "devil's advocate"—pardon the pun. Apparently, according to French, he learned much of his intimidation tactics as a debt collector from working with the Inland Revenue. According to French, the government "tax man" can be ruthless and employ psychological torture techniques when endeavoring to gain unpaid taxes back from the public. After explaining how he took over a furniture store because the owner had not paid ten thousand pounds in rent, French explains his logic in this manner:

> The beauty of the situation was that it was all legitimate business—tax paid. Again, it all came down to utilizing the skills I'd learned at the Inland Revenue—reputation and psychological intimidation. My unique selling point was that I could make debtors think that the moon was going to fall out of the sky and land on their house if they didn't pay (Johnson 2009, p. 211).

Stephen French was also a world champion in martial arts, and what he stated about the Inland Revenue certainly has legitimacy. If one does not pay taxes due then the wrath of psychological intimidation is heaped upon the person, mostly from poorer backgrounds, who fails to pay. One can actually sympathize with the logic of French in this sense. It sounds like he understood the ruthlessness of the Inland Revenue system. That is the nature of power and privilege. Therefore, who is "criminal" is a relative subject matter in the world of politics and *poli-tricks*.

Another notorious criminal who came out of the Liverpool Born Black experience is Curtis Warren—a boyhood friend of French but apparently their relationship turned sour as adults in criminal activity. In another sensationalized account, authors Tony Barnes, Richard Elias, and Peter Walsh tell his story from the streets of Liverpool to becoming "Britain's biggest ever drug baron." Their book was first published in 2000 and is titled *Cocky: The Rise and Fall of Curtis Warren.* Again, as with French, there is an interesting story of a Liverpool Born Black young man, raised in a tough environment, who gets into petty crime and becomes a mega-rich drug dealer of international proportions. Again, what is missed in these criminal-biographic stories is something very important related to one's socialization. For instance, what if Stephen French and Curtis Warren could have had genuine opportunities to have grown in an environment that made them feel needed. Where they had been able to express their obvious talents in another direction? Make no mistake, to have achieved what Curtis Warren supposedly did in terms of the accumulation of wealth via a complex international drug enterprise took exceptional mental ability. Significantly, for him to have negotiated on an international level in Europe, Latin America, and other parts of the world appears illogical for someone from his humble social background. How can such a complex network have been achieved given his limited opportunities in education? It certainly perplexes the mind, having myself gained three degrees from three universities, two from Britain, and one from the United States, I could not in a million years work out how Curtis Warren or Stephen French could do what they did in the underworld. It is rather perplexing and it must have taken great brain power to achieve what they each did in their criminal lives. Not to condone such criminal behavior but to suggest that minds like theirs could have been nurtured for greater use to humanity had the environment they grew up in offered such opportunity.

Another lesser-known Liverpool Born Black male, Robert Smith (though in the autobiography he says his last name is Suilerman) had his petty criminal life exposed by a local publisher, The Bluecoat Press, in 1996 titled *Born Under a Bad Sign*. Again, it is a story about a Black child coming to terms with his Blackness in Toxteth and learning the life of criminality. What is disquieting is in the way publishers are quick to circulate such negative stories surrounding Black Liverpudlians but fail markedly to share alternatively positive stories. It is no wonder then that the reading public should find it hard to see Blacks as anything but problematic in society. This is what has to change in mainstream culture, there needs to be a more holistic account of Black life and values that goes beyond the stereotypical drug dealing, violent, criminal portrayal. What should be brought more to the fore is a multifaceted aspect of Black British life. *Born Under a Bad Sign* only further perpetuates a genre of "Black criminality" while stifling so many optimistic stories of Black life in Liverpool and its history—regardless of the racism and discrimination that has impeded communities of color.

Crucially, Curtis Warren and Stephen French were extremely talented at what they did, and this is not to glorify their criminality. On the contrary, it is merely to expose the potential brain power of those men who could have been captains of industry. The point is also related to the waste of human talent, to the loss of such brain power in a community that needed them in a positive sense that is unutterably sad to contemplate. It is easy, way too easy, for Heseltine to pontificate from a lofty position in society about the rights and wrongs of poor communities like Toxteth. Yet a man like him would unlikely have prospered had he been born and raised in the same area as Curtis Warren and Stephen French. It is frustrating reading Heseltine because he is economical with the truth in his assessment of the poverty and racism that has blighted Liverpool 8. To suggest that the Liverpool 8 Defense Committee of 1981 was guided by criminals is an awful indictment and plainly untrue—that committee only had the best interests of all who resided in Toxteth. If criminality was a part of the experience, one should not be surprised. As the wonderful humanitarian Margaret Simey explained to the Gifford Inquiry in chapter five, "the harsh reality of racism":

> We are in a very bad way in Granby, and you are the only people ever, I think, who have actually come and sat here to listen to us, and so you are tremendously welcome. People don't know what to campaign for. They are completely turned adrift. The society is so disintegrated. The churches have disintegrated, the family has disintegrated, right down to the individual. Some have realised that there is an opportunity for free enterprise. You look for opportunities and you take them, and if the opportunities are fringe, if not straight crime, then you take them (cited in Gifford, Brown, and Bundey 1989, p. 63).

Margaret Simey was speaking in the post-1981-uprising era, some seven or more years later. She was an upright public servant who understood far more than a fabricated Tarzan, Michael Heseltine, who hid behind his privileged status and leveled attacks on community activists wanting some redress for Black Liverpudlians. In her assessment, one can read she is explaining that if no opportunities exist in the legitimate world, then some persons will take an illegitimate route to earn a living. This is not rocket science, but for men like Heseltine it would not fit his autobiographical narrative of "savior" and "entrepreneurial guru" who came and conquered the "natives" of Toxteth. His presence in Liverpool 8 in 1981, in hindsight, was an abject failure. In addition, Heseltine's autobiographical account of his time in Liverpool 8 is a farrago of twisted facts and stereotypes that may well appeal to the ignorant outsider, but does little to ameliorate the real social problems—of which many remain—such as widespread unemployment, deprivation, and yes, institutional racism.

One cannot comprehend the depth of structural racism unless there is a consideration of Heseltine, and ironically some of the research applied to the Liverpool Black experience by white researchers—who are either unresponsive in empathizing or cannot face the reality of "looking in the mirror" at their subconscious bias in maintaining the status quo. Only authentic utterances from Liverpool Black men and women can validate the lived experiences they have encountered in the city. When white researchers write on Black Liverpool, they should acknowledge their whiteness and few, if any, ever do. For example, there is a white researcher based currently at the University of Liverpool who deems herself an expert on Black Identity. Can you imagine a male researcher today having the audacity to promote himself as an "expert on Women's Identity"? It is ludicrous, but this is what white researchers in Liverpool have often done—put themselves as experts on Black life and experience. This is why the interpretation of Black Liverpool is often skewed and fails to have a Black perspective because the writer is of white heritage. However, being Black is not always the criteria for getting visceral knowledge of Black experience, but it is likely most often to be more efficacious in comprehending the life and times of a Black cultural group that she or he belongs to. Liverpool is unique, and this has been made manifest throughout this study—researchers need to read more deeply the accounts of Blacks who know the city, have lived in the city, and understand its depth.

John Belchem's study, *Before the Windrush: Race Relations in 20th-Century Liverpool* ends with an analysis of the 1981 uprising. His final chapter "It Took a Riot" is taken verbatim from Heseltine's autobiography and his chapter on Liverpool 8. Belchem discusses the Liverpool 8 Defense Committee that formed on July 6, 1981, and would be based at the Charles Wootton Centre in the basement where Heseltine, along with an armed undercover Special Branch officer, and advisors eventually met with the committee. I was a student at the Charlie at the time from 1980 to 1981. In one coincidental moment I am seen at the door of the Charles Wootton Centre inadvertently welcoming Heseltine to the institution on *News at 5:45pm*; the irony of that moment relates to me merely going to get my daily KitKat bar of chocolate from a local grocery store. I literally bumped into Heseltine at the entrance of the Charlie and he was being followed by group of national and international journalists with cameras. That stated, the Liverpool 8 Defense Committee gave no trouble during these crisis times. Why the committee was based at the Charlie was due to it being a comfort zone for all Black Liverpudlians. But the tone of Belchem is rather dismissive of this fact in his interpretation of the events—indeed the reason for the committee being based there is not even raised. To be sure, the Charlie was a place whereby Blacks felt culturally "at home" and this has been missed not only by Belchem (2014) but by two other white researchers who were endorsed by Belchem's Liverpool

University Press, Diane Frost and Richard Phillips. They edited a very short book titled *Liverpool '81: Remembering the Riots* (2011).These researchers had no direct contact with the time or place, yet were able to "shape" like Belchem how future generations will read the history. In comprehending the cultural relativity of the 1981 uprising, Frost and Phillips produced a rather turgid account that disregards the central role of the Charles Wootton Centre as a meeting place whereby the Liverpool 8 Defense Committee felt safe to articulate the grievances encountered by the community.

As mentioned, when one reads Heseltine's account, his ignorance of Black Liverpool flies off the pages of his autobiography. Like the dismissiveness of Frost and Phillips (2011), Heseltine fails to even capture the location of the Charlie correctly. Nor does he understand the essence of who made up the Liverpool 8 Defense Committee. This is a fundamental error, but it is highly relevant to what the white establishment, along with its academic cabal think of Liverpool Born Black heritage—those who were born in the city and not of immigrant status. In other words, the longevity of Black presence is summarily overlooked in the analysis. The fact that Black Liverpudlians were mainly Indigenous is not thoroughly tackled because it is an embarrassment to the established order. Heseltine recalls his second meeting with the Liverpool 8 Defense Committee, and his ignorance of all social facts shines through like a beacon light:

> The second meeting was arranged by my private office by telephone with the Afro-Caribbean leaders of the self-styled Liverpool 8 Defense Committee. We were escorted to it by armed policemen. We arrived at the door of a building on Princes Street, the Charles Wootton Centre, which was used by local community groups. It was made clear that only my political colleagues, my officials and I could attend the meeting. The police had to remain outside. They did (with the exception of one Special Branch constable, who handed his gun in a brown envelope to my private secretary and surreptitiously took his place) and the rest of us went in (Heseltine 2000, pp. 220–221).

Heseltine, in his reflection, clearly did not conduct impartial research on Black Liverpool for his autobiography; the Charles Wootton Centre was located on 248 Upper Parliament Street on the junction with Kingsley Road. But more than this, he deems the Liverpool 8 Defense Committee as merely "Afro-Caribbean leaders"—one can be sure he is endeavoring to make them out to be tough Yardies from Jamaica, as some may have been in Brixton—certainly not all. In relation to Liverpool, Heseltine was profoundly incorrect—the vast majority of the committee were born and raised in Liverpool of Black mixed heritage. To suggest they were "Afro-Caribbean" was purely his way of trying to demean them within the context of British politics at that time. Just as later studies would show, these men and women of the Liverpool 8 Defense Committee were concerned Liverpool Born Black individuals. They were not criminals and as mentioned earlier most went on to become prominent community leaders of grassroots organizations. Importantly, Heseltine goes on to state that the meeting was "brittle" but not aggressive, and it lasted about two hours. One can gauge that he was afraid by indicating it was "the most demanding meeting he had ever chaired"—another sign of his limited interaction with grassroots urban leaders who had survived generations of stigma and social exclusion.

Heseltine was basically out of his depth, and almost twenty years later his recollections only confirm the fact that his comprehension of those difficult days was at best hazy (Heseltine 2000). He could have at least got the location of this "unprecedented meeting" correct, along with the nuanced Black identity of the group. It is curious too how in not one page of his 560-page autobiography does he mention Patrick Minford, the economic advisor to Thatcher, who was based at the University of Liverpool during and after the 1981 uprising—but then again how could he? This would have proved how disastrous the Tory policies were for Liverpool. There can never be clarity when those at the top of society dictate how history shall be interpreted. Social change, as Margaret Simey aptly put it, for the better ultimately comes from the bottom up. If those who want to maintain the status quo are writing the history they interpret events merely for themselves—not for the greater good. A reading of Tarzan's autobiography is akin to the character he embellished while connected to Liverpool 8—hyperbolic fiction.

LIVERPOOL BLACK ORGANIZATIONS VERSUS A MILITANT COUNCIL

The years following 1981 were very difficult for Blacks in Liverpool. The Liverpool 8 Defense Committee morphed into the Liverpool Black Caucus. A Black organizational infrastructure formed in Liverpool 8 that proved very useful for empowering Liverpool Born Blacks who wanted to succeed in education and gain professional careers. This is also understated by white researchers from the University of Liverpool—who possibly saw the collective Black organizations as what they actually were: de facto segregated entities that were a safety net for Black Liverpudlians. It is worthwhile here to list those Black organizations that were important from the 1980s to 1990s in developing a sense of self-determination among the community. Yet, and this is a very important aspect in the fragility of these organizations: they relied heavily on funding from the Liverpool City Council and other government agencies (Lynch 1997). This made such organizations extremely vulnerable.

Nevertheless, there was a sense of "strength in numbers" in that if one was attacked the others could offer support and advocacy. Meanwhile, mainstream institutions tended to co-opt talented individuals from the grassroots and assimilate them into the majority cultural framework that was controlled in the main by white managerial staff.

Nevertheless, a grassroots infrastructure in Liverpool 8 made up of Black organizations began to take shape in the middle 1980s, and by then the Charles Wootton Centre was so well established that it spawned other organizations like the Black Sisters, and it had given experience to Black community persons like Claire Dove who went to create Blackburn House—an educational establishment for women. There was also the Liverpool 8 Law Centre that established a strong advocacy in defending mainly Black Liverpudlians from overzealous policing and issues related.

But first there was a major problem facing the Liverpool Black experience when the Militants, as they were known, took over the Liverpool City Council in 1983. They were collectively a nightmare for Black Liverpudlians—trying to impose a white working-class ideology (supposedly) that was to override Black cultural and political leadership. They also tried to enforce a "Black" leader on the community who was not from Liverpool, but London, nor did he have any experience in racialized issues—and particularly the complexity of Black Liverpool. This was to become widely known as the "Sam Bond Affair" that left a deep scar on relations between the Liverpool City Council and Black Liverpool. Dave Clay, a former member of the Liverpool 8 Defense Committee, did have a tad working relationship with the Militants in regard to their collective dislike to Margaret Thatcher's policies, but when it came to racialized matters there was no understanding whatsoever between the two groups (Clay 2020, pp. 89–90). This led to a long worn-out saga that eventually ended with Militants disbanding their "Race Relations Liaison Committee"—and Sam Bond, whom Belchem (2014, p. 267) describes as their "Militant toady from London," was left to meander in the corridors of the Liverpool City Council as a lame duck.

Meanwhile, Liverpool 8 fought on, and as poverty and discrimination lingered voluntary sector funding agencies grew, such as the Granby/Toxteth Task Force and European Anti-Poverty program and Objective 1. Liverpool was often exemplified as a "test case" for the worst ills a society can offer in terms of urban decay and the despondency of cultural groups who resided in such boundaries. The age-old problem with all these schemes is that they attracted outsiders and hangers-on who did not care for the local communities involved. It was the funding that came with ameliorating the social problems that most interested the outsiders. Again, it was most often a top-down social policy for urban renewal instead of a bottom-up. Always, either in the foreground or background, was a white man pulling the strings in terms of which organizations would be allocated funding—while voluntary sector groups scrambled to take some of the crumbs offered to keep whatever project afloat for a financial year or two. There was never any sustainability in these schemes and the irony is that most of the *existing* mainstream institutions like the University of Liverpool would guide the process in terms of uneven "partnerships" with various local Black organizations who were most often disempowered within these so-called partnerships.

Eric Lynch, as a renowned Liverpool Born Black and local historian relating to Liverpool and its involvement in the transatlantic slave system, made reference to contemporary problems facing Liverpool in terms of a lack of self-determination. He was perceptive enough to point out the problem of Black organizational reliance on external funding for economic survival. Lynch correctly forewarned the Liverpool 8 community with the following words:

> Too many Black organisations in the local community are dependent on external funding for survival and this is a regrettable state of affairs. The early Black organisations that were established in Liverpool, by the likes of African seamen, were self-reliant organisations. Black people were prepared to make sacrifices to help their brothers and sisters to gain a foothold in an often harsh economic and social environment. In helping one another, Black people were able to establish a real sense of community and pass on positive character-building values to up-and-coming generations of Black people. Black organisations today, dependent as they are on funding from agencies not controlled by Black people, send wrong messages to young Black people. The messages they learn are that it is O.K. to be dependent on the State, and financial survival is more important than retaining one's dignity and respect as a Black person (Lynch 1997, p. 54).

Eric Lynch certainly provided prophetic words and a caveat to Black organizations in the grassroots voluntary sector. Yet, always at the heart of the problem in Liverpool was its insuperable racism that caused a "uniquely horrific" form of poverty and racism—especially within the context of Granby/Toxteth. Black men and women needed livelihoods that mainstream Liverpool was simply not providing. This is why there was a strong and viable need for a grassroots Black community infrastructure that helped organize ways for tangible and effective improvement. The history of these struggles has been captured in numerous reports and newsletters that emanated from these organizations over the years. In fact, they represent a collective historical record from a grassroots point of view and are rarely cited in mainstream writings on the 1980s to 2000. These Black organizations were always up against the odds for survival due to having to rely on funding from precarious sources that did not desire, it seems, strong self-determined Black empowerment within the community of Liverpool 8. Anything "too Black" and independent was frowned upon by those who were involved in advising, editing, and shepherding funding to Black related voluntary groups—this has been deemed the "white liberal apparatus" who effectively controlled Black organizations via funding and political power that stemmed directly or indirectly from the business sector, local authority, and higher education institutions (Christian 1997b, pp. 73–76).

Take for example the London-based Commission for Racial Equality (CRE); from 1971 to 1993 it had its presence in Liverpool under the title Merseyside Racial Equality Council (MREC). The CRE decided to withdraw funding for the MREC from June 30, 1993. This is very odd as it was only two months after the murder of Stephen Lawrence in London by vicious racist thugs. Stephen was an eighteen-year-old student with dreams of becoming an architect when his life was brutally cut short while he waited for a bus to take him home. Now, two months later, in arguably the worst city known in Britain for Black survival, the CRE cut the funding. This is the inane reality of and decision making from those external to Liverpool who can defund an important organization for maintaining racialized harmony. Writing in the *Charles Wootton News* (CWN), the chairperson of the MREC stated:

> The Commission for Racial Equality (CRE) has dealt a fatal blow to Race Equality work and the fight against racism in the city, by withdrawing funding from the Merseyside Racial Equality Council (MREC). Following the CRE's decision, the [Liverpool City Council] gave notice to the MREC that their grant aid to the organisation will also cease (*Charles Wootton News*, June 1993, p. 9).

It was usually a domino effect whereby once one funding body ceased to fund an organization, another funder followed suit. That way it acted as an umbrella loss of funding to effectively break down an organization. Voluntary sector groups were particularly vulnerable when they relied so heavily for existence on Liverpool City Council funding—a notoriously racist institution in the life of the Liverpool Black experience (Gifford, Brown, Bundey 1989).

The early 1990s were particularly vibrant for grassroots community groups, yet the constant threat of closure due to funding issues meant that they could never be sustainable. A report on poverty from 1993 by the Granby/Toxteth Community Project, authored by Manneh Brown, which is hardly ever cited yet it is very well written and expertly produced, is aptly titled *They Haven't Done Nothing Yet* (taken from a song written and sung by Stevie Wonder from his 1974 album *Fulfillingness' First Finale*). This report consulted very important players in the grassroots sphere and went deep into the hypocrisy of local and national government agencies, as well as the University of Liverpool's lack of Black representation in their workforce. For example, it found that the Liverpool City Council boasted an equal opportunities policy but had nothing in place to actually measure such outcomes. In 1991 the council had a total workforce of 1,322, and only twenty-five employees were people of color. Likewise, the University of Liverpool employed 4,041 persons and only 107 had postcodes in Liverpool 8 and Liverpool 1, and a postcode does not indicate the cultural background of employees as many whites lived in these areas. There were no figures for Black and other people of color employees. The University of Liverpool was the largest employer and sat close to Liverpool 8. Crucially, Brown points out that the involvement of the university with the Granby/Toxteth Community Project was rather incongruous given its awful record with the Black community (Brown 1993, pp. 11–12).

Whenever one considered the employment statistics of larger employers in the city, and those close to Liverpool 8, there was a massive discrepancy. Clearly a game of "white exclusiveness in hiring" was at hand by those who had power to put an end to discrimination in employment practices. This brings us back to why there was a need for a grassroots institutional base; there had to be an infrastructure that developed a professional class of Black Liverpudlians and it was not happening rapidly enough within the sphere of mainstream employment opportunity. The only time these institutions opened their doors to Black Liverpudlians was indeed if they gained substantially from government grants. Moreover, during this period, in the 1980s–1990s there were millions of pounds being funneled to urban areas to provide training and educational opportunities for Black and low-income residents to overcome the dire impediments to their life chances. Again, the problem was that these "schemes" benefited the powerful institutions at the expense of the largely powerless voluntary organizations.

Chapter five of Manneh Brown's *They Haven't Done Nothing Yet* gives a breakdown of the key players in the Granby/Toxteth triangle who relied on funding from either the Granby Toxteth Task Force, the Merseyside Task Force, or the Liverpool City Council. Top of the list provided was the Charles Wootton College for Further Education, which was described as "a registered charity and its main aims and objectives being to promote the educational aspirations of local Black people" (Brown 1993, p. 29). Moreover, beyond the necessary English and arithmetic classes other courses it ran were, "a) black studies, b) medical secretarial course, c) law, d) economics." Brown explains that the college had a life going back twenty-plus years and had functioned as a community organization beyond its educational remit. This again, was due to the social exclusion emanating from the University of Liverpool and other local mainstream institutions that did not provide access or aid to the area. Now that there was money being funneled into the area the universities were *keen* to access it by exploiting the plight of underserved cultural groups such as Liverpool Born Blacks. The other organizations from *They Haven't Done Nothing Yet* highlighted were as follows:

> African Arts Collective
> Bangladeshi Association
> Somali Women's Group
> Merseyside Immigration Advice Unit
> South Liverpool Personnel [employment agency for local Blacks]
> Merseyside Somali Community Organisation
> Rialto Neighbourhood Council
> Liverpool Black Sisters
> ITEC CENTRE [Charles Wootton]
> East African Welfare Organisation
> Elimu Wan Nane/Study School [educational needs of local Black eleven- to eighteen-year-olds]
> Mary Seacole House [Health outreach to Liverpool 8 residents]
> South Liverpool Family Support Group [preventative drug use]
> Liverpool 8 Law Centre [help with police harassment and other issues]
>
> (Brown 1993, pp. 29–31).

This is a fairly representative list, but it excluded important grassroots organizations like the Caribbean Centre and other similar establishments that catered to Black youth, with social and recreational facilities. For intellectual knowledge on Black culture and resistance to mainstream racism Source Books in Myrtle Parade run by Adam Hussein was instrumental in providing an outlet to Black students and scholars who endeavored to comprehend Black history and culture from a historical perspective. Writers and artists often visited the bookstore when in town from overseas. Such as Maya Angelou who visited Source Books in June 1991, which gives an example of its importance to Liverpool's Black experience. Whenever a Black writer or artist was in town, they would ordinarily visit Source Books for a cultural respite from white Britain. The importance of such culturally relevant enterprises cannot be overstated.

The African American scholar and activist Dr. William Nelson Jr. completed a Fulbright Scholar research project in Liverpool 8 between 1990 and 1997, eventually publishing his research in 2000 titled *Black Atlantic Politics: Dilemmas of Political Empowerment in Boston and Liverpool*. This study, as with others written by Black scholars, has rarely been cited in any profound way, yet it offers relevant and judicial insight into the political structure of the Liverpool Black experience in comparison to another transatlantic city—Boston in the United States. Nelson provided a profound insight that gave a very useful analysis into the manner structural politics had played out in the city in relation to the Black communities of Liverpool. It is therefore curious why so few established white researchers have engaged with this perceptive analysis. Indeed, Belchem (2014) completely ignores Nelson's 2000 study, not even giving it a mention in his notes—which from a scholarly perspective is incredulous. To be sure, Dr. William Nelson Jr. offered a firm grasp on the historical significance of Black politics and resistance in the city, as he contended:

> Structural dimensions of the racial hierarchy and institutional environment operative in Liverpool have stimulated and nurtured a variety of Black political responses. Black resistance to racial oppression, in the form of organized protests, has been a prominent and persistent ingredient in the medley of strategies adopted and implemented by the Black community in Liverpool in its ongoing efforts to advance Black interests through political empowerment (Nelson 2000, p. 237).

One can only surmise that aspects of the mainstream scholarly community continue to dilute the significance of studies offered by Manneh Brown, Wally Brown, William Nelson Jr., Mark Christian, Madeline Heneghan, Emy Onuora, Stephen Small, and others, because these collective insights endeavor to empower the Liverpool Black experience. Moreover, they tend to offer perspectives that consider the empowerment of Black communities, unlike various white perspectives that tend to limit cultural racism as a primary factor. However, within the Black experience in Liverpool there have been some very honest white activists who have not exploited Black poverty and discrimination for their own ends. Included in this sense were Father Austin, Sylvia Brown, Ibrahim Thompson, Bill Harpe, to name a few. But in reality, the list is rather short *and* those listed progressive whites have not published accounts of their lived experiences in Liverpool. Most often, Black Liverpudlians have been largely exploited by those white researchers who were in positions of power to make social change or to speak truth to power on behalf of the disempowered. Unfortunately, in hindsight, some of them feathered their own nests by securing comfortable positions in the university sector while pontificating about urban poverty. The benefits provided to certain non-threatening Black Liverpudlians kept them in a state of acquiescence because at least they had acquired some form of livelihood via the funding of a project in the community. As Eric Lynch forewarned, nothing positive could come out of a situation whereby Black organizations depended on funding from external agencies who ultimately did not desire vibrant Black communities that thrived. Certainly, Black communities that prospered were usually regarded as a threat not an asset in such racialized hierarchies—and Liverpool was the personification of such. The status quo, it seems, merely wanted a situation where there was no conflict or unrest—it did not desire strong, culturally aware, and focused Black organizations that prospered in Liverpool.

THE 1990s BLACK STUDIES RENAISSANCE AND RESISTANCE

One area that succeeded in the 1990s was in the realm of Black history and culture in Liverpool. The Charles Wootton Centre in 1992 was upgraded to a college; and at the heart of its curriculum was Black studies, often known now as Africana studies. The Charlie had always offered Black history because it was the "Black" in the lives of its students. It was the fundamental reason they had walked through the doors of this special institution that provided educational opportunities to mainly young Black Liverpudlians who had been failed by the local schools. One has to disagree with Belchem (2014, p. 239) who deems the Charlie as a "second chance" educational establishment because most often it was the "only chance" to get qualifications for Black Liverpudlians—unless one was fortunate to have met a decent teacher and this was rare for Black children in Liverpool as discussed in chapter three. For example, out of the Christian family, five members of the family attended the Charlie: Janet, Rita, Mark, Jenny, and Kevin. That is an interesting *fact* because it is merely one Black Liverpool family highlighted of many who benefited greatly from this Black grassroots education institution.

To call the Charlie merely a "second chance" educational opportunity is to completely misunderstand the racialized discrimination in Liverpool. Belchem (2014) offers another mainstream liberal historical perspective on Black Liverpool, which dilutes the deep-rooted institutional racism that makes a mockery of the city being anything but cosmopolitan in any harmonious sense (Belchem 2006b). Studies that deftly maintain white supremacy are evident throughout the history relating to the Black experience, particularly when it relates to the historical amnesia of its slaving past. Significantly, Belchem does a disservice to historiography by avoiding the true nature of Liverpool's past—especially in relation to the deeply flawed editing in *Liverpool 800: Culture, Character and History* and chapter two on "Civic Liverpool 1680–1800" that airbrushes and euphemizes the ugliness of the city's slaving history. For example, there is no mention of the notorious Liverpool slaving vessel, the *Zong*, and the massacre of its enslaved Africans to gain insurance monies in 1781; nor the infamous *Brookes*, another Liverpool slaver, that is shown in a diagram displaying how the enslaved Africans were crammed tightly like sardines on the transatlantic voyages to misery. This is part of the untold history of Liverpool that is carefully and willfully disregarded by Belchem (2006a).

Yet it is this very type of history that needs to be taught and was imparted in Black studies classes at the Charles Wootton Centre back in the 1970s up to the 1990s when it would become a bona fide college. Black studies was not something appreciated by the city's powerbrokers in Liverpool 8 because it shined a light on the history of lies and avoidance that manifested in the majority of mainstream education curriculums in Liverpool and elsewhere. It was evident to anyone knowledgeable of the true essence of the Charlie that Black studies empowered Black Liverpudlians to reject any notion of mental inferiority that was implicitly instilled into their minds via their mainstream education experiences. One of the main aspects in denying the true history of Black experience is to blunt the self-assurance of the Black person. Once confidence is shattered there is no need to be concerned that the individual will be a threat; he or she will "know their place" and comply with the status of second-class citizenship. But this would not happen at the Charlie, where students were empowered to learn about those men and women of African heritage who resisted any assault on their humanity and fought back. When one is confronted with the history of Marcus Garvey or a Mary Seacole there is a sense of self-confidence that surges through one's veins as a person with Black heritage.

Lessons from the Charlie in Black history and culture would gradually increase the self-awareness of students. For example, the education in African cultures was just as worthy of historical analysis as any other cultural groups. Africa had a history that had long been maligned, misinterpreted, and misrepresented through generations of British miseducation. The Charlie had a library that was stacked with Black history books that would refute such misinformation. There were books on ancient and modern African history such as Chancellor Williams' *The Destruction of Black Civilization* and Basil Davidson's *The African Genius*. These books predated both Arab and European penetration into the African continent and gave an indication of great civilizations that thrived even before Europe existed. Now, this is powerful knowledge to a young Black Liverpudlian who had largely been taught that Africa had no history until Europe stumbled on the continent. Along with Basil Davidson and Peter Fryer, there was another white scholar, J. M. Blaut, who could be deemed in their caliber in terms of being honest and forthright in opposition to the imposition of Eurocentric/ethnocentric knowledge—something that is prevalent throughout many education systems across the globe. Blaut's study *The Colonizer's Model of the World* offers a refreshing perspective on world history that challenges the myth of white supremacy and domination that the likes of Margaret Thatcher and so many others had propagated during their lifetimes. Peter Fryer explained in brilliant prose the legacy of pseudoscientific racism in chapter seven of his *Staying Power: The History of Black People in Britain*. Blaut adds to Fryer's analysis by explaining the arrogance of European thought, as he contended:

> This belief is both historical and geographical [of white supremacy]. Europeans are seen as the "makers of history." Europe eternally advances, progresses, modernizes. The rest of the world advances more sluggishly, or stagnates: it is "traditional society." Therefore, the world has a permanent geographical center and a permanent periphery: an Inside and an Outside. Inside leads, Outside lags. Inside innovates, Outside imitates (Blaut 1993, p. 1).

It is difficult to disagree with Blaut and his thesis represents a way to comprehend how people of color have had to survive in this world of Eurocentric make believe that offers essentially ethnocentric delusions of grandeur in the nations like Britain, whereby people of color are never quite accepted, never quite British enough for the "British way of Life"—this is just as mythical as the notion of white supremacy itself. This is partly how the Charles Wootton College students would come to learn through Black studies a more balanced view of history. Sadly, this kind of knowledge and pedagogy was something that the white powerbrokers of the city did not want disseminated. In point of fact, during archival research for this study, I found the first ever edition of the *Charles Wootton News* from June 1987. On the front page there is a photograph of "victory" and the headline story relates to threats to the Charles Wootton Centre (as it was in 1987) being closed under a "City Council Compulsory Purchase Order"—apparently this threat had been hanging over the Charlie since 1984. This was probably an attempted reprisal against it for the role it played during the 1981 uprising whereby it allowed the Liverpool 8 Defense Committee to do their negotiations with the government in its building.

There was a two-day public inquiry in November 1986 to stop the compulsory purchase order and the secretary of state for environment finally rejected the Liverpool City Council's application to effectively demolish the Charlie. For a researcher, this was a revelation because it demonstrated with primary data that without Black organizations documenting history, in this case through publication of the *Charles Wootton News,* resistance to oppression can get lost. Moreover, it gives an account of the constant pressure grassroots organizations were under from those who had the power to defund them. It appears that the government stepped in on this occasion because it did not want the situation to escalate into another uprising—as it probably would have had the Liverpool City Council been allowed to demolish the Charlie building.

In a poignant reflection of this wonderful grassroots education establishment that persisted from 1974 to 2000 until it finally succumbed to a defunding entrapment, Dave Clay asks an open question in his chronicled study of Black presence in Liverpool: "Charles Wootton . . . What went wrong?" Such a request actually demands greater research, scrutiny of those involved in education funding policy at the Liverpool City Council, and local politicians who were in power during its closure. The director, Chief Ben Agwuna, passed away in February 2010, and with him went much of the economic history as to who was responsible at the council level, why, and how the Charles Wootton College was forced to close its doors in 2000. Clay (2020) writes that he was a former chair of the Charles Wootton College management committee in the late 1980s, and he explains that the college was always under a "funding crisis" due to the heavy reliance on the city council education department for funding. On reflection, it is fair to suggest that there was a rather anti-Charles Wootton College feeling in the city council from the very outset of its existence. Why? Perhaps because it catered to the needs and aspirations essentially of Liverpool Black youth.

The fact that the Liverpool City Council tried to demolish the building from 1984 to 1987 is not chronicled by Clay (2000), and it could well have been because he was unaware of this aspect of its struggle for survival. Indeed, until this study it has largely been hidden history or simply forgotten in the annals of Black Liverpool history. Basically, without there being full-blown access to city council documents and reports pertaining to the entire life of the Charles Wootton College from 1974 to 2000 there will be gaps in the knowledge of those who write about its history in relation to "Why the college closed its doors in 2000?" and what went wrong for this to happen. Clay does agree with some salient points that shed light on its importance to the Liverpool Black experience. The major point being it offered educational assistance to Black Liverpudlians who had been underserved by the mainstream education system in the city, and the Charlie therefore increased, directly, the number of Liverpool Born Blacks who would go on to universities to gain professional status and careers. Clay chronicled a photograph from the front page of the *Charles Wootton News* (Issue 12, December 1992) that celebrated changing its status from a "center" to a "college" in 1992. Again, this indicates the actual strength of the college at that point in time. Why? Because the list of names present that day reveal something rather curious. There were very powerful Liverpool City Council representatives at the celebration that day with the director, Chief Ben Agwuna. It is often stated that a picture says a thousand words, well this photograph says arguably more. Under the caption "Guests Toast College Status" the list of names followed from left to right: "Frank Cogley, Director of Education [Liverpool City Council]; Claire Dove, Chairperson Management Committee [Charles Wootton College] seen proposing a toast; Arif Ali, Editor of the *Caribbean Times*; Ben Agwuna, College Director; Rosemary Cooper, Lord Mayor [of Liverpool]; Bishop K. O'Connor, Archbishop's Representative and [Councillor]; and Gideon Ben-Tovim, Chair Liverpool Education Committee" (see appendix E).

By any standard, this is a significant group of dignitaries present to celebrate the status changing of *the* major grassroots education institution in Liverpool 8. Frank Cogley and Gideon Ben-Tovim represented the two most significant men in education for the Liverpool City Council. Ben-Tovim was also a prominent university lecturer, the editor of all things "Black Caucus," ironically, and the power behind many "Black" individuals who rose to prominence in the city: particularly Wally Brown and Dave Clay. To top that, he was also the councilor for the Princes Park ward that is an ethnically diverse area—containing mainly Black Liverpudlians—and the Charles Wootton College is located in the region.

Ben-Tovim was the labor councilor for Princes Park ward from 1987 to 2008. That is why it is curious to read some of his citations relating to the Charles Wootton College and other Black organizations—which are incongruous to his vast input on Black Liverpool issues. He was once apparently a card-carrying member of the Communist Party, which must have changed as he would settle for being a labor councilor. In relation to the Charles Wootton College from 1992 onward there's a contradiction with Ben-Tovim because he is there celebrating its status as a bona fide college in 1992, and still in 1996 he is citing it as a center in the media and research documents. This is not a mistake on his behalf because he was profoundly aware of the Charlie as an important institution via his role as the chair of the Liverpool Education Committee at the council and his relationship with Liverpool Black experience. Indeed, his influence in local Black politics was profound—editing and giving forewords to numerous books that focused on the issues encountered by Black Liverpudlians. So, the charge of "ignorant white man" cannot be put to Ben-Tovim—he systematically continued to reference the Charles Wootton as a "Centre" and not a "College" thereby limiting its status and further development.

This Machiavellian style of Clr./Lecturer Ben-Tovim is personified in Nelson (2000), *Black Atlantic Politics: Dilemmas of Political Empowerment in Boston and Liverpool*. Nelson explains that as the chair of the education committee on the Liverpool City Council, Councilor Ben-Tovim was disinclined to yield liberally to the college's requests for increased funding as he felt the requests were unrealistic. Nelson goes on to cite Ben-Tovim directly from 1996, four years since the Charles Wootton College had such status:

> The Charles Wootton Centre is going strong; it is still looking for resources. They've developed a good teaching staff the last few years, but I think one

of their problems is that they are carrying too much staff for the number of students they have. They've inherited a lot of staff from a number of programs in the past. These people are well known in the community, but the number of students, they've got problems justifying their funding to funding agencies (Ben-Tovim cited in Nelson 2000, p. 253).

In hindsight, there are major problems with Ben-Tovim's disingenuous perspective on the Charles Wootton College. He was fully aware of the many hundreds of Black Liverpudlians who had benefited due to the Charlie and its presence in Liverpool 8—which from a Black educational perspective was "priceless" to the communities it served. Moreover, he stated at the outset "The Charles Wootton Centre is going strong" again, dismissing its college status, *and* if it is going strong then why should there be a need to justify itself? He then hides behind the "numbers game" that white authority employs whenever it wants to defund a viable Black enterprise. "Oh well you just don't have the numbers of clients to justify your existence" or "well, we can't fund this because your product will not sell enough, it's only worthwhile to Black people." There are endless ways to "crunch numbers" to destroy a Black organization. Ben-Tovim was certainly economical with the truth and ahistorical in his comments to the African American political scientist when interviewed.

Going back to Dave Clay, who was a mentee of Ben-Tovim's, and worked closely with him on a number of Black grassroots projects—including a Race Equality Management Team that did not have longevity at the Liverpool City Council. Clay does get something right in regard to the funding of Black organizations, when he referred to the Charles Wootton College's role in Black community issues:

> It became clear that there was a thin line between education and (local) politics. This was no more apparent when the CWC allowed the "controversial" Liverpool 8 Defense Committee [which he was part of] to utilize their premises in 1981. This did not go down too well with their funding "masters" (Clay 2020, p. 62).

"This did not go down well with their funding 'masters'" is Dave Clay putting meat on the bones of his initial question in, what went wrong? The fact remains that the Charlie from the outset was an unwelcome grassroots institution for the Liverpool City Council due to the racialized factor in it highlighting the extremely poor experience of Black youth in Liverpool's schooling system. The very presence of it highlighted just how behind Liverpool was in providing proper education for Black Liverpudlians. What was an added problem related to the core of its curriculum being "Black studies" and Black perspectives in education that empowered students to embrace their collective

Blackness with self-confidence. Ben-Tovim knew this only too well being a university lecturer and a so-called expert on "race" and ethnicity. So, for him to suggest the Charles Wootton College had to justify itself was actually him acknowledging his credentials as a political charlatan to the Liverpool Black experience. He was actually a willing architect in the demise of the college because he never accepted it as a bona fide college—that is now historical fact—in his own words. Since he was *there* when it celebrated its status, and yet getting interviewed four years later he is still calling it a "center" and demeaning its justification—though being very careful to state, incongruously, that it is "going strong" but needed more funding.

By the mid-1990s the *Charles Wootton News* provided openly information that was related to the funding of the college. The issue from the June 1997 front page reads: "College Loses over £40,000 in Council Grants Cuts"—and reveals information relating to the struggle it has had historically with the Liverpool City Council. Again, behind these cuts were the names Frank Cogley, director of education, and Gideon Ben-Tovim, chair of the Liverpool Education Committee. Indeed, their roles in the council under education issues made it impossible for them *not* to have been central players in reducing funding to the college. For the year 1997/98 the council cut £19,000 from the grant, even though increasing numbers of Black Liverpudlian students were heading to universities (see appendix F). Clearly, there was a concerted effort to dismantle the college and destabilize its future on behalf of Cogley and Ben-Tovim. The irony is that the more success the college received with its outcomes, the more the Liverpool City Council turned the heat up by lessening its annual grant monies.

A frequent visitor and friend of the Charlie during this time was the late member of Parliament, Bernie Grant, MP for Tottenham in London. He literally loved coming to Liverpool to spend time at the Charles Wootton College. More importantly, he was made the first official patron of the college in 1997. He was indeed a champion for all Black British people and it was well known that he treasured his African heritage. Originally from Guyana, Bernie Grant was also a strong advocate for Black studies and an avid supporter and organizer for reparations. One may ask: was it because the Charles Wootton College raised awareness with the centrality of Black studies that the assault from the Liverpool City Council became so incessant during this period? Yet, it was out of necessity that Black studies emerged to offset the dire ignorance that mainstream Liverpool education inculcated. Is not "necessity the mother of invention"? Did not the profound isolation of Black Liverpudlians create the need for the Charles Wootton College? If so, then why defund it at the height of its power and influence, unless its effect did not coincide with the cultural hegemony of the existing order.

To give a contemporary example, currently in the United States the right-wing political sphere are attempting to dismantle "critical race theory" which simply deconstructs the reality of white supremacy and how it has manifested in American history and culture. Well, Black studies at the Charles Wootton College, a core aspect of its curriculum, was no different than critical race theory in exposing both historical and contemporary forms of institutional racism and how to combat it. When asked to share his feelings on how the Charles Wootton College maintained itself under such financial insecurity the director, Ben Agwuna, responded:

> When this problem started [decreasing funding for the college from the council] the Militants [far-left Liverpool City Council in power 1983–1986] did not suspend our grant. The money was there. Every month we had to apply to the city council for money to pay the rents, lights and so on. We had to justify our budget from month to month. The management team of the centre started panicking. We had to rush through our charitable status so that if the centre was bankrupt, the Management Committee would be protected from liability. It was only because the staff stood fast that the centre remained open (cited in Nelson 2000, p. 252).

It is certainly not the most optimal way to run a fiscal policy to have an important grassroots education organization in Liverpool 8 struggling on a month-to-month existence. This was clearly a maneuver by the Liverpool City Council to destabilize and destroy the Charlie, along with its attempt to demolish the building from 1984 to1987. This was left-wing politics in Liverpool and it did not improve much under other political parties, there was always financial insecurity. Nevertheless, there are those responsible for the demise of the Charles Wootton College other than Ben-Tovim, Cogley, and other Liverpool City Council actors. Maybe if the director Ben Agwuna had been less confrontational in his leadership, and more transparent with those involved in the decision-making, less openly African centered in his mannerism, the college could have been saved—this is all conjecture and for the history books to interpret. What is difficult to accept is a response to the closure of the college by Ben-Tovim over a decade later that is Machiavellian in scope, inculcating historical amnesia:

> With respect to community infrastructure some of the older community centres, for example Charles Wootton and the Liverpool 8 Law Centre have gone. Those were both quite dependent of [Liverpool] City Council funding, and ultimately came up against decisions linked to value for money. The closures of both the Charles Wootton and the Liverpool 8 Law Centre went without a great deal of community opposition and noise, although they both provided significant services in their time and were important institutions (cited in Frost and Phillips 2011, p. 132).

To suggest Ben-Tovim was being economical with the truth would be an understatement. As noted, he was at the center of the poli-tricks as to why the Charles Wootton College was forced to close its doors. To be at the core decision-making tables in all things "Black" in Liverpool was Ben-Tovim's remit at the council and in the community via his lectureship position at the University of Liverpool. There is nowhere to find him citing the Charles Wootton College as a college; even though he can be seen smarmily smiling when toasting its elevation from a "centre to college" on the front page of the December 1992 edition of the *Charles Wootton News* (appendix E). With certainty, Ben-Tovim could never have accepted a grassroots education organization led by Black men and women being a bona fide college. And certainly not one that offered a Black intellectual perspective at its core. One only has to read Ben-Tovim's quotes on the college that he never openly deemed to be a college. Few researchers would probably not even care to delve into such an obvious nuance because most white academics are not adept at considering power dynamics within the Liverpool Black experience.

Clay (2020, p. 60) was close to Ben-Tovim during the height of his community activism in Liverpool 8, yet he asked the question "what went wrong?" in relation to the demise of the Charles Wootton College in 2000. The question should have been far broader from Clay that covered a deeper inquiry. Like, what happened to the vibrant community infrastructure of Liverpool 8? Moreover, what happened to these following organizations in a collective sense: Liverpool South Personnel, Elimu Study School, LAARCA, Source Books, L8 Access to Higher Education, Charles Wootton College, Liverpool 8 Law Centre, Caribbean Centre, and the Race Equality Management Team, that Clay himself managed, at the Liverpool City Council? Because these organizations, along with others, were highly relevant to the Black community infrastructure in Liverpool 8. To suggest that they no longer had relevance is myopic. An explanation can be found by suggesting white cultural hegemony did not want the community to prosper and maintain a level of independence. Eric Lynch was correct when he stated, paraphrased, "Black organizations are too reliant on external funding" and this will be deleterious for Black communities in Liverpool if it continues (Lynch 1997). Not only was he prescient in his warning to Black organizations, he understood the importance of having a sense of independence among Black Liverpudlians who most often took the brunt of economic austerity whenever there was a downturn in the local economy. The Liverpool City Council has a history of defunding Black organizations (Lynch 1997), and some of the above-mentioned examples are more than adequate proof. It is imperative to comprehend grassroots Black communities often rely heavily on external funding, and if that revenue disappears then so it is likely that the organization does too.

AN EMPTY SLAVE TRADE APOLOGY AND RENEGED PROMISES BY THE LIVERPOOL CITY COUNCIL

This chapter concludes with a brief analysis of the formal "City of Liverpool Slave Trade Apology" that was sanctioned by the Liverpool City Council at the Town Hall on December 9, 1999. Due to the historical importance of the apology for Black communities, and it being largely disregarded by officialdom in the city to date, it ranks as imperative in holding the council responsible to its wording *within* the authorized apology. Moreover, the local historian John Belchem, who in editing *Liverpool 800: Culture, Character and History* (2006a), or even his *Before the Windrush: Race Relations in 20th- Century Liverpool* (2014), that focused directly on the Liverpool Black experience, failed to state *one* word about the city's official slavery apology. Now, how can it be possible for an academic focused on the history of Blacks in Liverpool to overlook the significance and historical relevance of an official slave trade apology that was ratified in December 1999? It is odd but not too surprising coming out of mainstream academia in Liverpool that has a propensity to dilute the veracity of Liverpool Black history. In point of fact, a recent study noted the apology in *The Persistence of Memory: Remembering Slavery in Liverpool, 'Slaving Capital of the World'* (2020) by Jessica Moody, and this research stems from her 2014 doctoral thesis at York University. Yet, in relation to the analysis of the "City of Liverpool Slave Trade Apology" there are certain discrepancies between a reading of the doctoral thesis and the book itself—especially in terms of direct references being omitted that would be more critical of the establishment in Liverpool. It appears that the book format diluted the context and deleted pertinent sources that would have given more relevance to the contemporary Liverpool Black experience (Christian 2002d). If the reader puts this point in context with the city's overall avoidance of the apology and its significance to contemporary Black Liverpudlians, then one can gauge a crafty dilution of historical veracity. To put this another way, it could be deemed that the powerbrokers in the city created another form of historical amnesia for future generations by simply denying the slavery apology and relevant source material. Certainly, obscuring the importance of Black scholarly and grassroots organizational contributions responsible for bringing about the slavery apology in the first instance is an act of definite avoidance.

To be sure, in the past I have provided two scholarly contributions related to the city's official apology in the form of a peer-reviewed journal article (Christian 2002d) and a public lecture presented at the International Slavery Museum on the Albert Dock in Liverpool—November 14, 2007. Rather than repeating the entire build-up to the slave trade apology that was put forward in November and ratified in December 1999 by Councilor Mirna Juarez, it would be more efficacious to simply provide an analysis of the slave trade apology wording itself for brevity's sake. Below is the actual verbatim that speaks to the City of Liverpool's profound involvement and its contrition, in relation the transatlantic enslavement system:

> At a special Meeting of the city council of the City of Liverpool held on Thursday, 9 December 1999 within the Town Hall, in the presence of The Right Worshipful, The Lord Mayor, Councillor Joe Devaney, it was moved by Councillor Mirna Juarez and seconded by Councillor Maggie McDaid and supported by all party leaders or their representatives, that;
>
> As its last formal act, at its last formal meeting of this millennium, the city council acknowledges Liverpool's responsibility for its involvement in the three centuries of the slave trade, a trade which influenced every aspect of the city's commerce and culture and affected the lives of all its citizens.
>
> Whilst bequeathing the city a rich diversity of people and cultures, learning, architecture and financial wealth, it also obscured the human suffering upon which it was built. The untold misery which was caused has left a legacy which affects black people in Liverpool today.
>
> On behalf of the city, the city council expresses its shame and remorse for the city's role in the trade in human misery. The city council makes an unreserved apology for its involvement in the slave trade and the continual effects of slavery on Liverpool's Black communities.
>
> The first-step towards reconciliation will be the basis upon which the city, and all its people and institutions, can grasp the challenges of the new millennium with a fresh and sustainable commitment to equality and justice in Liverpool.
>
> The city council hereby commits itself to work closely with all Liverpool's communities and partners and with the people of those countries which have carried the burden of the slave trade.
>
> The council also commits to programmes and action, with full participation of Liverpool's black communities, which will seek to combat all forms of racism and discrimination and will recognise and respond to the city's multi-racial inheritance and celebrate the skills and talents of all its people.
>
> The Motion was supported unanimously
>
> Lord Mayor [Councilor Joe Devaney]

In hindsight, it is interesting to read the official apology from the Liverpool City Council given that within one year it reneged on its promises to Black communities of the city—all of them. For example, in 2000 the council took away funding from the Charles Wootton College and the Liverpool 8 Law Centre, which effectively destroyed the Black community infrastructure of Liverpool 8 that was thriving in the 1990s to combat manifold forms of

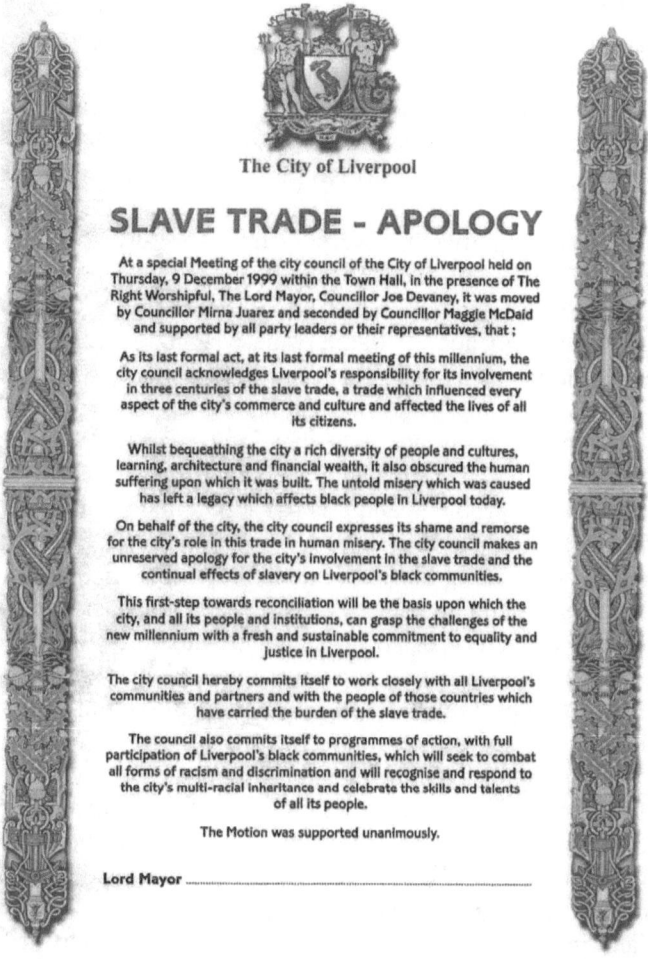

Figure 4.1 Formal Slave Apology Certificate from the Liverpool City Council—December 9, 1999.
Source: 352/MIN Liverpool Central Library and Archive for the Slavery Minutes and Apology reprinted with permission from the archive.

institutionalized racism. For the record here, Clr. Gideon Ben-Tovim for the Princes Park ward was not even present to vote on the Liverpool Slave Trade Apology on December 9, 1999. It is unutterably sad to consider him as a so-called advocate of the Liverpool Black experience when silent on such an important historical issue for Liverpool Black citizenry. It is doubtful that anyone has ever taken the time to follow his quotes and deeds as an elected councilor for an area that covered a large section of Liverpool 8. This study has been forced to do so in relation to the Charles Wootton College,

Liverpool 8 Law Centre, and other Black grassroots institutions. Clearly there should be a reassessment of all things Clr. Ben-Tovim was involved in with Black organizations as a council member and to consider why a self-styled communist/labor advocate could accept the demise of the Liverpool 8's grassroots community infrastructure. In January 2012, Clr. Ben-Tovim was awarded the OBE (Order of the British Empire) apparently for his "services to health" in the City of Liverpool—it would not be facetious to exclude the health of Black communities in Liverpool from this award. For example, in an article titled "Blacks Still Facing Hard Times in Liverpool's Own Form of Apartheid" by Kim Sengupta from the *Independent*, she cites Clr. Ben-Tovim, and an equal opportunity administrator, Anne Wright, regarding the Liverpool City Council's intransigent structural racism. Sengupta cited Clr. Ben-Tovim as stating, "The ethnic minorities now do have greater access to channels to the authorities, so in that respect things have improved, although they are far from perfect." Whereas the equal opportunity officer, Wright, stated, "We know there is a major problem, and it is not something we are taking lightly" (*Independent*, March 25, 1998).

To be sure, when reading his public and published comments, a pattern in Clr. Ben-Tovim's statements emerged. He had a propensity to quell Black protest, and then at the end of all his statements there is a tendency to state something to cover himself as an apparent advocate for Black struggle in the city. Most often this phrase is tacked on after subduing the protest of Black Liverpudlians in any given conflict: "but there's still a long way to go." Maybe this is the way of a politician and the emphasis is to keep social order. Yet it can be deemed an underhand way to control Black protest in Liverpool that has often been missed by researchers in his rhetoric and writings. As an elected official, it seems that Clr. Ben-Tovim was connected to Black struggle in Liverpool for merely self-interest, because the empowerment of Black Liverpudlians in the city who aimed for self-determination independently clearly waned under his leadership. It appears from his public comments and role in the council as an education officer that he would do what he could to destabilize Black grassroots independence of thought and action that genuinely gave any degree of autonomy—particularly in relation to the Charles Wootton College. Not only were the views of Black Liverpudlians most often ignored by the Liverpool City Council, they were usually dismissed outright and demeaned (Gifford, Brown, and Bundey 1989; Liverpool Black Caucus 1986).

Crucially, in considering this City of Liverpool Slave Trade Apology in regard to the history of Black Liverpudlians throughout this chapter, it was the height of hypocrisy and a cruel jest to confer this apology to Liverpool Black communities. Malcolm X in his many public addresses would inform his people that: "They'd been took" . . . "Bamboozled" . . . "Hoodwinked" by the establishment. Well, in relation to the Liverpool City Council and its apology for involvement in the transatlantic enslavement system, they turned out to be empty promises: "to commit itself to programmes of action" with the "full participation of Liverpool's Black communities"—the council simply reneged on these promises. On reflection, it has proved to be an empty statement and it is at best a fraudulent apology. It basically masked its design to dismantle through its consequent defunding of grassroots institutions. Those very organizations that aided Black Liverpudlians in their long night of institutionalized racism and oppression. Indeed it is a shameful act of betrayal that may never be put right—unless the good people of Liverpool become aware of what actually transpired in the Machiavellian post-Slave Trade Apology era: *the destruction of many viable Black grassroots institutions in Liverpool 8.*

However, there were those experienced grassroots advocates in Liverpool 8 that did not trust anything the Liverpool City Council proposed and therefore boycotted the December 9, 1999 meeting. Long-standing community activists Eric Lynch, Maria O'Reilly, and Albert Fontenot were there to protest the formal apology. The following day the *Daily Post* published a full-page article by Sol Buckner on the council meeting that ratified the apology. The report cited Mark Brown from the Consortium of Black Organisations, who stated: "We just feel that two days to consult the [B]lack community on such an important issue is an insult" (*Daily Post,* December 10, 1999, p. 3). Overall, there was grassroots skepticism in regard to whether the council had in place plans of action to ameliorate racism and discrimination in housing, jobs, and education.

Others felt that it was an important historical moment that future generations of Liverpool Blacks could hold the council accountable to the statement. To be fair, a formal slave trade apology offered hope for the future, and with it being in writing it could be used to show the public how distrusting the council could be if they reneged on the promises it made to improve the lot of Black Liverpudlians. Therefore, those who supported the apology were not naïve, they simply wanted something etched in stone to hold the council responsible going forward. That is why it is so important to hold the Liverpool City Council accountable now for the attempt to deny that a slavery apology even occurred. Indeed, as a researcher it has been a difficult task to locate evidence to prove the existence of this slavery apology in contemporary writings on Liverpool history.

In evaluating the apology holistically, and within the context of this entire chapter, it has been contended given the City of Liverpool and its Slave Trade Apology announcement, it should certainly be followed up by viable reparations (appendix B). However, Black grassroots organizations should also take some responsibility for the manner in which they folded, and how they happened to be defunded by the council. Particularly, in regard to the Charles Wootton College and the Liverpool 8 Law Centre which should both be here today due to their importance to the communities they served. Indeed, as Eric Lynch in 1997 warned the Liverpool 8 community, without having a strong degree of economic independence one cannot ever rely on external funding bodies to maintain Black community enterprise. The history of Liverpool has shown itself to be callous and dismissive of its Black settlement. Famous Black Liverpudlians such as Eric Lynch, Dorothy Kuya, Wally Brown, Ray Costello, Liz Drysdale, Levi Tafari, Anna Rothery, Gloria Hyatt, Howard Gayle, and many others have documented historical struggle the community has encountered in education, housing, employment, and culture. They have each played a part in pushing Black Liverpudlians forward—regardless of the various forms of racism they respectively met in life. Yet there are lesser known Black Liverpudlians who deserve to be known for the long years of grassroots activism in Liverpool 8, names such as: Louis Julienne, Alan Gayle, Eugene Weaver, Maria O'Reilly, Albert Fontenot, Joe Farrag, Peter Bassey, Solly Bassey, Dave Smith, Victor Christian, Karl Smith, Adam Hussein, Ray Quarless, Sonia Bassey, Ann Carney, Peter Eyo, Bobby Nyahoe, Joe Joel, Manneh Brown, Abdul Gayle, Dave Clay, Steve Smith, Alex Bennett, and so many others who have contributed to the historical struggle of Blacks in Liverpool but are rarely recognized.

It is now a concern for future generations to take up the baton to continue the fight for racialized equality in the city. A Black Liverpudlian family, the Christians, has been cited throughout as an example of the many other Black Liverpudlian families, particularly large, that have endured in the racialized hierarchy of the city, and have attained some individual success against the odds in education and/or cultural industries. However, there should never have had to be such adverse racialized obstacles placed in the way of celebrating *any* Black Liverpudlian talent. As the deceitful City of Liverpool Slave Trade Apology stated at the close of the twentieth century in 1999, it "will recognise and respond to the city's multi-racial inheritance and celebrate the skills and talents of all its people." Now, if only those words from the official slavery apology were to become a widespread reality—then we could truly celebrate in unison as one large family of Liverpool citizens. That day has yet to arrive; there has to be first a recognition of what took place almost immediately after the disingenuous apology was enacted: an assault on Black organizational funding throughout Liverpool 8 in the early 2000s via the Liverpool City Council.

Chapter 5

A Tale of Two Freedoms

Contemporary Self-Reflexivity and the Memory of Frederick Douglass

Frederick Douglass, a twenty-seven-year-old fugitive on the run from enslavement, was anxious to escape to Britain in 1845 because he had recently penned what would be the first of three autobiographical accounts of his life. He was in a very precarious situation having fled his slaveholder, with the aid of his eventual wife, Anna Douglass, in 1838 Maryland at the age of twenty years. Between 1841 and 1845 he had made a name for himself as an orator for the American Abolitionist movement led by William Lloyd Garrison, the fiery editor of the *Liberator*—a weekly newspaper employed solely for the destruction of the slave system. Garrison was a white man with a strong moral aversion to the enslavement of Africans in America. He detested the "peculiar institution" that dehumanized his fellow African American men and women. When Garrison met the young Frederick Douglass, whose name during his days in bondage was Frederick Augustus Washington Bailey, he was immediately taken back by the potential of his oratorical skills and acumen for revealing the horrors of servitude. Therefore, he encouraged Douglass to "tell his story" as a paid anti-enslavement lecturer in the abolitionist crusade, along with putting it into the written word. Hence, the publication of the *Narrative of the Life of Frederick Douglass, an American Slave, Written by Himself* in 1845—which became an immediate bestseller in the United States and Britain. Yet, the success of his autobiography also put his life in danger of being captured and returned to bondage—he had to leave America.

His destination was the British Isles where he would hopefully eventually find freedom from bondage. Douglass recalled his travel to Britain in this way:

> The writing of my pamphlet [autobiography], in the spring of 1845, endangered my liberty, and led me to seek a refuge from republican slavery in monarchial England. A rude, uncultivated fugitive slave was driven, by stern necessity, to that country to which young American gentlemen go to increase their stock of knowledge, to seek pleasure, to have their rough, democratic manners softened by contact with English aristocratic refinement. (Douglass 2019, p. 250).

Frederick was a Black man of mixed heritage. His mother, Harriet Bailey, being African American, and his "father" being an unknown white man—no doubt someone close to the plantation world in which he was born and raised. Douglass wrote: "The opinion . . . was whispered that my master was my father. . . . I know nothing; the means of knowing was withheld from me" (Douglass 1997, p. 2). After he escaped, he found his way to New York, finally settling in New Bedford, Massachusetts with his wife. From there he rose to become a popular abolitionist speaker in the cause for the freedom of his people. It was arranged for him to travel to Britain in August of 1845, escorted by a white abolitionist James Buffum. They were then to join forces with British abolitionists, first in Liverpool, England, and then conduct a speaking tour across the British Isles. At the venues he would share his autobiography that depicted the atrocities committed to enslaved African Americans.

Frederick Douglass' nineteenth century story is a transatlantic tale that also connects inextricably to other persons who endeavored to seek freedom from oppression and the stifling of one's humanity and life chances. When he boarded the Cunard-owned *Cambria* steamship in August of 1845 he was anxious, excited, and wary going into what was an entirely unknown adventure, sailing from Boston to Liverpool. Crossing the Atlantic Ocean took about twelve days and, in many respects, it was a turbulent voyage for this young Black man fleeing from persecution as an enslaved fugitive. His account of the journey and stay in the United Kingdom is well documented in chapter twenty-four of this second autobiographical book, *My Bondage and My Freedom,* and is titled "Twenty-One Months in Great Britain." It was not an easy journey as he was not allowed to mix freely on the vessel and confined to the steerage, lower deck, quarters of the ship due to his African American heritage. Moreover, there were a number of slave merchants on board from New Orleans and Georgia who were on route to do business in Liverpool and elsewhere in Britain—most probably related to cotton and other commodities that were brought from plantations to British seaports such as Liverpool to be manufactured in local factories. Slavery may well have been abolished in Britain in 1807, but the trading in enslaved-labored commodities continued uninterrupted.

Therefore, Douglass' physical presence on the *Cambria* caused angst among the agitated proslavery passengers who had a vested interest in keeping their notorious livelihoods in continued profitability. Douglass reveals that a passenger of goodwill requested that he give a lecture on enslavement. Reluctant to comply at first, he agreed only if Captain Charles Judkins would give his endorsement. Against threats to be thrown overboard by the slaveholders if he spoke on the horrors of enslavement, Douglass undeterred went forth with courage due to the support of the sea captain giving his approval. In a letter to Garrison dated early September 1845 that would be published in the *Liberator* later in the month, Douglass recounted the "melee" that occurred on the *Cambria* in this manner:

> Yes, they actually got up a MOB—a real American, republican, democratic, Christian mob,—and that, too, on the deck of a British steamer, and in sight of the beautiful high lands of Dungarvan [coast of Ireland]! I declare, it is enough to make a slave ashamed of the country that enslaved him, to think of it. Without the slightest pretensions to patriotism, as the phrase goes, the conduct of the monocratic Americans on board the Cambria almost made me ashamed to say I had run away from such a country. It was decidedly the most daring and disgraceful, as well as wicked exhibition of depravity, I have ever witnessed, North or South; and the actors in it showed themselves to be as hard in heart, as venomous in spirit, and as bloody in design, as the infuriated men who bathed their hands in the warm blood of the noble Lovejoy [Elijah Lovejoy (1802–1837), a martyred American who died for his publication promoting abolitionist propaganda] (*Liberator*, September 26, 1845).

There was something extraordinary in regard to the courage of Frederick Douglass, never did he shrink in the face of violent proslavery advocates during his lifetime. He had bones broken, was beaten up severely, yet never shrank in bravery. He was a man of conviction and honesty who believed viscerally that the cause he was involved in required the mastery of his nerves when it came to speaking on the abolition of enslavement in America. Douglass would not budge one iota in his belief that it was a heinous crime to shackle another human being, to take his or her liberty, and in the case of women their chastity. It was an evil system to the core and he was convinced that his role in its demise required an effort that surpassed the normal day-to-day existence of an average person. It was a full-time, seven days a week, task to fight with all his might the edifice that had made his life a living hell.

In the same letter to Garrison, he depicted the mix of passengers who were on board the *Cambria* with him during the tumultuous voyage to Liverpool, England:

> In the first place, our passengers were made up of nearly all sorts of people, from different countries, of the most opposite modes of thinking on all subjects. We had nearly all sorts or parties in morals, religion, and politics, as well as trades and callings, and professions. The doctor and the lawyer, the soldier and the sailor, were there. The scheming Connecticut wooden clock-maker, the large, surly, New-York lion-tamer, the solemn Roman Catholic bishop, and the Orthodox Quaker were there. A minister of the Free Church of Scotland, and a minister of the Church of England—the established Christian and the wandering Jew, the Whig and the Democrat, the white and the black—were there. There was the dark-visaged Spaniard, and the light-visaged Englishman—the man from Montreal, and the man from Mexico. There were slaveholders from Cuba, and slaveholders from Georgia. We had anti-slavery singing and pro-slavery grumbling; and at the same time that Governor Hammond's [James Henry Hammond (1807–1864), slaveholder and governor of South Carolina] Letters were being read, my Narrative was being circulated (*Liberator,* September 26, 1845).

In poetic form, Douglass uses dichotomy to explain the varied "opposites" on board the *Cambria* and it seems that he was able to balance the good with the bad experiences during the journey. Selling his *Narrative* was a boon for the young man with high aspirations. When they disembarked in the port of Liverpool, England he was met by British abolitionists who whisked the party off to a hotel about a half a mile away in Clayton Square. It was August 28, 1845 and he was in the bustling reality of life in Liverpool. It is interesting in reading the accounts of historians, American and British, who never juxtapose Liverpool's slave port history with that of Douglass' arrival. Even David Blight's mammoth biographical study, *Frederick Douglass: Prophet of Freedom* (2018), only mentions Liverpool passingly. He did speak in Liverpool in October 1846, which will be covered later, but given the legacy of the slave system to the city, it is not surprising that Douglass was not a "celebrated" African American figure there. On his second day in the city, August 29, he visited Eaton Hall, in the Chester region not far from Liverpool. This magnificent stately home was owned by the aristocratic Marquess of Westminster, Richard Grosvenor. Douglass may have largely moved in working-class circles in Britain, but the abolitionists were also very well connected to the higher echelon—this is also something largely ignored in the Douglass literature—he never fully embraced the Chartism or class struggle of his day, though he was sympathetic toward it (Blight 2018, p. 174). Douglass recalls the visit to the splendid Eaton Hall as something momentous due to the fact that there were some passengers from the *Cambria* also visiting, no doubt the slaveholding variety from gleaning his writing:

> They [his white compatriots] looked as sour as vinegar, and as bitter as gall, when they found I was to be admitted on equal terms with themselves. When the door was opened, I walked in, on an equal footing with my white fellow-citizens, and from all I could see, I have as much attention paid to me by the servants that showed us through the building, the statuary did not fall down, the pictures did not leap from their places, the doors did not refuse to open, and the servants did not say, *"We don't allow niggers in here!"* (Douglass 2019, p. 225).

The *italic* emphasis and use of profanity in Douglass' writing makes facetious mockery of the role segregation played in his life in America. He mentions how "sour" and "bitter" his countrymen were when the British aristocratic home was opened to him as it was to any other individual in the party that day, of which Douglass was the only Black person. Considering this is 1845 and he has not long arrived in Britain on his very first visit, it must have been a marvelous feeling for him to experience such opulence in the company of those from America who would have scorned him had it been in their nation. The absurdity is profound, a man who is a fugitive African American is in Britain in every sense of the word "free" and courted to speak about his experiences as an enslaved man via his autobiographical work. While there he meets with every kind of people, affluent, working class, and the poorest of the poor. His skin color and Afro hairstyle make him unique, his accent and eloquence framed in a handsome physique and face no doubt did him no harm. Douglass stood six foot and two inches, with a muscular toned body— in short, the man had the looks of an Adonis. It is little wonder the envy of his white compatriots spilled out on the *Cambria* because in their midst was a young and handsome African American male with profound eloquence. The same man who had spent the first twenty years of his existence in bondage, not being allowed to read or write, what an incredulous consideration. Indeed, it is astounding writing such a scenario in the third decade of the twenty-first century, yet there is no hyperbole in the prose. Frederick Douglass was a brilliant young man who captured the hearts of good British people wherever he went to speak and share his experience of enslavement. Audiences were simply captivated by his presence.

Maybe his lack of time spent actually in Liverpool was due to the fact that Douglass' impact in Scotland and Ireland was so powerful that it overshadowed his attendance in other British towns and cities. Overall, it has been argued that Douglass gave a staggering 184 speeches during his twenty-one months in Britain (Blight 2018, p. 175). The existing literature on his time in Ireland and Scotland is certainly a growing industry. Laurence Fenton's *Frederick Douglass in Ireland: 'The Black O'Connell'* and Tom Chaffin's *Giant's Causeway: Frederick Douglass's Irish Odyssey and the Making of an American Visionary*, both published in 2014, are certainly worth reading regarding his time spent with the Irish people. Then there is the recent study by Alasdair Pettinger (2020), *Frederick Douglass and Scotland, 1846: Living an Antislavery Life* that covers Douglass's speaking engagements throughout the Scottish region. These are fairly recent studies and highly engaging in terms of shedding further light onto the immense depth of his impact on the Irish and Scottish peoples. A fugitive Black man of mixed heritage speaking to crowds of between 2,000 and 2,500 is a tremendous feat for one so young and merely seven years divorced from servitude. In Ireland he was an admirer of the great "Irish Liberator" Daniel O'Connell, and even got to share the platform with him during his visit. Laurence Fenton argues that Douglass was inspired by O'Connell and regarded him as a "broad hearted philanthropist" (Fenton 2014, p. 89).

There are other studies that have focused on Douglass' British visits, though this chapter is concerned with only his first. Alan Rice and Martin Crawford edited a volume titled *Liberating Sojourn: Frederick Douglass and Transatlantic Reform* (1999). This volume focuses on the theme of special reform, such as religion and enslavement, Chartism and radicalism, with an emphasis on the Free Church of Scotland that infamously took donations from slaveholders. At the time of Douglass' sojourn in 1845–1847, there was a campaign to "Send the Money Back" taking place in Scotland, and Douglass would be in the forefront of these lively debates whereby getting heckled was a major part of his experiences. Yet, in all of these boisterous meetings, the contemporary press overwhelmingly rated Douglass a star of the show—a man of substance and great courage to share his ideas and lived experiences as to why enslavement needed to be abolished in the United States. Given the fact that so many British slave merchants continued to prosper from the commodities produced it is no wonder the "Send It Back" campaign largely failed to materialize—it seems that the glory of God was overcome by the power of the dollar.

Another edited volume on Frederick Douglass' British exploits was published in 2021 titled *Frederick Douglass in Britain and Ireland, 1845–1895*. What is unique about this study is in its focus on his writings and speeches that relate directly to his British experience and the related social connections. There is even a graph indicating the date and towns where he spoke during his visits. It is an incredibly useful volume and encapsulates the extent to which he traveled across the length and breadth of the British Isles speaking, sometimes without a break for weeks on end. It is curious that, according to the existing scholarship, he only spoke one time to an audience of over two thousand in Liverpool.

DOUGLASS SPEAKS IN LIVERPOOL—
OCTOBER 19, 1846

Often when Douglass spoke to an audience in Britain, he was self-deprecating and clearly humbled by the occasion. After all, he was not drenched in formal education and qualifications attained by the average middle-class white man who spoke to thousands of people in packed auditoriums. Too often white commentators fail to appreciate the immense stress a Black man or woman would have encountered just getting up to speak to a predominantly white audience in order to speak on abolition. It is not the cultural experience of white historians to even consider this as they would ordinarily not have ever experienced such pressure. Particularly those historians in the twenty-first century commentating on a nineteenth century Black man or woman who had lived their lives at one time in enslavement. That stated, it is useful before we consider Douglass' one major speech in Liverpool, which was mainly noted by local press and not transcribed fully in the history books, to reflect on his opening words from a speech he delivered in the month of May in London, 1846—about five months before his speech in Liverpool:

> I feel exceedingly glad of the opportunity now afforded me of presenting the claims of my brethren in bonds in the United States to so many in London and from various parts of Britain who have assembled here on the present occasion. I have nothing to commend me to your consideration in the way of learning, nothing in the way of education, to entitle me to your attention; and you are aware that slavery is a very bad school for rearing teachers of morality and religion. Twenty-one years of my life have been spent in slavery—personal slavery—surrounded by degrading influences, such as can exist nowhere beyond the pale of slavery; and it will not be strange, if under such circumstances, I should betray, in what I have to say to you, a deficiency of that refinement which is seldom ever found, except among persons that have experienced superior advantages to those which I have enjoyed. But I will take it for granted that you will know something about the degrading influences of slavery, and that you will not expect great things from me this evening, but simply such facts as I may be able to advance immediately in connection with my own experience of slavery. (*Frederick Douglass Papers*, Vol. 1, edited by Philip Foner 1950, p. 154)

How Douglass opened up this talk that spring May evening at Finsbury Chapel in London is a clear example of a humble man endeavoring to explain to his predominantly white British audience that he was not a man of letters but a man formerly enslaved. He simply had a story to tell that was valid and experiential. He went on to cite a number of notable individuals to back up this claim, including Charles Dickens, and yet the eloquence of the man shines through his words like a beacon light. He did not require to cite others to endorse his knowledge. That night he spoke about the scars on his back from the lashes he endured while enslaved, he spoke about his siblings still suffering under the yoke of bondage as he stood there on stage. There was no pretense about Douglass, and the audience could sense his depth of passion when he spoke with such knowingness about something he detested to the core of his being. As he stated:

> I have on my back marks of the lash; I have four sisters and one brother now under the galling chain. I feel it my duty to cry aloud and spare not. . . . I expose slavery in this country [Britain], because to expose it is to kill it. Slavery is one of those monsters of darkness to whom the light of truth is death. Expose slavery, and it dies. Light is to slavery what the heat of the sun is to the root of a tree; it must die under it. All the slaveholder asks of me is silence (p. 164).

When Douglass articulated the grievances of his people while in Britain it was a powerful indictment of American slavery. He spoke about a newly formed partnership in marriage between a male and female African American, the "marriage" being unlawful due to their enslavement, and how this couple were cruelly separated on the auction block. He also spoke that night in London about "slave-breeding" humans as they would dogs or sheep. Douglass was a powerful orator and could vividly share such horror due to his experiences in the same "peculiar institution" he had escaped. In Liverpool, given the assessment of all the places he spoke on numerous occasions, and this city being one of the key British locations for life and commerce via enslavement, it is fair to suggest that his words were largely unwelcome. Also, given the deeply-rooted reality of continued business between slaveholders in America and British merchants in Liverpool during the 1840s to 1860s. It is without much guesswork to suggest Douglass' message would largely fall on deaf ears when it came to endorsing the abolition of enslavement. This, in hindsight, is probably why his presence in any formal address has only been recorded on this one occasion. Therefore, what happened the night he spoke in Liverpool in October of 1846? How was he received, and what was his message to the audience that evening? Let us delve into these questions by employing a content analysis of the contemporary press reportage.

Prior to his engagement in Liverpool, Douglass had spoken in Newcastle on October 16th and after his engagement in Liverpool on the 19th he was off to speak in Edinburgh for the 21st—and then on to numerous speaking venues almost every day or with just a one-day break in between engagements throughout the month of October. The man was a speaking-machine during his time in Britain, an absolutely driven man who took every opportunity to expose the wrongs haunting his people in the United States as he enjoyed a degree of liberty and celebrity.

In Liverpool on October 19, the location for Douglass' oration was at the Concert Hall, a lavish setting located on Lord Nelson Street near Lime Street train station—the building still stands today but is now a block of luxury apartments. Back in 1846 it was used as a vaudeville venue and one of the best in the city at this time with a capacity of 2,700 persons. The local press reported an audience of 2,500 had attended the event. In reading the current literature, not much is stated about those who took to the stage with Douglass that Monday evening in Liverpool. Yet there was the great American abolitionist William Lloyd Garrison and his British collaborator—abolitionist George Thompson. Garrison needs little introduction, but Thompson deserves some attention here because not only was he a passionate white British abolitionist, the man was also born in Liverpool in 1804, three years prior to the formal abolition of international trading in enslaved Africans via British vessels. Thompson had the reputation of being a diehard radical abolitionist. A man of great courage and conviction for the cause of African American liberation. He had learned all about the inhumane treatment of enslaved Africans from his father who earned his living on slave ships that traveled the transatlantic from Liverpool. His son, thankfully, had a more humane disposition for his darker-hued brethren and grew to detest the notorious "slave trading" in human life. Thompson had first visited the United States in 1834 when Douglass was a mere sixteen-year-old boy; he made two further visits in 1851 and 1865 (Rice 1968, p. 16). Indeed, Thompson had longevity in his activist struggle for the liberation of those shackled under the strain of American servitude.

C. Duncan Rice in a rare essay on Thompson gives a brief outline of his career as a talented British abolitionist, very close to Thomas Clarkson in prestige, who had died just weeks prior to the Liverpool meeting. Rice contends:

[George] Thompson dominated the connexion between the extremist wings of the British and American anti-slavery movements . . . leading back to his father's experience in the crew of a slave-ship. He . . . painstakingly educated and equipped himself as a first-rate public speaker and debater. From 1831 until the passage of the Emancipation Act, he toured the country incessantly, stirring up opinion in the constituencies to support the campaign at Westminster. During this time, he was the only lecturer continually in the employment of the Agency Committee . . . he gained the reputation in many quarters as the man who was second only to Clarkson in his contribution to the triumph of 1833 [British West Indies Abolition of Enslavement]. A young man of twenty-nine at the time the Emancipation Act passed, he naturally continued using his talents in the same field. With the British nonconformists awakening to their universal moral responsibility for world abolition, there was plenty of employment for him (Rice 1968, pp. 16–17).

Thompson went on to be a British member of Parliament, but he never stopped advocating for the abolition of enslavement in the United States. The Garrisonian abolitionists were in unison with Frederick Douglass that October night in Liverpool. Though later there would be ideological friction based on numerous issues—at this stage there was unity among friends fighting the same foe: slaveholding America. The title of Douglass' address in Liverpool that night was "Slavery Exists Under the Eaves of the American Church," and from the various press reports compiled in *The Frederick Douglass Papers, Series One: Speeches, Debates, and Interviews,* Vol. 1: 1841–1846, edited by John Blassingame, one can glean that it was a rousing performance by the young fugitive from bondage. However, he was highly critical of the Church in the United States that evening and unrelenting in his articulation depicting the inherent hypocrisy involved in the condoning of enslavement by a supposedly sacred institution. This is how a reporter recounted his criticism:

> Under the drippings of the American sanctuary slavery has its existence. Whips, chains, gags, blood-hounds, thumb-screws, and all the bloody paraphernalia of slavery lie right under the drippings of the sanctuary, and instead of being corroded and rusted by its influence, they are kept in a state of preservation. Ministers of religion defend slavery from the Bible—ministers of religion own any number of slaves—bishops trade in human flesh—churches may be said to be literally built up in human skulls, and their very walls cemented with human blood—women are sold at the public block to support a minister, to support a church—human beings sold to buy sacramental services, and all, of course, with the sanction of the religion of the land. It was with such religionists as these that the Evangelical Alliance would have the Christians of this country link and interlink themselves. (Applause) A multitude of resolutions could be read, showing the support given to slavery by the churches of America.

The newspaper report continued,

> He could not misrepresent, he could not exaggerate the state of things in America. He would give them a specimen of the religious teaching of these men to their slaves, and for this purpose he begged to be permitted to preach them a sermon,—a slave-holder's sermon. He wished also to use the canting tones of the minister, for even these slave holding divines affected a pious whine in their sermons and gave them with a sanctimonious air. He had listened to them, and if their preaching was calculated to do any good at all, of course he had had the benefit of their teaching. They had only one text: there were only two texts in the Bible that suited them. They did not like the present translation at all. He should not wonder if they got out another translation, more in accordance with their views of the original. (Laughter)

By all accounts, Douglass engaged in both pathos and mimicry of a slaveholding preacher that evening in Liverpool to expose the evil of a system that had snared him and his family, his brethren, into a long night of captivity. There was plentiful applause for his logic, and laughter for his irony of a system that branded humans with hot irons, among other cruelties (Dickens 1989, pp. 232–235), while those with the power behind such malevolence prayed and espoused their allegiance to Christianity. To be sure, Douglass was on fire with his oratorical skills that night in Liverpool. His calling was confirmed by the Liverpool people who attended. It was also reported how Douglass revealed some of the statistics of the Church's involvement and the extent of its ownership of enslaved African Americans:

> After describing other punishments which can be inflicted upon slaves, and detailing one or two affecting incidents, he said all denominations in the United States, with a few, and only a few, exceptions, were implicated in this guilt. The Methodist church, through its members and its ministers, held no fewer than 250,000 slaves, the Presbyterians 90,000, the Episcopalians 80,000, and the Baptists 125,000. Indeed, they had men sold to build churches, women sold to support missionaries, babes sold to buy Bibles to send to the heathen. The slaves' prison and the church stand in the same street—the gates of heaven and the gates of hell being in the same avenue. The pulpit and the auctioneer's block are in the same neighbourhood, and the blood-stained gold, received for the sale of human flesh on the auction block (*Frederick Douglass Papers, Vol. 1*, Blassingame 1979, pp. 446–474).

According to the accounts recorded by contemporary newspaper reporters, there was no booing that night in Liverpool. Therefore, when one considers Frederick Douglass, at twenty-eight years of age, an African American fugitive in Britain, he was not alone that evening. In Liverpool he was clearly in the company of very robust advocates for the abolition of enslavement in United States—British and American advocates. Again, there is that nagging conundrum knowing George Thompson, a Liverpudlian, is with Douglass during this period and only on one occasion is there an event held in Liverpool. Given the importance of the city to the "peculiar institution" one can only guess that it was too dangerous or difficult a task to have such a subject matter discussed in Liverpool in 1846. It is mere conjecture, but looking at the many engagements Douglass had in cities across Britain and Ireland, and the fact that he disembarked in Liverpool from the United States, and left from Liverpool to return, it is incredulous that there is just one significant reference to a speech he gave in the city. Indeed, historians and collectors of his writings and speeches tend to bypass this evening in Liverpool. Instead, there is a focus on his London "farewell speech" in March 1847. Had it not been for the late African American historian, John Blassingame, compiling the evidence it could well have been lost to generations. However, the Liverpool speech by Douglass has recently been captured in the work of Hannah-Rose Murray and John McKivigan, *Frederick Douglass in Britain and Ireland, 1845–1895* (2021, p. 46). But in David Blight's 2018 celebrated biography of Douglass there is no mention of this event, whereby Douglass is in top form imitating, ridiculing slaveholders, and cajoling a 2,500- strong Liverpool audience on a topic that made the city rich. To be sure, most if not all of its civic splendor, its architectural inheritance, had come from the profits accrued out of the transatlantic slave system. Douglass did not criticize Liverpool's slaving past; he was diplomatic enough to know, with a high degree of precocity, to focus on the present and his brothers and sisters' plight in America suffering under the yoke of oppression. Monday October 19, 1846 was not the time to provoke a Liverpool audience with its shameful past—he concentrated instead on the current task in hand serving to secure the freedom of his people. He did that successfully, with the assistance of some British and American abolitionist friends, one of whom was famously born in Liverpool—a scouser.

FREDERICK AND KARL—PEERS BUT NOT BROTHERS IN ARMS

Something that has often puzzled me as a thinker relates to the lives of Frederick Douglass and Karl Marx, because they were in fact peers, not in an equal sense of existing in the social world on parity, but in terms of age—and in intellect if all in life had been impartial. Douglass was born enslaved in Maryland, America sometime in February 1818, while Marx was born in Germany on May 5, 1818. Therefore, it can be stated with assurance that Douglass was merely three months Marx's senior. They were in a real sense, equal in age, and the reason this is important relates to the sheer avoidance Marx had for anything to do with the abolitionists of his era, whether in Britain or in the United States. Marx was exiled from Paris in 1845 and moved to Brussels before settling in London around 1849. Certainly, he had to be aware of Douglass' presence in the Britain between 1845 and 1847, and the work he was doing to end enslavement for his people. For Marx to have missed this episode as a journalist and writer, given the uproar Douglass and his team of abolitionists were creating across Britain at the time, is extremely doubtful—we can assume then that Marx knew something about Douglass.

Why is this of importance? It is because Marx has influenced generations of Black thinkers and scholars that have literally worshipped him. Probably most exemplified by the twentieth century Black activist, Claudia Jones, who is buried "left of Marx" in Highgate Cemetery in London and adopted a Marxist-Leninist approach to the struggle of Africana peoples, with a focus on Black women (Boyce Davies 2007, p. 2). This is not a digression; Jones is merely one example of many Blacks who adapted the "historical materialism" theories of Karl Marx and his friend in white working-class activism—Frederick Engels—to fit Black struggles for social equality. For Marx and Engels, the major argument related to the exploitative nature of the capitalist system, and how the white working class or proletariat needed to unite and develop a "class consciousness" to overcome the underhandedness of the bourgeoisie who controlled the means of production in the burgeoning industrial societies of mid-nineteenth century Europe. Yet, one could ask, why was Marx not there beside the abolitionists and writing about Frederick Douglass in the affirmative, and others who sought freedom?

Today there are Marxist thinkers who still largely sugarcoat the reality that Marx was fundamentally not concerned about the liberty of African peoples in America—even though their unfree labor was the producer of the vast amount of raw materials that would be supplied to the factories of Liverpool, Manchester, and elsewhere in Britain. Karl Marx was silent on Frederick Douglass and other men of African heritage who were literally fighting for their humanity and liberation in *his* day and this should not be airbrushed out of historiography. Indeed, over seventy years after the Civil War ended in 1865, twentieth century Marxists put together a compilation of Marx and Engels' writings on *The Civil War and the United States* and there is not a single word on Frederick Douglass, who by the 1850s was the undisputed leader among African Americans. Crucially, when one juxtaposes Douglass with Marx there is a glaring incongruity in terms of why Marx specifically did not share in Douglass' struggle. Ultimately, the culpability, if any, must fall at the feet of Marx and Engels, who did not mention one word about *American* enslavement in their 1848 *Communist Manifesto*. They do mention "freeman and slave" but it is in relation to past history and not the contemporary time they were writing in. The outset of their famous pamphlet reads:

> The history of all hitherto existing society is the history of class struggles. Freeman and slave, patrician and plebian, lord and serf, guild-master and journeyman, in a word, oppressor and oppressed, stood in constant opposition to one another, carried on an uninterrupted, now hidden, now open fight, a fight that each time ended, either in a revolutionary reconstitution of society at large, or in the common ruin of the contending classes (Marx and Engels, 2021, p. 9).

Marx and Engels were a complicated duo when one endeavors to understand why they did not see the fight for freedom that Douglass pursued for the African Americans as relevant to be analyzed deeply. Alternatively, they deemed the "wage-laborer" a "slave to capitalism"—there is need for further research into this area because it is difficult to be convinced that Marx was a friend of peoples of African heritage. His calling was to free the white working classes of Europe. That is a fair assessment at this juncture in considering the life and times of Douglass in Britain—who witnessed the squalor and poverty of the Irish during the famine—and the struggle of Daniel O'Connell for Irish freedom. Douglass was no fair-weather friend to the working-class poor in Britain, he could see there was a connection between the struggle of the Irish poor and the enslaved African American—though he stayed clear of interfering directly in Irish politics because to tell *his* story was his reason to be on a speaking tour. As Fenton (2014) has contended, Douglass was an "Anglophile" due to his immediate situation and the tangible aid he had received from British abolitionists. Nevertheless, he was likewise a great admirer of Daniel O'Connell who clearly inspired him with his quest for Irish liberation. As such, Douglass was a tad conflicted pleading the case of the enslaved in America, but having witnessed the plight of the Irish poor at the hands of the British (Fenton 2014, p. 165). Yet one cannot find an excuse for Marx and Engels ignoring outright Douglass the man, the enslaved African American who had suffered the fruits of his labor being robbed from him by his master, Thomas Auld.

Other contemporaries of Douglass whom he, in retrospect, naïvely admired were Charles Dickens and Thomas Carlyle. Dickens was a friend of the poor, had written some notes relating to the condemnation of American slavery (Dickens 1989); but if one follows his life-path holistically, Dickens was at best a hypocrite and at worst a subconscious racist tinged with the dis-*ease* of white supremacy. His support for Governor Ayre during the Morant Bay Rebellion in 1865 Jamaica testifies to his underlying acceptance of racial hierarchy. Yet Dickens twenty years earlier was someone Douglass admired largely due to his 1842 publication of *American Notes* that in part condemned enslavement. To be fair to Dickens, his chapter on slavery in this travelogue is powerful in reproving the cruelty of enslavement. Maybe this was because he was a relatively young man, in his late twenties, when he witnessed America firsthand—there was an idealism in Dickens that may have diminished later in his life.

Likewise, Thomas Carlyle was admired by Douglass in the early 1840s, yet he wrote a notorious pamphlet in 1849 and updated in 1853 titled the "Occasional Discourse on the Nigger Question" that focused on an undeniably white supremacist view in holding that the Jamaicans and other British Caribbean colonials should not have been emancipated in 1833/4—it is an explicitly racist tract from the pen of the "socialist" Thomas Carlyle. Douglass, however, would have a precarious relationship with most of the learned white men he admired—it was in a sense "the price of the ticket" to self-discovery—ultimately, white liberals can be the worst of enemies to Black liberation.

Specifically in relation to Liverpool, Herman Melville and Charles Dickens are often cited due to their trivial depictions of Black representation in the city. Melville's *Redburn* and Dickens' *The Uncommercial Traveller* each give accounts of African heritage and other persons of color who were evident in the dockland area of Liverpool. Yet though they capture Black presence, there is no depth in the characterizations, just stereotypical "otherness" and rather banal depictions of the Black men they witness. Dickens' chapter five of *The Uncommercial Traveller* titled "Poor Mercantile Jack" is particularly stereotyped and hackneyed in its portrayal of the Black persons he encountered via an internship with the local police superintendent's patrol of the dockland area. This is how Dickens writes about an experience in a dockland public house (pub):

> The male dancers were all blacks, and one was an unusually powerful man of six feet three or four. The sound of their flat feet on the floor was as unlike the sound of white feet as their faces were unlike white faces. They toed and heeled, shuffled, double-shuffled, double-double-shuffled, covered the buckle, and beat the time out, rarely, dancing with a great show of teeth, and with a childish good-humoured enjoyment that was prepossessing. They generally kept together, these poor fellows, said Mr. Superintendent, because they were at a disadvantage singly, and liable to slights in the neigbouring streets (Dickens 1987, pp. 46–47).

Dickens conjured up the "dancing, childlike Black men" typecast in his depiction, but often there is a kernel of truth in any stereotype. In this case it is the impending violence that lurked in the dockland area if Black men were alone on the streets of Liverpool. Though this is not a literary criticism exercise, the entire "Poor Mercantile Jack" story is riddled with mumbo jumbo—it reads like he wrote the piece without any thought for psychological nuance or character building. And the main legible word from Dickens in the following extract relates to the usual negativity toward Blacks: "Dat hair nigger by 'um fireplace 'hind a' time, shake it out o' yerselbs, gib 'ell a breakdown" (p. 46). Gibberish from Dickens and a distinct lack of viability in his prose, yet because of his fame as a writer this nonsensical babble is viewed as satirical British literature. Well, Douglass may have found him worthy of his respect, but in hindsight he should have taken his time in praising both him and Thomas Carlyle—another incipient racist around at the time Douglass was on his tour across the British Isles.

Lastly, Herman Melville's *Redburn* was published in 1849, apparently written in ten weeks, which makes sense because it too is rather superficial in its prose and characterization of African heritage humanity. Again, perhaps because it is Melville the *Moby Dick* writer, as with Dickens, that he gets to be cited within the context of Liverpool and Black presence. Though in fact Melville states nothing much of substance, other than acknowledging Black men were evident in Liverpool during his time. It is interesting, however, how the Liverpool white historian John Belchem in reading *Redburn* fails to pick up on one glaring observation from the great American writer. That is, Melville recognized the absence of Black men and women among the destitute in the areas where he pondered in the city center. Well, this again speaks to what Dickens alluded to in his writing on Liverpool: *it was not safe for Black persons to roam about in Liverpool.* Here is how Melville explained his perplexity in not seeing Black Liverpudlians in the city center:

> I must not omit one thing, that struck me at the time [he was in Liverpool]. It was the absence of negroes; who in the large towns in the "free states" of America, almost always form a considerable portion of the destitute. But in these streets, not a negro was to be seen. All were whites; and with the exception of the Irish, were natives of the soil: even Englishmen (Melville 1986, p. 277).

Melville, just as Dickens or later J. B. Priestly, was a visitor. He also confuses the reader about Black settlement in Liverpool by sharing his observation of an African American seaman walking briskly and confidently in Liverpool with a "good-looking English woman"—but what he fails to comprehend is that Black seaman is from America, he is away from the shackles and prejudice of his own nation and probably does not think he is in any danger in Liverpool. However, it is with confidence here that had Melville stalked that very couple all their walking steps and days he would have witnessed a different scenario than the one depicted in *Redburn*. This is why to rely merely on Dickens or Melville to comprehend Black settlement in Liverpool is problematic. What they offer due to their fame is credence to "Black presence" in the city. What historians today should be asking is why Dickens and Melville were not writing about the Frederick Douglass phenomenon? Why, if they were genuine humanitarians, would they avoid extoling such men like Douglass who spoke to multitudes in Britain? As with Marx and Engels, Dickens and Melville did not "see" Douglass as a holistic man, nor did they want to as he was a beacon light that disturbed and unsettled age-worn stereotypes relating to white superiority. Indeed, Douglass and other fellow African Americans like him unsettled the consciences of privileged white men and confused them with their innate and largely self-taught intellect.

FREEDOM SECURED THROUGH WHITE-FEMALE-LED PHILANTHROPY

Interestingly, few people recognize the significance of Frederick Douglass gaining his freedom from his slaveholder, Thomas Auld, while in Britain during the twenty-one months of his stay. Had it not been mainly for the guile and ingenuity of two white women from Newcastle, Ellen and Anna Richardson, he may not have gained his manumission. It is a sobering fact to contemplate given the force of this man requiring the aid of white British women—who would support his quest for freedom—and who were clearly moved by his stature and eloquence. It was not long after his October 1846 speaking engagement in Liverpool that his "English friends" as he called them raised the then £150/$750 (equivalent in 2022 to over £12,000/$16,000). This was a lot of money and it indicates the depth of feeling his British and Irish friends had for the brilliant and relatively young man. Douglass had certainly defied the odds and astounded audiences from the length and breadth of the British Isles with his passionate eloquence.

However, not everyone was pleased for Douglass; the Garrisonian philosophy was quite simple: no man/woman should or could buy another human being as he or she was a creation of God. William Lloyd Garrison was initially supportive of Douglass paying for his freedom, but some of the other Garrisonians, like Henry C. Wright, were firmly against the idea of Douglass having to pay for his "God-given freedom." It was in the interest of the abolitionist movement for him to remain a fugitive rather than be a designated freeman. Yet he faced not being able to return to the United States without being hounded by slave-catchers who could easily have returned him to the wretched life of enslavement. Douglass found this dilemma imposed by the white abolitionists unacceptable. Therefore, if he had an opportunity to return to his family a free man and work for the liberty of his people, without looking over his shoulder constantly, with the threat of being hauled back into bondage he would take it.

Douglass responded to the criticism of Henry C. Wright, who had written a letter to him, dated December 12, 1846, advising that buying his freedom in this manner was not a good idea. In a profound response to Wright that was written in a letter from his Manchester, England hotel on December 22, 1846, Douglass made clear that it was easy for those outside of his experience to suggest him being manumitted was unfavorable, but to have his freedom, by any means necessary, was a visceral instinct. To use a twentieth century example, Douglass' letter is as profound as the "Letter from Birmingham Jail" that would be penned over six score years later by a young African American preacher also fighting for the dignity of his people—Martin Luther

King Jr. Why this letter from Douglass is not a major part of education in the United States and elsewhere is incredulous as it is a masterpiece in terms of logical argument for pursuing his liberty. Douglass writes:

> I am in England, my family are in the United States. My sphere of usefulness is in the United States; my public and domestic duties are there; and there it seems my duty to go. But I am *legally* the property of Thomas Auld, and if I go to the United States (no matter to what part, for there is no City of Refuge there, spot sacred to freedom there) Thomas Auld, *aided by the American Government,* can seize, bind and fetter, and drag me from my family, feed his cruel revenge on me, and doom me to unending slavery. In view of this simple statement of facts, a few friends, desirous of seeing me released from the terrible liability, and to relieve my wife and children from the painful trepidation, consequent upon the liability, and to place me on an equal footing of safety with all other anti-slavery lecturers in the United States, and to enhance my usefulness by enlarging the field of my labors in the United States, have nobly and generously paid Hugh Auld, the agent of Thomas Auld, £150—in consideration of which Hugh Auld (acting as his agent) and the Government of the United States agree, that I shall be free from all further liability (cited in Foner and Taylor 1999, p. 50).

The letter from Douglass to Wright in December 1846 goes on to give a powerful example of the hypocrisy in the latter condemning the action done to gain his freedom. Douglass explained to Wright that just as you are against the "passport system" that was instigated for foreign travel, he felt that any human being should be free to travel anywhere on God's Earth, using Wright's language, and that it was unfair to introduce passports for foreign travel. Douglass deftly points out to him that he, Wright, *still* went ahead and got the passport and how much in philosophical difference is this to Douglass gaining his freedom so that he too can move about the world freely with his family, and fight for the greater liberation of his people with less hindrance. Certainly, there was powerful logic throughout the letter and it is clearly a piece of literary genius in the rhetoric of liberty from oppression—even though one has to pay to keep the bully off one's back. It is indeed the shame of the bully who carries the weight of such a transaction, and not the victim of the oppressor who has been robbed of £150 in 1846 to be free from his clutches.

This incident likewise brought to light the consistent paternalism that Douglass endured from white abolitionists. Yes, he was grateful for all that they had done for him but he was also growing as a human being, as an intellect, and could not be shackled by the philosophy of white men like Garrison, Wright, or others who felt he should "stick to the facts" and leave the philosophy of liberation to them (McKivigan et al. 2018, pp. 519–522). Douglass was supposed to just "play the slave on the run" while on the platform and the white abolitionists would do the bidding for his freedom. This situation would inevitably turn intolerable for a man of Douglass' intellect, and the more he experienced life abroad, the more he encountered his freedom to think on his toes during lectures, the more his burgeoning intelligence expanded his mental horizon. Douglass could never be confined to merely "sticking to facts" in explaining how horrible enslavement was for him and his people. He desired and needed to expand his repertoire and critique the essence of American hypocrisy—and that sometimes led to disputes with his white abolitionist colleagues who meant good but did bad. Douglass bought his freedom, yes, but he did not yield one iota to enslavement being evil and inhumane. It was Auld who would carry the weight on *his* conscience if he saw it accurate to yield £150 from Douglass in turn for his liberty. This had nothing to do with Douglass surrendering to the injustice of such a cruel system; he did it only to gain a "passport" to travel and speak more freely—and he would do just that until the emancipation of his people arrived almost twenty years later in 1865.

It too should be noted that Douglass did not exist in a vacuum; there were transatlantic pioneers before him, like Henry Highland Garnet, and there would be those who followed his path in their pursuit of individual liberation for the good of others, like William Wells Brown. There was also James W. C. Pennington, a fugitive African American who escaped bondage, and was in England with abolitionists in 1843 (Webber 2011, pp. 186–201). Indeed, there were numerous talented African American abolitionists. Some were born free but took up the fight to end enslavement in America—they too spoke in the British Isles on the abolitionist platform prior to Douglass. Charles Lenox Remond worked with Garrison; he was a talented orator and a hair stylist, indeed his hair style of the 1840s could fit the 1970s and beyond—he was a great personality. Douglass even named one of his sons after him: Charles Remond Douglass. His sister too, Sarah Parker Remond, was a pioneering activist for women and men in bondage. Crucially, there were *many* African Americans who fought with the abolitionist cause, free men and women, as well as fugitives who, as Douglass, had published their autobiographies: *Slave Narratives*. Yet Douglass appears to stand out due to his sheer star quality, good looks, and his extraordinary charisma, combined with a rare talent as an orator-intellect, who possessed exceptional courage in terms of speaking truth to power. His talk in Liverpool on October 19, 1846 is certainly a prime example of his audacity to critique the Christian Church, both in America and Britain, and the hypocrisy in it being highly involved in the enslavement system due to the profits that could be accrued. Douglass criticized the Christian Church that night in Liverpool with statistical data that was printed in the local press—he clearly went beyond the confines of a "slave narrative"; his criticism was political and it went straight to the heart of what was required to be heard from the perspective of enslaved people of African heritage.

Something important should be considered here, given the scope of this study revealing Black mixed heritage history in Liverpool and beyond. It is in relation to the fallacy of Black mixed heritage persons like Douglass being more "superior" to so-called "full Black" persons. This was a theme that would emerge from writers like Robert E. Park in the 1920s to 1930s under the ruse of eugenic racism. His writings should today be regarded as undeniably pseudoscientific and racist but like other dubious thinkers he continues to hold some sway as a classical sociological theorist, especially his notion of the "Marginal Man" (Goldberg 2012). Park explains his dubious notion in this manner:

> Ordinarily the margin man is a mixed blood [unstable in character, yet superior to "full Blacks"], like the Mulatto in the United States . . . but that is apparently because the man of mixed blood is one who lives in two worlds, in both of which he is more or less a stranger (Park 1928, p. 893).

Park regards a Black man of mixed heritage like Frederick Douglass or Barack Obama as living in two worlds and having unstable characters. Well, let us state for brevity that Park was unstable in his analysis. Any person in the United States, for example, was socially deemed "Black" if he or she had "one drop" of African ancestry. This is a social fact. W. E. B. Du Bois spoke of a "double consciousness" encountered by *all* African Americans, from vanilla to blue Black in shade. What is rather disingenuous of Park and others of his ilk is in the manner he would endeavor to divide African Americans on the basis of how "white" the Black man or woman was. According to Park, the lighter he or she was of Black heritage would mean the brighter, or more intelligent. The problem with this is he conveniently left out brilliant "full Black" men and women like: Alexander Crummell, Henry Highland Garnet, Samuel Ringgold Ward, Charles Lenox Remond, Harriet Tubman, and Sarah Parker Remond to name just a few who were colleagues of Douglass and often good friends in the cause of liberation. Moreover, there were contemporaries too of Park himself, like George Washington Carver and Clement Garnett Morgan who were so-called "full Blacks" and brilliant in mind, body, and soul.

But more than this, Robert E. Park got his start professionally working at Tuskegee Institute with a Black man of mixed heritage, Booker T. Washington. Surely Park could not have failed to witness the different shades of Black men and women working side by side in the thrall of white supremacy in Alabama. Park traveled widely *with* Washington and worked with him as a ghostwriter on a study published in 1912 titled *The Man Farthest Down: A Record of Observation and Study in Europe*, which considered the white poor of London, England and other parts Europe. In other words, Park knew better than to write humbug in relation to Black men and women of mixed heritage. If indeed Black men and women of *all* shades were "marginal" it was due to the vicissitudes and vitriolic nature of white supremacy and the legacy of enslavement. Not to forget the reality of segregation when Park was writing his pseudoscientific racist diatribe. Significantly, whether a man or woman was of Black mixed heritage or "full Black" was largely irrelevant—they lived in "two worlds" and fought hard for their collective humanity as abolitionists. Those who tried to divide and conquer African Americans on the basis of human biology were able to have access to mainstream journals and book publishing to disseminate balderdash that has come down the centuries to miseducate generations of white minds into believing they had superior faculties to men and women of color—this is on reflection unutterably sad. Crucially, Frederick Douglass and many others who fought for freedom from racialized oppression are testimony to the strength and power of one set of human beings to overcome the evil of another set of human beings. When one considers the eugenics movement that Park was involved with, one should also keep in mind it being inextricably interwoven to the development of Nazi ideology that advanced in earnest during WW2.

FREDERICK LEAVES RACIST LIVERPOOL FOR AMERICA

After his farewell speech to his British friends in London, March 30, 1847, Frederick Douglass had to set his sight on returning to the United States. He would travel again on the steamship *Cambria* from Liverpool to Boston. A copy of the report that indicates who was on board has Frederick Douglass as passenger number 48; and in a twist of fate, it would be the same Captain Charles Judkins in charge of the steamship that brought Douglass to Liverpool some twenty-one months earlier. Being an organized man, Douglass had bought a first-class ticket from a Cunard shipping sales officer, Mr. Ford, while in London on March 4, 1847. In purchasing the steamship ticket, he was accompanied by Mr. George Moxhay, of the Hall of Commerce, a white man of importance in London and a good witness to have in case anything untoward took place while doing business with Mr. Ford of the Cunard line. The cost of the first-class ticket was approximately £41 (or about £4,500/$6,000 in 2022); Douglass inquired if there were any second-class tickets available; he was informed there were none and that there was one first- class fare cost only. He therefore paid the monies and took his ticket/receipt for cabin berth number 72 on the *Cambria* to sail from the port of Liverpool to Boston on April 6, 1847.

Unfortunately, when he took his luggage on board the *Cambria*, he found out that the Liverpool agent for Cunard, Mr. McIver, who had an office based on Water Street in the city not far from the quay, had given his cabin to another passenger. Frederick Douglass, who had spent almost two years being greeted as a man and a champion of human rights, was now treated again as a second-class citizen. Yet, lost by historians is the fact that this was Liverpool where he was having his first-class cabin return ticket taken from him; Douglass is blinded by his British adulation to view the incident as racist action in Liverpool, England. He relented, and determined his journey home would be in steerage, with other cargo like mail and bottled beverages. His recent biographer David Blight puts this scenario in some context:

> [O]n a quay in Liverpool [April 1847], Douglass lifted his trunk onto the *Cambria* . . . for the return voyage to America. He was a changed man, an experienced orator-writer and professional abolitionist with an international reputation, an "illustrious transatlantic," as a Sheffield newspaper had called him. He would never again be a good follower; from this day he did not take direction well from abolitionist handlers, although he would remain a constant learner and seeker of new strategies, new methods of mingling the power of the word with the power of politics. Douglass boarded the ship, again under humiliating conditions of segregated quarters, [steerage] (Blight 2018, p. 177).

Blight explains how Douglass had grown into an experienced orator and thinker/writer who would never be the same after his British sojourn. However, Blight states nothing about the circumstances behind the "humiliation" that the great man encountered in Liverpool. His cabin ticket was literally stolen, and his monies were not returned considering he would suffer a much lower grade of comfort. This, in terms of Africana critical studies, is where most white historians and biographers cannot comprehend the visceral aspect in how these daily acts of racism hurt the soul. How it can impact the life of a man or woman of Africana heritage deeply, yet it is overlooked by Blight (2018).

Nor does he mention Douglass' aggrieved letter dated April 3, 1847 to the *London Times* and published three days later, the day he set sail for America. In the letter Douglass explained the incident and the discrimination he encountered via the Liverpool agent of the Cunard shipping line, Mr. McIver. Captain Judkins even took the time to go with Douglass in person to the agent's office on Water Street to seek redress. But Douglass was told by McIver that the London agent had acted incorrectly "without authority" and was told that the only way he could travel is if he ate alone, did not interact with any passengers in the saloon area, and to give up the cabin berth that he had paid in full for. Douglass had no choice but to accept the new travel restrictions. He needed to return home and therefore accepted the conditions, the humiliation, and took a place on the steamship with the cargo in steerage (*London Times,* April 6, 1847).

When news of this was publicized the boss of the Cunard shipping line sent Douglass a written apology, mainly because of the uproar it had caused in British circles. Douglass was now a much-loved celebrity in Britain—even though when it came to the everyday realties of racism, he was still a Black man and open to the slights and microaggressions that beset most people of color in the mid-nineteenth century. What is problematic from Douglass in his letter related to his misunderstanding of Liverpool racism. He wrote, "I have travelled this country 19 months, and have always enjoyed equal rights and privileges with other passengers, and it was not until I turned my face towards America that I met anything like the proscription on account of my colour" (ibid.). What Douglass misses here, and probably due to him not wanting to slight his British friends, is the racist actions of a Liverpool shipping agent, who no doubt knew something about him or how would he have known to take the cabin from him in the first place? The name "Frederick Douglass" was probably famous in Britain by March 1847, and McIver who stole his cabin on the *Cambria* made a small fortune by selling it to a white traveler. This is overlooked by white historians because it does not fall into a deeper understanding of racism and its tentacles in all spheres of British society.

Frederick Douglass arrived back in the United States a free man on April 20, 1847 after a fifteen-day transatlantic journey. He was in effect a manumitted person, freed by his master for the sum of $750—another small fortune had been stolen from Douglass. More importantly, he would go on for almost another fifty years fighting for the civil and human rights of African Americans. He would travel again to Europe to meet up with his "British friends" and some would actually travel to America to work and support his endeavors. By all accounts, he had a full life; Douglass is a marvel in human endurance and an inspiration to anyone who studies his path from enslavement to freedom and his fight for the liberty of all African Americans. His time in the British Isles from August 1845 to April 1847 is now folklore history—indeed it is hard to believe all that he achieved in such a short space of time. Douglass arrived in Liverpool and he left from Liverpool—a tale of freedom for the ages, interspersed with acts of British racism and paternalism against his humanity that he largely chose to ignore.

****

It was a cold December 2015 evening in New York City. As a Black Liverpudlian, I was excited to see the *Hamilton* musical on Broadway. I had been a full-time professor in the United States for fifteen years, having spent eleven years at Miami University of Ohio. I had relocated to the City University of New York in 2011 where I would endeavor to enjoy anything on Broadway that spoke to my interests in Africana history and culture. When I had first arrived in America to read for a master's degree in Black studies at Ohio State University in 1992, I did not think that I would end up eventually living and working here for thirty-plus years. After completing my master's degree, I returned to England in 1993 to work in Liverpool 8 as an educational guidance officer for GOAL8, as well as teaching part-time at Elimu Study School where I taught Black studies to young students aged eleven to eighteen years. I continued to work with the Charles Wootton College on a voluntary basis pushing the need to have Black studies taught in the city's mainstream educational sphere. By 1994 I decided to read for my doctoral degree and took up an offer to do so at the University of Sheffield with the Department of Sociological Studies. The subject for my dissertation would be Black settlement and Black Identity in Liverpool, 1919–1996. I had chosen this subject because while completing the master's degree in America my professors and peers all wanted to know what Black Britain was about—some did not even believe Black communities existed in the United Kingdom.

After completing my doctorate in 1997 I was fortunate to gain a senior postdoctoral Fulbright scholarship to teach about Black Britain at the Department of Pan African Studies, Kent State University—1997/8. I had certainly come a long way from my days as a student at the Charlie where in 1981 I had written and published my first pieces of poetry as a teenager, where I had experienced close up the uprising in the Liverpool 8 area. Here I was now, waiting in line to view *Hamilton* the musical, as a full and tenured professor, established in the fields of Africana studies and sociology. I had certainly come a long way—and one of my most respected historical figures is Frederick Douglass. I had read his autobiographies and a number of his many speeches and articles. However, I was never arrogant enough to state that I had read *all* of whatever Douglass had written, or what others had written about him. Yet I could call myself a dedicated "Douglass scholar" being very well versed in his life and times—and an expert in African American history from the nineteenth to twentieth centuries.

As I stood in the line waiting on that cold December evening, I was feeling in a nostalgic mood. I thought back to my days at Primary School, and wondered what Mr. Redburn would think of me now as a professor—the nine-year-old Black Liverpudlian he had scolded and refused to accept had written a biographical sketch of the Brazilian footballer, Pelé. I also drifted memory-wise to my Comprehensive School that never allowed me to grow as a young scholar—where I was never taken seriously as a student. What would my former teachers think of full and tenured "Professor Christian" teaching at the City University of New York? As the line inched forward, I noticed a poster of the *Hamilton* creator, Lin-Manuel Miranda. He is a born and bred New Yorker of Puerto Rican heritage—a young man who loves Hip Hop. Apparently, after reading a biography on one of the Founding Fathers of America, Alexander Hamilton (1757?–1804) by Ron Chernow, he was inspired to create in his mind what would be the acclaimed *Hamilton* musical that would eventually reach the heights of success on Broadway in 2015. What is quite astounding about this creative adventure is in the way Miranda combined Hip Hop culture with eighteenth century American history—with a cast of predominantly young people of color. In essence, it was creative genius as the cast literally would "Rap" the lyrics in poetic form.

I was enthralled observing this unique display of artistic talent and began to think of Frederick Douglass, and how well something similar could be imagined. In being inspired by the art and vision of Miranda, I decided to think of a way to put Douglass' journey to Britain in 1845 in context to my passage in the other direction, America, in 1992. Were there any similarities? Did the life of Douglass have anything in common with mine? These questions began to resonate in my mind. Of course, at the outset I considered such a notion ridiculous; how could one compare the life of an enslaved African American born in 1818 and it have relevance to a Black Liverpudlian born in 1961? Yet there was something that kept resonating in my mind. Douglass largely had no formal education other than his wit and ingenuity to learn to read and write; he began to learn most once free from enslavement, joining the abolitionist movement, and developing an avarice for reading. Douglass gradually gained confidence and strength of character having experienced life abroad. As Blight argued, "He would never be the same" after his first trip to Britain. Well, I had not gained much from my initial mainstream schooling in Liverpool. It was not until I enrolled at the Charles Wootton in 1980 as a teenager that my hunger for education began to change. Yes, I could read and write well after leaving the mainstream education system, but it was the Charlie that gave me the passion, the desire, the inclination to believe I could be successful in life. I was particularly elevated by my interaction with Ron "Babatunde" Phillips, who taught Black history lessons and gave me the self-confidence to write poetry.

Like Douglass, as a young man I went abroad and had such a wonderful experience in the Department of Black Studies at Ohio State University. After that experience I too "would never be the same" on my return to Britain in 1993. I then focused my sights on becoming an expert in Black history and culture; I would eventually become a professor and research the experiences of transatlantic Africana peoples. Moreover, I would learn in time more about my ancestral roots and that my grandfather from Jamaica, George Rupert Christian, was an active member of the Universal Negro Improvement

Association (UNIA) and had worked with Marcus Garvey directly. The more I delved into my family history, the more I connected with the transatlantic history that allowed me to study the life and times of Frederick Douglass. Indeed, I read how Douglass could sing and play the violin; I had sung a cappella with my brothers for seven years between 1977 and 1984, and played acoustic guitar. Douglass was six foot, two inches in height; I am six foot, two inches and a half (but tend to round it up to six foot, three inches). Douglass was a passionate advocate for social justice, while I also developed an activist zeal for promoting the importance of Africana studies to be taught in Liverpool and beyond. In Liverpool I would become a grassroots advocate for Black studies in Liverpool 8, and then I would go on to teach courses as an adjunct at Liverpool John Moores University, Liverpool Hope University, and would be a director of a Black studies summer school at the University of Liverpool. I also went back to teach at the Charles Wootton College while completing my doctoral studies in the mid-1990s.

By 1992, Frederick Douglass and I were almost 150 years apart in biography and history, but there were aspects to these lives that had connection—this is not hyperbole. We were each young Black men of mixed heritage seeking freedom from oppression and lack of opportunity when we crossed the transatlantic for sojourns in the opposite direction. Liverpool was not a place for a Black Liverpudlian to succeed career-wise, even with a doctorate in the 1990s or early 2000s. The reality of institutional racism and exclusion of Black Liverpudlians from full-time employment in British academia made it necessary to seek pastures new elsewhere—the United States being the most favorable. The overall statistical data in 2022 still remains poor for Black British academics, and generally, which can be exemplified by Meghan Markle's experiences in the Royal Family (Ducey and Feagin 2021). Crucially, Douglass clearly had a different and harsher life compared to mine. He endured a much tougher physical and psychological one, yet the reality of nineteenth century racialized oppression is also relative to the twentieth and twenty-first centuries in terms of legacy. Racism and its concomitant prejudices live on, hurt individuals, in a given society.

The life of the enslaved Douglass in America, who fought for his freedom in Britain in 1845, has relevance to the life of a Black Liverpudlian who sought his intellectual freedom in 1992 America. Two young Black men, though traveling in different directions of the transatlantic, finding liberty in different ways, but reaching similar outcomes: self-confidence, self-awareness, and self-determination. One hundred and forty-seven years apart, each holding on to dreams of opportunity, but being determined not to leave those whom they left behind—each man returned to aid in the struggle against racialized oppression. As Miranda created an Alexander Hamilton for the twenty-first century—likewise, I was determined to have Frederick Douglass speak to the Black Liverpudlian experience.

In September 2016, I arrived in my hometown to present a seminar at a Liverpool university. The title of my presentation was: "Frederick Douglass and His Trip to Britain, 1845–1847, with Special Reference to Liverpool" and the abstract read:

> Frederick Douglass (1818–1895) provides a powerful example of the human spirit in terms of his endurance to withstand a manifold array of life obstacles. This presentation is concerned with his trip to Britain in 1845 as an escaped fugitive from enslavement. There is the notion of migration, abolitionist friends, the women, and his encounter with freedom in Britain. There is also the conundrum of Liverpool's deeply rooted connection to the Slave Trade in regard to Frederick's experience of wide acceptance as an African American in Britain during his trip in 1845–1847. Juxtaposed by the author's own migration to the US some 147 years later, this paper is both historical and contemporary in Black Atlantic themes.

The seminar room was packed full. I had been escorted to the event by Clr. Anna Rothery, a Black Liverpudlian woman with a strong spirit for social justice in the city. Also in our party was the director of the International Slavery Museum based on the Albert Dock, Liverpool—close to where Douglass had disembarked from Boston in August of 1845. The packed seminar room surprised me because the actual start of the British academic year did not commence until a few weeks, so to have full attendance was somewhat surprising. The atmosphere was a little stiff, typical British academia with sterile, lifeless, countenances looking at you. Coming back to Liverpool always gives me mixed feelings, both joy and pain. The university where the seminar took place was a particularly unwelcoming institution for me to endure, where I had experienced the "cold chill" of white academics too many times in the past to ever feel a sense of comfort there. Nevertheless, this was a new day, I was by now a firmly established academic in the United States, and fairly well known in Britain.

To be fair to this group of white British academics, and graduate students from what I could gather, they had no idea that I had been inspired by the *Hamilton* musical on Broadway when considering the topic of Frederick Douglass' trip to Britain. Yet, as seminars go, I was there simply to introduce the topic and bounce ideas around—or so I thought. In opening up with the usual appreciation to those who had organized the seminar, I then began to outline an understanding of Liverpool's Slave Trade history—which is crucial in comprehending the irony of Douglass disembarking there from Boston. This took about twenty minutes because it was a foundational aspect as to why I had to eventually leave the city to find my freedom and life opportunity in the early 1990s. In brief, the seminar was a precursor to the chapter that has been written here, a window into understanding how it could be tackled and how one could integrate a nineteenth century American figure into the life of a twentieth century Black Liverpudlian. It was certainly early days in the thought process. One thing that began to make sense was that this idea immensely confused the traditional British historian—it was too unconventional for that kind of sterile mind.

Moreover, for a Black Liverpudlian to have the audacity to link his life to that of Frederick Douglass was unfathomable heresy to a typical historian. Indeed, the average white British academic has no real appreciation for the racialized experiences Black Liverpudlians have encountered historically. They mainly consider "slavery to be in the past" and if present day racism can be found it is nothing like it used to be, and so forth. The problem with this kind of thinking relates to the fact that exclusion and a denial of one's worth is often a universal phenomenon met by people of color. The fact that I could be escorted to this talk by a sitting Black Liverpudlian councilor and the director of the International Slavery Museum, who was a Black man of mixed heritage from Yorkshire, is quite remarkable in itself. However, it would be wrong to view token representation as a broad sign of equality in action—especially in Liverpool.

There is indeed a legacy to enslavement, racialized oppression, and second-class citizenship that often does not resonate with white academics. They consider it all most often in past tense and fail to comprehend how history has a holistic impact on the present—especially in regard to racialized relations. In short, Douglass *can* link with the life of a Black Liverpudlian and that is why often he himself would be writing for "future generations" that were not yet born.

I regarded the seminar experience as unhealthy in terms of gaining a positive reaction. This of course was of no surprise as I would ordinarily not expect anything else. It has such a poor record in regard to improving institutional racism, as noted by Manneh Brown in 1993. Yet, what I noticed that day was a group of white men at the end being disrespectful beyond normal academic criticism. One comment that stuck was "everything that needs to be stated about Frederick Douglass has been said"—this was prior to the plethora of Douglass studies that have emerged since 2016. The depth of ignorance that day was disbelieving. Another comment from a white academic was: "Douglass never was with aristocrats in Britain"—that person was clearly ignorant of Douglass' visit to Eaton Hall in Chester on the second night of his arrival in Liverpool, August 29, 1845. Douglass moved in all social circles comfortably, and it was fairly wealthy white abolitionists who paid heavily in cost for his freedom. It is difficult to consider anything other than a group of white academics wanting to destabilize or even sabotage the seminar, but they could not. As Douglass met with loutish fools on the *Cambria*, I did think it would be an important topic to write about this seminar within the context of a Black Liverpudlian "coming home" and receiving such a negative welcome. It actually endorsed the very reason that made me seek a life on the other side of the transatlantic, away from Liverpool and its chilly British academic climate.

In a sense, the life of Frederick Douglass can collide with mine and many others who have lived within the context of the Africana world. Regardless of our lives being a century and a half apart—the legacy of Douglass' life can at the very least inspire any Africana generation who learns his story. To be sure, as I conclude this study of a transatlantic experience, within a Black Atlantic frame of reference, one key aspect of this research is to claim that Africana critical studies should endeavor to comprehend the historical and contemporary connections of Africana peoples. Although Douglass may have lived long before my existence, it is not hyperbole to juxtapose aspects of his experiences of white domination with that of contemporary Black souls. Indeed, in the twenty-first century Africana peoples in the Diaspora continue to deal with the psychology of racism and its foibles. Whether it be a scholar in academia, or any other occupation, racism is tangible in the United Kingdom or the United States. Moreover, there can be no substitute for learning from history; the point is not to repeat the mistakes of the past. The argument herein, in part, relates to the "legacy of enslavement, colonialism, and postcolonialism" in the twenty-first century. Much of what has been discussed within this study relates to the City of Liverpool and how its Black settlement has had longevity under excruciatingly difficult circumstances that continue to this very day. What can be done to improve things? Well, white people in Liverpool and beyond could take time to read and listen to the many stories that reveal the life experiences of Black Liverpudlians, and their families. The Christians, for example, do not differ much from any other large Black family. Yes, there is a musical talent in the Christian brothers, and a proclivity for education captured in our forebears from Jamacia, and in the life of Victor the music teacher and social justice activist; or in Tina who was a head teacher at an elementary school in Liverpool and a pioneer for *all* women in engineering. Lastly myself, as an international scholar in Africana critical studies—who now offers this study as a small contribution to the history of Black Liverpudlians within the context of the Black Atlantic paradigm that is forever expanding its realm.

Appendix A

The City of Liverpool

CITY OF LIVERPOOL

9TH DECEMBER 1999

Special Meeting of the City Council held on Thursday, 9th December 1999 at 5.00 p.m. in the Town Hall.

091299

9th December, 1999

- 115 -

PRESENT

THE LORD MAYOR
(Councillor Joe Devaney)

COUNCILLORS: Karen Afford, Peter Allen, Dave Antrobus, Rose Bailey, Vera Best, Paul Brant, Peter Brennan, Jan Clein, Flo Clucas, Barbara Collinge, Pauline Connolly, Donald Craig, Alan Dean, Frank Doran, Steve Ellison, Marilyn Fielding, Ron Gould, Dave Hanratty, Herbert Herrity, Alfie Hincks, Daniel Hughes, David Irving, Lady Doreen Jones, Mirna Juarez, Malcolm Kelly, Erica Kemp, Malcolm Kennedy, Margaret McDaid, Marie McGiveron, Barbara Mace, Andrew Makinson, Richard Marbrow, Peter Millea, Patrick Moloney, Jean Newton, Frank O'Donoghue, Ian Phillips, Cathy Prayle, Frank Prendergast, Steve Radford, Sylvia Renilson, Richard Roberts, Frank Ruse, Gerry Scott, George Smith, Jack Spriggs, Mike Storey, Berni Turner, Len Tyrer, Peter Tyrrell and Hazel Williams.

Apologies for absence were submitted from Councillors Joe Anderson, Gideon Ben-Tovim, Tom Carter, Eddie Clein, Paul Clein, Chris Curry, Chris Dooley, Kevin Firth, Alf Flattery, Beatrice Fraenkel, Dorothy Gavin, Jimmy Gouldbourne, Ann Hines, Richard Kemp, Frances Kidd, Elaine Kinahan, George Knibb, Bob Lancaster, John McIntosh, Oliver Martins, Steve Munby, Chris Newby, Bob Ousby, Ed Phelan, Keith Turner, Alan Walker and Richard White.

PERMISSION FOR FILMING

Resolved that authority be granted for filming to take place at this meeting of the Council.

COUNCIL MINUTES

The Minutes of the two meetings of the City Council held on 24th November 1999 were submitted and signed by the Lord Mayor.

CONSORTIUM OF BLACK ORGANISATIONS

With the permission of the Council Ms. Adele Ambrose addressed the meeting on behalf of the Consortium of Black Organisations.

9th December, 1999

CANON NICHOLAS FRAYLING

At the invitation of the Lord Mayor, Canon Nicholas Frayling addressed the meeting.

SLAVE TRADE

Motion by Councillor Mirna Juarez, seconded by Councillor Maggie McDaid and supported by all Party Leaders or their representatives,

That –

As its last formal act, at its last formal meeting of this Millennium, the City Council acknowledges Liverpool's responsibility for its involvement in three centuries of the slave trade, a trade which influenced every aspect of the City's commerce and culture and affected the lives of all its citizens.

Whilst bequeathing the city a rich diversity of people and cultures, learning, architecture and financial wealth, it also obscured the human suffering upon which it was built. The untold misery which was caused has left a legacy which affects Black people in Liverpool today.

On behalf of the city, the City Council expresses its shame and remorse for the city's role in this trade in human misery. The City Council makes an unreserved apology for the city's involvement in the slave trade and the continual effects of slavery on Liverpool's Black communities.

This first step towards reconciliation will be the basis upon which the city, and all its people and institutions, can grasp the challenges of the new Millennium with a fresh and sustainable commitment to equality and justice in Liverpool.

The City Council hereby commits itself to work closely with all Liverpool's communities and partners and with the peoples of those countries which have carried the burden of the slave trade.

The Council also commits itself to programmes of action, with full participation of Liverpool's Black communities, which will seek to combat all forms of racism and discrimination and will recognise and respond to the city's multi-racial inheritance and celebrate the skills and talents of all its people.

9th December, 1999

- 117 -

As part of the way forward, an appropriate event will be organised in the new millennium in full consultation with all communities in Liverpool possibly including a further meeting of the full Council.

The Motion was supported unanimously.

091299

Figure A.A Liverpool City Council Slave Apology Minutes—from December 9, 1999.
Source: 352/MIN Liverpool Central Library and Archive for the Slavery minutes and apology reprinted with permission from the archive.

Appendix B

INTERNATIONAL SLAVERY MUSEUM – ALBERT DOCK, LIVERPOOL, ENGLAND.

NOVEMBER 14, 2007 – 7pm-9pm

In this free lecture Dr. Mark Christian, associate professor of Sociology and Black World Studies at Miami University uses the case study of Liverpool's apology for its role in the Transatlantic Slave Trade to explore the concept of slave apologies. He examines the substance of such an apology and what it has meant for Liverpool's Black communities in the contemporary sense.

Mark Christian: Before I start I'd like to thank Dr. Richard Benjamin and his staff for all the support they've shown me in bringing me here tonight. It's a wonderful opportunity to come back home. It's a strange place Liverpool, it kind of draws you away and pulls you back. Well, we'll get into that.

The age of slave apologies. We're living in a very crucial time in a sense when it comes to reflection on the history of enslavement. So that's where I want to go with this tonight and to then bring in the slave apology that took place in Liverpool.

Now I don't like to just flick through things but this guy here is so sorry, yeah? He's part of the church actually. This is the triangular trade, here we have the Albert Dock all spruce and Liverpool 800 on the top there.

OK, some recent examples of this apology. What is this slave apology? Why do they seem to be ubiquitous at the moment? Liverpool's in 1999, London's in 2007, the Church of England 2006/7 began to apologise and one of their members said "We the Church of England were at the heart of it". So out of this remembrance and apology era many things are coming to light about the actual extent of this experience.

To put this into some kind of context I wrote what's called 'A slavery apology from Western European nations and the legacy of racialised discrimination'. I did this in order to put some meat on the apology for you. It's done in hopefully a creative way for you to understand where I'm coming from and what I understand of these apologies and what they are actually apologising for, which is a very sensitive issue as you all know.

Historical context, I'm going to run through until the 19th century.

- We collectively apologise for the era of European enslavement and its legacy that developed in the 15th century and did not cease formally until the mid-19th century, depending on the region.
- We apologise for the disruption, plunder and rape of the African continent and to the indigenous peoples decimated by our arrival to the region known euphemistically and erroneously as the new world.
- We apologise to the millions of African sons and daughters kidnapped directly from the continent who suffered profound physical and mental abuse. This is at the heart of our apology.
- We apologise moreover to their intercultural offspring born in the new world plantation system as chattel, whom continue to suffer under the heavy burden of toiling unpaid from dawn to dusk or from can't see in the morning to can't see at night.
- We apologise for the laws put in place to prevent anyone with any degree of African heritage the opportunity to educate oneself. Although these severe laws did not totally deny the intellectual development of all enslaved peoples they did curtail the vast majority from cultural advancement. We apologise for this wholeheartedly.
- We apologise for branding the enslaved with hot irons, for raping the enslaved women at will, for breaking up enslaved families by selling of their children, siblings or partners to other plantations and for crippling or dismembering those defiant enough to want to escape enslavement.
- We apologise for stifling the normal growth of a people due to the enforcement of enslavement in the historical sense. That is from the 15th century to the 19th centuries.
- We hope that our apology will help heal the wounds of the past and make the future more equitable.

That puts some meat and bones on the apology in historical context. But I'm interested in the here and now as well as history and I write now about the contemporary context with a focus not on France or any other European nation but the British slave trade legacy. And I argue the latter part of the 19th Century though to the 20th Century saw the aftermath of enslavement replaced by colonialism for peoples of African heritage and for those nations that would gain independence there would be the spectre of neo-colonialism in Africa and the Caribbean.

On Peter Fryer's powerful book, I was speaking to some colleagues earlier about Peter Fryer's *Staying Power: The History of Black People in Britain*. It is a powerful book from 1984 published by Pluto Press. I heard the man died last year and I'm very sorry to hear that. He had a style, a clarity and a readability that is not often the case in many academic books I can tell you. Although he was known as a journalist maybe that's why his prose is so clear. Peter Fryer, chapter seven, if there are any young people in here please look up *Staying Power* and go to chapter seven because there's a powerful analysis of how in the 18th and 19th centuries pseudo-scientific racial theories were developed and disseminated by universities, popular culture and across generations to cement into the social consciousness the fallacious notion of white racial superiority over all peoples of colour. And some white groups were not white enough but we don't have time to go into that right now.

It would take a century to counter such pseudo-racialised theories and they still have life today in the 2000s. In relation to the Black British settlement in the 20th Century both World Wars brought a major influx of Africans and African Caribbean from the colonies to work in the armed services and later to kick start the British economy in the 40s and 50s.

During the 1960s and the 1970s those born of African heritage in Britain and particularly in Liverpool would suffer from the many forms of institutionalised racism, poor education, and poor job prospects. Stifled opportunities all round meant difficult times for all Black communities.

The 1980s and the 1990s brought riots, the militant left council and regeneration not to mention, or not to forget to mention, Alan Bleasdale's acclaimed *Boys from the Blackstuff*. A Liverpool drama that captured the pain and struggle of working class Liverpool under Thatcher's government. My first home away from the family home was in Kelvin Grove and that was the street where they filmed Yosser's home. So it is very poignant to understand that I was living in the same street at Yosser Hughes, it gives you an indication of my life past. "Gissa job" [laughter]. OK, we'll move on. [Yosser was a key character in the series, working class and out of work.]

Liverpool saw the development of the Albert Dock complex after the 1981 riots. I remember asking Tarzan, the then-Tarzan of the Thatcher government Michael Heseltine, in the Liver Buildings behind us, from the International Slavery Museum, I was a Charles Wootton student: "Can you assure", I said, "Can you assure that there will be jobs for Black people at the Albert Dock complex?" He answered in the political affirmative, talking through both sides of his mouth. In hindsight we now know that few jobs, if any, at the Albert Dock complex went to Liverpool born Blacks.

On a positive note, because we have to keep positive, we have to keep hope alive, indeed Jesse Jackson was here not long ago to open the International Slavery Museum. Well, access to higher education has opened up for those willing to defer gratification and take the long road to academic success. Some Black Liverpudlians took up the opportunities to further themselves via education and/or training.

But even in the first decade of the 21st century the Liverpool economy has not fully opened up its opportunity doors to Liverpool Black people. The city centre remains today largely a white enclave of economic activity. In 2007 there are few Black faces still in the city centre places. Or let me be more poetic: *There are few Black faces in city centre places*.

So let me move on to this PowerPoint. To summarise thus far, I've put some meat on this talk tonight and we've gone through history and we've moved up to the present times. I want to speak about an apology and if I hurt somebody or we hurt somebody there are 3 components to an apology. First, say we're sorry, or "I'm sorry I hurt you" and second, we then we admit to doing the wrong. Finally it's the third component: what can I do or what can we do to make it right? We must understand those three components to an apology. What can we do to make it right? Let that run around your head - what can we do to make it right? We know that something bad went wrong in the past and the legacy of that is quite profound. What can we do to make it right?

In terms of the Liverpool apology, and my focus on the Liverpool slave trade apology as a case study, because I was inextricably interwoven into this apology as a historical agent. There's a hidden history to it. I don't know whether many of you know this but a very quiet young lady, former student of the Charles Wootton, Myrna Juarez, from Belize I believe. Many students of Charles Wootton came through and got into professional activity via the Charles Wootton Centre and then College. She was a Liberal councillor in 1999, very green, a little bit nervous. She used to live in Parkfield Road, I knew her from the Charles Wootton and we used to touch base and talk in Parkfield Road at the time, September/October 1999. She was a very new councillor,

Appendix B

Liberal, and was asking me because she knew I was interested in Black history and culture she'd say: "Mark what do you think about a slave apology?" I'd say "I think it would be good as long as there is some substance behind an apology". This young lady went ahead with this proposal and it is strange how this diminutive quiet soul could shake up the city to create a slave apology. Maybe if myself or Dave Smith, a Liverpool born Black grassroots activist in the audience, had went knocking on the Liverpool City Council door [chuckles] it would have been closed or the police would have arrived, you know how it is.

So this young lady she gets things moving and I think in hindsight that that could be a good thing. She put forward this proposal and there was a guy there, the Lord Mayor at the time, Joe Devaney - am I pronouncing his name right? He was a very positive guy, he was all for it. So basically through the Liverpool Council minutes I found them - and the Liverpool City Council have been very gracious because I asked for these minutes and they did send them through via email. I found a note here, again inextricably interwoven into this history that the Liverpool City Council meeting of November 4th 1999, they would produce a report with appropriate members, the Lord Mayor and Dr. Mark Christian. We never did write that report by the way but at least we were moving in the right direction. But we did meet with Liverpool Black organisations at the Liverpool 8 Law Centre and we drafted notes on what we desired in the apology. They sent their version of the apology, and we tweaked it and we came to an agreement on what should be written in the formal apology.

So let me read you the formal apology. This is a Liverpool slave trade apology December of 1999, this is how it looks [indicates slide in PowerPoint presentation and reads it out].

At a special Meeting of the city council of the City of Liverpool held on Thursday, 9 December 1999 within the Town Hall, in the presence of The Right Worshipful, The Lord Mayor, Councillor Joe Devaney, it was moved by Councillor Mirna Juarez and seconded by Councillor Maggie McDaid and supported by all party leaders or their representatives, that;

As its last formal act, at its last formal meeting of this millennium, the city council acknowledges Liverpool's responsibility for its involvement in three centuries of the slave trade, a trade which influenced every aspect of the city's commerce and culture and affected the lives of all its citizens.

Appendix B

Whilst bequeathing the city with a rich diversity of people and cultures, learning, architecture and financial wealth, it also obscured the human suffering upon which it was built. The untold misery which was caused has left a legacy which affects black people in Liverpool today.

On behalf it the city, the city council expresses its shame and remorse for the city's role in this trade in human misery. The city council makes an unreserved apology for the city's involvement in the slave trade and the continual effects of slavery on Liverpool's black communities.

The first-step towards reconciliation will be the basis upon which the city, and all its people and institutions, can grasp the challenges of the new millennium with a fresh and sustainable commitment to equality and justice in Liverpool.

The city council hereby commits itself to work closely with all Liverpool's communities and partners and with people of those countries which have carried the burden of the slave trade.

The Council also commits itself to programmes of action, with full participation of Liverpool's black communities, which will seek to combat all forms of racism and discrimination and will recognise and respond to the city's multi-racial inheritance and celebrate the skills and talent of all its people.

The Motion was supported unanimously

Lord Mayor..

All its people. So that's a very profound slave apology. That's very powerful. The problem is now, what do we do? How do we make things right? And here we are eight years, almost a decade later in 2007.

Let us look at Liverpool itself in terms of "race" and racism. I understand this is a sensitive issue but we have to bear with it and cross to the valley of optimism, yeah? From Charles Wootton in 1919, for those of you who don't know, he was a Bermudan sailor who was murdered in Liverpool and a subsequent during the anti-Black riots of 1919. Apparently, Charles Wootton [sometimes spelt Wooten] was actually chased to the docks by a mob, here at the International Slavery Museum area, and he tried to swim away but he was ripped and pelted with bricks by the mob, in presence of police – this was June of 1919.

And then Anthony Walker's murder in July 2005. We've never really analysed the death of Anthony Walker, a horrible death, such a waste. Let me say that 2005 for me, that people I don't think have written about, I think the swell of discontent towards people of colour, particularly anybody who looked Arab actually at that time because of 7/7 bombing in London. I think there was the problem of the media, and there was an upsurge again of hate/xenophobia and Anthony Walker may have been in the wrong place at the wrong time during that swell of retribution towards people of colour from the ignorant section of our community. And I think when time settles people will analyse Anthony Walker in the context of the broader national situation of 7/7 rather just a parochial Liverpool incident. But that's for future analysis.

But we can say that Liverpool's Black experience has been one of a constant battle against structural and individual acts of racism. If you look at some of the disturbances that have taken place throughout Liverpool there's a systematic issue, what I would consider race and class. Some say 1919 had something to do with sexual jealousy of the white community against Black people who consorted with white women, that's when I read the documents, but I think we're dealing with "race" and class essentially in all of these issues.

OK the longevity of institutional racism. We have the Swann Report from 1985 and that actually gave a special reference to Liverpool-born Blacks in chapter fifteen, because those of us of Black heritage in Liverpool, my heritage is Jamaican father, and my mother was of Spanish and British heritage, so a lot of people forget the Spanish Moors, so there's Black on both sides of my family, but a lot of Spanish people don't know that or will not acknowledge it. But anyway, the Jamaican side of my heritage is very prominent but we Liverpool-born Blacks speak with the same accent as the average Liverpudlian. We understand the nuances of what it is to be in the city of Liverpool. But we have this historical experience of being socially marginalised and the Swann Report actually gives a chapter on that uniqueness because the issue was back then "Well if these immigrants learn the English language then everything will be OK". But that didn't suit the Liverpool Black experience because we did speak a Liverpudlian, British language. English language, with a twist of course [laughter].

So we have that historical record which clearly situates Liverpool-born Blacks as having a problem with social inclusion. The Liverpool 8 Inquiry, *Loosen the Shackles*, comes by in 1989 and that had a profound impact on Liverpool in terms of our understanding of institutionalised racism. The authors of that book, Lord Gifford, Wally Brown, and Ruth

Bundey, they said that they'd work in different cities and out of all of that experience their experience in Liverpool was "uniquely horrific" in terms of racism.

Ten years later we had the Stephen Lawrence MacPherson report in 1999. We have a definition that mainstream organisations all began to use - this is the definition of institutionalised racism: *It is the collective failure of an organisation to provide an appropriate and professional service to people because of their colour, culture or ethnic origin.* That's what MacPherson called institutionalised racism.

But what was profound about this report is that the tragedy of Stephen Lawrence is only one side of it, the broader tragedy is in the millions of young Blacks who are suffering in the institutional sense of British society. Not coming through the education system. Tapering off. Being excluded more than their white counterparts and so on and so forth. We are conspicuous by our absence in most key echelons of power. This is what was powerful about this Stephen Lawrence/MacPherson report. It acknowledged that not only the Police have institutionalised racism but other institutions in society.

So I'm giving you a context here of problems. We're coming to the 2000s and equality continues on a broad scale to evade Liverpool-born Blacks and others. My focus here is on the Liverpool slave trade in relation to the people of African heritage in all of their social and cultural complexity. But I'm not mindful of the other inequalities that exist - sexism against Asian and people of Arab heritage. I'm aware of all of that but my focus tonight is on Liverpool Blacks specifically.

The Liverpool City Council came up with a report in 2000. It took place between May 99 and January 2000. Made up of seven councillors and seven residents. This is some of their key findings: Liverpool City Council's practices are discriminatory. Liverpool City Council continues to exclude many people in its workforce. Individuals and communities do not receive a fair equal service. Liverpool City Council has an appalling record on equal opportunities with its image, its ethos and its culture.

That's a very damning report, very depressing. 2000, a year after the apology to put it in context.

This is what I came across because I had to prepare for this and I knew somebody would ask me about up-to-date references. Here we have something from 2007, it's a report I found by the Merseyside Black Police Association. Their annual report, on page

Appendix B

12 so you can take a record of this if you like. In a section entitled "Liverpool Apartheid" which is a very powerful phrase to use in 2007, they say – and this is the Merseyside Black Police Association, this is not the Charles Wootton College or the Liverpool 8 Law Centre, the usual suspects in truth-telling:

> "Very few indigenous black people could be seen in employment in Liverpool city centre. Where black people were employed it tended to be in low-paid positions where little training or skills are required." (Merseyside Black Police Association, 2007 report, p. 12).

What do we do with that quote? What is happening in Liverpool for this to continue decade after decade, this exclusion of Black people in the city centre?

So Liverpool-born Black exclusion, let's try and understand it. I was speaking with Gloria Hyatt, who's very famous now, she has an MBE. An MBE. I've said that twice. I'm very happy for her, I would not be happy for myself to accept an MBE, to be a Member of the British Empire, but that's another story. Me and Gloria, we speak on this topic all the time and we will continue tonight after the lecture.

She's done very well as an educational activist in this city. There's no doubt about that.

She says, if I'm citing her right, that there continues to be exclusionary tactics regarding the monitoring of indigenous Liverpool-born Blacks who she says are still the largest racialised minority group in the city. And this is by the Liverpool Education Authority.

My argument is more focused on those cultural groups who have English as a second language seems to be the strategy. That there's more focus still on groups that need to learn English, but what about the Liverpool-born Blacks? It seems that those in power have forgotten the Swann Report of 1985 - indigenous Liverpool-born Blacks have a specific history of being racially stigmatised and that's been well documented.

I want you to see the Charles Wootton College. I took this picture two months ago. If you take a drive to 248 Upper Parliament Street you will see it on your right. A dilapidated English Heritage building I believe. It's going to be turned into a block of flats and offices – apparently.

But once this disappears a generation will come and go and will not even know where the Charles Wootton was once located. It will be a folklore history like many other buildings in the city. But this building has so much history. That building there produced the majority of Liverpool Black organisations in the late seventies, early eighties. The Liverpool 8 Defense Committee met with Heseltine there in the basement in July 1981. While they were meeting, I was doing algebra, my math teacher was Chief Ben Agwuna. I used to look out of this window, [pointing to photo of Charles Wootton College] dreaming about life and the future. I see this now, this dilapidated building and I think of the slave apology, and I think of the Liverpool City Council, and I think of its promise to work with the Black community.

Is this dilapidation all the fault of the Liverpool City Council? I would say here no. We too must take responsibility, those Black people who had power and the last Director of the Charles Wootton College, Chief Ben Agwuna, and I spent a lot of time as a student supporting his work, he did not do the right thing in the end to pass on to the next generation. I'll leave it there because it gets a little bit tricky. But what we can say is that we can't blame everything on the Liverpool City Council. Although they don't have a great record, we were given this opportunity and we could have built that college into something really special.

So many individuals have come out of that dilapidated building, myself included. I had no qualifications when I left school so I went back to the Charles Wootton like many other Liverpool Blacks because that's how we filtered through the system. The ones who have got a little bit of talent, it doesn't emerge until their late teens and early twenties. I came through that route. Without that, I wouldn't be here. You see? That's 25-plus years ago. I remember meeting Heseltine. I remember coming out of this door [pointing to the Charles Wootton College] here and Heseltine comes walking forward with all the press behind him and I'm going for a Kitkat at the local convenience store. And later that day I'm on the 5.45 pm news shaking Heseltine's hand on the steps of the Charles Wootton – and I was simply going for a Kitkat [a chocolate bar]. It was break time!

Then I met him. We were a group of Liverpool-born Blacks, and because when anything Black happened in Liverpool outsiders came to the Charles Wootton to find out information about the Liverpool 8 community. When anything happened they would call the Charles Wootton. There was a press release once a month. It had a profound effect on my consciousness. That's why I have this passion for maintaining a historical record.

I was very disappointed to see the outcome of the Charles Wootton, because I think it's still needed today.

This historical and important building, let me move on, is going to be flats and offices, I don't know who owns it or what will happen. Will they have a Black perspective involved in that, I'm not sure, I would say no. It's a symbol of regeneration but it's also for me a symbol of reneging on promise because we had an educational institution there that had a powerful record in developing young Black individuals and giving them a chance to grow in life. Not only that, many Black teachers who were being shunned in mainstream would congregate, or gain employment there, at the Charles Wootton and teach courses.

I remember a visitor to the Charles Wootton said "You guys have got more qualifications than I've got across my university department". There was a lot of professional talent at the Charles Wootton. It was a place for educational discourse from a Black perspective. That's a very powerful story for you to think about. It was a very important base for Black intellectuals.

Now let's focus on Toxteth or Liverpool 8, the media's baby. Selected Toxteth statistics. Granby Street, still largely dilapidated. This is what we have in the area. High unemployment, low education. High deprivation, low housing expectation. High on drug use, low on book use. High on gentrification in the best areas, low on egalitarianism. A high percentage of Liverpool-born Blacks without work, a low percentage of anyone who cares it seems.

So, in conclusion, I'm coming up with some recommendations. They're not etched in stone, it's just something for us to think about. As we consider the Liverpool slave trade apology as a sincere apology, I've read those words and they're very powerful words to hold the city council responsible to its word, we must also consider the third component of an apology, what can we do to make things right. Without concrete measurement of progress, the slave trade apology has no substance. You cannot apologise in 1999 and then close down the Charles Wootton in 2000. That is the height of hypocrisy.

It would be no more than a hollow statement. There should be more done to eradicate structural inequality and racism in Liverpool. It goes beyond rhetoric. Don't set up another task force. Don't set up another committee to come up with a report that's going to tell us the same depressing statistics. Just do something.

This is what I've come up with that's tangible and this relates to reparations. I know it's a tricky term this, reparations, there's a lot of cynical people out there you know, for example, those that state: "My grandfather had nothing to do with slavery". If you understand white privilege and "race" and ethnicity, if you have a white skin and you look white, then you've got better life chances than people of colour. That's the social reality of our world, I'm sorry but that's the way it goes.

These are the recommendations for an action plan. A ten point slavery legacy plan for Liverpool-born Blacks. And it should be supported by the Liverpool City Council.

- I believe the wealth of our universities can come up with education scholarships that can help that specific target group. Those young people who come to get a scholarship must have at least showed the energy for wanting to be successful. I think we could come up with, these universities of ours, with scholarships that meet this discussion. It's not much to ask for.

- I think there should be a housing council tax deduction on those that can deem themselves Liverpool-born Blacks. Why should people pay higher taxes when they have low services? This is a very controversial question/point and it will probably hit a brick wall but I'm going to say it anyway.

- Employment, internships in local politics, media. I met a young man today who writes a column for the Liverpool Echo. That is like breaking through a rock, a boulder, to get a young Black individual, he's not online yet which means he's not being read but it's a step in the right direction. This is what I mean by if the Liverpool Echo opens its doors to a young Black writer then we hear a different voice. That's diversity, then we need women, you know the story. But it has to be tangible.

- I believe the bank sector, particularly Barclays, if you study Barclays it goes right back to the Heywood Bank which was developed out of the profits of enslavement. You know all this - the Bank of Liverpool and then we lead to Martins Bank through to Barclays Bank. Surely Barclays Bank can come up with some internship for Liverpool-born Blacks who want to take up banking for a career. I don't think this is too much to ask.

- Christian scholarships. I mention Christian because I hear the Church is very sorry and you know the Church branded enslaved Africans with their emblem - they called it the Society in something I read, I'm recalling the article - the Society, Christian

Church, branding. Well "brand" some scholarships in the memory of those enslaved Africans you branded with hot irons with your emblem.

- Police and law training scholarships. We need police. We need the police. People are critical of the Police and I've been very critical of the Police but in relation to the Anthony Walker affair I was very impressed that they apprehended the ones who did it, they called it a racially motivated crime and they put the guys behind bars. They did a very good job. They didn't do that with Stephen Lawrence. So, let's give something but there's still a long way to go for the Police to get the whole thing right in Liverpool. Young Black people can be still criminalised unfortunately.
- There should be apprenticeships in construction trades. I've gone through Liverpool today, I visited in September and took a few photos and I'm seeing massive reconstruction taking place. How many young Blacks or young Whites from Liverpool are working in these building sites?
- Affordable housing in prime city centre regions. We have something taking place in Liverpool that is profoundly beneficial economically, but will young Liverpool people be able to draw into that. I'm not sure. Particularly Liverpool Black people. There should be some way and I don't know how but if they can create the slave trade they can create some housing for Blacks. And I don't mean segregated housing, I just mean affordable space.
- There should be a childcare voucher for Liverpool Blacks. Considering this historical discrimination which has stifled Black development in this city, let's give some childcare vouchers to get women, young children, young men who look after their children a chance to get into education. They'll probably be in their mid-twenties if they do, in Liverpool.
- I think there should be a retirement home that the City Council can set up, particularly for Liverpool Blacks. It could be open to the relatives of Liverpool Blacks, whom many are white. I'm not talking about segregated housing here, I'm talking about a home specifically for Liverpool-born Blacks and their families. This is something structural that could be there and we could all celebrate.

This is small. This is a small-scale and do-able action plan.

I also believe there should be a Liverpool-born Black institute for social economic and cultural research by the Liverpool City Council. I think I've just relayed to you some of the historical paths we're taking in terms of reports and you know and I know that the same findings keep emerging - a lack of Black empowerment is a constant theme.

As we open up for questions, I want all of you to think about what is this longevity of institutionalised racism? How do you think as white people in this audience? Does race matter? Maybe it doesn't matter to you. How does it manifest itself? How does it manifest itself when people go for jobs?

We have ageism, sexism and racism in jobs still. How do we get across this in future?

Note: This article is based on a public lecture Dr. Mark Christian gave on November 14, 2007 at the International Slavery Museum at the Albert Dock in Liverpool, England. It has been mildly edited to erase transcription errors, spelling is in British English, and the *essence* of the talk remains the same as when it was delivered to the audience.

Figure A.B "The Age of Slave Apologies: The Case of Liverpool, England"—transcript of a public lecture presented by Dr. Mark Christian, November 14, 2007.
Source: Reprinted with permission from the International Slavery Museum.

Appendix C

ISSUE No. 26   DECEMBER 1999

CHARLES WOOTTON NEWS

Lord Mayor endorses a City of Liverpool Apology for the 'Slave Trade' era

FOLLOWING on from the 1998 United Nations Educational, Scientific and Cultural Organisation's (UNESCO) decision to pass a resolution establishing an International Day for the Remembrance of the infamous Slave Trade and its Abolition (23rd August each year), Bernie Grant MP, came to the city of Liverpool to unveil a plaque at the Albert Dock complex in commemoration of this. Along with the Lord Mayor and other civic dignitaries, members of the Liverpool Black community also attended the unveiling which was organised by the National Museums & Galleries on Merseyside.

In line with this and according to the *Liverpool Echo* (16 October 1999), the Lord Mayor, Joseph Devaney, later announced that he wants the city of Liverpool to formally 'express remorse over the slave trade'. The *Liverpool Echo* further stated that the the Lord Mayor intends to write to the US President Bill Clinton and Civil Rights activist Jesse Jackson, in order to invite them to take part in what would be Liverpool City Council's 'final deed of 1999'. We commend this verbal gesture in helping to heal the wounds of the past. We also hope that it is followed through with dignity and genuine recognition of the city's role in the enslavement of African humanity. This is the only way forward for reconciliation and to deal with the contemporary discrimination faced by Black people in Liverpool at the dawn of 2000.

(See Editorial for further comment).

● *Lord Mayor, Councillor Joe Devaney, with Bernie Grant, MP, under the portrait of the first Black British Lord Mayor, John Archer (Battersea, 1913).*

The Staff and Students at the Charles Wootton College wish all our Readers and Advertisers a Happy Christmas and a prosperous New Millennium!

£2.50 per copy
FREE to Staff & Students

Figure A.C Front cover: *CWCN* reports on historic Slave Apology (Issue 26: December 1999).

Source: 340/LAW Liverpool Central Library and Archive for the Charles Wootton College publications reprinted with permission from the archive.

Appendix D

**CONSORTIUM OF BLACK ORGANISATIONS
STATEMENT RESPONSE TO LIVERPOOL CITY COUNCIL**
Apology for 'Liverpool's Significant role in European Slave Trade'
9 December 1999

WE WISH TO LODGE A COMPLAINT IN THE STRONGEST TERMS regarding the Principal Officers of the Central Policy Unit, in particular, the Community Development and Equality Unit's involvement in today's historic motion. The approach to this issue epitomises their poor approach to 'race relations' in this city.

After consulting with the Consortium of Black Organizations in regard to the Liverpool City Council's Special Meeting to formally 'Apologize' for the city's role in the inhumane 'European Slave Trade', collectively its members agree that the 'consultation process' on behalf of the Council with Black community representatives has been abysmal. Indeed it has been handled by city council officials in a colonial administrative fashion. In other words, we feel highly patronized and insulted at the lack of genuine consultation in regard to this highly emotive and sensitive aspect of our history. For example, two days cannot be considered adequate time to respond properly to such an important and far-reaching motion- and this is what we were given. WE WILL NOT ALLOW A 'WINDOW DRESSING' EXERCISE ON SUCH AN IMPORTANT SOCIAL ISSUE.

Moreover, given the fact that there is a contemporary attack on Liverpool's already depleted Black organizational infrastructure (e.g. the cut to MIAU, the sole independent Immigration Advice service to Refugees and Asylum Seekers), along with the continued high levels of racial discrimination and exclusion in the local labour market, and mainstream institutions such as Education, we need GENUINE ASSURANCES that this will be addressed IMMEDIATELY in the form of a PUBLIC INQUIRY. Indeed, it is now 10 years since the GIFFORD INQUIRY stated that the city has a 'uniquely horrific' racist culture and there is again clearly a need to re-examine the issue of 'poor race relations' in the city of Liverpool. This contemporary form of racism must be acknowledged in the form of an inquiry, along with the 'unreserved apology' for the 'slave-trading era'.

CONSORTIUM OF BLACK ORGANISATIONS
STATEMENT RESPONSE TO LIVERPOOL CITY COUNCIL
Apology for 'Liverpool's Significant role in European Slave Trade'
9 December 1999

WHAT DO WE WANT?

The Public Inquiry will focus on the extent of Black social exclusion in the city and should cover the extent of institutionalized racism in:

- Liverpool City Council
- Educational institutions
- Employment (especially in the city centre service industries and the professions)
- Housing
- Nursery provision
- Health facilities
- Business training
- Leisure activities (especially in terms of Social Clubs, Restaurants, Bars)

Primary Focus for Positive Outcomes

We focus on the dire need for 'Black role models' in this city.

Our main concern is for the **BLACK YOUTH** of today and the next generation of Black communities in the city of Liverpool. We are determined to make a collective stand on this issue. At present we are not convinced that the representatives of the Liverpool City Council have the interest of Black Communities at heart in regard to this 'apology' for the city's involvement in the 'European Slave Trade'. This is more than evident in the shabby and offhand manner in which we were 'consulted'.

Crucially, WE WANT A TANGIBLE, LONG-TERM, END TO RACIAL EXCLUSION AND DISCRIMINATION IN THIS CITY. THIS CAN ONLY BE ACHIEVED THROUGH AN ARRAY OF POSITIVE ACTION PROGRAMMES AND **DIRECT** INVOLVEMENT AND PARTNERSHIP WITH BLACK COMMUNITY ACTIVISTS.

Figure A.D Consortium of Black Organizations–Liverpool, response to LCC Slave Apology.
Source: 352/MIN Liverpool Central Library and Archive for the Slavery minutes and apology reprinted with permission from the archive.

Appendix E

ISSUE No. 12   DECEMBER 1992

CHARLES WOOTTON NEWS

GUESTS TOAST COLLEGE STATUS

Guests at the 1992 Open Day Celebrations toast Charles Wootton College Status, Left to right: Frank Cogley, Director of Education; Claire Dove, Chairperson Management Committee seen proposing the toast; Arif Ali, Editor Caribbean Times; Ben Agwuna, College Director; Rosemary Cooper, Lord Mayor; Bishop K. O'Connor, Archbishop's Representative and Cllr. Gideon Ben-Tovim, Chair Liverpool Education Committee.

Wedding of the Year Elaine & Eugene

Staff & Students at The Charles Wootton College for Further Education wish all our readers Seasons Greetings

Black Police Chief from U.S.A. Ron Hampton talks to local reporter during his visit to Liverpool last summer.

First Pre-H.E. Entry Programme Students with their tutors on weekend orientation at Burton Manor College, before the start of the course
(See page 11 for more photographs)

Figure A.E Front cover: *CWCN* **celebration of college status (Issue 12: December 1992).**
Source: 340/LAW Liverpool Central Library and Archive for the Charles Wootton College publications reprinted with permission from the archive.

Appendix F

ISSUE No. 21   JUNE 1997

CHARLES WOOTTON NEWS

COLLEGE LOSES OVER £40,000 IN COUNCIL GRANT CUTS

"SHOCK and dismay!" This was how one Charles Wootton College management member summed up reaction to the news of the City Council's decision to cut £19,000 from the College's 1997/98 grant. After all, this is a college working on a shoe-string budget since it was set up in the early 1970s and which has accomplished a great deal for education in Toxteth. (*see brief Progression statistics below).

The college, which was established in 1974 as a result of the failure of the state education system to provide *adequate and relevant education* for local Black and ethnic minority groups. The recent cut in the college grant rises to well over £40,000 when account is taken of inflation and cost of living rises.

Since the John Ord affair, the Compulsory Purchase Order and the ill-fated attempt to build a new Adult Education Centre opposite the Charles Wootton College were halted by local community action in the late 80s and early 90s, the college and the City Council has built up a good working relationship. However, the present cut in the college grant is bound to put strains on this relationship. Also, new information reaching the *Charles Wootton News* that the cuts were not really across the board will further test the relationship in the coming months. It is a fact that most other voluntary organisations got off lightly: e.g. Youth Section. The questions that need answering are: "Why the Charles Wootton College", and "Who made the recommendation?'

The college management has vowed to fight all the way to recover all the money cut from the college grant.

Today, as shown by the figures below, the college is sending increasing numbers of students to universities and other H.E. institutions all over the country. Also, a significant number of those not going into Higher Education have found good full-time jobs.

Progression from C.W.C. to H.E. Institutions in the U.K.

1993/94 .... 38%
1994/95 .... 58%
1995/96 .... 73%

BERNIE GRANT, MP, BECOMES THE FIRST PATRON OF CHARLES WOOTTON COLLEGE

Dr. Bernie Grant, MP

BERNIE Grant MP, is the member of Parliament for Tottenham in London. First elected to Parliament in 1987, Mr Grant has diligently fought for the rights of his constituents and for Black people all over the world. Mr Grant was born in Guyana in 1944 and came to Britain in 1963 with his family. After working as a railway clerk and then as a telephonist Mr Grant became a full-time trade union official and in 1978 he became a local councillor. In 1985 he became the leader of the Haringey Council before moving to parliament in 1987. Mr Grant is well known for standing up for the rights of Black people and is the Chair of the African Reparations Movement and The Standing Conference Against Racism in Europe (SCORE). He actively campaigned against the Apartheid regime of South Africa and had the privilege of greeting Nelson Mandela on his release from prison. In 1993 he was awarded an Honorary Doctorate from Pace University in New York in recognition of his great work in fighting for justice and equal rights. However, not resting on his laurels, Bernie Grant continues to strive for equity and justice for oppressed peoples and that is why the Charles Wootton College is delighted to honour him as the first patron of Britain's best known Black educational establishment.

Figure A.F *CWCN* editorial denounces drastic cuts to funding by LCC (Issue 21: June 1997).

Source: 340/LAW Liverpool Central Library and Archive for the Charles Wootton College publications reprinted with permission from the archive.

Appendix G

Figure A.G *Liverpool Echo* **(August 27, 1997)—report praised CWC teaching.**
Source: 340/LAW Liverpool Central Library and Archive for the Charles Wootton College publications reprinted with permission from the archive.

Appendix H

Charles Wootton News
'Charles Wootton Lives'

Issue No.1.
June 1987

Public Enquiry Victory Celebration by Staff.

Since 1984 Charles Wootton Centre has been threatened with closure under the City Council Compulsory Purchase Order. We are very delighted to announce that last April we won a sensational victory after a hard-fought two-day Public Inquiry in November 1986. The Secretary of State for Environment has finally rejected Liverpool City Council's application to demolish our Centre. We wish to thank all those individuals and organisations who gave us their support in our campaign against the City Council's action.

While we congratulate and welcome the new Labour City Administration leader, Cllr. Harry Rimmer, we hope that his election means the end of the long war of attrition waged against the Centre from the City and that steps will be taken by the new Administration to initiate better lines of communication and support that will enable the Centre to continue with its fine educational and community work.

May I welcome our readers to the first edition of our new quarterly newspaper. This paper will aim largely to provide information for the local Community on the work done by our two Centres- Charles Wootton Centre for Further Education, and Charles Wootton Technology Centre Ltd.

We are going to include also a varied selection of articles and features directly related to activities and events as they happen in our local community.

Do not miss our special feature called, 'Spotlight', which will be looking at current social issues as they affect the lives of Black People in the society.

We welcome any contribution from individuals or organisations in the local community who wish to be featured in future editions of 'Charles

Figure A.H Front cover: *CWCN* **(Issue 1: June 1987)—evidence of LCC fight to close CWC in 1987.**

Source: 340/LAW Liverpool Central Library and Archive for the Charles Wootton College publications reprinted with permission from the archive.

Appendix I

ISSUE No. 25   JUNE 1999

CHARLES WOOTTON NEWS

The Lawrence Inquiry offers new hope for Multicultural Education

WITH the February publication of the Lawrence Inquiry there is now the opportunity to discuss openly the issue of multicultural education. The role of Black Studies in this will be crucial and it is necessary for it to be considered a vital component in the elimination of racism in society. The Charles Wootton College openly acknowledges the courage and dignity of both Doreen and Neville Lawrence in their fight for social justice. Let us hope that the education system will take heed of the recommendations in the report that concerns the eradication of racism. Indeed, without tackling this endemic problem at the school, college and university levels of education there can be little hope in eliminating racist attitudes in society.

Neville and Doreen Lawrence at the publication of the Lawrence Inquiry Report.

Figure A.I Front cover: *CWCN* **(Issue 25: June 1999)—reports on Lawrence Inquiry and racism.**
Source: 340/LAW Liverpool Central Library and Archive for the Charles Wootton College publications reprinted with permission from the archive.

Appendix J

America through busing. Though she now lives on the radical fringes of Cambridge she clearly remembers those childhood days. "They had desegregated all the schools". So, essentially all the schools were intergrated but the neighbourhoods everyone came from weren't.

It was an odd situation because the friendships Tracy made with people, would not go beyond school time. There were a lot of really bad things that happened. Those bad things formed a basis for her debut album. Those that had seen Tracy's style compared her to the likes of Bob Dylan and Joan Armatrading. Writing protest songs like Talking About The Revolution and Behind The Wall, the singer/song writer raised fundamental questions concerning, racism, justice and peoples reaction to the like.

What causes Tracy to be that much more exposed than other singers in her field however, is the sheer force of reality in her lyrics. She compels people to look at issues other-wise passed over.

Tracy began writing poetry, prose and songs in her adolescence, she gained scholarships to a private school in Danbury, Connecticut and to Tufts University in Medford, Massachusetts where she graduated with a degree in Anthropology. Even

before she graduated Tracy was regularly in coffee-houses, clubs and performing at special events.

The energy and force of Tracy's music is channelled into becoming known as far and wide as possible and continue to bear forth home truths.

Jackie Brown – Black American Research Scholar

Jackie Brown, originally from Brooklyn, N.Y., was here in Liverpool in 1991 and 1992. She was conducting research on **history and identity** in the Black Community for her Ph.D. in Antropology. She attends Stanford University, and hopes to graduate in June of 1994. From there she will become a University Lecturer, teaching courses on African Communities in Europe.

Jackie may be reached at the following address:-

> Department of Antropology,
> Building 10
> Stanford University
> Stanford
> California 94305

Figure A.J *CWCN* (Issue 12: December 1992, p. 13)—proof of Jacqueline N. Brown visiting CWC.
Source: 340/LAW Liverpool Central Library and Archive for the Charles Wootton College publications reprinted with permission from the archive.

Appendix K

ISSUE No. 8   DECEMBER 1990

CHARLES WOOTTON NEWS

*Staff and Students at
The Charles Wootton Centre
for Further Education
wish all our readers
Seasons Greetings*

Figure A.K Front cover: *CWCN* **(Issue 8: December 1990)—Dr. William E. Nelson Jr. at CWC.**

Source: 340/LAW Liverpool Central Library and Archive for the Charles Wootton College publications reprinted with permission from the archive.

Appendix L

Dr. Mark Christian Community Education Award from the *Voice* 1999.
Source: 340/LAW Liverpool Central Library and Archive for the Charles Wootton College publications reprinted with permission from the archive.

Bibliography

PRIMARY SOURCES

Archives

Black Cultural Archives–London
Imperial War Museum–London
Liverpool City Council, Central Library, Archives–Liverpool Record Office

Note:

The references to the Slave Trade Apology and Minutes from the Liverpool City Council can be found under: LRO, Liverpool, Liverpool City Council Minutes, 352 MIN/COU, Community, Equality and Values Select Committee Meeting, November 4, 1999; and LRO, Liverpool, Special Meeting of the Liverpool City Council, December 9, 1999, Council Minutes, 352 MIN/COU.

References for the Charles Wootton Newsletters, Consortium of Black Organisations, and related information on Liverpool grassroots organizations can be found at the Liverpool Record Office, Central Library: LRO 340LAW.

Newspapers and Magazines

Anti-Slavery Reporter
Black Linx
Charles Wootton News
Chares Wootton College: Special 20th Anniversary Report, 1994
Daily Mail
Guardian, UK
Independent
Listener
Liverpool Courier

Liverpool Echo
Liverpool Post
Liverpool Mercury
Liverpool Weekly Post
Merseyside Against Racism: First Annual Report of MARA: Merseyside Anti-Racist Alliance, September 1979
Merseyside Community Relations Council, 10th and 11th Anniversary Annual Reports, 1980 and 1981
New York Times
Spectator
Times, UK

*There are other primary texts embedded within the secondary sources as they can be deemed as both primary and secondary in context being books and reports focused primarily on Black experience in Liverpool. Most notably, the archive at the Liverpool Central Library, Liverpool Record Office, is building a substantial record of Liverpool Black experience material.

SECONDARY SOURCES

Achebe, Chinua. *The African Trilogy: Things Fall Apart, Arrow of God, No Longer at Ease.* New York: Penguin, 2017.

Ackah, William. "Pan-African Consciousness and Identity: Reflections on the Twentieth Century." In *Black Identity in the 20th Century: Expressions of the US and UK African Diaspora*, edited by Mark Christian, 3–31. London: Hansib, 2002.

———, and Mark Christian, eds. *Black Organisation and Identity in Liverpool: A Local, National and Global Perspective.* Liverpool, UK: Charles Wootton College, 1997.

Adams, Tony E., et al., eds. *Handbook of Autoethnography, 2nd Edition.* New York: Routledge, 2021.

———, with Stacy Holman Jones and Carolyn Ellis. *Autoethnography: Understanding Qualitative Research.* Oxford, UK: Oxford University Press, 2015.

Adi, Hakim. *Pan-Africanism: A History.* London: Bloomsbury, 2018.

———. *Pan-Africanism and Communism: The Communist International, Africa and the Diaspora, 1919–1939.* Trenton, NJ: Africa World Press, 2013.

———. "West Africans and Political Identity in Britain: 1900–1960." In *Black Identity in the 20th Century: Expressions of the US and UK African Diaspora*, edited by Mark Christian, 33–57. London: Hansib, 2002.

———. *West Africans in Britain: 1900–1960: Nationalism, Pan-Africanism and Communism.* London: Lawrence & Wishart, 1998.

———, and Marika Sherwood. *The 1945 Manchester Pan-African Congress Revisited.* London: New Beacon, 1995.

Adorno, Theodor W. "On Jazz." Translated by Jamie Owen Daniel. *Discourse* 12, no.1 (Fall–Winter 1989–90 [1936]): 45–69.

———, et al. *The Authoritarian Personality.* New York: Harper & Brothers, 1950.

Agozino, Biko. *Counter-Colonial Criminology: A Critique of Imperialist Reason.* London: Pluto, 2003.

———. "The Politics of Cultural Identity." In *Black Organisation and Identity in Liverpool: A Local, National and Global Perspective,* edited by William Ackah and Mark Christian, 80–97. Liverpool, UK: Charles Wootton College Press, 1997.

Akbar, Na'im. *Know Thy Self.* Tallahassee, FL: Mind Productions, 1998.

Aldridge, Delores P., and E. Lincoln James, eds. *Africana Studies: Philosophical Perspectives and Theoretical Paradigms.* Pullman, WA: Washington State University Press, 2007.

Ali, Muhammad, with Richard Durham. *The Greatest: My Own Story.* London: Mayflower Books, 1976.

Alland, Alexander, Jr. *Race in Mind: Race, IQ, and Other Racisms.* New York: Palgrave, 2002.

Anderson, Benedict. *Imagined Communities: Reflections on the Origins and Spread of Nationalism.* Revised Edition. London: Verso, 1991.

Andrews, Williams L., ed. *The Oxford Frederick Douglass Reader.* New York: Oxford University Press, 1996.

Ani, Marimba. *Yurugu: An African-Centered Critique of European Cultural Thought and Behavior.* Trenton, NJ: Africa World Press, 1994.

Appiah, Kwame Anthony. *In My Father's House: Africa in the Philosophy of Culture.* New York: Oxford University Press, 1992.

Araujo, Ana Lucia, ed. *Paths of the Atlantic Slave Trade: Interactions, Identities, and Images.* New York: Cambria Press, 2011.

Arnold, Millard, ed. *Steve Biko: Black Consciousness in South Africa.* New York: Vintage, 1979.

Asante, Molefi. *Revolutionary Pedagogy: Primer for Teacher of Black Children.* Brooklyn, NY: Universal Write Publications, 2017.

———. *Maulana Karenga: An Intellectual Portrait.* Malden, MA: Polity, 2009.

———. *The History of Africa: The Quest for Eternal Harmony.* New York: Routledge, 2007a.

———. "The Afrocentric Metatheory and Disciplinary Implication." In *The African American Studies Reader,* edited by Nathaniel Norment Jr., 506–518. Durham, NC: Carolina Academic Press, 2007b.

———. "The Ideological Origins of Chattel Slavery." Inaugural Slavery Remembrance Lecture. Liverpool Town Hall, City of Liverpool (August 21, 2007c), accessed November 1, 2021:

———. *Race, Rhetoric and Identity: The Architecton of Soul.* New York: Humanity Books, 2005.

———. "Afrocentricity and the Decline of Western Hegemonic Thought: A Critique of Eurocentric Thought and Practice." In *Black Identity in the 20th Century: Expressions of the US and UK African Diaspora,* edited by Mark Christian, 101–118. London: Hansib, 2002.

———. *The Painful Demise of Eurocentrism: An Afrocentric Response to Critics.* Trenton, NJ: Africa World Press, 1999.

———. *Afrocentricity.* Trenton, NJ: Africa World Press, 1988.

———. *The Afrocentric Idea.* Revised and expanded. Philadelphia, PA: Temple University Press, 1998.

———, and Nah Dove. *Being Human Being: Transforming the Race Discourse.* New York: Universal Write Publications LCC, 2021.

———, and Maulana Karenga, eds. *Handbook of Black Studies.* Thousand Oaks, CA: Sage, 2006.

———, and Ama Mazama, eds. *Encyclopedia of Back Studies.* Thousand Oaks, CA: Sage, 2005.

Babbitt, Susan E., and Sue Campbell, eds. *Racism and Philosophy.* Ithaca: Cornell University Press, 1999.

Bailey, F. A., and R. Millington. *The Story of Liverpool.* Liverpool, UK: The Corporation of the City of Liverpool, 1957.

Bainbridge, Beryl. *English Journey: Or the Road to Milton Keynes.* New York: Carroll & Graf, 1997; first published 1984.

Baker, Houston A., Jr., et al., eds. *Black Cultural Studies: A Reader.* Chicago: University of Chicago Press, 1996.

———. *Black Studies, Rap, and the Academy.* Chicago: University of Chicago Press, 1993.

Baldwin, James. *Notes of a Native Son.* Boston, MA: Beacon, 2012; first published 1955.

———. *The Fire Next Time.* New York: Penguin, 1964.

Banton, Michael. *Racial Consciousness.* London: Longman, 1988.

Baraka, Amiri. *The Autobiography of Leroi Jones.* New York: Lawrence Hill, 1997.

———. *Blues People: The Negro Experience in White America and the Music That Developed from It.* New York: Morrow Quill, 1963.

———, with William J. Harris. *The Leroi Jones/Amiri Baraka Reader.* New York: Basic Books, 2009.

Barnes, Tony, Richard Elias, and Peter Walsh. *Cocky: The Rise and Fall of Curtis Warren.* Wrea Green, UK: Milo Books, 2000.

Barton, Brian. *The Belfast Blitz: The City in the War Years.* Belfast: Ulster Historical Foundation, 2015.

Bassey, Magnus O. "What Is Africana Critical Theory or Black Existential Philosophy?" *Journal of Black Studies* 37, no. 6 (July 2007): 914–935.

Bates, Stephen. "Sir Ken Robinson Obituary." *Guardian.* (August 26, 2020) Accessed July 16, 2021: https://www.theguardian.com/education/2020/aug/26/sir-ken-robinson-obituary

Baxter, Paul, and Basil Sansom, eds. *Race and Social Difference: Selected Readings.* Middlesex, England: Penguin, 1972.

Beaver, Harold. "Introduction." In *Redburn: His First Voyage, Being the Sailor-Boy Confessions and Reminiscences of a Son-of-a-Gentleman, in the Merchant Service,* by Herman Melville, 7–30. London: Penguin, 1986.

Becker, Howard S. "Whose Side Are We On?" *Social Problems* 14, no. 3 (Winter 1967): 239–247.

———. *Outsiders: Studies in the Sociology of Deviance.* New York: The Free Press, 1963.

Beckert, Sven, and Seth Rockman, eds. *Slavery's Capitalism: A New History of American Economic Development.* Philadelphia, PA: University of Pennsylvania Press, 2016.

———. *Doing Things Together: Selected Papers.* Evanston, IL: Northwestern University Press, 1986.

Beckles, Hilary McD. *Britain's Black Debt: Reparations for Caribbean Slavery and Native Genocide.* Kingston, JA: The University of West Indies Press, 2013.

Belchem, John. *Before the Windrush: Race Relations in 20th-Century Liverpool.* Liverpool, UK: Liverpool University Press, 2014.

———. *Irish, Catholic and Scouse: The History of the Liverpool-Irish, 1800–1939.* Liverpool, UK: Liverpool University Press, 2007.

———, ed. *Liverpool 800: Culture, Character & History.* Liverpool, UK: Liverpool University Press, 2006a.

———. "An Accent Exceedingly Rare." In *Merseyside: Essays in Liverpool Exceptionalism,* edited by John Belchem, 31–66. Liverpool, UK: Liverpool University Press, 2000a.

———. "Liverpool's Story Is the World's Glory." In *Merseyside: Essays in Liverpool Exceptionalism,* edited by John Belchem, 3–30. Liverpool, UK: Liverpool University Press, 2000b.

———, and Donald M. MacRaild. "Cosmopolitan Liverpool." In *Liverpool 800: Culture, Character and History,* edited by John Belchem, 311–392. Liverpool, UK: Liverpool University Press, 2006b.

Bell, Derrick. *Confronting Authority: Reflections of an Ardent Protestor.* Boston: Beacon, 1994.

———. *Faces at the Bottom of the Well: The Permanence of Racism.* New York: Basic Books, 1992.

———. *And We Are Not Saved: The Elusive Quest for Racial Justice.* New York: Basic Books, 1989.

Benjamin, Richard. "Museums and Sensitive Histories: The International Slavery Museum." In *Politics of Memory: Making Slavery Visible in the Public Space,* edited by Ana Lucia Araujo, 178–196. New York: Routledge, 2012.

Bennett, Evelyn. *Frederick Douglass and the War against Slavery.* Brookfield, CT: Millbrook Press, 1993.

Bennett, Lerone, Jr. *Forced into Glory: Abraham Lincoln's White Dream.* Chicago: Johnson Publishing, 2000.

Benson, Susan. *Ambiguous Ethnicity: Interracial Families in London.* Cambridge, UK: Cambridge University Press, 1981.

Ben-Tovim, Gideon. "Foreword." *Conference Report: Raising Achievement and Promoting Equality Within Education,* 3. Liverpool: LCC, 1998.

Ben-Tovim, Gideon, John Gabriel, Ian Law, and Kathleen Stredder. *The Local Politics of Race.* London: Macmillan, 1986.

Benyon, John, and John Solomos, eds. *The Roots of Urban Unrest.* Oxford, UK: Pergamon Press, 1987.

Bernier, Celeste-Marie, ed. *My Bondage and My Freedom.* Oxford, UK: Oxford University Press, 2019.

Bhabha, Homi. "Foreword; Remembering Fanon: Self, Psyche and the Colonial Condition." In *Black Skin, White Masks,* by Frantz Fanon, translated by Charles Lam Markmann. London: Pluto Press, 1986; first published 1952.

Bhambra, Gurminder K., and John Holmwood. *Colonialism and Modern Social Theory.* Cambridge, UK: Polity Press, 2021.

Biko, Steve, with Aelred Stubbs. *I Write What I Like: A Selection of His Writings.* Randburg, SA: Ravan Press, 1996; first published 1978.

Biondi, Martha. *The Black Revolution on Campus.* Berkeley, CA: University of California Press, 2012.

Blaisdell, Bob, ed. *Selected Writings and Speeches of Marcus Garvey.* New York: Dover, 2004.

Blassingame, John W. *Frederick. Douglass, the Clarion Voice.* Middletown, DE: MLibrary, 2021; first published 1976.

———. *The Slave Community: Plantation Life in the Antebellum South, Revised Edition.* New York: Oxford University Press, 1979.

Blaut, J. M. *Eight Eurocentric Historians.* New York: Guilford Press, 2000.

———. *The Colonizer's Model of the World: Geographical Diffusionism and Eurocentric History.* New York: Guilford Press, 1993.

Blight, David W. *Frederick Douglass: Prophet of Freedom.* New York: Simon & Schuster, 2018.

Bloch, Maurice. "Foreword." In *Prospero and Caliban: The Psychology of Colonization,* by O. Mannoni. Ann Arbor, MI: University of Michigan Press, 2001.

Bolt, Christine. *Victorian Attitudes to Race.* London: Routledge & Kegan Paul, 1971.

Bonilla-Silva, Eduardo. *Racism without Racists: Color-Blind Racism and the Persistence of Racial Inequality in the United States.* Lanham, MD: Rowman & Littlefield, 2003.

Bonnett, Alastair. *Multiracism: Rethinking Racism in Global Context.* Cambridge, UK: Polity Press, 2022.

Boodry, Kathryn. "Against Belmont and the World the Slaves Made." In *Slavery's Capitalism: A New History of American Economic Development,* edited by Sven Beckert and Seth Rockman, 163–178. Philadelphia, PA: University of Pennsylvania Press, 2016.

Bottomore, T. B. *The Frankfurt School.* London: Tavistock, 1984.

Boxhill, Bernard R. *Blacks and Social Justice.* Lanham, MD: Rowman & Littlefield, 1992.

Boyce Davies, Carolyn. *Left of Karl Marx: The Political Life of Black Communist Claudia Jones.* Durham, NC: Duke University Press, 2007.

Brace, C. Loring. *"Race" Is a Four-Letter Word: The Genesis of the Concept.* New York: Oxford University Press, 2005.

Bradbury, Richard. "Frederick Douglass and the Chartists." In *Liberating Sojourn: Frederick Douglass and Transatlantic Reform,* edited by Alan J. Rice and Martin Crawford, 169–206. Athens, GA: University of Georgia Press, 1999.

Brown, Jacqueline N. *Dropping Anchor, Setting Sail: Geographies of Race in Black Liverpool.* Princeton, NJ: Princeton University Press, 2005.

Brown, Manneh K. *They Haven't Done Nothing Yet: L8.* Liverpool, UK: University of Liverpool, Race and Social Policy Unit, 1993.
Brown, Wally. "Foreword." In *No One Ever Mentions Love: An Inside View of Black and White Relationships,* Second Chance to Learn Women's History Group, 4. Liverpool, UK: Liverpool Community College, 1997.
———. *Race, Class and Educational Inequality: A Case Study of Liverpool Born Blacks.* Master's degree thesis, University of Liverpool, 1986.
———. "Unemployment and the Black Community on Merseyside." Edited by Merseyside Area Profile Group, 103–108. Liverpool, UK: Merseyside Area Profile Group, 1983.
———. *How Liverpool Has Underdeveloped Its Blacks.* Unpublished paper, Manchester Polytechnic, 1979.
Broyard, Bliss. *One Drop: My Father's Hidden Life—A Story of Race and Family Secrets.* New York: Black Bay Books, 2007.
Buccola, Nicholas. *The Essential Douglass: Selected Writings and Speeches.* Indianapolis, IN: Hackett Publishing, 2016.
———. *The Political Thought of Frederick Douglass: In Pursuit of American Liberty.* New York: New York University Press, 2012.
Buckner, Sol. "Children of Slavery: Black City's 'Quick-Fix' Apology." *Daily Post* (December 10, 1999): 10.
Burdsey, Daniel, ed. *Race, Ethnicity and Football: Persisting Debates and Emergent Issues.* London: Routledge, 2011.
Butler, Alice. "Toxic Toxteth: Understanding Press Stigmatization of Toxteth during the 1981 Uprising." *Journalism* 21, no. 4 (2020): 541–556.
Butler, Johnnella E. "Black Studies and Sensibility: Identity, the Foundation for a Pedagogy." In *Africana Studies: Philosophical Perspectives and Theoretical Paradigms,* edited by Delores P. Aldridge and E. Lincoln James, 96–100. Pullman, WA: Washington State University Press, 2007.
Bygott, David. *Black and British.* London: Oxford University Press, 1992.
Cabral, Amilcar. *Unity and Struggle: Speeches and Writings of Amilcar.* Translated by Michael Wolfers. New York: Monthly Review Press, 1979.
———, ed. Africa Information Service. *Return to the Source: Selected Speeches of Amilcar Cabral.* Cape Verde Islands: Africa Information Service and PAIGC, 1973.
Cameron, Gail, and Stan Crooke. *Liverpool: Capital of the Slave Trade.* Liverpool, UK: Picton Press, 1992.
Campbell, Horace. *Rasta and Resistance: From Marcus Garvey to Walter Rodney.* London: Hansib, 1985.
Carby, Hazel V. *Cultures in Babylon: Black Britain and African America.* London: Verso, 1999.
Carew, Jan. *Ghosts in Our Blood: Malcolm X in Africa, England, and the Caribbean.* Chicago: Lawrence Hill, 1994.
Carew, Joy Gleason. *Blacks, Reds, and Russians: Sojourners in Search of the Soviet Promise.* New Brunswick, NJ: Rutgers University Press, 2008.
———. "Culture and Rebellion." *Race and Class* 35, no. 1 (July–September 1993): 1–8.

Carr, Greg E. "Towards an Intellectual History of Africana Studies: Genealogy and Normative Theory." In *The African American Studies Reader, 2nd Edition*, edited by Nathaniel Norment Jr., 438–452. Durham, NC: Carolina Academic Press, 2007.

Carruthers, Jacob H. *Intellectual Warfare*. Chicago: Third World Press, 1999.

Carter, Trevor, with Jean Coussins. *Shattering Illusions: West Indians in British Politics*. London: Lawrence & Wishart, 1986.

Caute, David. *Frantz Fanon*. New York: Viking Press, 1970.

Césaire, Aimé. *Discourse on Colonialism*. Translated by Joan Pinkham. New York: Monthly Review Press, 1972; originally published 1955.

Chabal, Patrick. *Amilcar Cabral: Revolutionary Leadership and People's War*. London: Cambridge University Press, 1983.

Chaffin, Tom. *Giant's Causeway: Frederick Douglass's Irish Odyssey and the Making of an American Visionary*. Charlottesville, VA: University of Virginia Press, 2014.

Chamoiseau, Patrick. *School Days*. Translated by Linda Coverdale. Lincoln, NE: University of Nebraska Press, 1997.

Chapman, Frank. *Marxist-Leninist Perspectives on Black Liberation and Socialism*. Middletown, DE: F.R.S.O., 2021.

Chestnutt, Charles. *Frederick Douglass*. New York: Dover, 2002; first published 1899.

Chrisman, Laura. "Journeying to Death: Paul Gilroy's Black Atlantic." In *Postcolonial Contraventions: Cultural Readings on Race, Imperialism and Transnationalism*, edited by Laura Chrisman, 73–88. Manchester, UK: Manchester University Press, 2003.

Christian, Mark. "Striving to Sing Our Own Songs: Notes on the Left Not Right in Africana Studies." In *The Discipline and the African World: An Annual Report on the State of Affairs for Africana Communities*, edited by Serie McDougal III, 186–192. Cincinnati, OH: National Council for Black Studies, 2022.

———. *Booker T. Washington: A Life in American History*. Santa Barbara, CA: ABC-CLIO, 2021a.

———. *The 20th Century Civil Rights Movement: An Africana Studies Perspective*. Dubuque, IA: Kendall Hunt, 2021b.

———. "Race and Social Identity in the Obama Age: A View from Behind the Veil." In *Race in America: How a Pseudoscientific Concept Shaped Human Interaction*, edited by Patricia Reid-Merritt, 125–142. Santa Barbara, CA: Praeger, 2017a.

———. "From Liverpool to New York City: Behind the Veil of a Black British Male Scholar Inside Higher Education." In *Race Ethnicity and Education* 20, no. 3 (2017b): 414–428.

———. "To Sir, with Love: A Black British Perspective." In *Poitier Revisited: Reconsidering a Black Icon in the Obama Age*, edited by Ian G. Strachan and Mia Mask, 129–143. New York: Bloomsbury, 2015.

———, ed. *Integrated but Unequal: Black Faculty in Predominately White Space*. Trenton, NJ: Africa World Press, 2012a.

———. "Philosophical Racism, Mobbing, and Other Infractions on Black Male Faculty in Majority White Space." In *Integrated but Unequal: Black Faculty in*

Predominately White Space, edited by Mark Christian, 125–152. Trenton, NJ: Africa World Press, 2012b.

———. "Mixing Up the Game: Social and Historical Contours of Black Mixed Heritage Players." In *British Football,* edited by Daniel Burdsey, 131–144. London: Routledge, 2011.

———. "Black Studies in the US and UK: A Comparative Analysis." In *African American Studies,* edited by Jeanette R. Davidson, 149–167. Edinburgh, UK: Edinburgh University Press, 2010.

———. Book review of, *Dropping Anchor, Setting Sail: Geographies of Race in Black Liverpool.* Princeton, NJ: Princeton University Press, 2005. *Journal of Black Studies* 39, no. 4 (March 2009a): 657–659.

———. "African Diaspora Connections and Gilroy's Denial." In *Racial Structure and Radical Politics in the African Diaspora,* edited by James L. Conyers, 45–60. New Brunswick, NJ: Transaction Publishers, 2009b.

———. "The Fletcher Report 1930: A Historical Case Study of Contested Black Mixed Heritage Britishness." *Journal of Historical Sociology* 21, no. 2/3 (June/September 2008a): 213–241.

———. guest ed. "Marcus Garvey and the Universal Negro Improvement Association: New Perspectives on Philosophy, Religion, Micro-Studies, Unity and Practice." Special Issue, *Journal of Black Studies* 39, no. 2 (November 2008b).

———. "Notes on the European Capital of Culture 2008." *Diverse,* (2008c): 8–9.

———. "The Age of Slave Apologies: The Case of Liverpool, England. Lecture at the International Slavery Museum Public Lecture Series Albert Dock, Liverpool, UK" (November 14, 2007): https://www.liverpoolmuseums.org.uk/transcript-of-age-of-slave-apologies-case-of-liverpool-england. Accessed July 7, 2021.

———. "Philosophy and Practice for Black Studies: The Case of Researching White Supremacy." In *Handbook of Black Studies,* edited by Molefi K. Asante and Maulana Karenga, 76–88. Thousand Oaks, CA: Sage, 2006a.

———. guest ed. "The State of Black Studies in the Academy." Special Issue. *Journal of Black Studies* 36, no. 5 (May 2006b).

———. "Why Do We Go Abroad? There Are No Opportunities for Us in Britain." *Times Higher Education Supplement (*March 4, 2005a): 20–21.

———. "The Politics of Black Presence in Britain and Black Male Exclusion in the British Education System." *Journal of Black Studies* 35, no. 33 (January 2005b): 327–346.

———. "Marcus Garvey and the Universal Negro Improvement Association: With Special Reference to the 'Lost Parade' in Columbus, Ohio, September 25, 1923." *Western Journal of Black Studies* 28, no. 3 (2004): 424–434.

———, ed. *Black Identity in the 20th Century: Expressions of the US and UK African Diaspora.* London: Hansib, 2002a.

———. "Reflections on the 1997 European Year against Racism: A Black British Perspective." In *Black Identity in the 20th Century: Expressions of the US and UK African Diaspora,* edited by Mark Christian, 59–77. London: Hansib, 2002b.

———. "The Black Intellectual/Activist Tradition: Notes on the Past, Present and Future." In *Black Identity in the 20th Century: Expressions of the US and UK African Diaspora,* edited by Mark Christian, 119–136. London: Hansib, 2002c.

———. "An African Centered Perspective on White Supremacy." *Journal of Black Studies* 33, no. 2 (November 2002d): 179–198.

———. "African Centered Knowledge: A Black British Perspective." *Western Journal of Black Studies* 25, no. 1 (2001): 12–20.

———. *Multiracial Identity: An International Perspective.* London: Macmillan/Palgrave, 2000.

———. "Empowerment and Black Communities in the UK: With Special Reference to Liverpool." *Community Development Journal: An International* 33, no.1 (January 1998a): 18–31.

———. "An African Centered Approach to the Black British Experience: With Special Reference to Liverpool." *Journal of Black Studies* 28, no. 3 (January 1998b): 291–308.

———. "A Case Study of Mixed Racial Origin Identity in the City of Liverpool, England: 1919–1996." PhD diss., The University of Sheffield, 1997a.

———. "Black Identity in Liverpool: An Appraisal." In *Black Organisation and Identity in Liverpool: A Local, National and Global Perspective,* edited by William Ackah and Mark Christian, 62–79. Liverpool, UK: Charles Wootton College Press, 1997b.

———. "Black Organisation and Policy in Context." In *Black Organisation and Identity in Liverpool: A Local, National and Global Perspective,* edited by William Ackah and Mark Christian, 9–12. Liverpool, UK: Charles Wootton College Press, 1997c.

———. "The Black Community in Liverpool: Current Perspectives and Issues." *Charles Wootton News (*June 1995a): 3–5.

———. "Black Struggle for Historical Recognition in Liverpool." *North West Labour History* 20 (1995/96b): 58–66.

———. "The Charles Wootton College (1974–1994): 20 Years of Struggle and Achievement." *Charles Wootton News-Special 20th Anniversary Report,* 1994, 17.

Christie, Alvin. *Toxteth: Merseybeat: A Black Perspective.* Accessed October 16, 2021: http://merseybeat.toxteth.com/merseybeat/index.html (Copyright 2018).

Chukwuemeka, Angus. "The Economic Dimensions of Local Black Community Organisation." In *Black Organisation and Identity in Liverpool: A Local, National and Global Perspective,* edited by William Ackah and Mark Christian, 42–51. Liverpool, UK: Charles Wootton College Press, 1997.

———. "Closure of Merseyside Racial Equality Council as of 30 June, 1993." *Charles Wootton News,* Issue 13 (June 1993): 9–10.

Church Terrell, Mary. *A Colored Woman in a White World.* New York: Humanity Books, 2005; first published 1940.

Clark Hine, Darlene, et al. eds. *Black Europe and the African Diaspora.* Urbana and Chicago: University of Illinois Press, 2009.

Clarke, John Henrik. "Africana Studies, a Decade of Change, Challenge and Conflict." In *The African American Studies Reader*, edited by Nathaniel Norment Jr., 292–301. Durham, NC: Carolina Academic Press, 2007.

———. *My Life in Search of Africa*. Ithaca, NY: Africana Research Center, 1994.

———, ed. *Marcus Garvey and the Vision for Africa*. New York: Vintage, 1974.

Class of 1981. *Speaking for Ourselves: Poems from the Charles Wootton Centre*. Liverpool, UK: Charles Wootton Press, 1981.

Clay, Dave. *A Liverpool Black History—100 Years: 1919–2019*. Milton Keynes, UK: Liverpool City Council, 2020.

———. *10 Years On: 1981–1991: Looking Back Over the Years*. Unpublished manuscript, 1991.

Coard, Bernard. *How the West Indian Child Is Made Educationally Sub-normal in the British School System*. London: Karia Press, 1991; first published in 1971.

Coates, Ta-Nehisi. *Between the World and Me*. Melbourne, AU: Text Publishing, 2015.

Cohen, Stanley. *Folk Devils and Moral Panics: The Creation of Mods and Rockers*. London: Routledge, 2011.

Collier, Betty J., and Louis N. Williams. "An Ideology for Liberation: A Response to Amiri Baraka and Other 'Marxists.'" In *Africana Studies: Philosophical Perspectives and Theoretical Paradigms*, edited by Delores P. Aldridge and E. Lincoln James, 47–57. Pullman, WA: Washington State University Press, 2007.

Collins, Sydney F. "The Social Position of White and 'Half-Caste' Women in Colored Groupings in Britain." *American Sociological Review* 16, no. 6 (1951): 796–802.

Commission on Race and Ethnic Disparities. *The Report*. London: HMSO (March), 2021.

Commission for Racial Equality. *Five Views of Multi-Racial Britain*. London: Commission for Racial Equality, 1978.

———. *Educational Needs of Children from Minority Groups*. London: Commission for Racial Equality, 1974.

Connelly, Michelle, et al. *Black Youth in Liverpool*. Amsterdam: Giordano Bruno Culemborg, 1992.

Constantine, Learie. *The Colour Bar*. London: Stanley Paul, 1954.

Conyers, James L., ed. *Qualitative Methods in Africana Studies: An Interdisciplinary Approach to Examining Africana Phenomena*. Lanham, MD: University Press of America, 2016.

———. ed. *Racial Structure and Radical Politics in the African Diaspora*. Brunswick, NJ: Transaction Books, 2009.

Cornelius, John. *Liverpool 8*. London: John Murray, 1982.

Costello, Ray. *Black Tommies: British Soldiers of African Descent in the First World War*. Liverpool, UK: Liverpool University Press, 2015.

———. *Liverpool Black Pioneers*. Liverpool, UK: The Bluecoat Press, 2007.

———. *Black Liverpool: The Early History of Britain's Oldest Black Community, 1730–1918*. Birkenhead, UK: Birkenhead Press, 2001.

Cress Welsing, Frances. *The Isis Papers: Keys to the Colors*. Chicago: Third World Press, 1991.

Cronon, E. David. *Black Moses: The Story of Marcus Garvey and the Universal Negro Improvement Association.* Madison, WI: The University of Wisconsin Press, 1981; first published 1955.

Cross, William E., Jr. *Shades of Black: Diversity in African-American Identity.* Philadelphia, PA: Temple University Press, 1991.

Crouch, Stanley. *The All-American Skin Game, or The Decoy of Race.* New York: Vintage, 1997.

Curry, Tommy J. *The Man-Not: Race, Class, Genre, and the Dilemmas of Black Manhood.* Philadelphia, PA: Temple University Press, 2017.

Dabydeen, David, et al., eds. *The Oxford Companion to Black British History.* Oxford: 2008.

———, and Nana Wilson-Tagoe, eds. *A Reader's Guide to West Indian and Black British Literature.* Surrey, UK: Rutherford Press, 1987.

Darda, Joseph. *The Strange Career of Racial Liberalism.* Stanford, CA: Stanford University Press, 2022.

Davenport, C. B., and Morris Steggerda. *Race Crossing in Jamaica.* Washington, DC: Carnegie Institute, 1929.

Davidson, Basil. *The Black Man's Burden: Africa and the Curse of the Nation-State.* New York: Times Books, 1992.

———. *The African Genius: An Introduction to African Social and Cultural History.* Boston: Atlantic Little Brown, 1969.

———. *The African Slave Trade: Precolonial History, 1450–1850.* Boston: Atlantic Little Brown, 1961.

———. *The Lost Cities of Africa.* Boston: Little Brown, 1959.

Davis, Angela. *Angela Davis: An Autobiography.* New York: International Publishers, 1988; first published 1974.

Davis, Angela Y. *Narrative of the Life of Frederick Douglass: An American Slave Written by Himself. A New Critical Edition by Angela Y. Davis featuring Her "Lectures on Liberation."* San Francisco, CA: City Lights, 2010.

Davis, F. James. *Who Is Black? One Nation's Definition.* University Park, PA: Pennsylvania State University, 1991.

Dent, Gina, ed. *Black Popular Culture.* Seattle, WA: Bay Press, 1992.

Dickens, Charles. *The Uncommercial Traveller and Reprinted Pieces Etc.* Oxford, UK: Oxford University Press, 1987; first published 1860.

———. *American Notes for General Circulation and Pictures from Italy.* New York: Oxford University Press, 1989; first published 1842.

Dickerson, Vanessa D. *Dark Victorians.* Urbana, IL: University of Illinois Press, 2008.

Diedrich, Maria. *Love Across Color Lines: Ottilie Assing and Frederick Douglass.* New York: Hill and Wang, 1999.

Dilbeck, D. H. *Frederick Douglass: American's Prophet.* Chapel Hill, NC: University of North Carolina Press, 2018.

Diop, Cheikh Anta. *The African Origin of Civilization: Myth or Reality.* Chicago, IL: Lawrence Hill, 1974.

Discussants. In *Black Popular Culture*, edited by Gina Dent, 139–149. Seattle, WA: Bay Press, 1992.

Dhondy, Farrukh, Barbara Beese, and Leila Hassan. *The Black Explosion in British Schools.* London: Race Today Publications, 1985.

Donington, Katie, et al., eds. *Britain's History and Memory of Transatlantic Slavery: Local Nuances of a 'National Sin.'* Liverpool: Liverpool University Press, 2016.

Douglass, Frederick. *My Bondage and My Freedom.* New York: Oxford University Press, 2019; first published 1855.

———. *Narrative of the Life of Frederick Douglass, an American Slave, Written by Himself.* New York: Dell Publishing, 1997; first published 1845.

———. *Douglass Autobiographies: Narrative of the Life of Frederick Douglass, an American Slave, My Bondage and My Freedom, Life and Times of Frederick Douglass*, edited by Henry Louis Gates Jr. New York: The Library of America, 1994.

———. *The Frederick Douglass Papers*, 5 volumes, edited by John W. Blassingame et al. New Haven, CT: Yale University Press, 1979–1992.

———. *Frederick Douglass in Britain and Ireland, 1845–1895*, edited by Hannah-Rose Murray and John R. McKivigan. Edinburgh: University of Edinburgh Press, 2021.

———. *The Heroic Slave: A* Cultural *Critical Edition*, edited by Robert S. Levine et al. New Haven, CT: Yale University Press, 2015.

———. *The Frederick Douglass Papers.,* 5 volumes, edited by Philip S. Foner. New York: International Publishers, 1950–1975.

Drake, St. Clair. "What Happened to Black Studies?" In *The African American Studies Reader,* edited by Nathaniel Norment Jr., 338–349. Durham, NC: Carolina Academic Press, 2007.

———. "The 'Colour Problem' in Britain: A Study in Social Definitions." *Sociological Review* 3, no. 2 (December 1955): 197–217.

———, and Horace R. Cayton. *Black Metropolis: A Study of Negro Life in a Northern City.* Chicago: University of Chicago Press, 2015; first published 1945.

Draper, Nicholas. *The Price of Emancipation: Slave-Ownership, Compensation and British Society at the End of Slavery.* Cambridge, UK: Cambridge University Press, 2010.

Ducey, Kimberley, and Joe R. Feagin. *Revealing Britain's Systemic Racism: The Case of Meghan Markle and the Royal Family.* London: Routledge, 2021.

Edwards, Paul, ed. *Equiano's Travels: The Interesting Narrative of the Life of Olaudah Equiano or Gustava Vassa the African.* London: Heinemann, 1996.

Ehrlich, Scott. *Paul Robeson: Athlete, Actor, Singer, Activist.* Los Angeles, CA: Melrose Square, 1988.

Epstein, Kitty Kelly, and Bernard Stringer. *Changing Academia Forever: Black Student Leaders Analyze the Movement They Led.* Gorham, ME: Myers Education Press, 2020.

Essien-Udom, E. U., and Amy Jacques Garvey, eds. *More Philosophy and Opinions of Marcus Garvey, Vol. III.* London: Frank Cass, 1977.

Ethiopian Progressive Association. *Constitution of the Ethiopian Progressive Association: Founded A.D. 1904.* Liverpool, UK: D. Marples & Co., 1905.

Etoke, Nathalie. *Melancholia Africana: The Indispensable Overcoming of the Black Condition.* Translated by Bill Hamlett. New York: Rowman & Littlefield, 2019.

Ewey Johnson, Melissa. *Halle Berry: A Biography.* Santa Barbara, CA: ABC-CLIO, 2010.

Fanon, Frantz. *Toward the African Revolutions: Political Essays.* Translated by Haakon Chevalier. New York: Grove Press, 1988a; first published 1964.

———. *The Wretched of the Earth.* Translated by Constance Farrington. New York: Grove Press, 1988b; first published 1961.

———. *A Dying Colonialism.* Translated by Haakon Chevalier. London: Writers & Readers, 1980; first published 1959.

———. *Black Skin, White Masks.* Translated by Charles Lam Markmann. London: Pluto Press, 1986; first published 1952.

Farred, Grant. "You Can Go Home Again, You Just Can't Stay: Stuart Hall and the Caribbean Diaspora." *Research in African Literatures* 27, no. 4 (Winter 1996): 28–48.

Fenton, Laurence. *Frederick Douglass in Ireland: 'The Black O'Connell.'* Cork, Ireland: The Collins Press, 2014.

Ferber, Abby L. *White Man Falling: Race, Gender and White Supremacy.* Lanham, MD: Rowman & Littlefield, 1999.

Ferreira, Patricia J. "Frederick Douglass and the 1846 Dublin Edition of His Narrative." *New Hibernia Review* 5, no. 1 (Spring 2001): 53–67.

File, Nigel, and Chris Power. *Black Settlers in Britain, 1555–1958.* London: Heinemann Education, 1981.

Fleming, Rachel M. "Human Hybrids: Racial Crosses in Various Parts of the World." *Eugenics Review* 21, no. 4 (January 1930): 257–263.

———. "Anthropological Studies of Children." *Eugenics Review* 18, no. 4 (January 1927): 294–301.

Fletcher, Muriel E. *Report on an Investigation into the Color Problem in Liverpool and Other Ports.* Liverpool, UK: The Liverpool Association for the Welfare of Half-Caste Children, 1930.

Flood, Alison. "Cornel West Accuses Harvard University of 'Spiritual Bankruptcy.'" *Guardian* (July 16, 2021). Accessed July 18, 2021: https://www.theguardian.com/books/2021/jul/16/cornel-west-accuses-harvard-university-of-spiritual-bankruptcy?CMP=Share_AndroidApp_Other

Foner, Philip S., ed. *Frederick Douglass on Women's Rights.* New York: Da Capo Press, 1992; first published 1976.

———, ed. *Paul Robeson Speaks: Writings, Speeches, Interviews, 1918–1974.* New York: Citadel, 1978.

———, and Yuval Taylor, eds. *Frederick Douglass: Selected Speeches and Writings.* Chicago, IL: Lawrence & Wishart, 1999.

Forman, James. "The Black Manifesto—1969." [And criticisms of] In *Reparations for Slavery: A Reader,* edited by Ronald P. Salzberger and Mary C. Turck, 70–90. Lanham, MD: Rowman & Littlefield, 2004.

Freire, Paulo. *Pedagogy of the Oppressed.* New York: Continuum, 2002.

Frost, Diane. "Why Black History Matters." (October 13, 2020): University of Liverpool, School of Law and Social Justice Blog accessed November 9, 2020: https://www.liverpool.ac.uk/law-and-social-justice/blog/why-black-history-matters/

———. "Ambiguous Ethnicities: Constructing and De-Constructing Black and White 'Scouse' Identities in Twentieth Century Liverpool." In *Northern Identities: Historical Interpretations of the 'North and Northernness,'* edited by Neville Kirk, 195–229. Aldershot, UK: Ashgate, 2000.

———. "Ethnic Identity, Transience and Settlement: The Kru in Liverpool Since the Nineteenth Century." In *Africans in Britain,* edited by David Killingray, 88–106. London: Frank Cass, 1994.

———. "West Africans, Black Scousers and the Colour Problem in Inter-war Liverpool." *North West Labour History* 20 (1995/6): 50–57.

———, and Richard Phillips, eds. *Liverpool '81: Remembering the Riots.* Liverpool, UK: Liverpool University Press, 2011.

———, et al. "'We Are Not Separatist Because So Many of Us Are Mixed': Resisting Negative Stereotypes of Neighbourhood Ethnic Residential Concentration." *Journal of Ethnic and Migration Studies.* (Published online April 2021) accessed May 31, 2021: https://doi.org/10.1080/1369183X.2021.1912590

Fryer, Peter. *Black People in the British Empire.* London: Pluto, 1988.

——— *Staying Power: The History of Black People in Britain.* London: Pluto, 1984.

Garland, Jon, and Michael Rowe. *Racism and Anti-Racism in Football.* London: Palgrave, 2001.

Garrett, Paula, and Hollis Robbins, eds. *The Works of William Wells Brown: Using His "Strong and Manly Voice."* New York: Oxford University Press, 2006.

Garrison, William Lloyd. *Letters of William Lloyd Garrison.* Vol. 3, *No Union with Slave-Holders, 1841–1849,* edited by Walter M. Merrill. Cambridge, MA: Harvard University Press, 1973.

Garvey, Amy Jacques. *Garvey and Garveyism.* London: Collier, 1970.

Garvey, Marcus, with Amy Jacques Garvey. *The Philosophy and Opinions of Marcus Garvey, or Africa for the Africans, Vols. I and II.* Dover, MA: The Majority Press, 1986.

Gates, Henry Louis, Jr. *Tradition and the Black Atlantic: Critical Theory in the African Diaspora.* New York: Basic Civitas, 2010.

———. "Foreword." In *The Works of William Wells Brown: Using His "Strong and Manly Voice,"* edited by Paula Garrett and Hollis Robbins, ix–xiv. New York: Oxford University Press, 2006.

———. *Lincoln on Race and Slavery.* Princeton, NJ: Princeton University Press, 2009.

———. "Introduction." In *Narrative of the Life of Frederick Douglass: An American Slave, Written by Himself.* New York: Dell, 1997.

———, and William L. Andrews. *Pioneers of the Black Atlantic: Five Slave Narratives from the Enlightenment, 1772–1815.* Washington, DC: Civitas, 1998.

Gayle, Howard, with Simon Hughes. *61 Minutes in Munich: The Story of Liverpool FC's First Black Footballer Howard Gayle.* Liverpool: deCoubertin Books, 2016.

Gibson, Nigel C., ed. *Rethinking Fanon: The Continuing Dialogue.* New York: Humanity Books, 1999.
Gifford, Lord, Wally Brown, and Ruth Bundy. *Loosen the Shackles: First Report of the Liverpool 8 Inquiry in Race Relations in Liverpool.* London: Karia, 1989.
Gilbert, Nigel, ed. *Researching Social Life.* London: Sage, 1993.
Gill, Anton. *Ruling Passions: Sex, Race and Empire.* London: BBC Books, 1995.
Gillborn, David. "Education Policy as an Act of White Supremacy: Whiteness, Critical Race Theory and Education Reform." *Journal of Education Policy* 20, no. 4 (2005): 485–505.
Gilroy, Beryl. *Black Teacher.* London: Cassell, 1976.
Gilroy, Paul. "From a Colonial Past to a New Multiculturalism." *The Chronicle Review* (January 7, 2005): B7–B10.
———. *After Empire: Melancholia or Convivial Culture?* London: Routledge, 2004.
———. *Against Race: Imagining Political Culture Beyond the Color Line.* Cambridge, MA: Harvard University Press, 2000.
———. "British Cultural Studies and the Pitfalls of Identity." In *Black British Cultural Studies: A Reader,* edited by Houston A. Baker Jr. et al., 223–239. Chicago: University of Chicago Press, 1996.
———. *The Black Atlantic: Modernity and Double Consciousness.* London: Verso, 1993a.
———. *Small Acts: Thoughts on the Politics of Black Cultures.* London: Serpent's Tail, 1993b.
———. *There Ain't No Black in the Union Jack.* London: Routledge, 1987.
Givens, Jarvis R. *Fugitive Pedagogy: Carter G. Woodson and the Arts of Black Teaching.* Cambridge, MA: Harvard University Press, 2021.
Glazer, Nathan. *We Are All Multiculturalists Now.* Cambridge, MA: Harvard University Press, 1998.
Glissant, Édouard. *Poetics of Relation.* Translated by Betsy Wing. Ann Arbor, MI: University of Michigan Press, 1997.
Goffman, Erving. *Stigma: Notes on the Management of Spoiled Identity.* New York: Touchstone, 1986; first published 1963.
———. *The Presentation of Self in Everyday Life.* New York: Anchor Books, 1959.
Goldberg, Chad Alan. "Robert E. Park's Marginal Man: The Career of a Concept in American Sociology." *Labortorium* 4, no. 2 (2012): 199–217.
Gomez, Michael A. *Diasporic Africa: A Reader.* New York: New York University Press, 2006.
Gordon, Lewis R. "Fanon, Philosophy, and Racism." In *Racism and Philosophy,* edited by Susan E. Babbitt and Sue Campbell, 32–49. Ithaca: Cornell University Press, 1999.
———, et al., eds. *Fanon: A Critical Reader.* Oxford, UK: Blackwell, 1996.
Graham, Mekada. *Black Issues in Social Work and Social Care.* London: Polity Press, 2007.
Gramsci, Antonio. *Selections from the Prison Notebooks.* Translated and edited by Quintin Hoare and Geoffrey Nowell Smith. London: Lawrence & Wishart, 1996.

Grant, Colin. *Negro with a Hat: The Rise and Fall of Marcus Garvey.* New York: Oxford University Press, 2008.

Greenspan, Ezra. *William Wells Brown: An African American Life.* New York: W.W. Norton, 2014.

Gregory, James M. *Frederick Douglass: The Orator.* Springfield, MA: Willey and Co., 1893.

Griffin, Farah J., and Cheryl J. Fish, eds. *A Stranger in the Village: Two Centuries of African-American Travel Writing.* Boston, MA: Beacon, 1998.

Guptara, Prahbu. *Black British Literature: An Annotated Bibliography.* London: Dangeroo Press, 1986.

Gutman, Amy, ed. *Multiculturalism: Examining the Politics of Recognition.* Princeton, NJ: Princeton University Press, 1994.

Gutzmore, Cecil. "Carnival, the State and the Black Masses in the United Kingdom." In *Inside Babylon: The Caribbean Diaspora in Britain,* 207–230. London: Verso, 1993.

Haggerty, Sheryllyne, et al., eds. *The Empire in One City? Liverpool's Inconvenient Past.* Manchester, UK: Manchester University Press, 2008.

Hall, Catherine. *Civilising Subjects: Metropole and Colony in the English Imagination, 1830–1867.* Chicago, IL: University of Chicago Press, 2002.

Hall, Stuart, Paul Gilroy, and Ruth Wilson Gilmore, eds. *Selected Writings on Race and Difference.* Durham, NC: Duke University Press, 2021.

Hall, Stuart. "New Ethnicities." In *Black British Cultural Studies: A Reader,* edited by Houston A. Baker Jr., et al, 163–172. Chicago: University of Chicago Press, 1996.

———. "Racism and Reaction." In *Five Views on Multiracial Britain*, edited by the Commission for Racial Equality, 23–35. London: CRE, 1978.

———. "What Is This 'Black' in Black Popular Culture?" In *Black Popular Culture,* edited by Gina Dent, 21–36. Seattle, WA: Bay Press, 1992.

Hall, Stuart, Paul Gilroy, and Ruth Wilson Gilmore, eds. *Selected Writings on Race and Difference.* Durham, NC: Duke University Press, 2021.

Hamilton, Charles V. "Foreword." In *The Case for Identity Politics: Polarization, Demographic Change, and Racial Appeals*, by Christopher T. Stout. Charlottesville, VA: University of Virginia Press, 2020.

Hammersley, Martyn. *Taking Sides in Social Research: Essays in Partisanship and Bias.* London: Routledge, 2000.

———. "Racism and Reaction." In *Five Views of Multi-Racial Britain,* edited by the Commission for Racial Equality, 23–35. London: Commission for Racial Equality, 1978a.

———, et al. *Policing the Crisis: Mugging, the State, and Law and Order.* London: Macmillan, 1978b.

Hare, Nathan. "The Challenge of the Black Scholar." In *The Death of White Sociology: Essays on Race and Culture,* edited by Joyce A. Ladner, 67–78. Baltimore, MD: Black Classic Press, 1998.

———, and Julia Hare. *The Miseducation of the Black Child.* San Francisco, CA: Banneker Books, 1991.

Harris, Herbert W., et al. *Racial and Ethnic Identity: Psychological Development and Creative Expression.* New York: Routledge, 1995.

Harris, Joseph E. *Africans and Their History.* New York: Mentor, 1987; first published 1972.

Harris, Roxy, and Sarah White. *Changing Britannia: Life Experience with Britain.* London: New Beacon Books, 1999.

Harrison, Faye V. *Decolonizing Anthropology: Moving Further toward an Anthropology for Liberation.* 2nd Edition. Arlington, VA: American Anthropological Association, 1997a.

———. "Ethnography as Politics." In *Decolonizing Anthropology: Moving Further toward an Anthropology for Liberation,* edited by Faye V. Harrison, 88–110. Arlington, VA: American Anthropological Association, 1997b.

Harry, Bill. *The Beatles Encyclopedia: Revised and Updated.* London: Virgin Publishing, 2000.

Heneghan, Madeline, and Emy Onuora. *Great War to Race Riots: Black Experience in Post-WW1 Liverpool.* Liverpool, UK: Writing on the Wall, 2019.

Heseltine, Michael. *Life in the Jungle: My Autobiography.* London: Hodder & Stoughton, 2000.

Hesse, Barnor, ed. *Un/Settled Multiculturalisms: Diasporas, Entanglements, Disruptions.* London: Zed Books, 2000.

———. "Black to Front and Black Again." In *Writing Black Britain: An Interdisciplinary Anthology,* edited by James Proctor, 78–82. Manchester: Manchester University Press, 2000.

Hill, Dave. *Out of His Skin: The John Barnes Phenomenon.* London: WSC Books, 2001.

Hill, Robert A., and Barbara Bair, eds. *Marcus Garvey: Life and Lessons.* Berkeley, CA: University of California Press, 1987.

Hilliard, Asa G. *The Maroon Within Us: Selected Essays on African American Community Socialization.* Baltimore, MD: Black Classic Press, 1995.

Hitchens, Christopher. *Why Orwell Matters.* New York: Basic Books, 2002.

Hitler, Adolf. *Mein Kampf.* Translated by Ralph Manheim. London: Pimlico, 1993.

Hobsbawn, E. J. *The Age of Empire: 1875–1914.* London: Guild Publishing, 1987.

Holmes, Martin, ed. *The Eurosceptical Reader.* London: Macmillan, 1996.

Holland, Frederic May. *Frederick Douglass: The Colored Orator, Revised Edition.* New York: Funk and Wagnalls, 1895. Accessed July 16, 2021: https://docsouth.unc.edu/neh/holland/holland.html

Howart, Gerald. *Learie Constantine.* Great Britain: Readers Union, 1976.

Howe, Stephen. *Afrocentrism: Mythical Past and Imagined Homes.* London: Verso, 1998.

Hudson-Weems, Clenora, ed. *Contemporary Africana Theory, Thought and Action: A Guide to Africana Studies.* Trenton, NJ: Africa World Press, 2007.

Huggins, Nathan I. *Slave and Citizen: The Life of Frederick Douglass.* New York: Harper Collins, 1980.

Hughes, Langston. *The Ways of White Folks.* New York: Vintage, 1990; first published 1933.

Humphry, Derek, and Gus John. *Because They're Black.* Middlesex, England: Pelican, 1971.
Humphry, Derek. *Police Power and Black People.* London: Panther, 1972.
———, and Gus John. *Because They're Black.* Middlesex, England: Pelican, 1971.
Ifekwunigwe, Jayne O. *'Mixed Race' Studies: A Reader.* London: Routledge, 2004.
Imam, Umme, et al. "Black Perspectives." *Youth and Policy* 49 (Summer 1995).
Isenberg, Nancy. *White Trash: The 400-Year Untold History of Class in America.* New York: Penguin, 2016.
James, C. L. R. *A History of Pan-African Revolt.* Oakland, CA: PM Press, 2012.
———. "Africans and Afro-Caribbeans: A Personal View." In *Writing Black Britain: An Interdisciplinary Anthology,* 60–63. Manchester: Manchester University Press, 2000.
———. *Beyond a Boundary.* Durham, NC: Duke University Press, 1993; first published 1963.
James, William. *Talks to Teachers on Psychology: And to Students on Some of Life's Ideals.* Rockville, MD: Arc Manor, 2008; first published 1899.
James, Winston, and Clive Harris, eds. *Inside Babylon: The Caribbean Diaspora in Britain.* London: Verso, 1993.
Jefferies, Stuart. "Was This Britain's First Black Queen?" *Guardian* (March 11, 2009), accessed October 4, 2021. https://www.theguardian.com/world/2009/mar/12/race-monarchy
Jenkinson, Jacqueline. *Black 1919: Riots, Racism and Resistance in Imperial Britain.* Liverpool, UK: Liverpool University Press, 2019.
Johnson, Graham. *The Devil: Britain's Most Feared Underworld Taxman.* Edinburgh: Mainstream Publishing, 2009.
Johnson, Linton Kwesi. *Bass Culture.* Island Records, 1980.
Jones, Claudia. "The Caribbean Community in Britain." In *Writing Black Britain 1948–1998: An Interdisciplinary Anthology,* 68–71. Manchester: Manchester University Press, 2000.
Jones, Greta. "Eugenics and Social Policy between the Wars." *Historical Journal* 25, no. 3 (September 1982): 717–728.
Jones, Owen. *Chavs: The Demonization of the Working Class.* London: Verso, 2012.
Jones, Ron. *The American Connection: The Story of Liverpool's Links with America from Christopher Columbus to The Beatles.* Merseyside: Author, 1992.
Julienne, Louis. *Charles Wootton: 1919 Race Riots in Liverpool.* Liverpool, UK: Charles Wootton College, 1979.
Karenga, Maulana. *Introduction to Black Studies, 4th Edition.* Los Angeles, CA: The University of Sankore Press, 2010.
Keenan, Sheila. *Frederick Douglass: Portrait of a Freedom Fighter.* New York: Scholastic Press, 1995.
Keith, Michael. "The 1948 Race Riots in Liverpool: A Synopsis." *Migration: A European Journal of International Migration and Ethnic Relations* 13 (1992): 5–30.
Kelley, Robin D. G. *Freedom Dreams: The Black Radical Imagination.* Boston: Beacon, 2002.

———. "Foreword." In *Black Marxism: The Making of the Black Radical Tradition*, Cedric J. Robinson, xi–xxvi. Chapel Hill, NC: University of North Carolina Press, 2000.

———. *Race Rebels: Culture, Politics, and the Black Working Class*. New York: Free Press, 1996.

Kennedy, Randall. "Confronting the Truth about Frederick Douglass." *The Atlantic* (December 2018). Accessed July 21, 2021: https://www.theatlantic.com/magazine/archive/2018/12/the-confounding-truth-about-frederick-douglass/573931/

Kershaw, Terry. "The Emerging Paradigm in Black Studies." In *Africana Studies: Philosophical Perspectives and Theoretical Paradigms*, edited by Delores P. Aldridge and E. Lincoln James, 185–196. Pullman, WA: Washington State University Press, 2007.

Khan, Kazim, and Neville Leroy Smith. *Race, Ethnicity and Culture in the British Context*. London: Avaanca Publications, 1995.

Killingray, David, editor. *Africans in Britain*. Great Britain: Frank Cass, 1994.

King, Martin Luther, Jr. *Where Do We Go from Here: Chaos or Community?* Boston: Beacon Press, 1968.

Kuumba Imani Millennium Centre. *Passing the Baton: The Story of L8, a Better Place: 2018–2021*. Liverpool: Kuumba Imani Millennium Centre, 2021.

Ladner, Joyce A., ed. *The Death of White Sociology: Essays on Race and Culture*. Baltimore, MD: Black Classic Press, 1998; first published 1973.

Lamming, George. *In the Castle of My Skin*. Ann Abor, MI: University of Michigan Press, 1991; first published 1953.

———. "Sea of Stories." *Guardian* (October 23, 2002). Accessed September 18, 2021. https://www.theguardian.com/books/2002/oct/24/artsfeatures.poetry

Lane, Tony. "The Political Imperatives of Bureaucracy and Empire: The Case of the Coloured Alien Seam Order, 1925." *Immigrants and Minorities* 13, no. 2/3 (1995): 104–129.

———. *Liverpool: Gateway to Empire*. London: Lawrence & Wishart, 1987.

Lanier, Shannon. *Jefferson's Children: The Story of One American Family*. New York: Random House, 2002.

Law, Ian, and June Henfrey. *A History of Race and Racism in Liverpool, 1660–1950*. Liverpool, UK: Merseyside Community Relations Council, 1981.

Lawrence, Doreen. *And Still I Rise: Seeking Justice for Stephen*. London: Faber and Faber, 2006.

Lee, Maurice S., ed. *The Cambridge Companion to Frederick Douglass*. Cambridge, MA: Cambridge University Press, 2009.

Lefkowitz, Mary. "In Wars of Words, a Role for Rules of Etiquette." *Chronicle of Higher Education* (February 1998): A64.

———. *Not Out of Africa: How Afrocentricism Became an Excuse to Teach Myth as History*. New York: Basic Books, 1997.

Leonard, Marion, and Robert Strachan. *The Beat Goes On: Liverpool, Popular Music and the Changing City*. Liverpool, UK: Liverpool University Press, 2010.

Levine, Robert S. *The Lives of Frederick Douglass*. Cambridge, MA: Harvard University Press, 2016.

———. *Martin Delany, Frederick Douglass, and the Politics of Representative Identity.* Chapel Hill, NC: University of North Carolina Press, 1997.

———, and Samuel Otter. *Frederick Douglass and Herman Melville: Essays in Relation.* Chapel Hill, NC: University of North Carolina Press, 2008.

Lewis, Rupert. C. *Walter Rodney's Intellectual and Political Thought.* Kingston, JA: The Press University of West Indies, 1998.

Liebow, Elliot. *Tally's Corner: A Study of Negro Streetcorner Men.* Boston: Little, Brown and Company, 1967.

Linebaugh, Peter, and Marcus Rediker. *The Many-Headed Hydra: Sailors, Slaves, Commoners, and the Hidden History of the Revolutionary Atlantic.* Boston: Beacon Press, 2000.

Liverpool Black Caucus. *The Racial Politics of Militant in Liverpool: The Black Community's Struggle for Participation in Local Politics.* Liverpool, UK: Merseyside Area Profile Group, 1986.

Liverpool City Council. *The Index of Multiple Deprivation 2019: A Liverpool Analysis.* Liverpool, UK: LCC, 2020.

Liverpool Primary Care Trust. *Annual Report: 2012–2013.* London: National Health Service, 2013.

Loewen, James W. *Lies My Teacher Told Me: Everything Your American History Textbook Got Wrong.* New York: Touchstone, 1996.

Lohmann, Christoph, ed. *Radical Passion: Ottilie Assing's Reports from America and Letters to Frederick Douglass.* New York: Peter Lang, 1999.

Longmore, Jane. "Civic Liverpool: 1680–1800." In *Liverpool 800: Culture, Character and History,* edited by John Belchem, 113–170. Liverpool, UK: Liverpool University Press, 2006.

Lynch, Eric. "Discipline in the Black Community." In *Black Organisation and Identity in Liverpool: A Local, National, and Global Perspective,* edited by William Ackah and Mark Christian, 52–54. Liverpool, UK: Charles Wootton College Press, 1997.

———. "Transcript of Speech Given by Eric Lynch in 1980." In *Loosen the Shackles: First Report of the Liverpool 8 Inquiry in Race Relations in Liverpool,* edited by Lord Gifford, Wally Brown, and Ruth Bundey, 247–250. London: Karia, 1988.

Macdonald, Sharon, and Gordon Fyfe. *Theorizing Museums: Representing Identity and Diversity in a Changing World.* Oxford, UK: Blackwell, 1996.

Macey, David. *Frantz Fanon: A Biography.* New York: Picador, 2000.

Mackie, Liz. *The Great Marcus Garvey.* London: Hansib, 2001.

MacPherson, William. *The Stephen Lawrence Inquiry.* London: HMSO, 1999.

MacRitchie, David. *Ancient and Modern Britons, 2 Vols.* Freeman, SD: Pine Hill Press, 1991.

Malcolm X, with Alex Haley. *The Autobiography of Malcolm X.* Middlesex, England: Penguin, 1987.

Malcomson, Scott L. *One Drop of Blood: The American Misadventure of Race.* New York: Farrar, Straus & Giroux, 2000.

Mannoni, Octave. *Prospero and Caliban: The Psychology of Colonization.* Ann Arbor, MI: University of Michigan Press, 2001; first published 1950.

Manpower Service Commission. *Ethnic Minorities in Liverpool: Problems Faced in Their Search for Work.* Liverpool, UK: Merseyside Area Manpower Board, 1985.

Marable, Manning. "Beyond Racial Identity Politics: Toward a Liberation Theory for Multiracial Democracy." *Race and Class* 35, no. 1 (July–September 1993): 113–130.

———. *How Capitalism Underdeveloped Black America: Problems in Race, Political Economy and Society.* London: Pluto Press, 1983.

Marcuse, Herbert. *An Essay on Liberation.* Great Britain: Pelican Books, 1972.

Marke, Ernest. *Old Man Trouble.* London: Weidenfeld and Nicolson, 1975.

Martin, S. I. *Britain's Slave Trade.* London: Macmillan, 1999.

Martin, Tony. *The Pan-African Connection: From Slavery to Garvey and Beyond.* Dover, MA: The Majority Press, 1983.

———. *Race First: The Ideological and Organizational Struggles of Marcus Garvey and the Universal Negro Improvement Association.* Dover, MA: The Majority Press, 1976.

Martin, Waldo E. *The Mind of Frederick Douglass.* Chapel Hill, NC: University of North Carolina Press, 1984.

Marx, Karl, and Frederick Engels. *The Communist Manifest.* New York: International Publishers, 2021; first published 1848.

———. *The Civil War and the United States.* Edited by Richard Enmale. New York: International Publishers, 1937.

Mason, Peter. *Learie Constantine.* Oxford: Signal Books, 2008.

Matory, J. Lorand. *Stigma and Culture: Last-Place Anxiety in Black America.* Chicago: University of Chicago Press, 2015.

May, Roy, and Robin Cohen. "The Interaction between Race and Colonialism: A Case Study of the Liverpool Race Riots of 1919." *Race and Class* 16, no. 2 (1974): 111–126.

Mazama, Ama, ed. *The Afrocentric Paradigm.* Trenton, NJ: Africa World Press, 2003.

Mazrui, Ali A. *The African Condition: The Reith Lectures.* London: Heinemann, 1979.

M'Baye, Babacar. "The Representation of Africa in Black Atlantic Studies of Race and Literature." *Thamyris/Intersecting,* no. 11 (2003): 151–162.

McDougal, Serie, III, ed. *The Discipline and the African World 2022 Report: An Annual Report on the State of Affairs for Africana Communities.* Cincinnati, OH: National Council for Black Studies, 2022.

———. *Research Methods in Africana Studies.* New York: Peter Lang, 2014.

McFeely, William S. "Visible Man: Frederick Douglass for the 1990s." In *Liberating Sojourn: Frederick Douglass and Transatlantic Reform,* edited by Alan J. Rice and Martin Crawford, 15–27. Athens, GA: University of Georgia Press, 1999.

———. *Frederick Douglass.* New York: W.W. Norton, 1991.

McKivigan, John R., et al., eds. *The Speeches of Frederick Douglass: A Critical Edition.* New Haven, CT: Yale University Press, 2018.

McNeil, Daniel. *Sex and Race in the Black Atlantic.* London: Routledge, 2010.

McWhiney, Grady. *Cracker Culture: Celtic Ways in the Old South.* Tuscaloosa, AL: University of Alabama Press, 1988.

Meegan, Richard. "Urban Policy: National, Local and European Perspectives." In *Black Organisation and Identity in Liverpool: A Local, National and Global Perspective*, edited by William Ackah and Mark Christian, 13–41. Liverpool, UK: Charles Wootton College Press, 1997.

Meer, Sarah. "Public and Personal Letters: Julia Griffiths and *Frederick Douglass' Paper*." *Slavery and Abolition* 33, no. 2 (June 2002): 251–264.

Melville, Herman. *Redburn: His First Voyage, Being the Sailor-Boy Confessions and Reminisces of the Son-of-a-Gentleman, in the Merchant Service*. London: Penguin, 1986; first published 1849.

Members of Merseyside Socialist Research Group. *Genuinely Seeking Work: Mass Unemployment on Merseyside in the 1930s*. Birkenhead, Merseyside: Liver Press, 1992.

Memmi, Albert. *The Colonizer and the Colonized*. Translated by Howard Greenfeld. London: Earthscan, 1990; first published 1965.

———. *Decolonization and the Decolonized*. Translated by Robert Bononno. Minneapolis, MN: University of Minnesota Press, 2006; first published 2004.

Merseyside Anti-Racialist Alliance. *Merseyside against Racism: First Annual Report of MARA*. Liverpool, UK: Author, September 1979.

Merseyside Area Profile Group. *Racial Disadvantage in Liverpool: An Area Profile*. Liverpool, UK: Author, 1986.

———. *Equal Opportunities and the Employment of Black People and Ethnic Minorities on Merseyside*. Liverpool, UK: Author, 1983.

Migliorino, Ellen Ginzburg, and Giorgio G. Campanaro. "Frederick Douglass's More Intimate Nature as Revealed in Some of His Unpublished Letters." *Southern Studies* 18 (Winter 1979): 480–487.

Miles, Robert. *Racism and Migrant Labour*. London: Routledge & Kegan, Paul, 1982.

Miller, Anthony. *Poverty Deserved: Relieving the Poor in Victorian Liverpool*. Merseyside: Liver Press, 1988.

Mills, C. Wright. *The Sociological Imagination*. London: Oxford University Press, 1959.

Mills, Charles W. *Black Rights/White Wrongs: The Critique of Racial Liberalism*. New York: Oxford University Press, 2017.

———. "The Racial Polity." In *Racism and Philosophy*, edited by Susan E. Babbitt and Sue Campbell, 13–31. Ithaca: Cornell University Press, 1999.

———. *Blackness Invisible: Essays on Philosophy and Race*. Ithaca: Cornell University Press, 1998.

———. *The Racial Contract*. Ithaca: Cornell University Press, 1997.

Mirza, Heidi, ed. *Black British Feminisms: A Reader*. London: Routledge, 1997.

Modood, Tariq, et al. *Ethnic Minorities in Britain*. London: Policy Studies Institute, 1997.

Monteiro-Ferreira, Ana. *The Demise of the Inhuman: Afrocentric, Modernism, and Postmodernism*. Albany: State University of New York Press, 2014.

Moody, Jessica. *The Persistence of Memory: Remembering Slavery in Liverpool, 'Slaving Capital of the World.'* Liverpool, UK: Liverpool University Press, 2020.

———. "The Memory of Slavery in Liverpool in Public Discourse from the Nineteenth Century to the Present Day." PhD diss. University of York, 2014.

Moore, Carlos. "Were Marx and Engels White Racists? The Prolet-Aryan Outlook of Marxism." *Berkeley Journal of Sociology* 19 (1974–75): 125–156.

Moore, Robert. *Ethnic Statistics and the 1991 Census: The Black Populations of Inner Liverpool.* London: Runneymede Trust, 1994.

Morris, Michael. "Robert Burns: Recovering Scotland's Memory of the Black Atlantic." *Journal of Eighteenth-Century Studies* 37, no. 3 (July 2013): 343–359.

Morrison, Toni. *The Source of Self-Regard: Selected Essays, Speeches, and Meditations.* New York: Vintage, 2020.

———. *The Origin of Others.* Cambridge, MA: Harvard University Press, 2017.

———. *Playing in the Dark: Whiteness and the Literary Imagination.* New York: Vintage, 1993.

Muir, Ramsay. *A History of Liverpool.* London: Liverpool University Press, 1907; reproduced 2013 by Neil Mackenzie.

Munford, Clarence J. *Race and Reparations: A Black Perspective for the 21st Century.* Trenton, NJ: Africa World Press, 1996.

Murari, Timeri. *The New Savages.* London: Macmillan, 1975.

Murphy, Andrea. *From the Empire to the Rialto: Racism and Reaction in Liverpool, 1918–1948.* Merseyside, UK: Liver Press, 1995.

Myers, Norma. *Reconstructing the Past: Blacks in Britain: 1780–1830.* London: Frank Cass, 1994.

Myers, Peter C. *Frederick Douglass: Race and the Rebirth of American Liberalism.* Lawrence, KS: University of Kansas Press, 2008.

Nazel, Joseph. *Paul Robeson: Biography of a Proud Man.* Los Angeles, CA: Holloway House, 1980.

Nelson, William E., Jr. *Black Atlantic Politics: Dilemmas of Political Empowerment in Boston and Liverpool.* Albany, NY: State University of New York Press, 2000.

———. "Africology: Building an Academic Discipline." In *The African American Studies Reader,* edited by Nathaniel Norment Jr., 68–73. Durham, NC: Carolina Academic Press, 2007.

———, and Gideon Ben-Tovim. "Race, Class, Equal Opportunity Policies and Local Government: The Case of Liverpool." *The National Political Science Review* 7 (1999): 53–63.

Nkrumah, Kwame. *Africa Must Unite.* London: Panaf, 1985; first published 1985.

Norment, Nathaniel, Jr., ed. *The African American Studies Reader, 2nd Ed.* Durham, NC: Carolina Academic Press, 2007.

Nott, Josiah, and George Gliddon. *Types of Mankind: Or, Ethnological Researches, Based upon the Ancient Monuments, Paintings, Sculptures, and Crania of Races, and upon Their Natural, Geographical, Philological, and Biblical History.* Charleston, SC: BiblioBazaar, 2016; first published 1855.

Nzegwu, Nkiru. "Colonial Racism: Sweeping Out Africa with Mother Europe's Broom." In *Racism and Philosophy,* edited by Susan E. Babbitt and Sue Campbell, 124–156. Ithaca: Cornell University Press, 1999.

Obama, Barack. *Dreams from My Father: A Story of Race and Inheritance.* New York: Three Rivers Press, 1995.
Olusoga, David. *Black and British: A Forgotten History.* London: Macmillan, 2016.
O'Mara, Pat. *The Autobiography of a Liverpool Slummy.* Liverpool, UK: The Bluecoat Press, n.d.
Orwell, George. *Why I Write.* New York: Penguin, 2005.
———. *Animal Farm.* London: Penguin, 1989; first published 1945.
Ouseley, Herman. "Preface." In Bernard Coard, *How the West Indian Child Is Made Educationally Sub-normal in the British School System,* 9–10. London: Karia Press, 1991.
Outlaw, Lucius T., Jr. "On Race and Philosophy." In *Racism and Philosophy,* edited by Susan E. Babbitt and Sue Campbell. Ithaca: Cornell University Press, 1999.
Painter, Nell Irvin. *The History of White People.* New York: W.W. Norton, 2010.
Panaf Editors. *Frantz Fanon.* London: Panaf Books, 1975.
Parekh, Bhikhu. *Rethinking Multiculturalism: Cultural Diversity and Political Theory.* Cambridge, MA: Harvard University Press, 2000.
———. "Asians in Britain." In *Five Views on Multi-Racial Britain,* edited by the Commission for Racial Equality, 36–55. London: Commission for Racial Equality, 1978.
Park, Robert E.. "Mentality of Racial Hybrids." *The American Journal of Sociology* 36, no. 4 (January 1931): 534–551.
———. "Human Migration and the Marginal Man." *The American Journal of Sociology* 33, no. 6 (May 1928): 881–893.
Park, Robert E., with Everett Cherrington Hughes, et al., eds. *Race and Culture.* Glencoe, IL: The Free Press, 1950.
Parker Rhodes, Jewell. *Douglass' Women.* New York: Washington Square Press, 2002.
Pensoneau-Conway, Sandra L., et al. eds. *Doing Autoethnography.* Rotterdam: Sense Publishers, 2017.
Pettinger, Alasdair. *Frederick Douglass and Scotland, 1846: Living an Antislavery Life.* Edinburgh: University of Edinburgh Press, 2020.
———, ed. *Always Elsewhere: Travels of the Black Atlantic.* London: Cassell, 1998.
———. "Send Back the Money: Douglass and the Free Church of Scotland." In *Liberating Sojourn: Frederick Douglass and Transatlantic Reform,* edited by Alan J. Rice and Martin Crawford, 31–55. Athens, GA: University of Georgia Press, 1999.
Phillips, Caryl. *Color Me English: Migration and Belonging Before and After 9/11.* New York: The New Press, 2011.
———. *The Atlantic Sound.* New York: Alfred A. Knopf, 2000a.
———. *The European Tribe.* New York: Vintage Books, 2000b.
———. *Crossing the River.* New York: Alfred. A. Knopf, 1994.
Phillips, Mike, and Trevor Phillips. *Windrush: The Irresistible Rise of Multiracial Britain.* London: Harper Collins, 1998.
Phillips, Ron Babatunde. *Ndidi's Story by Babatunde.* Manchester, England: Pan-African Institute Publications, 1980.

Phoenix, Ann, et al. "Viewpoint: 'When B.lack Lives Matter All Lives Will Matter'—A Teacher and Three Students Discuss the BLM Movement" *London Review of Education* 18, no. 3 (November 2020): 519–523.

Pouchet Paquet, Sarah. "Foreword." In *In the Castle of My Skin,* by George Lamming, iv–xxxiii. Ann Abor, MI: University of Michigan Press, 1991.

Pope, David. "The Wealth and Social Aspirations of Liverpool's Slave Merchants of the Second Half of the Eighteenth Century." In *Liverpool and Transatlantic Slavery*, edited by David Richardson, Anthony Tibbles, and Suzanne Schwarz, 164–226. Liverpool: Liverpool University Press, 2007.

Poulos, Christopher N. *Essentials of Autoethnography*. Washington, DC: American Psychological Association, 2021.

Poulos, William. "Adorno and Jazz." *Varsity* (June 9, 2021). Accessed June 9, 2021. https://www.varsity.co.uk/music/15086#:~:text=Writing%20in%20the%201930s%2C%20Adorno,was%20not%20expressive%20and%20spontaneous.&text=Jazz%20may%20have%20its%20roots,can%20be%20a%20mass%2Dproduced.

Powell, Enoch. "Britain and Europe." In *The Eurosceptical Reader,* edited by Martin Holmes, 75–87. London: Macmillan, 1996.

Preston, Dickson, F. *Young Frederick Douglass: The Maryland Years.* Baltimore, MD: John Hopkins University Press, 2018.

Priestly, J. B. *English Journey: Being a Rambling but Truthful Account of What One Man Saw and Heard and Felt and Thought during a Journey through England during the Autumn of 1933.* London: Penguin, 1977; first published 1934.

Proctor, James, ed. *Writing Black Britain: An Interdisciplinary Anthology.* Manchester: Manchester University Press, 2000.

Pryce, Ken. *Endless Pressure: A Study of West Indian Life-styles in Bristol.* London: Bristol, 1979.

Quarles, Benjamin. *Frederick Douglass.* Washington, DC: Associated Publishers, 1948.

Quinn, John F. "'Safe in Old Ireland': Frederick Douglass's Tour, 1845–1846." *The Historian* 64, no. 3/4 (Spring/Summer 2002): 525–550.

Rabaka, Reiland. *W.E.B. Du Bois and the Problems of the Twenty-First Century: An Essay on Africana Critical Theory.* Lanham, MD: Lexington Books, 2007.

———. *Africana Critical Theory: Reconstructing the Black Radical Tradition, from W.E.B. Du Bois and C.L.R. James to Frantz Fanon and Amilcar Cabral.* Lanham, MD: Lexington Books, 2010.

Race Equality Management Team, Liverpool City Council, Liverpool Anti-Racist Community Arts Association and the European Social Fund. *Raising Achievement and Promoting Equality within Education: Conference Report.* Liverpool, UK: Liverpool City Council, 1998.

———. *Slavery: An Introduction to the African Holocaust.* Liverpool, UK: Liverpool Education Directorate, 1995.

Rampton Report. *West Indian Children in Our Schools.* London: Her Majesty's Sorting Office, 1981.

Rediker, Marcus. *The Slave Ship: A Human History.* London: Penguin, 2008.

Reid-Merritt, Patricia, ed. *Race in America: How a Pseudoscientific Concept Shaped Human Interaction*, 2 Vols. Santa Barbara, CA: Praeger, 2017.
Reuter, Edward Byron. *The Mulatto in the United States: Including a Study of the Role of Mixed-Blood Races throughout the World.* Chicago: University of Chicago, 1918.
Reynolds, David S. *Lincoln's Selected Writing: A Norton Critical Edition.* New York: W.W. Norton, 2015.
Rice, C. Duncan. "The Anti-Slavery Mission of George Thompson to the United States, 1834–1835." *Journal of American Studies* 2, no. 1 (April 1968): 13–31.
Rich, Paul B. *Prospero's Return? Historical Essays on Race, Culture and British Society.* London: Hansib Publications, 1994.
———. *Race and Empire in British Politics.* Cambridge, UK: Cambridge University Press, 1986.
———. "Philanthropic Racism in Britain: The Liverpool University Settlement, the Anti-Slavery Society and the Issue of 'Half-Caste' Children, 1919–1951." *Immigrants and Minorities* 3, no. 1 (1984): 69–88.
Richards, Dona. "The Ideology of European Dominance." In *Africana Studies: Philosophical Perspectives and Theoretical Paradigms*, 86–95. Pullman, WA: Washington State University Press, 2007.
Richardson, David, et al. *Liverpool and Transatlantic Slavery.* Liverpool, UK: Liverpool University Press, 2007.
Richmond, Anthony H. *Colour Prejudice in Britain: A Study of West Indian Workers in Liverpool, 1941–1951.* London: Routledge & Kegan Paul, 1954.
Roberts, Dorothy. *Fatal Invention: How Science, Politics, and Big Business Re-create Race in the Twenty-First Century.* New York: The New Press, 2011.
Robeson, Paul. *Paul Robeson Speaks.* Edited by Philip Foner. New York: Citadel Press, 1978.
Robeson, Paul, with Lloyd L. Brown. *Here I Stand.* London: Cassell, 1988; first published 1958.
Robinson, Cedric. *Black Marxism: The Making of the Black Radical Tradition.* Chapel Hill, NC: University of North Carolina Press, 2000; first published 1983.
———. "Introduction." In *White Man Listen! Lectures in Europe, 1950–1956*, by Richard Wright, viii–xxv. New York: HarperPerennial, 1995.
———. "The Appropriation of Frantz Fanon." *Race and Class* 35, no. 1 (July–September 1993): 79–91.
Robinson, Ken, with Lou Aronica. *The Element: How Finding Your Passion Changes Everything.* New York: Penguin, 2009.
Robinson, Randall. *The Debt: What America Owes to Blacks.* New York: Plume, 2001.
Rodney, Walter. *Groundings with My Brothers.* London: Bogle-L'Ouverture, 1975.
———. *How Europe Underdeveloped Africa.* London: Bogle-L'Ouverture, 1972.
———. *A History of the Upper Guinea Coast: 1545–1800.* New York: Monthly Review Press, 1970.

Rogers, Ibram H. *The Black Campus Movement: Black Students and the Racial Constitution of Higher Education, 1965–1972.* New York: Palgrave Macmillan, 2012.

Rojas, Fabio. *From Black Power to Black Studies: How a Radical Social Movement Became an Academic Discipline.* Baltimore, MD: The John Hopkins University Press, 2007.

Russell, Bertrand. *The Problems of Philosophy.* London: Dover, 1999.

Saakana, Amon Saba, and Adetokunbo Pearse, eds. *Towards the Decolonization of the British Education System.* London: Karnak House, 1986.

Sadhguru. *Inner Engineering: A Yogi's Guide to Joy.* New York: Spiegel & Grau, 2016.

Salzberger, Ronald P., and Mary C. Turck, eds. *Reparations for Slavery: A Reader.* Lanham, MD: Rowman & Littlefield, 2004.

Sam, Dicky.* *Liverpool and Slavery: An Historical Account of the Liverpool-African Slave Trade.* Liverpool, UK: Scouse Press, 1984; originally published in 1884 by A. Bowker & Son. *Author used a pseudonym.

Sanello, Frank. *Halle Berry: A Stormy Life.* London: Virgin Books, 2004.

Sarich, Vincent, and Frank Miele. *Race: The Reality of Human Differences.* Boulder, CO: Westview Press, 2005.

Scobie, Edward. *Black Britannia: A History of Blacks in Britain.* Chicago: Johnson Publishing, 1972.

Schuyler, George S. *Black No More: A Novel.* New York: Modern Library, 1999; first published 1931.

Second Chance to Learn Women's History Group. *No One Ever Mentions Love: An Inside View of Black and White Relationships.* Liverpool, UK: Liverpool Community College, 1997.

Segal, Ronald. *The Race War: The World-wide Conflict of Races.* Middlesex, England: Penguin, 1967.

Seltzer, Richard, and Nicole E. Johnson. *Experiencing Racism: Exploring Discrimination through the Eyes of College Students.* Lanham, MD: Lexington, 2009.

Selvon, Sam. *The Lonely Londoners.* London: Longman, 1987; first published in 1956.

Shankly, Bill. *Shankly: My Story.* Great Britain: Sports Media, 2009.

Shaw, Claire. "Liverpool's Slave Trade Legacy." *History Today* 70, no. 3 (March 2020). Accessed July 10, 2021: https://www.historytoday.com/history-matters/liverpool%E2%80%99s-slave-trade-legacy

Sengupta, Kim. "Blacks Still Facing Hard Times in Liverpool's Own Form of Apartheid." *The Independent* (March 25, 1998). Accessed November 16, 2021: https://www.independent.co.uk/news/blacks-still-facing-hard-times-in-liverpool-s-own-form-of-apartheid-1152284.html

Shephard, David. *Steps Along Hope Street: My Life in Cricket, the Church and the Inner City.* London: Hodder & Stouton, 2002.

Shepperson, George. "Frederick Douglass and Scotland." *Journal of Negro History* 38, no.3 (July 1953): 307–321.

Shermerhorn, Calvin. "The Coastwise Slave Trade and a Mercantile Community of Interest." In *Slavery's Capitalism: A New History of American Economic Development*. Philadelphia, PA: University of Pennsylvania Press, 2016.
Sherwood, Marika. *Pastor Daniels Ekarte and the African Churches Mission*. London: Savannah Press, 1995.
———. *Many Struggles: West Indian Workers and Personnel in Britain (1939–45)*. London: Karia Press, 1985.
Shyllon, Florin. *Black People in Britain, 1553–1833*. Oxford, UK: Oxford University Press, 1977.
Simey, Margaret. *Democracy Rediscovered: A Study of Police Accountability*. London: Pluto, 1988.
Simon, Roger. *Gramsci's Political Thought: An Introduction*. London: Lawrence & Wishart, 1988.
Sivanandan, A. "Britain's Gulags." In *Writing Black Britain, 1948–1998: An Interdisciplinary Anthology*, edited by James Proctor, 149–153. Manchester, UK: Manchester University Press, 2000.
———. *Communities of Resistance: Writings on Black Struggles for Socialism*. London: Verso, 1990.
———. *From Resistance to Rebellion: Asian and Afro-Caribbean Struggles in Britain*. London: The Institute of Race Relations, 1986.
———. *A Different Hunger: Writings on Black Resistance*. London: Pluto, 1982.
———. *Race and Resistance: The IRR Story*. London: Race Today, 1974.
Skellington, Richard, with Paulette Morris. *'Race' in Britain Today*. London: Sage, 1992.
Small, Stephen. *20 Questions and Answers on Black Europe*. The Hague, NL: Amrit Publishers, 2018.
———. "Black People of Mixed Origins and the Politics of Identity." In *Black Identity in the 20th Century: Expressions of the US and UK African Diaspora*, edited by Mark Christian, 167–194. London: Hansib, 2002.
———. *Racialised Barriers: The Black Experience in the United States and England in the 1980s*. London: Routledge, 1994a.
———. "Racist Ideologies." In *Transatlantic Slavery: Against Human Dignity*, edited by Anthony Tibbles, 111–115. London: Her Majesty's Sorting Office, 1994b.
———. "Racialised Relations in Liverpool: A Contemporary Anomaly." *New Community* 17, no. 4 (1991): 511–537.
———. "Raising Achievement and Promoting Equality Within Education." Conference Presentation dated 11/6/1997. Conference Report, 9–13. Liverpool: LCC, 1998.
Smedley, Audrey. *Race in North America: Origin and Evolution of a Worldview*, 3rd Edition. Boulder, CO: Westview, 2007.
Smith, Robert. *Born Under a Bad Sign*. Liverpool, UK: The Bluecoat Press, 1996.
Smith, Susan. *The Politics of 'Race' and Residence: Citizenship, Segregation and White Supremacy in Britain*. Cambridge: Polity Press, 1989.
Smith, Zadie. *Changing My Mind: Occasional Essays*. New York: Penguin, 2009.

Soyinka, Wole. *The Man Died: Prison Notes.* London: Arrow Books, 1985; first published 1972.
Snowden, Frank M., Jr. *Before Color Prejudice: The Ancient View of Blacks.* Cambridge, MA: Harvard University Press, 1983.
Spencer-Strachan, Louise. *Confronting the Color Crisis in the Afrikan Diaspora: Emphasis Jamaica.* New York: Afrikan World InfoSystems, 1992.
Stampp, Kenneth M. *The Peculiar Institution: Slavery in the Ante-Bellum South.* New York: Vintage, 1956.
Staples, Robert. *Introduction to Black Sociology.* New York: McGraw-Hill, 1976.
Stein, Judith. *The World of Marcus Garvey: Race and Class in Modern Society.* Baton Rouge, LA: Louisiana State University Press, 1986.
Stephens, Ronald J., and Adam Ewing, eds. *Global Garveyism.* Gainesville, FL: University Press of Florida, 2019.
Steward, James, and Talmadge Anderson. *Introduction to African American Studies, Revised and Expanded.* Baltimore, MD: Black Classic Press, 2015.
Stewart, James B. "Reaching for Higher Ground: Toward an Understanding of Black/Africana Studies." In *The African American Studies Reader*, edited by Nathaniel Norment Jr., 420–437. Durham, NC: Carolina Academic Press, 2007.
Stout, Christopher T. *The Case for Identity Politics: Polarization, Demographic Change, and Racial Appeals.* Charlottesville, VA: University of Virginia Press, 2020.
Sussman, Robert Wald. *The Myth of Race: The Troubling Persistence of an Unscientific Idea.* Boston, MA: Harvard University Press, 2014.
Swann Report. *Report of the Committee of Enquiry into the Education of Ethnic Minority Groups.* London: Her Majesty's Sorting Office, 1985.
Sweeney, Fionnghuala. *Frederick Douglass and the Atlantic World.* Liverpool, UK: Liverpool University Press, 2007.
Swindall, Lindsey R. *Paul Robeson: A Life of Activism and Art.* Lanham, MD: Rowman & Littlefield, 2013.
Tafari, Levi. *Liverpool Experience. Lautertal*: Michael Schwinn, 1989.
Taiwo, Olufemi. "Reading the Colonizer's Mind: Lord Lugard and the Philosophical Foundations of British Colonialism." In *Racism and Philosophy*, edited by Susan E. Babbitt and Sue Campbell, 157–186. Ithaca: Cornell University Press, 1999.
Talty, Stephan. *Mulatto America: At the Crossroads of Black and White Culture, a Social History.* New York: Perennial, 2003.
Tate, Shirley. "Colour Matters, 'Race' Matters: African Caribbean Identity in the 20th Century." In *Black Identity in the 20th Century: Expressions of the US and UK African Diaspora,* edited by Mark Christian, 195–212. London: Hansib, 2002.
Taylor, Paul C. *Race: A Philosophical Introduction, 3rd Ed.* Cambridge, UK: Polity Press, 2022.
Taylor, Ula Yvette. *The Veiled Garvey: The Life and Times of Amy Jacques Garvey.* Chapel Hill, NC: The University of North Carolina Press, 2002.
Temple, Christel N. *Transcendence and the Africana Literary Enterprise.* Lanham, MD: Lexington Books, 2018.

Thatcher, Margaret. "The European Family of Nations." In *The Eurosceptical Reader,* edited by Martin Holmes, 88–96. London: Macmillan, 1996.

Thomas, W. I., and Dorothy Swaine Thomas. *The Child in America: Behavior Problems and Programs.* New York: Alfred Knopf, 1928.

Thompson, John, with William L. Andrews, ed. *The Life of John Thompson, a Fugitive Slave.* New York: Penguin, 2011; first published 1856.

Thompson, Vincent B. *Africans of the Diaspora: The Evolution of African Consciousness and Leadership in the Americas, from Slavery to the 1920s.* Trenton, NJ: Africa World Press, 2000.

Thompson, Vincent Bakpetu. *The Making of the African Diaspora in the Americas, 1441–1900.* New York: Longman, 1987.

Tibbles, Anthony, ed. *Transatlantic Slavery: Against Human Dignity.* London: Her Majesty's Sorting Office, 1994.

Torkington, Ntombenhle Protasia K. *Black Health: A Political Issue: The Health and Race Project.* London: Catholic Association for Racial Justice & Liverpool Institute of Higher Education, 1991.

Trollop, Anthony. *The West Indies and the Spanish Main.* New York: Hippocrene Books, 1985; first published 1859.

———. *The Racial Politics of Health: A Liverpool Profile.* Liverpool, UK: The University of Liverpool, 1983.

Turley, David. "British Unitarian Abolitionists, Frederick Douglass, and Racial Equality." In *Liberating Sojourn: Frederick Douglass and Transatlantic Reform,* edited by Alan J. Rice and Martin Crawford, 56–70. Athens, GA: University of Georgia Press, 1999.

Turner, James E. "Historical Dialectics of Black Nationalist Movements in America." In *Africana Studies: Philosophical Perspectives and Theoretical Paradigms,* edited by Delores P. Aldridge and E. Lincoln James, 8–39. Pullman, WA: Washington State University Press, 2007.

———. "Introduction." *David Walker's Appeal: To the Coloured Citizens of the World, but in Particular, and Very Expressly, to Those of the United States of America.* Baltimore, MD: Black Classic Press, 1993.

———. "Ideology and Pan-Africanism: Historical Dialectics of Black Nationalist Movements in America." *Western Journal of Black Studies* 1, no. 3 (September 1977): 164–183.

Twine, France Winddance. *A White Side of Black Britain: Interracial Intimacy and Racial Literacy.* Durham, NC: Duke University Press, 2011.

University of London. "A Voice for Freedom: The Life of Sarah Parker Remond." Accessed July 16, 2021: https://london.ac.uk/news-and-opinion/leading-women/a-voice-freedom-life-sarah-parker-remond

Van Deburg, William L., ed. *Modern Black Nationalism: From Marcus Garvey to Louis Farrakhan.* New York: New York University Press, 1997.

Van Helmond, Marie, and Donna Palmer. *Staying Power: Black Presence in Liverpool.* Liverpool, UK: National Museums and Galleries on Merseyside, 1991.

Van Sertima, Ivan, ed. *Golden Age of the Moor.* New Brunswick, NJ: Transaction Publishers, 1996.

———. *African Presence in Early Europe*. Brunswick, NJ: Transaction Publishers, 1990.

Vincent, Theodore G. *Black Power and the Garvey Movement*. Baltimore, MD: Black Classic Press, 2006; first published 1970.

Walker, Aswad. *Princes Shall Come Out of Egypt: A Comparative Study of the Theological and Ecclesiological Views of Marcus Garvey and Albert B. Cleage, Jr.* Dubuque, IA: Kendall Hunt, 2012.

Walker, David. *David Walker's Appeal: To the Coloured Citizens of the World, but in Particular, and Very Expressly, to Those of the United States of America*. Baltimore, MD: Black Classic Press, 1993; first published 1830.

Walker, Martin. *The National Front*. Glasgow: Fontana Books, 1977.

Walvin, James. *A World Transformed: Slavery in the Americas and the Origins of Global Power*. Oakland, CA: University of California Press, 2022.

———. *Making the Black Atlantic: Britain and the African Diaspora*. London: Cassell, 2000.

———. *The Slave Trade*. Stroud, UK: Sutton Publishing, 1999.

———. *Black Ivory: A History of British Slavery*. Washington, DC: Howard University Press, 1992.

Ware, Leland. *A Century of Segregation: Race, Class, and Disadvantage*. Lanham, MD: Lexington Books, 2018.

———. "A Comparative Analysis of Unconscious and Institutional Discrimination in the United States and Britain." *Georgia Journal of International and Comparative Law* 36, no.1 (Fall 2007): 89–157.

Warrington, Paul. *Black British Intellectuals and Education: Multiculturalism's Hidden History*. London: Routledge, 2014.

Washington, Booker T., with Robert E. Park. *The Man Furthest Down: A Record of Observation and Study in Europe*. New York: Doubleday, Page & Company, 1912.

———, with Ellis Paxson Oberholtzer, ed. *Frederick Douglass*. Honolulu, HI: University Press of the Pacific, 2003; first published 1906.

Webber, Christopher L. *American to the Backbone: The Life of James W.C. Pennington, the Fugitive Slave Who Became One of the First Black Abolitionists*. New York: Pegasus Books, 2011.

Welborn, Jaime, E., et al. *Leading Change through the Lens of Cultural Proficiency: An Equitable Approach to Race and Social Class in Our Schools*. Thousand Oaks, CA: Corwin, 2022.

Wells-Barnett, Ida B. *On Lynchings*. New York: Humanity Books, 2002; first published 1892–1900.

———, and Alfreda M. Duster, ed. *Crusade for Justice: The Autobiography of Ida B. Wells*. Chicago: The University of Chicago Press, 1970.

Wells Brown, William. *The Black Man: His Antecedents, His Genius, and His Achievements*. Savanah, GA: James M. Symms, 1863.

West, Cornel. *The Cornel West Reader*. New York: Basic Civitas Books, 1999.

———. *Race Matters*. New York: Vintage, 1994.

West, Michael O. "Decolonization, Desegregation, and Black Power: Garveyism in Another Era." In *Global Garveyism,* edited by Ronald J. Stephens and Adam Ewing, 265–286. Gainesville, FL: University Press of Florida, 2019.
Weyl, Nathaniel. *Karl Marx: Racist.* New York: Arlington House, 1979.
Wideman, John Edgar. *Fanon: A Novel.* Boston: Houghton Mifflin, 2008.
Williams, Chancellor. *The Destruction of Black Civilization: Great Issues of a Race from 4500 BC to 2000 A.D.* Chicago: Third World Press, 1976.
Williams, Eric. *Capitalism and Slavery.* London: Andre Deutsch, 1964; first published 1944.
Williamson, Scott C. *The Narrative Life: The Moral and Religious Thought of Frederick Douglass.* Macon, GA: Mercer University Press, 2002.
Willis, Paul. *Learning to Labour: How Working-Class Kids Get Working-Class Jobs.* New York: Columbia University Press, 2017; first published 1977.
Wilson, Carlton E. "Racism and Private Assistance: The Support for West Indian and African Missions in Liverpool, England during the Interwar Years." *African Studies Review* 35, no. 2 (1992): 55–76.
Windbush, Raymond A., ed. *Should America Pay? Slavery and the Raging Debate on Reparations.* New York: Amistad, 2003.
Witkin, Robert W. "Why Did Adorno 'Hate' Jazz?" *Sociological Theory* 18, no. 1 (2000): 145–70. Accessed June 10, 2021. http://www.jstor.org/stable/223286.
Wolf-Robinson, Maya. "'Liverpool Is Built on Transatlantic Slavery': How City's Museums Are Tackling Racism." *Guardian* (May 21, 2021). https://www.theguardian.com/uk-news/2021/may/26/liverpool-is-built-on-transatlantic-slavery-how-the-citys-museums-are-tackling-race-issues?CMP=Share_AndroidApp_Other Accessed June 10, 2021.
Wong, Maria Lin. *Chinese Liverpudlians: A History of the Chinese Community in Liverpool.* Merseyside: Liver Press, 1989.
Woodward, Komozi. *A Nation within a Nation: Amiri Baraka (Leroi Jones) and Black Power Politics.* Chapel Hill, NC: University of North Carolina Press, 1999.
Wright, Richard. "Introduction." In *The Black Metropolis: A Study of Negro Life in a Northern City,* St. Clair Drake and Horace R. Cayton, ix-xxvi. Chicago: University of Chicago Press, 2015; first published 1945.
———. *White Man Listen! Lectures in Europe, 1950–1956.* New York: HarperPerennial, 1995a; first published 1957.
———. *Black Power: A Record of Reactions in a Land of Pathos.* New York: HarperPerennial, 1995b; first published 1954.
———. *The Color Curtain: A Report on the Bandung Conference.* Jackson, MS: Banner Books, 1994; first published 1956.
Yancy, George. *Backlash: What Happens When We Talk Honestly about Racism in America.* Lanham, MD: Rowman & Littlefield, 2018.
———. *On Race: 34 Conversations in a Time of Crisis.* New York: Oxford University Press, 2017.
Yeboah, Samuel K. *The Ideology of Racism.* London: Hansib, 1988.

Yee, Shirley. "Charles Lenox Remond (1810–1873)." *Black Past* (June 4, 2008). Accessed July 16, 2021: https://www.blackpast.org/african-american-history/remond-charles-lenox-1810-1873/

Yekwai, Dimela. *British Racism: Miseducation and the Afrikan Child.* London: Karnak House, 1988.

Yogananda, Paramahansa. *Autobiography of a Yogi.* Los Angeles, CA: Self-Realization Fellowship, 1974; first published 1946.

Young, Robert J. C. *Colonial Desire: Hybridity in Theory, Culture and Race.* London: Routledge, 1995.

Zack-Williams, Alfred B. "African Diaspora Conditioning: The Case of Liverpool." *Journal of Black Studies* 27, no. 4 (March 1997): 528–542.

Zephaniah, Benjamin. "What Stephen Lawrence Has Taught Us." In *Writing Black Britain, 1948–1998: An Interdisciplinary Anthology*, edited by James Proctor, 259–261. Manchester: Manchester University Press, 2000.

———. *Inna Liverpool.* Chico, CA: AK Press, 1992.

Zuberi, Tukufu, and Eduardo Bonilla-Silva, eds. *White Logic, White Methods: Racism and Methodology.* Lanham, MD: Rowman & Littlefield, 2008.

Index

abolition and abolitionism, 40–41; Douglass, F., in movement for, 221; of Thompson, G., 229–30
accents, 32
Ackah, William, 9
Adorno, Theodor, 51
Africana Britain, complexity of, 31–33
Africana critical studies, 1–3, 5–6, 26, 166, 242; colonialism and, 10–11; emergence of field of, 49–50; theoretical grounding in, 10–14; on unity, 29
African Americans, 161
African Churches Missions, 78
African Diaspora, 13, 28, 70; Blackness in relation to, 32; Cabral on, 30–31; evolution of, 51
The African Genius (Davidson), 148, 207
Afrocentrism, 12–13, 50; Gilroy, P., on, 45–46, 52, 58
Afro hairstyle, 115–16, 152
After Empire (Gilroy, P.), 4
Agwuna, Ben, 148–49, 160, 209, 213
Ahearn, Fred, 130, 143
Albert Dock, 7, 215–16
Aldo, Steve, 89
Alexander, Arthur, 89
Ali, Arif, 210

Ali, Muhammad, 150–51, 158
alienation, 11
Alland, Alexander, Jr., 101
alterity, Gilroy, P., on, 45–47
Always Elsewhere (Pettinger), 68–69
American Civil War, 14
American Notes (Dickens), 234
American studies, 158–61
Amoo, Chris, 124
Amoo, Eddie, 88, 124
ancient Romans, 100
Angelou, Maya, 7, 13, 204
Ani, Marimba, 58
Ankrah, Edmund, 88
Ankrah, Joe, 88
anticolonialism, 25, 52–53
anti-essentialism, 45
anti-Semitism, 54
Araujo, Ana Lucia, 2
Asante, Molefi K., 12–13, 47, 52, 58–59
Aspinall, James, 39
assimilation, 149
Atlantic Records, 88
The Atlantic Sound (Phillips), 16, 63–64
August Bank Holiday, 180–81
Auld, Thomas, 234, 237, 239
autoethnography, 15–20; Poulos on, 15

323

Babatunde. *See* Phillips, Ron "Babatunde"
Bailey, Harriet, 222
Baker, Jennifer, 150
Baldwin, James, 15, 25, 69, 158; on American history, 161; on writing, 1–2
Baraka, Amiri, 47, 185
Barbados, 60
Barnes, John, 6, 101, 136, 137, 138–39
Barnes, Tony, 195
Barrett, Janet, 147
Barrett, Richard, 89
Bass Culture, 61
Bassey, Peter, 193, 220
Bassey, Solly, 220
Bassey, Sonia, 220
BBP. *See* British Black Panther Party
the Beatles, 35, 51, 88–89, 134
Before the Windrush (Belchem), 77, 197, 215
Being Human Being (Asante & Dove, N.), 58
Belchem, John, 17–18, 34, 83, 102–3, 111, 156–57, 205; on Black Liverpudlians, 77, 122–23; on Falkner Estate attacks, 183; on Liverpool 8 Defense Committee, 197–98; slave trade airbrushed by, 206–7, 215
Bennett, Alex, 220
Ben-Tovim, Gideon, 17, 168, 210–14, 217; on Charles Wootton College, 210–11; Clay and, 214; Nelson on, 210–11
Berman, Marshall, 46
Berry, Chuck, 89
Berry, Halle, 90–92
Beyond a Boundary (James), 81
biraciality, 89–90
Birkenhead, 96
Black 1919 (Jenkinson), 170
Black and British (Olusoga), 155–56

The Black Atlantic (Gilroy, P.), 2, 15, 32; publication of, 45–46; reception of, 50
Black Atlantic paradigm, 20, 32–33, 41–42, 249; criticism of, 51; essentialism in paradigm of, 49–59; refinement of, 70; transatlantic in context of, 66–68
Black Atlantic Politics (Nelson), 9, 204–5, 210–11
Black British people, 2–3; exodus of scholars, 5–7; historiographical counter-narratives, 3–9; in transatlantic context, 59–66; in World War I, 74–75; in World War II, 74–75
Blackburn House, 200
Black empowerment, 205; in Liverpool, 18; white liberals as enemies of, 234–35
the Blackie, 182, 184
Black Ivory (Walvin), 37, 38
Black Liverpool and Liverpudlians, 18, 20–21; Belchem on, 77, 122–23; Charles Wootton College benefiting, 211; counterhegemonic studies on, 156–57; Dickens on, 235–36; experience of, 41–44; fight for equality for, 220; grassroots perspective on, 43; Melville on, 235–36; mixed heritage, 89–97; music and, 85–89, 105–10; population of, 106–7; Richmond on, 77–78; Small on, 161–62; social exclusion of, 43–44; stigmatization of, 19; transatlantic history and, 44; white activists and, 205. *See also* Liverpool Born Blacks
Black Nationalism, 46; white nationalism contrasted with, 49
Blackness, 90–91, 97; African diaspora related to, 32; in Britain, 32; differences in experiences of, 47, 70
blackness, Gilroy, P., on, 49
Black Panthers, 57–58, 87

Black Rights/White Wrongs (Mills), 12
Black Skin, White Masks (Fanon), 10, 29, 92
Black Studies: at Charles Wootton College, 211–12; at Elimu, 158; in 1990s, 206–14. *See also* Africana critical studies
Blassingame, John, 230, 231–32
Blaut, J. M., 207–8
Blight, David, 224, 232; on Douglass, F., 242
Bolt, Christine, 42
Born Under a Bad Sign (Smith, R.), 195–96
Braithwaite, E. R., 59
Brexit, 113, 147
bricklaying, 154–55
Bristol, 44
British Black Panther Party (BBP), 58, 61
Brookes slave ship, 38–40, 206
Brooks, Joseph, Jr., 36, 38
Brown, Jacqueline Nassy, 17–18, 157; on Liverpool, 103–5
Brown, James, Jr., 43–44
Brown, Manneh, 120, 193, 202–4, 205, 220, 248
Brown, Mark, 218
Brown, Sylvia, 205
Brown, Tommy, 87–88
Brown, Wally, 86, 144, 156, 167, 205; on Liverpool Born Blacks invisibility, 119–20
Brown, William Wells, 92, 239
Brown Baby Problem, 121–22
Buckner, Sol, 219
Buffum, James, 222

Cabral, Amilcar, 10, 27–28, 46, 53–54, 85, 149; on African diaspora, 30–31; assassination of, 31; on colonialism, 28
calypso, 89
Cambria steamship, 222–25, 241–42
Cameron, Gail, 32, 34

Cameroon, 30
Campaign Against Racial Discrimination (CARD), 58
capitalism, 169
Capitalism and Slavery (Williams, E.), 53
Carby, Hazel, 5, 7
CARD. *See* Campaign Against Racial Discrimination
Cardiff, 44
Caribbean, 2, 17, 33, 60–61
Caribbean Football Club, 139–40
Carlyle, Thomas, Douglass, F., and, 234–35
Carney, Ann, 220
Carruthers, Jacob, 58
Carver, George Washington, 240
Catholics, 169, 174
Celts, 100
Césaire, Aimé, 10, 29; on colonialism, 24–26; on Negritude, 23–25
Chaffin, Tom, 225–26
Chamoiseau, Patrick, 125
the Chants, 88–89
Charles Wootton College, 8, 104, 160, 166–68, 171, 198, 207; Ben-Tovim on, 210–11; Black Liverpudlians benefited by, 211; Black Studies at, 211–12; Christian, M., at, 143–54; Clay on, 209; closing of, 214; defunding of, 220; funding of, 212, 214, 216–17
Charles Wootton News, 208, 214
Charlotte (Queen), 101–2
Chartists, 44
Chernow, Ron, 245
Chrisman, Laura, on Gilroy, P., 55–56
Christian, Ada Jane, 72, 94, 126, 127; children of, 86–87, 114–15; Christian, G. F., and, 75–76, 84–85, 105–6; as household leader, 95–96; as singer, 116
Christian, Denny, 87–88, 96
Christian, Garry, 107–8, 110, 116, 124–25, 139

Christian, George Rupert, 72, 94; in UNIA, 245–46
Christian, Gladstone Forbes, 71, *73*, 77–78, 94; automobile accident of, 87; children of, 86–87, 114–15; Christian, A. J., and, 75–76, 84–85, 105–6; retirement of, 95
Christian, Ian, 96, 115
Christian, Janet, 96–97, 105–6, 115
Christian, Jenny, 96–97
Christian, Kevin, 116–17
Christian, Mark, 7, 9, 16, 107–9, 205; on American studies, 158–60; at Charles Wootton College, 143–54; Douglass, F., and, 244–49; education of, 125–32; on family history, 245–46; football played by, 139–42; speech in Liverpool, 247–49
Christian, Pam, 96–97, 105–6
Christian, Rita, 96–97, 105–6, 115, 147
Christian, Roger, 87–88, 107–10
Christian, Russell, 107–8, 124
Christian, Tina, 96–97, 105–6
Christian, Victor, 107–9, 125, 129–30, 143, 220
Christianity: Douglass, F., on, 231, 239; slavery interwoven with, 14
Christie, Alvin, 89, 123
The Chronicle Review, 3
Churchill, Winston, 112
"Civic Liverpool" (Longmore), 34–35
Civil Rights Movement, 15, 49–50, 188
The Civil War and the United States (Marx & Engels), 233
Clarke, John Henrik, 58, 148
Clarkson, Thomas, 38, 229–30
Clay, Dave, 140, 167, 184, 193, 211, 220; activism of, 181–82; Ben-Tovim and, 214; on Charles Wootton College, 209; on the Militants, 200
Clemence, Ray, 136
clubs, Liverpool 8, 83–84, 123–24
Coard, Bernard, 128–29, 131
Cocky (Barnes, T., Elias, & Walsh), 195
Cogley, Frank, 209–10, 212, 213

Collingwood, Luke, 39–40
colonialism, 32, 170; Africana critical studies emerging from, 10–11; Cabral on, 28; Césaire on, 24–26; education and, 62
The Colonizer's Model of the World (Blaut), 207–8
colonizer's paradigm, 77
colorism, 93–94; racialized hierarchies and, 90, 97
color line, music and, 105–10
Color Me English (Phillips), 16
Colour Prejudice in Britain (Richmond), 77
Columbus, Christopher, 32
Commission for Racial Equity (CRE), 202
The Communist Manifesto (Marx & Engels), 14, 169, 233
Consortium of Black Organisations, 218
Constantine, Learie, 11, 60, 79–80, 95
Cooke, Stan, 33, 34
Cooper, Anna Julia, 46, 92
Cooper, Leroy, 150, 187
Costello, Ray, 43
counterculture, 49–50
counter-hegemony, 1–2; creation of, 24–26
Crawford, Martin, 226
CRE. *See* Commission for Racial Equity
cricket, 79–83; James on, 81–83
criminalization, 193
critical race theory, 26; right-wing attacks on, 213
Crosby, Bing, 84
Crossing the River (Phillips), 63–64
Crummell, Alexander, 240
"A Cry from Africa," 63
Cullen, Anna Maria, 97
Cullen, Countee, 69
Cullen, Joanna, 97
Cullen, Susannah, 97

Dalglish, Kenny, 136
dance, 84–85

Davidson, Basil, 148–49, 155, 207
Davis, Angela, 46, 69, 115–16
Davis, Kenny, 124
Democracy Rediscovered (Simey), 187–88, 189
The Destruction of Black Civilization (Williams, C.), 207
The Devil (Johnson, G.), 194
Diana (Princess), 101
Dickens, Charles, 13, 227–28; on Black Liverpool, 235; Douglass, F., and, 234
Dimbleby, Jonathan, 183
Diop, Cheikh Anta, 85
Discourse on Colonialism (Césaire), 24, 25, 26
diversity, unity and, 47–49
Doo Wop, 108
Doreen Lawrence (Lawrence), 8–9
double consciousness, 50, 240
Douglass, Anna, 221; at Eaton Hall, 224–25, 248
Douglass, Charles Remond, 239
Douglass, Frederick, 13–14, 15, 20, 51, 69, 92; in abolitionist movement, 221; in America, 241–43; autobiographies of, 221–22; Blight on, 242; in British Isles, 221–22; on *Cambria* steamship, 222–25, 241–42; Carlyle and, 234–35; Christian, M., and, 244–49; on Christianity, 231, 239; Dickens and, 234; freedom of, 237–41, 243; in Ireland, 225–26; legacy of, 249; in Liverpool, 14, 227–32; *London Times* letter, 242–43; Marx and, 14, 232–36; mixed heritage of, 222; oratorical style of, 231; paternalism of white abolitionists towards, 238–39; in Scotland, 225–26; slavery indicted by, 228; speeches by, 225–26; white female philanthropy towards, 237–41; Wright, H. C., and, 237
Dove, Claire, 200, 209–10
Dove, Nah, 58

Drake, St. Clair, 120, 121–22
Dropping Anchor, Setting Sail (Brown, J. N.), 103–4
Drysdale, Liz, 120, 193
Du Bois, W. E. B., 47, 52, 57, 92, 240

Eaton Hall, Douglass, F., at, 224–25, 248
education and education system: of Christian, M., 125–32; colonialism and, 62; grassroots, 143–54, 167–68; higher education access, 154–63; Lamming on, 62–63; of LBBs, 120, 143; problems in, 132–34; racialized hierarchies in, 133–34; racism in, 131–32
Edward III (King), 101
Edward of Woodstock (Prince), 101
EFC. *See* Everton Football Club
Ekarte, Daniel, 78, 120–21
The Element (Robinson, K.), 132
Elias, Richard, 195
Elimu Wa Nane, Black Studies at, 158
Elizabeth II (Queen), 102
Ellison, Ralph, 52
Emecheta, Buchi, 11
emergent convivialities, Gilroy, P., on, 3–4
Emerson, Ralph Waldo, 99
Empire Windrush, 4, 7, 59, 177
Engels, Frederick, 14, 169; on slavery, 233–34
English purity, as myth, 100–102
Enlightenment, 12, 32, 55; Eurocentrism of, 40
Epstein, Brian, 88
equality, fight for, 220
Equal Temperament, 124–25
Equiano, Olaudah, 39; marriage and children of, 97–98
essentialism, 7, 23, 68; strategic, 57. *See also* ethnic absolutism
ethnic absolutism, 49, 52; Gilroy, P., on, 46

Etoke, Nathalie, on racialized hierarchies, 29–30
eugenics. *See* pseudoscientific racism
Eurocentrism, 46–47; in academia, 51; of Enlightenment, 40; Gilroy, P., and, 51–52; oppression from, 2; uncoupling from, 11–12
European exceptionalism, 11–12
The European Tribe (Phillips), 63–64
Everton Football Club (EFC), 135
Eyo, Peter, 185, 220

Falkner Estate, 182
false consciousness, 170, 183
Fanon, Frantz, 10, 26, 46, 53–54, 85; on internalized racism, 92–93; on Negritude, 23–24; on racialized hierarchy, 96–97
Farrag, Joe, 120, 220
Fatal Invention (Roberts), 98
Fenton, Laurence, 225, 234
Fish, Cheryl, 69
Fletcher, Muriel, 102–5; pseudoscientific racism of, 102–3; racism of, 187–88
Fletcher Report, 102–3; Simey on, 187–88
Foner, Philip, 227
Fontenot, Albert, 219, 220
football, 126; Christian, M., playing, 139–42; in Liverpool 8, 139–42; racism in, 135–39
Fortune, T. Thomas, 92
Foucault, Michel, 46
Frankfurt School, 51
Franklin, Aretha, 116
Frederick Douglass (Blight), 224
Frederick Douglass and Scotland (Pettinger), 226
Frederick Douglass in Britain and Ireland (Murray & McKivigan), 226, 232
Frederick Douglass in Ireland (Fenton), 225–26
The Frederick Douglass Papers, 230

freedom, defining, 69
French, Stephen, 194
"From a Colonial Past to a New Multiculturalism" (Gilroy, P.), 3
Frost, Diane, 17–18, 41, 198
Fryer, Peter, 36, 42, 98, 155, 156, 168–69, 172, 176, 180–81; on pseudoscientific racism, 207–8

Garnet, Henry Highland, 239, 240
Garrison, William Lloyd, 221, 223, 229, 237
Garvey, Marcus, 47, 54, 72, 153
Gaye, Marvin, 130
Gayle, Abdul, 220
Gayle, Howard, 137
Ghana, 53
Giant's Causeway (Chaffin), 225–26
Gifford Inquiry, 107, 186–87, 196
Gilroy, Beryl, 11, 59, 101
Gilroy, Paul, 2–3, 7, 10–11, 15, 112, 139, 177; as academic writer, 49; on Afrocentrism, 45–46, 52, 58; on alterity, 45–47; on Black Atlantic, 20, 32–33, 41–42, 45–47; on blackness, 50; Chrisman on, 55–56; critiques of, 5–6, 51–59; on emergent convivialities, 3–4; essentialism in Black Atlantic paradigm of, 49–59; on ethnic absolutism, 46; as Eurocentrist, 51–52; M'Baye on, 57; on melancholia, 4; non-racialized world envisioned by, 5–6. *See also* Black Atlantic paradigm
Glissant, Édouard, 23
Goffman, Ervin, on stigmatization, 19
Goldberg, Chad Allen, 145, 147
Grace, W. C., 81
Granby/Toxteth Community Project, 202–3
Granby/Toxteth Task Force, 200, 203
Grant, Bernie, 212
grassroots organization: on Black Liverpool and Liverpudlians, 43; defunding of, 219–20; destruction

of, 218; education, 143–54, 167–68; Lynch on, 201–2; mainstream scholarly community undermining, 205–6; in 1990s, 202–3
Great War to Race Riots (Heneghan & Onuora), 173–74
Greenidge, Michael, 153
Gregson, James, 39
Gregson, John, 39
Gregson, William, 39
Gregson Syndicate, 39
Griffin, Farah, 69
Griffin, Lawrence, 87–88
Grosvenor, Richard, 224
Guinea-Bissau, 26–27

Habermas, Jurgen, 46
half-caste, 9, 89–90, 121, 124
Hall, Stuart, 2–3, 5–6, 10–11, 46, 97, 177; on Black British people, 31–32; on historical amnesia, 110–12; on internalized racism, 93–94; on racism, 114
Hamilton, 243–45, 247
Hamilton, Alexander, 245, 246
Harding, Alan, 88
Harpe, Bill, 182, 205
Harrison, Faye, 105
Harrison, George, 133
Harry (Prince), 101, 102
Hawkins, Judith Ann, 90
Hegel, George, 52, 54, 68
Hemings, Sally, 101
Henchard, Francis, 168
Heneghan, Madeline, 173–74, 205
Heseltine, Michael, 190–92; on Liverpool 8, 191, 193, 196–97; on Liverpool 8 Defense Committee, 198–99; structural racism and, 197
Hesse, Barnor, 5, 66–67, 177, 180
higher education, in Liverpool 8, 154–63
Hill, Dave, 138
Hilliard, Asa, III, 58

historical amnesia: Hall on, 110–12; racism and, 110–14
A History of the Upper Guinea Coast (Rodney), 27
The History of White People (Painter), 99
Hitler, Adolf, 102–3
Holocaust Studies, 56
hooks, bell, 46
Howart, Gerald, 79
Howe, Stephen, 59
How Europe Underdeveloped Africa (Rodney), 26, 28
How the West Indian Child is Made Educationally Sub-Normal in the British School System (Coard), 128
Hudson-Weems, Clenora, 47, 58
Hughes, Emlyn, 136
human hybridity, 144–45
Humphry, Derek, 185–86
Hurston, Zora Neale, 52
Hussein, Adam, 120, 193, 204, 220
Hyatt, Gloria, 157

indentured servants, European, 160
Indigenous peoples, 33
"Inglan is a Bitch," 61–62, 63
Inland Revenue, 194
Inna Liverpool (Zephania), 17
institutionalized racism, of Liverpool, 162–63
institutional racism, 8–9
internalized racism, 10; Fanon on, 92–93; Hall on, 93–94
International Slavery Museum, 7, 215–16, 247
In the Castle of My Skin (Lamming), 60, 62
Ireland, Douglass, F, in, 225–26

Jackson, Jessie, 7, 13
Jackson 5, 115
Jamaica, 9, 69; Christian, G. F., in, 72–74
Jamaica Producer, 72–73, 80, 94

James, C. L. R., 10–11, 46, 54, 60, 63, 74, 79; on cricket, 81–83
Jameson, Frederic, 46
Jazz, 51
Jefferson, Thomas, 101
Jeffries, Stuart, 101
Jenkinson, Jacqueline, 170
Joel, Joey, 140, 193, 220
John, Gus, 161, 185–86
Johnson, Graham, 194
Johnson, Linton Kwesi, 11, 59, 63; Lamming and, 60–62
Jones, Claudia, 46, 232–33
Jordan, June, 69
Juarez, Mirna, 216
Judkins, Charles, 223
Julienne, Louis, 171, 172–73, 220

Karenga, Maulana, 28, 58, 153
Keegan, Kevin, 136
Keith, Michael: on racism, 177–80; on Small, 180
Kelsal, James, 40
Kent State University, 244
Kenya, 63
Kenyatta, Jomo, 63
Khader, Brian, 155
King, Martin Luther, Jr., 150–52, 237–38
Kingsley Road, 198
Kojack, 141
Kuya, Dorothy, 120
Kwanzaa, 153

Lake, Ray, 124
Lamming, George, 11, 59, 74; on education, 62–63; Johnson and, 60–62
Lawrence, Doreen, 8
Lawrence, Stephen, 8, 9, 67, 202
LBBs. *See* Liverpool Born Blacks
League of Colored Peoples (LCP), 121
Learning to Labour (Willis), 127–28
Lee, John, 40
Lee, Spike, 46

Leeds, 64
LFC. *See* Liverpool Football Club
liberalism: whiteness and, 12. *See also* white liberals
Liberating Sojourn (Rice, A., & Crawford), 226
Liebow, Elliot, 184
Little Richard, 89
Liverpool, 2–3; Black empowerment in, 18; Brown, J. N., on, 103–5; Christian, M., speaking in, 247–49; demographics, 106–7; Douglass, F., in, 14, 227–32; institutionalized racism of, 162–63; London contrasted with, 32; Phillips on, 18–19; population of, 42; racialized discrimination in, 3; racialized violence in, 167–71; slave ships in, 36–41; slave trade in, 33, 206–7; social system of, 41–42; teaching in, 20–21. *See also specific topics*
Liverpool 8, 16, 66, 75, 79, 162–63, 182; clubs in, 83–84, 123–24; football in, 139–42; Heseltine on, 191, 193, 196–97; higher education in, 154–63; Lynch on, 201–2; uprising of 1981 in, 186–99
Liverpool 8 Defense Committee, 193–94; Belchem on, 197–98; Heseltine on, 198–99
Liverpool 8 Law Centre, 200, 216–17; defunding of, 220
Liverpool '81 (Frost & Phillips, R.), 198
Liverpool 800 (Belchem), 34, 111, 206, 215
Liverpool Black Caucus, 199–200
Liverpool Black Pioneers (Costello), 43
Liverpool Born Blacks (LBBs), 9, 11, 16–17, 19–20; Brown, W., on invisibility of, 119–20; education options for, 120, 143; unemployment of, 143
Liverpool - Capital of the Slave Trade (Cameron & Cooke), 33

Liverpool City Council: accountability for, 218; apology for slave trade, 215–20, *217*
Liverpool Echo, 80–81
"Liverpool Experience" (Tafari), 11
Liverpool Football Club (LFC), 135, 136
Liverpool Mercury, 44
Liverpool Police Force, 181
Liverpool University Press, 198
London, 11, 44; Liverpool contrasted with, 32
London Times, 242–43
The Lonely Londoners (Lamming), 60
Longmore, Jane, 34–35
The Lost Cities of Africa (Davidson), 148
Lynch, Eric, 120, 165; on economic independence, 220; on grassroots organization, 201–2; on Liverpool 8 community, 201–2

Maiden Castle, 100
Making the Black Atlantic (Walvin), 42
Malcolm X, 2, 45–46, 54, 67, 69, 128, 150–51, 158, 182; on racism, 178
Malcolm X (film), 46
Mandela, Nelson, 110–11
The Man Farthest Down, 240–41
Many Struggles (Sherwood), 83
marginal man, 145; Park on, 240
Maritime Museum, 7
Marke, Ernest, 174
Markle, Meghan, 101, 102, 246
Marley, Bob, 115
Martinique, 23
Marx, Karl, 169; Douglass, F., and, 14, 232–36; on slavery, 233–34
Marxism, 182–83
Mau Mau uprising, 63
M'Baye, Babacar: on Gilroy, P., 57; on strategic essentialism, 57
McCartney, Paul, 133–34
McIver, 242–43
McKivigan, John, 226, 232

McPherson Report, 8
Mein Kampf (Hitler), 102–3
melancholia, Gilroy, P., on, 4
Melancholia Africana (Etoke), 29–30
Melville, Herman, 13, 17; on Black Liverpool, 235–36
Memi, Albert, 10
Mento, 84
Merseybeat, 89, 123–24
Merseyside Hospitality Council (MHC), 79
Merseyside Racial Equality Council (MREC), 202
MHC. *See* Merseyside Hospitality Council
Michael Heseltine (Heseltine), 190–91
microaggressions, 160
Miele, Frank, 98
the Militants, 199–206; Clay on, 200
Mills, Charles, 11–12, 19, 99; on white supremacy, 12
Minford, Patrick, 199
Miranda, Lin-Manuel, 245
mixed heritage: of Black Liverpudlians, 89–97; of Douglass, F., 222; historical contours of, 97–100; from non-consensual unions, 98; Park on, 144–47, 240–41
mixed racial unions, as social problem, 97–98
Mohammed, Ahmed Y., 150
Moody, Harold, 121
Morgan, Clement Garnett, 240
Motown, 88, 115
Moxhay, George, 241
MREC. *See* Merseyside Racial Equality Council
Mullard (professor), 159
multiculturalism, of Britain, 4
Multiracial Identity (Christian), 7, 188
Munford, Clarence, 58
Murari, Timeri, 183–86
murders, racist, 8–9
Murphy, Andrea, 167–68
Murray, Hannah-Rose, 226, 232

music, 84–85; Black Liverpudlians and, 85–89, 105–10; Christian family and, 107–9, 115–16, 124–25; color line and, 105–10. *See also specific topics*
My Bondage and My Freedom (Douglass, F.), 222
The Myth of Race (Sussman), 99

Narrative of the Life of Frederick Douglass, An American Slave, Written by Himself (Douglass, F.), 221, 224
nationalism, 45. *See also* Black Nationalism; white nationalism
National Union of Seamen, 178, 192
Native Son (Wright, R.), 52–53
Nazis, 72–73
Negritude: Césaire on, 23–25; Fanon on, 23–24
Nelson, William E., Jr., 9, 58, 204–5; on Ben-Tovim, 210–11
Newcastle, 228
The New Savages (Murari), 183–86
New World, 2, 32–33, 38, 68
New York City, 243–44
1919-2019 (Clay), 181–82, 185
Nkrumah, Kwame, 53
Notes of a Native Son (Baldwin), 1, 25
Nyahoe, Bobby, 185, 220

Obama, Barack, 90–92, 240
Objective 1, 200
O'Connell, Daniel, 234
Old Man Trouble (Marke), 174
Olusoga, David, 155–57
one drop rule, 70, 86, 90, 92, 101
Onuora, Emy, 173–74, 205
O'Reilly, Maria, 120, 193, 219, 220
otherness, 11
Ousley, Herman, 128–29
Out of his Skin (Hill), 138
Oxford, Kenneth, 187; Simey on, 188–89
Oye, Chris, 140

Padmore, George, 120
Painter, Neil Irvin, 99
Paisley, Bob, 137
Pan Africanism, 47, 54–55, 63, 149, 153
Park, Robert E.: on marginal man, 240; on mixed heritage, 144–47, 240–41; pseudoscientific racism of, 145–46
Parks, Rosa, 188
Pastor Daniels Ekarte and the African Churches Mission (Sherwood), 120
Paths of the Atlantic Slave Trade (Araujo), 2
Pearl Harbor, 72
Pele, 126, 244
Pennington, James W. C., 239
The Persistence of Memory (Moody), 215
Pettinger, Alasdair, 68–69, 226
Philippa of Hainault (Queen), 101
Phillips, Mike, 177
Phillips, Richard, 198
Phillips, Trevor, 177
Phillips, Caryl, 11, 15–18, 63–64; on Liverpool, 18–19
Phillips, Ron "Babatunde," 149–50, 151, 245
Pitt, Ada. *See* Christian, Ada Jane
Pitt, Frederick, 76
Poetics of Relation (Glissant), 23
police: brutality in 1919, 173–76; racism of, 185–86
Police Power and Black People (Humphry), 185–86
Policing the Crisis (Hall), 6
postmodernism, 32
Poulos, Christopher, on autoethnography, 15
Powell, Enoch, 95–96; racism of, 4
The Presentation of Self in Everyday Life (Goffman), 19
Priestly, J. B., 236
Princes Park, 210, 217
Prospero's Return? (Rich), 85
Protestants, 169

pseudoscientific racism, 33, 42, 90, 98–99, 122, 124; of Fletcher, 102–3; Fryer on legacy of, 207–8; of Park, 145

Quarless, Ray, 220
Quarry Bank Comprehensive, 125
Quarry Bank School, 110

race, as social construct, 98–100, 180
Race Equality Management Team, 211
Race in the Mind (Alland), 101
race riots, 74, 157, 166, 169; in 1948, 176–81; in 1919, 174–76
The Racial Contract (Mills), 11–12
racialization, 10
racialized discrimination, in Liverpool, 3
racialized hierarchies, 4, 98, 162; colorism and, 90, 97; combating, 50; defining, 10; in education system, 133–34; Etoke on, 29–30; Fanon on, 96–97; impacts of, 10–11, 29, 57; unraveling, 13, 26
racial purity: defining, 100–101; myth of English, 100–102
racism, 48; of British, 110–14, 170–71; in education system, 131–32; fights against, in 1960s, 87–88; of Fletcher, 187–88; in football, 135–39; Hall on, 114; historical amnesia and, 110–14; impact of, on soul, 242; institutional, 8–9; internalized, 10, 92–94; Keith on, 177–80; Malcolm X on, 178; in 1970s, 181–86; of police, 185–86; of Powell, 4; pseudoscientific, 33, 42, 90, 98–99, 102–3, 122, 124, 145–46, 207–8; Simey on, 196; structural, 121; Sussman on, 99–100; of Thatcher, 110–14, 189–90
Racism and Antiracism in Football, 138
"Racism and Reaction" (Hall), 111
RAR. *See* Rock Against Racism
R&B, 108
the Real Thing, 124

Redburn (Melville), 17, 235–36
Redburn (schoolteacher), 126–30, 161, 244
Rediker, Marcus, on slave trade, 36–37, 39
Reggae, 84
Regis, Cyrille, 138–39
Reid-Merritt, Patricia, 58
Remond, Charles Lenox, 239, 240
Remond, Sarah Parker, 239, 240
Report on an Investigation into the Color Problem in Liverpool and Other Ports (Fletcher), 102
Return to the Source (Cabral), 28
Rialto, 84
Rice, Alan, 226
Rice, C. Duncan, 229–30
Rich, Paul, 85
Richardson, Anna. *See* Douglass, Anna
Richardson, Ellen, 237
Richmond, Anthony, 83; on Black Liverpudlians, 77–78
Rimmer (schoolteacher), 130
Roberts, Dorothy, 98
Robeson, Paul, 69, 135
Robinson, Cedric, 53–54
Robinson, Ken, 132–34, 161
Rock Against Racism (RAR), 109
Rodney, Walter, 26, 46, 47, 50; assassination of, 31
Rogers, Joy, 153
the Rolling Stones, 88
Rothery, Anna, 247
Royal Ordnance Factory, 75, 76, 80–81
Russian revolution, 173

Saana FC, 141–42
Sarich, Vincent, 98
Scarman (Lord), 190
School Days (Chamoiseau), 125
Scotland, Douglass, F, in, 225–26
Seacole, Mary, 207
Selvon, Samuel, 11, 59
Sengupta, Kim, 218
Sennett, Richard, 46

Sertima, Ivan Van, 58
Shakur, Assata, 47
Shankly, Bill, 135–37
Sharp, Granville, 39
Sherwood, Marika, 83, 120; on Brown Baby Problem, 121–22
Sierra Leone, 174
Simey, Margaret, 193; on Fletcher Report, 187–88; on Oxford, 188–89; on racism, 196; on social justice, 188, 199
Sinatra, Frank, 158
Sivanandan, A., 11, 46, 50
Ska, 84
slave merchants, 34–35
slavery: Christian Church interwoven with, 14; Douglass, F., indicting, 228; end of, 40–41; Engels on, 233–34; historical data on, 42; hybridity ushered in by, 45; impact of, 13–14; Marx on, 233–34
The Slave Ship (Rediker), 36
slave ships, 206–7; in Liverpool, 36–41
slave trade: barbarity of, 38–39; Belchem airbrushing, 206–7, 215; in Liverpool, 33–36, 206–7; Liverpool City Council apology for, 215–20; Rediker on, 36–37, 39
Slave Trade Apology, City of Liverpool, 21
Small, Stephen, 156, 205; on Black Liverpool, 162; Keith on, 180
Small Acts (Gilroy, P.), 67
Smeda, Nat, 88
Smith, Dave, 124, 193, 220
Smith, Karl, 220
Smith, Robert, 195–96
Smith, Zadie, 11, 65
The Sociological Imagination (Mills), 19, 22
Speaking for Themselves, 150
Stanley House, 122–23
Staying Power (Fryer), 42, 98, 155, 156, 168–69, 176
Stephen Lawrence Report, 8

stereotypes, 170
Stigma (Goffman), 19
stigmatization: of Black Liverpudlians, 19; Goffman on, 19
A Stranger in the Village, 69
strategic essentialism, M'Baye on, 57
Strong, Barrett, 89
structural racism, 121; Heseltine and, 197
Sussman, Robert Wald, on racism, 99
Swann Report, 143, 146, 162

Tafari, Levi, 11
Tally's Corne (Liebow), 184
Tarzan. *See* Heseltine, Michael
taxes, 194
Taylor, Odie, 124
the Temptations, 87, 107, 115, 130
Terrell, Mary Church, 92
Thatcher, Margaret, 61, 186; racism of, 110–14, 189–90
There Ain't No Black in the Union Jack (Gilroy, P.), 6, 59, 139
They Haven't Done Nothing Yet (Brown, M.), 202, 203–4
Thomas, W. I., 99
Thompson, George, 231; abolitionism of, 229–30
Thompson, Ibrahim, 205
Toshack, John, 136
Toxteth. *See* Liverpool 8
transatlantic history, 26–31; Black Atlantic paradigm and, 66–68; Black British people in context of, 59–66; Black Liverpudlians and, 44
trauma, 26
Trump, Donald, 6
Trumpism, 147
Tubman, Harriet, 240
Ture, Kwame, 47
Twine, France Winddance, 103, 105
Tyler, Martin, 138
The Uncommercial Traveller (Dickens), 235

undercover police, 173–76
unemployment, of LBBs, 143
UNIA. *See* Universal Negro Improvement Association
unions, 86
unity: Africana critical studies on, 29; diversity and, 47–49; uniformity and, 50, 68
Unity and Struggle (Cabral), 28
Universal Negro Improvement Association (UNIA), 73, 94, 153; Christian, G. R., in, 245–46
University of Liverpool, 43

Victoria I (Queen), 101–2
Victorian Attitudes to Race (Bolt), 42
violence, racialized, in Liverpool, 167–71

Walcott, Derek, 60, 63, 74
Wales, 100
Walker, Anthony, 8, 9
Walker, Juanita, 8
Walsh, Peter, 195
Walters, Ronald, 58
Walvin, James, 37, 38, 42–43, 155
Ward, Samuel Ringgold, 240
war on terror, 3
Warren, Curtis, 194–96
Washington, Booker T., 92, 122, 155
Washington, Denzel, 46
Weaver, Eugene, 220
Wells-Barnet, Ida B., 46, 47
West, Cornel, 46
West Indians, 77–78
white liberals, 188, 202; as enemies of Black empowerment, 234–35

White Man Listen! (Wright, R.), 53
white nationalism, 5–6, 147; Black Nationalism contrasted with, 49
whiteness, 51; liberalism and, 12; as myth, 99
white supremacy: challenges to, 207–8; Mills on, 12
White Teeth (Smith, Z.), 65
Wilberforce, William, 39
Wilkie, Derry, 89
Williams, Allan, 89
Williams, Chancellor, 207
Williams, Eric, 53
Williams, Josiah, 168
Willis, Paul, 127–28
Wilson, Edward, 39
Windrush (Philips, M., & Philips, T.), 177
Woodbine (Lord), 89
Wootton, Charles (aka Wotten), murder of, 171–73
World War I, 173; Black British people in, 74–75
World War II, 72; Black British people in, 74–75
Wright, Anne, 218
Wright, Henry C., 237
Wright, Richard, 2, 52, 57, 158; Nkrumah and, 53; Robinson, C., on, 53–54
writing, Baldwin on, 1–2

Yale University, 5
Yemen, 141

Zephaniah, Benjamin, 11, 17
Zong slave ship, 39–40

About the Author

Dr. Mark Christian is a tenured and full professor in the Department of Africana Studies at the City University of New York, where he joined in August 2011 from Miami University of Ohio after eleven years there. He received his BA (Honors) in sociology and American studies from Liverpool Hope University, UK; his MA in Africana/Black studies from the Ohio State University; and his PhD in sociology from the University of Sheffield, UK. Dr. Christian was a senior Fulbright Scholar with the Department of Pan African Studies at Kent State University (1997–1998) and a research fellow at the University of London's Commonwealth Institute. He was a board member of the National Council for Black Studies (2006–2008). He is the author of *Multiracial Identity: An International Perspective* (Palgrave, 2000) and editor of *Black Identity in the 20th Century: Expressions of the US and UK African Diaspora* (London: Hansib, 2002), and two other edited books. He has been a guest editor of three special issue journals (2006, 2008, and 2010). He has been the book review editor for the *Journal of African American Studies* (2007–2014), and is a major reviewer for *Choice*, which reviews books for the entire US library system. Dr. Christian's award-winning book concerns the issue of Black faculty in majority white university and college settings. It is an edited volume titled *Integrated but Unequal: Black Faculty in Predominately White Space* (Trenton, NJ: Africa World Press, 2012). His latest books are: *Booker T. Washington: A Life in American History* (ABC-CLIO, 2021), for which he gained a 2022 RUSA Award from the American Library Association for "Outstanding Reference for Adults," and *The 20th Century Civil Rights Movement: An Africana Studies Perspective* (Kendall Hunt, 2021).

www.ingramcontent.com/pod-product-compliance
Lightning Source LLC
Chambersburg PA
CBHW021341300426
44114CB00012B/1038